Dynamical Aspects in Fuzzy Decision Making

Studies in Fuzziness and Soft Computing

Editor-in-chief
Prof. Janusz Kacprzyk
Systems Research Institute
Polish Academy of Sciences
ul. Newelska 6
01-447 Warsaw, Poland
E-mail: kacprzyk@ibspan.waw.pl
http://www.springer.de/cgi-bin/search_book.pl?series=2941

Further volumes of this series can be found at our homepage.

Vol. 50. F. Crestani and G. Pasi (Eds.)
Soft Computing in Information Retrieval, 2000
ISBN 3-7908-1299-4

Vol. 51. J. Fodor, B. De Baets and P. Perny (Eds.)
Preferences and Decisions under Incomplete Knowledge, 2000
ISBN 3-7908-1303-6

Vol. 52. E.E. Kerre and M. Nachtegael (Eds.)
Fuzzy Techniques in Image Processing, 2000
ISBN 3-7908-1304-4

Vol. 53. G. Bordogna and G. Pasi (Eds.)
Recent Issues on Fuzzy Databases, 2000
ISBN 3-7908-1319-2

Vol. 54. P. Sinčák and J. Vaščák (Eds.)
Quo Vadis Computational Intelligence?, 2000
ISBN 3-7908-1324-9

Vol. 55. J.N. Mordeson, D.S. Malik and S.-C. Cheng
Fuzzy Mathematics in Medicine, 2000
ISBN 3-7908-1325-7

Vol. 56. L. Polkowski, S. Tsumoto and T.Y. Lin (Eds.)
Rough Set Methods and Applications, 2000
ISBN 3-7908-1328-1

Vol. 57. V. Novák and I. Perfilieva (Eds.)
Discovering the World with Fuzzy Logic, 2001
ISBN 3-7908-1330-3

Vol. 58. D.S. Malik and J.N. Mordeson
Fuzzy Discrete Structures, 2000
ISBN 3-7908-1335-4

Vol. 59. T. Furuhashi, S. Tano and H.-A. Jacobsen (Eds.)
Deep Fusion of Computational and Symbolic Processing, 2001
ISBN 3-7908-1339-7

Vol. 60. K.J. Cios (Ed.)
Medical Data Mining and Knowledge Discovery, 2001
ISBN 3-7908-1340-0

Vol. 61. D. Driankov and A. Saffiotti (Eds.)
Fuzzy Logic Techniques for Autonomous Vehicle Navigation, 2001
ISBN 3-7908-1341-9

Vol. 62. N. Baba, L.C. Jain (Eds.)
Computational Intelligence in Games, 2001
ISBN 3-7908-1348-6

Vol. 63. O. Castillo, P. Melin
Soft Computing for Control of Non-Linear Dynamical Systems, 2001
ISBN 3-7908-1349-4

Vol. 64. I. Nishizaki, M. Sakawa
Fuzzy and Multiobjective Games for Conflict Resolution, 2001
ISBN 3-7908-1341-9

Vol. 65. E. Orłowska, A. Szalas (Eds.)
Relational Methods for Computer Science Applications, 2001
ISBN 3-7908-1365-6

Vol. 66. R.J. Howlett, L.C. Jain (Eds.)
Radial Basis Function Networks 1, 2001
ISBN 3-7908-1367-2

Vol. 67. R.J. Howlett and L.C. Jain (Eds.)
Radial Basis Function Networks 2, 2001
ISBN 3-7908-1368-0

Vol. 68. A. Kandel, M. Last and H. Bunke (Eds.)
Data Minining and Computational Intelligence, 2001
ISBN 3-7908-1371-0

Vol. 69. A. Piegat
Fuzzy Modeling and Control, 2001
ISBN 3-7908-1385-0

Vol. 70. W. Pedrycz (Ed.)
Granular Computing, 2001
ISBN 3-7908-1387-7

Vol. 71. K. Leiviskä (Ed.)
Industrial Applications of Soft Computing, 2001
ISBN 3-7908-1388-5

Vol. 72. M. Mareš
Fuzzy Cooperative Games, 2001
ISBN 3-7908-1392-3

Yuji Yoshida
Editor

Dynamical Aspects in Fuzzy Decision Making

With 35 Figures
and 34 Tables

Springer-Verlag Berlin Heidelberg GmbH

Prof. Yuji Yoshida
The University of Kitakyushu
Faculty of Economics and Business Administration
4-2-1 Kitagata, Kokuraminami
Kitakyushu 802-8577
Japan
yoshida@kitakyu-u.ac.jp

ISSN 1434-9922

DOI 10.1007/978-3-7908-1817-8

Cataloging-in-Publication Data applied for
Die Deutsche Bibliothek - CIP-Einheitsaufnahme
Dynamical aspects in fuzzy decision making: with 34 tables / Yuji Yoshida ed. -
Springer-Verlag Berlin Heidelberg 2001
(Studies in fuzziness and soft computing; Vol. 73)

Originally published by Physica-Verlag Heidelberg New York in 2001
MyCopy version of the original edition 2001

Hardcover Design: Erich Kirchner, Heidelberg

SPIN 10833235 88/2202-5 4 3 2 1 0 - Printed on acid-free paper
www.springer.com/mycopy

Preface

The concept of fuzziness, inspired by Zadeh (1965), brings us fruitful results when it is applied to problems in decision making. Recently, problems in fuzzy decision making are getting more complex, and one of the most complex factors is dynamics in systems. Dynamical approach to fuzzy decision making has been proposed by Bellman and Zadeh's celebrated paper "Decision-making in a fuzzy environment" (1970). The idea has developed into fuzzy mathematical programming and has been applied in many fields including management science, operations research, control theory, engineering, systems analysis, computer science, mathematical finance etc. Dynamic programming, advocated in Bellmans book "Dynamic programming" (1957), is one of the most powerful tools to deal with dynamics in systems, and Bellman and Zadeh (1970) has proposed the optimality principle in fuzzy decision making by introducing fuzzy dynamic programming. Fuzzy dynamic programming and fuzzy mathematical programming has been making remakable progress after they were given life by Bellman and Zadeh's paper (1970).

In this volume, various kinds of dynamics, not only time but also structure of systems, are considered. This volume contains ten reviewed papers, which deal with dynamics in theory and applications and whose topics are potentially related to dynamics and are expected to develope dynamical study in near future. first, fuzzy dynamic programming is reviewed from a viewpoint of its origin and consider its developement in theory and applications. Next, the structure of dynamics in systems is considered in relation to fuzzy mathematical programming. Further, some topics potentially related to dynamics are discussed: financial management, fuzzy differential for fuzzy optimization of continuous-time fuzzy systems, and fuzzy ordering in multi-objective fuzzy systems. finally, a unified approach in fuzzy decision making is developed.

J. Kacprzyk and A.O.Esogbue *(Fuzzy Dynamic Programming: Basic Issues and Problem Classes)* give a brief review of developments on fuzzy dynamic programming. The cases of a deterministic, stochastic, and fuzzy state transitions, and of the fixed and specified, implicitly given, fuzzy, and infinite times termination time are analyzed. This chapter also presents the framework for fuzzy criterion set and fuzzy criterion dynamic programming that is a general tool for dealing with many decision and control situations exemplified by the stochastic reservoir operation and stochastic inventory control models of operations research and engineering, and discusses computational complexity of fuzzy dynamic programs.

S. Iwamoto *(Fuzzy Dynamic Programming in the Stochastic Environment)* reconsiders the decision making models in a fuzzy and stochastic enviroment in Bellman and Zadeh's paper (1970) from the essential viewpoint of dynamic programming. He shows that a common optimal general policy for minimum criterion has been obtained through three – membership-parametric, history-parametric and multi-stage stochastic decision tree-table – methods. Further he illustrates that Markov class is not enough for stochastic system with minimum criterion. We see that an invariant imbedding method takes an important part in deriving a recursive formula for stochastic system with nonadditive criterion.

L.F. Sugianto *(Management of Data Uncertainty in Dynamic Programming)* presents an innovative approach to dynamic programming optimization to deal with data uncertainty problem. The proposed approach incorporates confidence measure which enables the utilization of alternative data sources for estimating uncertain data. An algorithm of fuzzy optimization is applied to optimize the spare parts inventory of an electrical power plant, and the technique in this chapter is generally applicable to optimize similar categories of objective functions when fuzzy aggregators can be determined by empirical research.

H.-S. Shih and E.S. Lee *(Discrete Multi-Level Programming in a Dynamic Environment)* present a multi-stage process of the discrete multi-level programming, extending their previous results on fuzzy approach for the multi-level programming, a supervised search procedure to simplify the complex structure. Taking advantage of recursive formulation in the dynamic programming for simplifying the process, the overall satisfaction of decision makers is evaluated through a stage-wise max-min operation and of hierarchical structure as well. Furthermore, an application to resource allocation is developed and a solution procedure is illustrated step by step.

M. Sakawa and I. Nishizaki *(Interactive Fuzzy Programming for Multi-Level Nonconvex Nonlinear Programming Problems Through Genetic Algorithms)* present interactive fuzzy programming through genetic algorithms for multi-level nonconvex nonlinear programming problems with the essentially cooperative decision makers. In the proposed method, mathematical programming problems for obtaining satisfactory solutions concerned in some groups of all the decision makers are successively solved to lead to a global satisfactory solution such that the decision makers at relatively upper levels are esteemed and satisfactory degree of each decision maker balances with those of the others.

M. Inuiguchi and T. Tanino *(Two-Stage Linear Recourse Problems under Non-Probabilistic Uncertainty)* discuss two-stage recourse programming for linear programming problems with uncertain parameters under an assumption that the set of possible realizations of uncertain parameters is known as a polytope. A two-stage recourse problem is formulated from pessimistic viewpoint, and it is shown that this problem is a convex programming problem with respect to the first stage variable vector and a large-scale linear programming problem when all vertices of the polytope representing possible realizations of uncertain parameters are given. A solution algorithm based on a relaxation procedure is proposed.

J. Watada *(Fuzzy Portfolio Model for Decision Making in Investment)* deals with decision making in financial management. He discusses an investment under uncertain environment which is much influenced by the disturbance of social and economical circumstances. He employs the aspiration level on the base of past experiences and knowledge possessed by a decision maker to treat a problem. Portfolio selection problems are formulated as a fuzzy mathematical programming with two objectives to minimize risk and maximize the expected return within a vague aspiration level and a fuzzy goal.

S. Saito, H. Ishii and M. Chen *(Fuzzy Diffrentials and Deterministic Approaches to Fuzzy Optimization Problems)* consider some types of fuzzy differentials of fuzzy functions which map from open sets in normed spaces to sets of fuzzy sets. There are many results in the field of fuzzy differentials which are strongly related to decision making in continuous fuzzy systems. This chapter introduces some fuzzy differentials which apply a deterministic method to some fuzzy optimization problems.

M. Kurano, M. Yasuda, J. Nakagami and Y. Yoshida *(Order Relations and a Monotone Convergence Theorem in the Class of Fuzzy Sets on R^n)* discuss fuzzy sets on R^n as an extension of fuzzy numbers, concerning with the topics of fuzzy rewards in fuzzy decision processes. This extension is a pseudo order defined by a non-empty closed convex cone and characterized by the projection into its dual cone. Especially a structure of the lattice is presented on the class of pyramid-type fuzzy sets. These results are applied to obtain the limit theorem for a sequence of fuzzy sets defined by the dynamic fuzzy system with a monotone fuzzy relation.

D. Dubois and H. Prade *(Advances in the Egalitarist Approach to Decision-Making in a Fuzzy Environment)* propose a unified approach to decision-making in a fuzzy environment, based on the original idea of Bellman and Zadeh, encompassing fuzzy optimization, fuzzy relational calculus and possibility theory. This approach encompasses the paradigm of constraint-directed reasoning in artificial intelligence and allows for flexible or prioritized constraints. This chapter suggests that the maximin approach to decision is potentially very fruitful both from an algorithmic and application-oriented point of view.

Kitakyushu, Japan
December, 2000

Yuji Yoshida

Contents

Fuzzy Dynamic Programming: Basic Issues and Problem Classes

Janusz Kacprzyk and Augustine O. Esogbue***

* Systems Research Institute, Polish Academy of Sciences
ul. Newelska 6, 01–447 Warsaw, Poland

Warsaw University of Applied Informatics and Management
ul. Newelska 6, 01–447 Warsaw, Poland
E-mail: kacprzyk@ibspan.waw.pl

** School of Industrial and Systems Engineering
Georgia Institute of Technology
Atlanta, GA 30332–0205, USA
E-mail: aesogbue@isye.gatech.edu

Abstract. A brief review of basic problem classes and developments of fuzzy dynamic programming is given. It is shown that fuzzy dynamic programming may be a promising tool for dealing with multistage decision making and optimization problems under fuzziness [under fuzzy constraints on decisions (controls) applied and fuzzy goals on states attained]. The cases of a deterministic, stochastic, and fuzzy state transitions, and of the fixed and specified, implicitly given, fuzzy, and infinite times termination time are analyzed.

Keywords: multistage decision making under fuzziness, multistage optimization under fuzziness, fuzzy dynamic programming, fuzzy set, fuzzy system, fuzzy criterion set and fuzzy criterion dynamic programming.

1 Introduction

The essence of multistage decision making, or multistage control, problems may be summarized – for the purposes of our discussion – as follows. First, the problem is dynamic in that some of its characteristics, exemplified by its state (output), evolve in time as a result of their present values and some decisions made (controls applied). There are some stages, exemplified by time (temporal) instants, discrete or continuous, at which a decision is to be made.

A decision made at a given stage, and at a given state, induces a change in the output of the process (e.g. in the total return on investment, hence has clearly an impact on what will happen in the future. The performance of the process is measured over some planning horizon, and is expressed by an aggregate of partial scores that expresse the performance of the particular stage decisions. This aggregate may take on various forms as, e.g, from a pessimistic, "safety-first" minimum to an optimistic maximum, through all intermediate cases exemplified by an (weighted) average. An optimal sequence of decisions or controls at the consecutive stages over the planning horizon (policy) is then sought.

Dynamic programming is a powerful formal tool for dealing with a large spectrum of multistage decision making and control problems. Since its inception in the mid-1950's (cf. Bellman, 1957), dynamic programming has become a standard tool in many fields including operations research, control theory and engineering, systems analysis, engineering, data analysis, control, computer science, etc.

Normally, however, we are faced with imperfect information (data). We have to deal with, e.g., uncertain, imprecise, vague, etc. data available. In such a case, previous works tended to equate all aspects of imperfect information with uncertainty (of a random character), and various probabilistic models were proposed, also in the context of dynamic programming.

No simple and adequate formal tool for handling imprecise data – which may stem, e.g., from the use of natural language by humans – was however available until the mid-1960's when Zadeh (1965) proposed fuzzy sets theory.

Dynamic programming has been one of the earliest general techniques to which fuzzy sets theory has been applied (cf. Chang, 1969; Bellman and Zadeh, 1970; Esogbue and Ramesh, 1970). These pioneering works have been followed by numerous contributions of both a foundational and applied character. They have been reviewed in many surveys as, e.g., by Esogbue and Bellman (1984), Esogbue, Fedrizzi and Kacprzyk (1988), Esogbue and Kacprzyk (1996, 1998), Kacprzyk (1994), Kacprzyk and Esogbue (1996) as well as in Kacprzyk (1983b, 1997). A recent increased interest in fuzzy dynamic programming is also well documented in Kacprzyk's (1997) book.

We will provide here a short, up-to-date survey of fuzzy dynamic programming by reviewing main problem classes, foundations, developments, and more relevant applications.

First, in Section 2 we present the essence of Bellman and Zadeh's (1970) general approach to decision making under fuzziness which is our point of departure. Next, we consecutively present formulations of various dynamic programming problem classes: in Section 3 the basic case of a fixed and specified termination time, in Section 4 the case of a fuzzy termination time, and in Sections 5 and 6 the cases of an implicit and infinite termination times. In Section 7 stochastic multistage decision making under fuzzy criteria is examined, while in Section 8 the computational complexity of fuzzy dynamic programming is briefly discussed. In Section 9 we mention main applications, and in Section 10 give some concluding remarks.

2 Multistage decision making (control) under fuzziness

In this section we will briefly present the well-known general framework for the analysis of multistage decision making (control) under fuzziness which is due to Bellman and Zadeh (1970).

2.1 Decision making under fuzziness – Bellman and Zadeh's approach

The basic elements of Bellman and Zadeh's (1970) general approach are: a fuzzy goal G in X, a fuzzy constraint C in X, and a fuzzy decision D in X; X is a (nonfuzzy) space of options (alternatives, variants, decisions, ...). We wish to:

"satisfy C and attain G"

and this leads to the fuzzy decision

$$\mu_D(x) = \mu_C(x) \wedge \mu_G(x), \forall x \in X \tag{1}$$

which expresses the "goodness" of an $x \in X$ as a solution to the decision making problem considered: from 1 for definitely good (perfect) to 0 for definitely bad (unacceptable), through all intermediate values. The "$a \wedge b = \min(a, b)$" operation is commonly used and is assumed throughout this paper though many other operations can also be employed – see Kacprzyk's (1983b, 1997) books for more detail.

For an optimal (nonfuzzy) solution to this problem, an $x \in X$ such that

$$\mu_D(x^*) = \sup_{x \in X} \mu_D(x) = \sup_{x \in X} (\mu_C(x) \wedge \mu_G(x)) \tag{2}$$

is a natural (but not the only possible – cf. Kacprzyk, 1997) choice.

An analogous reasoning may be performed for the case of multiple fuzzy constraints and fuzzy goals, even if defined in different spaces. Suppose that the fuzzy constraint C is defined as a fuzzy set in $X = \{x\}$, the fuzzy goal G is defined as a fuzzy set in $Y = \{y\}$, and a function $f : X \longrightarrow Y$, $y = f(x)$, is known. Typically, X and Y may be sets of decisions and their outcomes, respectively.

Now, the *induced fuzzy goal* G' in X generated by G in Y is defined as

$$\mu_{G'}(x) = \mu_G[f(x)], \qquad \text{for each } x \in X \tag{3}$$

and notice that by introducing the induced fuzzy goal, both G' and C are defined as fuzzy sets in the same space X.

The (min-type) fuzzy decision is

$$\mu_D(x) = \mu_{G'}(x) \wedge \mu_C(x) = \mu_G[f(x)] \wedge \mu_C(x), \qquad \text{for each } x \in X \tag{4}$$

Then, if we have n fuzzy constraints defined in X, $C_1, \ldots, C_n$, m fuzzy goals defined in Y, $G_1, \ldots, G_m$, and a function $y = f(x)$, then the (min-type) fuzzy decision is

$$\begin{aligned} \mu_D(x) = \mu_{G_1}[f(x)] \wedge \ldots \wedge \mu_{G_n}[f(x)] \wedge \\ \wedge \mu_{C_1}(x) \wedge \ldots \wedge \mu_{C_m}(x) \end{aligned} \tag{5}$$

for each $x \in X$.

Now we will proceed to the multistage decision making case within the above general framework.

2.2 Multistage decision making (control) under fuzziness – Bellman and Zadeh's approach

We will follow the exposition adopted in Bellman and Zadeh (1970) and Kacprzyk (1983b, 1997). First, we assume that the dynamics of the deterministic dynamic system under control is described by a state transition equation

$$x_{t+1} = f(x_t, u_t), \qquad t = 0, 1, \ldots \tag{6}$$

where $x_t, x_{t+1} \in X = \{x\} = \{s_1, \ldots, s_n\}$ are the states (equated here, for simplicity but without loss of generality, with outputs) at time (stage) t and $t+1$, respectively, and $u \in U = \{u\} = \{c_1, \ldots, c_m\}$ is the decision (control or input) at t; X and U, are assumed finite.

The essence of multistage decision making (control) under fuzziness may then be depicted as in Figure 1: we start from an initial state at stage (time) $t = 0$,

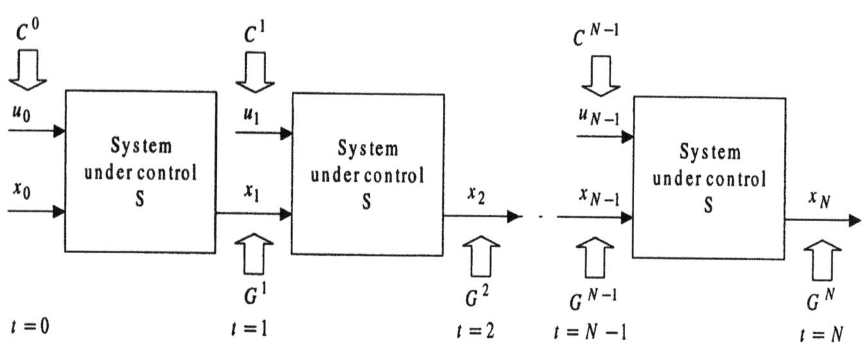

Fig. 1. A general framework for multistage decision making (control) under fuzziness

x_0, make a decision at $t = 0$, u_0, attain a state at time $t = 1$, x_1, make a decision $u_1, \ldots$. Finally, being at $t = N-1$ in x_{N-1} we apply u_{N-1} and attain the final state x_N.

The state transitions are given by (6), the the consecutive decisions u_t are subjected to fuzzy constraints C^t, and on the states x_{t+1} fuzzy goals G^{t+1} are imposed, $t = 0, 1, \ldots, N-1$.

The performance of the multistage decision making process is evaluated by the fuzzy decision which, assumed to be a decomposable fuzzy set in $U \times X \times \ldots \times U \times X$, is

$$\begin{aligned} &\mu_D(u_0, \ldots, u_{N-1} \mid x_0) = \\ &= \mu_C^0(u_0) \wedge \mu_{G^1}(x_1) \wedge \mu_{C^{N-1}}(u_{N-1}) \wedge \mu_{G^N}(x_N) = \\ &= \bigwedge_{t=0}^{N-1} [\mu_{C^t}(u_t) \wedge \mu_{G^{t+1}}(x_{t+1})] \end{aligned} \tag{7}$$

where N is some termination time which is fixed and specified in the basic case.

The problem is to find and optimal sequence of decisions $u_0^*, \ldots, u_{N-1}^*$ such that

$$\begin{aligned}
&\mu_D(u_0^*, \ldots, u_{N-1}^* \mid x_0) = \\
&= \max_{u_0, \ldots, u_{N-1}} [\mu_C^0(u_0) \wedge \mu_{G^1}(x_1) \wedge \mu_{C^{N-1}}(u_{N-1}) \wedge \mu_{G^N}(x_N)] = \\
&= \max_{u_0, \ldots, u_{N-1}} \bigwedge_{t=0}^{N-1} [\mu_{C^t}(u_t) \wedge \mu_{G^{t+1}}(x_{t+1})]
\end{aligned} \tag{8}$$

For simplicity, it is often assumed (also here, if not otherwise specified) that and a fuzzy goal , $\mu_{G^N}(x_N)$, is only imposed on the final state x_N. Then, the fuzzy decision is

$$\begin{aligned}
&\mu_D(u_0, \ldots, u_{N-1} \mid x_0) = \\
&= \mu_C^0(u_0) \wedge \ldots \wedge \mu_{C^{N-1}}(u_{N-1}) \wedge \mu_{G^N}(x_N)
\end{aligned} \tag{9}$$

and the problem is to find $u_0^*, \ldots, u_{N-1}^*$ such that

$$\begin{aligned}
&\mu_D(u_0^*, \ldots, u_{N-1}^* \mid x_0) = \\
&= \max_{u_0, \ldots, u_{N-1}} [\mu_C^0(u_0) \wedge \ldots \wedge \mu_{C^{N-1}}(u_{N-1}) \wedge \mu_{G^N}(x_N)]
\end{aligned} \tag{10}$$

This general problem formulation may be extended, mainly with respect to (cf. Kacprzyk, 1983b, 1997):

- The type of the termination time: fixed and specified in advance, fuzzy, implicitly given (by entering a termination set of states), infinite
- The type of the dynamic system: deterministic, stochastic, fuzzy, and fuzzy-stochastic.
- The type of objective function: cost minimization, profit/benefit maximization, and fuzzy criterion set based satisfactory degree maximization,

and in virtually all cases a dynamic-programming-type algorithm can be devised.

3 Fuzzy dynamic programming for the case of a fixed and specified termination time

The case of a fixed and specified (in advance) termination time is basic, and provides a suitable point of departure for extensions. We will therefore discuss it now considering consecutively a deterministic, stochastic, fuzzy dynamic system, and fuzzy criterion set dynamic program.

3.1 The case of a deterministic dynamic system

A deterministic system is described by its state transition equation (6), i.e. $x_{t+1} = f(x_t, u_t); x_t, x_{t+1} \in X = \{s_1, \ldots, s_n\}, u_t \in U = \{c_1, \ldots, c_m\}; t = 0, 1, \ldots, N-1; x_0 \in X$ is the initial state, and $N < \infty$ is a fixed and specified termination time (planning horizon).

The fuzzy constraints are $\mu_{C^0}(u_0), \ldots, \mu_{C^{N-1}}(u_{N-1})$ and the fuzzy goal is $\mu_{G^N}(x_N)$. The fuzzy decision is

$$\mu_D(u_0, \ldots, u_{N-1} \mid x_0) = \\ = \mu_{C^0}(u_0) \wedge \ldots \wedge \mu_{C^{N-1}}(u_{N-1}) \wedge \mu_{G^N}(x_N) \tag{11}$$

and the problem is to find $u_0^*, \ldots, u_{N-1}^*$ such that

$$\mu_D(u_0^*, \ldots, u_{N-1}^* \mid x_0) = \\ = \max_{u_0, \ldots, u_{N-1}} [\mu_{C^0}(u_0) \wedge \ldots \wedge \mu_{C^{N-1}}(u_{N-1}) \wedge \mu_{G^N}(x_N)] \tag{12}$$

Clearly, the two last terms in this problem, i.e.

$$\mu_{C^{N-1}}(u_{N-1}) \wedge \mu_{G^N}(f(x_{N-1}, u_{N-1}))$$

depend on u_{N-1} (and not on other decisions), hence (12) can be rewritten as

$$\mu_D(u_0^*, \ldots, u_{N-1}^* \mid x_0) = \\ = \max_{u_0, \ldots, u_{N-1}} [\mu_{C^0}(u_0) \wedge \ldots \wedge \mu_{C^{N-1}}(u_{N-1}) \wedge \mu_{G^N}(x_N)] = \\ = \max_{u_0, \ldots, u_{N-2}} [\mu_{C^0}(u_0) \wedge \ldots \wedge \mu_{C^{N-2}}(u_{N-2}) \wedge \\ \wedge \max_{u_{N-1}} (\mu_{C^{N-1}}(u_{N-1}) \wedge \mu_{G^N}(f(x_{N-1}, u_{N-1})))] \tag{13}$$

On repeating this backward iteration for $u_{N-2}, \ldots, u_0$, we obtain the set of dynamic programming recurrence equations

$$\begin{cases} \mu_{G^{N-i}}(x_{N-i}) = \max_{u_{N-i}} [\mu_{C^{N-i}}(u_{N-i}) \wedge \mu_{G^{N-i+1}}(x_{N-i+1})] \\ x_{N-i+1} = f(x_{N-i}, u_{N-i}); i = 1, \ldots, N \end{cases} \tag{14}$$

where $\mu_{G^{N-i}}(.)$ is a fuzzy goal at $t = N-i$ induced by a fuzzy goal at $t = N-i+1$.

An optimal sequence of decisions sought, $u_0^*, \ldots, u_{N-1}^*$, is given by the successive maximizing values of u_{N-i} in (14). It is convenient to represent the solution, u_t^*, by an optimal policy $a_t^* : X \longrightarrow U$, such that $u_t^* = a_t^*(x_t), t = 0, 1, \ldots, N-1$, i.e. relating an optimal decision to the current state.

3.2 The case of a stochastic dynamic system

The stochastic system is assumed to be a Markov chain whose temporal evolution is described by a conditional probability

$$p(x_{t+1} \mid x_t, u_t)$$

such that $x_t, x_{t+1} \in X = \{s_1, \ldots, s_n\}$, $u_t \in U = \{c_1, \ldots, c_m\}$, $x_0 \in X$ is an initial state, $t = 0, 1, \ldots, N-1$, and $N < \infty$ is a fixed and specified termination time.

We have now the following two problem formulations:

- due to Bellman and Zadeh (1970): find an optimal sequence of decisions $u_0^*, \ldots, u_{N-1}^*$ to maximize the probability of attainment of the fuzzy goal subject to the fuzzy constraints, i.e.

$$\begin{aligned} &\mu_D(u_0^*, \ldots, u_{N-1}^* \mid x_0) = \\ &= \max_{u_0, \ldots, u_{N-1}} [\mu_{C^0}(u_0) \wedge \ldots \wedge \mu_{C^{N-1}}(u_{N-1}) \wedge E\mu_{G^N}(x_N)] \end{aligned} \tag{15}$$

  where the fuzzy goal is viewed to be a fuzzy event in X whose (nonfuzzy) probability is (cf. Zadeh, 1968)

$$E\mu_{G^N}(x_N) = \sum_{x_N \in X} p(x_N \mid x_{N-1}, u_{N-1}) \cdot \mu_{G^N}(x_N) \tag{16}$$

- due to Kacprzyk and Staniewski (1980): find an optimal sequence of decisions $u_0^*, \ldots, u_{N-1}^*$ to maximize the expectation of the fuzzy decision's membership function, i.e.

$$\begin{aligned} &\mu_D(u_0^*, \ldots, u_{N-1}^* \mid x_0) = \\ &= \max_{u_0, \ldots, u_{N-1}} E[\mu_{C^0}(u_0) \wedge \ldots \wedge \mu_{C^{N-1}}(u_{N-1}) \wedge \mu_{G^N}(x_N)] \end{aligned} \tag{17}$$

and these formulations are clearly not equivalent.

Bellman and Zadeh's approach Since in (15) $\mu_{C^{N-1}}(u_{N-1}) \wedge E\mu_{G^N}[f(x_{N-1}, u_{N-1})]$ depend only on u_{N-1}, the next two right-most terms depend only on u_{N-2}, etc., the structure of (15) is essentially the same as that of (13), and the set of fuzzy dynamic programming recurrence equations is

$$\begin{cases} \mu_{G^{N-i}}(x_{N-i}) = \max_{u_{N-i}} [\mu_{C^{N-i}}(u_{N-i}) \wedge E\mu_{G^{N-i+1}}(x_{N-i+1})] \\ E\mu_{G^{N-i+1}}(x_{N-i+1}) = \sum_{x_{N-i+1} \in X} p(x_{N-i+1} \mid x_{N-1}, u_{N-1}) \times \\ \qquad \times \mu_{G^{N-i+1}}(x_{N-i+1}); \qquad i = 1, \ldots, N \end{cases} \tag{18}$$

and we consecutively obtain u_{N-i}^* or, in fact, optimal policies a_{N-i}^* such that $u_{N-i}^* = a_{N-i}^*(x_{N-i}), i = 1, \ldots, N$.

Kacprzyk and Staniewski's approach To solve problem (17), we first introduce a sequence of functions $h_i : X \times \times_{j=1}^{i} U \longrightarrow [0,1]$ and $g_j : X \times \times_{l=1}^{j+1} U \longrightarrow [0,1]$; $i = 0, 1, \ldots, N$; $j = 1, \ldots, N-1$; such that

$$\begin{cases} h_N(x_N, u_0, \ldots, u_{N-1}) = \mu_{C^0}(u_0) \wedge \ldots \wedge \mu_{C^{N-1}}(u_{N-1}) \wedge \\ \qquad \wedge \mu_D(u_0, \ldots, u_{N-1} \mid x_0) \\ \cdots\cdots\cdots\cdots\cdots\cdots\cdots\cdots\cdots\cdots \\ g_k(x_k, u_0, \ldots, u_k) = \sum_{i=1}^{n} h_{k+1}(s_i, u_0, \ldots, u_k)\, p(s_i \mid x_k, u_k) \\ h_k(x_k, u_0, \ldots, u_{k-1}) = \max_{u_k} g_k(x_k, u_0, \ldots, u_k) \\ \cdots\cdots\cdots\cdots\cdots\cdots\cdots\cdots\cdots\cdots \\ h_0(x_0) = \max_{u_0} g_0(x_0, u_0) \end{cases} \tag{19}$$

If the consecutive decisions and states are $u_0, \ldots, u_j$ and $x_0, \ldots, x_j$, respectively, then g_j is the expected value of $\mu_D(. \mid x_0)$ provided that the next decisions are optimal, i.e., $u_{j+1}^*, \ldots, u_{N-1}^*$.

It can be shown (Kacprzyk and Staniewski, 1980; Kacprzyk, 1983b, 1997) that there exist functions $w_k : X \times \times_{i=1}^{k} U \longrightarrow U$ such that $h_k(x_k, u_0, \ldots, u_{k-1}) = g_k(x_k, u_0, \ldots, u_{k-1}, w_k(x_k, u_0, \ldots, u_{k-1}))$. Then, an optimal policy sought, a_t^*, $t = 0, 1, \ldots, N-1$, is given by

$$\begin{cases} a_0^* = w_0(x_0) \\ a_1^*(x_0, x_1) = w_1(x_1, a_0^*(x_0)) \\ \cdots\cdots\cdots\cdots\cdots\cdots\cdots\cdots\cdots\cdots \\ a_{N-1}^*(x_0, \ldots, x_{N-1}) = \\ \qquad = w_{N-1}(x_{N-1}, b_{N-2}^*(x_0, \ldots, x_{N-2}, \ldots, b_0^*(x_0)) \ldots) \end{cases} \tag{20}$$

and it depends now not only on the current state but also on the trajectory.

Needless to say that the solution of this formulation is more difficult than of that due to Bellman and Zadeh.

3.3 The case of a fuzzy dynamic system

In this challenging case the system is fuzzy and its dynamics is governed by a state transitions equation

$$X_{t+1} = F(X_t, U_t), \qquad t = 0, 1, \ldots \tag{21}$$

where X_t, X_{t+1} are fuzzy states at time (stage) t and $t+1$, and U_t is a fuzzy decision at t, characterized by their membership functions $\mu_{X_t}(x_t), \mu_{X_{t+1}}(x_{t+1})$, and $\mu_{U_t}(u_t)$, respectively; (21) is equivalent to a conditioned fuzzy set $\mu_{X_{t+1}}(x_{t+1} \mid x_t, u_t)$ (cf. Kacprzyk, 1983b, 1997).

Notice that the fuzzy state transition equation (21) is just a general form which can be given as, e.g., a set of IF–THEN rules or a neural network.

Baldwin and Pilsworth (1982) proposed a dynamic programming scheme. First, for each $t = 0, 1, \ldots, N-1$ a fuzzy relation $\mu_{R^t}(u_t, x_{t+1}) = \mu_{C^t}(u_t) \wedge$

$\mu_{G^{t+1}}(x_{t+1})$ is constructed. The degree to which U_t and X_{t+1} satisfy C^t and G^{t+1} is

$$\begin{aligned}&\mu_T(u_t, \mu_{R^t}(u_t, x_{t+1}), x_{t+1}) = \\ &= \max_{u_t}[(\mu_{U_t}(u_t) \wedge \mu_{C^t}(u_t)) \wedge \max_{x_{t+1}}(\mu_{X_{t+1}}(x_{t+1}) \wedge \mu_{G^{t+1}}(x_{t+1}))]\end{aligned} \tag{22}$$

The fuzzy decision is

$$\begin{aligned}&\mu_D(U_0, \ldots, U_{N-1} \mid X_0) = \\ &= \max_{u_0}[\mu_{U_0}(u_0) \wedge \mu_{C^0}(u_0)) \wedge \ldots \wedge \max_{u_{N-1}}((\mu_{U_{N-1}}(u_{N-1}) \wedge \\ &\quad \wedge \mu_{C^{N-1}}(u_{N-1})) \wedge \max_{x_N}(\mu_{X_N}(x_N) \wedge \mu_{G^N}(x_N))]\end{aligned} \tag{23}$$

and we seek an optimal sequence of fuzzy decisions $U_0^*, \ldots, U_{N-1}^*$ such that

$$\begin{aligned}&\mu_D(U_0^*, \ldots, U_{N-1}^* \mid X_0) = \\ &= \max_{U_0, \ldots, U_{N-1}} \mu_D(U_0, \ldots, U_{N-1} \mid X_0) = \\ &= \max_{U_0} \max_{u_0}[\mu_{U_0}(u_0) \wedge \mu_{C^0}(u_0)) \wedge \ldots \\ &\quad \ldots \wedge \max_{U_{N-1}((\max_{u_{N-1}}} (\mu_{U_{N-1}}(u_{N-1}) \wedge \mu_{C^{N-1}}(u_{N-1}) \wedge \\ &\quad \wedge \max_{X_N \max_{x_N}} (\mu_{X_N}(x_N) \wedge \mu_{G^N}(x_N)))]\end{aligned} \tag{24}$$

hence the set of dynamic programming recurrence equations is

$$\begin{cases} \mu_{\overline{G}^N}(X_N) = \max_{x_N}[\mu_{X_N}(x_N) \wedge \mu_{G^N}(x_N)] \\ \mu_{\overline{G}^{N-i}}(X_{N-i}) = \max_{U_{N-i}[(\max_{u_{N-i}}}(\mu_{U_{N-i}}(u_{N-i}) \wedge \mu_{C^{N-i}}(u_{N-i})) \wedge \\ \qquad \wedge \mu_{\overline{G}^{N-i+1}}(X_{N-i+1})] \\ \mu_{X_{N-i+1}}(x_{N-i+1}) = \max_{x_{N-i}[\max_{u_{N-i}}}(\mu_{U_{N-i}}(u_{N-i}) \wedge \\ \qquad \wedge \mu_{X_{N-i+1}}(x_{N-i+1} \mid x_{N-i}, u_{N-i})] \wedge \mu_{X_{N-i}}(x_{N-i})) \\ i = 1, \ldots, N-1 \end{cases} \tag{25}$$

Though this may be solved, a prohibitive difficulty is that $\mu_{\overline{G}^{N-i}}(X_{N-i})$ must be specified for all the possible X_{N-i}'s, and the maximization is to proceed over all the possible U_{N-i}'s. As the number of both of them may be very high (theoretically infinite), Baldwin and Pilsworth (1982) predefine some (sufficiently small) number of reference (standard) fuzzy states and fuzzy controls. Then, they redefine their problem formulation in terms of the reference fuzzy states and fuzzy decisions to finally make (25) solvable. For details, see the source (Baldwin and Pilsworth, 1982) or a readable coverage in Kacprzyk (1983b, 1997) and Zimmermann (1987). The idea of using a small number of reference fuzzy sets is not new (cf. Kacprzyk and Staniewski, 1982), and has also been recently advocated for solving larger fuzzy dynamic programming problems (cf. Kacprzyk, 1993a, b).

Experience with Baldwin and Pilsworth's (1982) approach is often not encouraging (cf. Zimmermann, 1987) and an earlier and simple branch-and-bound approach by Kacprzyk (1979) may be a better choice.

4 Fuzzy dynamic programming for the case of a fuzzy termination time

In many real-world problems it may be more adequate to assume a fuzzy termination time as *more or less 5 years, a couple of days, ten years or so ....* This idea appeared in Fung and Fu (1977) and Kacprzyk (1977).

Let $R = \{0, 1, \ldots, K-1, K, K+1, \ldots, N\}$ be the set of decision making stages. At each $t \in R$ we have a fuzzy constraint $\mu_{C^t}(u_t)$, and a fuzzy goal $\mu_{G^v}(x_v)$, $v \in R$, is imposed on the final state. The fuzzy termination time is given by $\mu_T(v), v \in R$, which can be viewed as a degree of how preferable v is as the termination time.

The fuzzy decision is now (Kacprzyk, 1977, 1978b, c)

$$\mu_D(u_0, \ldots, u_{v-1} \mid x_0) = \mu_{C^0}(u_0) \wedge \ldots \wedge \mu_{C^{v-1}}(u_{v-1}) \wedge \mu_T(v) \cdot \mu_{G^v}(x_v) \quad (26)$$

and the problem is to find an optimal termination time v^* and an optimal sequence of decisions $u_0^*, \ldots, u_{v^*-1}^*$ such that

$$\mu_D(u_0^*, \ldots u_{v^*-1}^* \mid x_0) = \\ = \max_{v, u_0, \ldots, u_{v-1}} [\mu_{C^0}(u_0) \wedge \ldots \wedge \mu_{C^{v-1}}(u_{v-1}) \wedge \mu_T(v) \cdot \mu_{G^v}(x_v)] \quad (27)$$

4.1 The case of a deterministic dynamic system

Problem (27) was formulated and solved by Kacprzyk (1977, 1978b). Then, Stein (1980) presented a computationally more efficient model and solution.

Kacprzyk's approach In Kacprzyk's (1977, 1978c) formulation the set of possible termination times is $\{v \in R : \mu_T(v) > 0\} = \{K, K+1, \ldots, N\} \subseteq R$, hence an optimal sequence of decisions is $u_0^*, \ldots, u_{K-2}^*, u_{K-1}^*, \ldots, u_{v^*-1}^*$.

The part $u_{K-1}^*, u_K^*, \ldots, u_{v^*-1}^*$ is determined by solving

$$\begin{cases} \mu_{G^{v-i}}(x_{v-i}, v) = \max_{v_{v-i}} [\mu_{C^{v-i}}(u_{v-i}) \wedge \mu_{G^{v-i+1}}(x_{v-i+1}, v)] \\ x_{v-i+1} = f(x_{v-i}, u_{v-i}) \\ i = 1, \ldots, v-i+1; v = K, K+1, \ldots, N-1 \end{cases} \quad (28)$$

where $\mu_{G^v}(x_v, v) = \mu_T(v) \mu_{G^v}(x_v)$.

An optimal termination time v^* is then found by the maximizing v in

$$\mu_{G^{K-1}}(x_{K-1}) = \max_v \mu_{G^{K-1}}(x_{K-1}, v) \quad (29)$$

The part $u_0^*, \ldots, u_{K-2}^*$ is then determined by solving

$$\begin{cases} \mu_{G^{K-i-1}}(x_{K-i-1}) = \max_{u_{K-i-1}} [\mu_{C^{K-i-1}}(u_{K-i-1}) \wedge \mu_{G^{K-i}}(x_{K-i})] \\ x_{K-i} = f(x_{K-i-1}, u_{K-i-1}); i = 1, \ldots, K-1 \end{cases} \quad (30)$$

Stein's approach Stein (1980) presented a computationally more efficient dynamic programming approach. At $t = N-i, i \in \{1, \ldots, N-1\}$, we can either stop and attain $\mu_{\overline{G}^{N-i}}(x_{N-i}) = \mu_T(N-i)\,\mu_{G^{N-i}}(x_{N-i})$, or apply u_{N-i} and attain $\mu_{C^{N-i}}(u_{N-i}(u_{N-i}) \wedge \mu_{G^{N-i+1}}(x_{N-i+1})$. The better alternative should evidently be chosen, and this is repeated for $t = N-i-1, N-i-2, \ldots, 0$.

The set of recurrence equations is therefore

$$\begin{cases} \mu_{G^{N-i}}(x_{N-i}) = \mu_{\overline{G}_{N-i}}(x_{N-i}) \wedge \\ \qquad \wedge \max_{u_{N-i}}[\mu_{C^{N-i}}(u_{N-i}) \wedge \mu_{G^{N-i+1}}(x_{N-i+1})] \\ x_{N-i+1} = f(x_{N-i}, u_{N-i}); i = 1, 2, \ldots, N \end{cases} \tag{31}$$

and an optimal termination time is such a $t = N-i$ at which the terminating decision, $u^*_{v^*-1}$, occurs, i.e., when

$$\mu_{G^{N-i}}(x_{N-i}) > \max_{u_{N-i}}[\mu_{C^{N-i}}(u_{N-i}) \wedge \mu_{G^{N-i+1}}(x_{N-i+1})] \tag{32}$$

4.2 The case of a stochastic dynamic system

This case was first formulated and solved in Kacprzyk (1978b, c) by combining the elements of Sections 3.2.1 and 4.1. We seek an optimal termination time v^* and an optimal sequence of decisions $u^*_0, \ldots, u^*_{v^*-1}$ such that

$$\begin{aligned} &\mu_D(u^*_0, \ldots, u^*_{v^*-1} \mid x_0) = \\ &= \max_{v, u_0, \ldots, u_{N-1}} [\mu_{C^0}(u_0) \wedge \ldots \wedge \mu_{C^{v-1}}(u_{v-1}) \wedge E\mu_{G^v}(x_v)] \end{aligned} \tag{33}$$

where $\mu_{G^v}(x_v) = \mu_T(v)\,\mu_{G^v}(x_v)$; moreover, $\{v : \mu_T(v) > 0\} = \{K, K+1, \ldots, N\}$.

As in Section 3.2.1, we determine v^* and $u^*_{K-1}, u^*_K, \ldots, u^*_{v^*-1}$ by solving

$$\begin{cases} \mu_{G^{v-i}}(x_{v-i}) = \max_{u_{v-i}}[\mu_{C^{v-i}}(u_{v-i}) \wedge E\mu_{G^{v-i+1}}(x_{v-i+1})] \\ E\mu_{G^{v-i+1}}(x_{v-i+1}) = \sum_{x_{v-i+1} \in X} p(x_{v-i+1} \mid x_{v-1}, u_{v-1}) \times \\ \qquad \times \mu_{G^{v-i+1}}(x_{v-i+1}); i = 1, \ldots, N \end{cases} \tag{34}$$

and v^* is given by the maximizing v in

$$\mu_{G^{K-1}}(x_{K-1}) = \max_v \mu_{G^{K-1}}(x_{K-1}, v) \tag{35}$$

The remaining part $u^*_{K-2}, u^*_{K-3}, \ldots, u^*_0$ is obtained by solving

$$\begin{cases} \mu_{G^{K-1-i}}(x_{K-1-i}) = \max_{u_{K-1-i}}[\mu_{C^{K-1-i}}(u_{K-1-i}) \wedge E\mu_{G^{K-i}}(x_{K-i})] \\ E\mu_{G^{K-i}}(x_{K-i}) = \sum_{x_{K-i} \in X} p(x_{K-i} \mid x_{K-1-i}, u_{K-1-i}) \times \\ \qquad \times \mu_{G^{K-1-i}}(x_{K-1-i}); i = 1, \ldots, K-1 \end{cases} \tag{36}$$

In the later Stein's (1980) formulation the problem is solved by the following set of recurrence equations

$$\begin{cases} \mu_{G^{N-i}}(x_{N-i}) = \mu_{\overline{G}_{N-i}}(x_{N-i}) \wedge \\ \qquad \wedge \max_{u_{N-i}}[\mu_{C^{N-i}}(u_{N-i}) \wedge E\mu_{G^{N-i+1}}(x_{N-i+1})] \\ E\mu_{G^{N-i+1}}(x_{N-i+1}) = \sum_{x_{K-i} \in X} p(x_{K-i+1} \mid x_{N-i}, u_{N-i}) \times \\ \qquad \times \mu_{G^{N-i+1}}(f(x_{N-i}, u_{N-i})); i = 1, 2, \ldots, N \end{cases} \tag{37}$$

where v^* occurs when

$$\mu_{G^{N-i}}(x_{N-i}) > \max_{u_{N-i}}[\mu_{C^{N-i}}(u_{N-i}) \wedge E\mu_{G^{N-i+1}}(x_{N-i+1})] \tag{38}$$

4.3 Remarks on the case of a fuzzy dynamic system

In this case we fix some (finite and relatively small) number of reference fuzzy states (and possibly decisions), and obtain an auxiliary approximate system whose state transitions are of a deterministic system type (cf. Section 3.3 or Kacprzyk, 1983b and Kacprzyk and Staniewski, 1982). Then, Stein's approach can be employed. In many cases, however, a simple Kacprzyk's (1983b) branch-and-bound algorithm is a better choice.

5 Multistage decision making (control) with an implicitly specified termination time

Now the process terminates when the state enters for the first time a termination set of states $W = \{s_{p+1}, s_{p+2}, \ldots, s_n\} \subset X$. The problem is to determine an optimal sequence of decisions $u_0^*, \ldots, u_{\overline{N}-1}^*$ such that

$$\mu_D(u_0^*, \ldots, u_{\overline{N}-1}^* \mid x_0) = \\ = \max_{u_0, \ldots, u_{\overline{N}-1}} [\mu_C(u_0 \mid x_0) \wedge \ldots \wedge \mu_C(u_{\overline{N}-1} \mid x_{\overline{N}-1}) \wedge \mu_{G^{\overline{N}}}(x_{\overline{N}})] \tag{39}$$

where $x_0, \ldots, x_{\overline{N}-1} \in X \setminus W$, and $x_{\overline{N}} \in W$; we seek an optimal stationary strategy in fact.

The solution of (39) may proceed by using:

- Bellman and Zadeh's (1970) iterative approach,
- Komolov's *et et al.* (1979) graph-theoretic approach, and
- Kacprzyk's (1978a. b) branch-and-bound approach,

and the first one is somehow related to dynamic programming. For details we refer the reader to, e.g., Kacprzyk's (1983b, 1997) books.

6 Multistage decision making (control) with an infinite termination time

In all the problems considered so far the solution process required some iterations over consecutive stages. This may be justified when the number of stages is not too high, and when the process itself exhibits a sufficient variability over time. However, this is not always the case. Then it may expedient to assume an infinite termination time and seek an optimal stationary strategy.

In the fuzzy setting, the multistage decision making (control) problem with an infinite termination time was first formulated and solved by Kacprzyk and Staniewski (1982, 1983) – see also Kacprzyk's (1983b, 1997) books.

For the deterministic dynamic system (6), the fuzzy decision is

$$\begin{aligned}\mu_D(u_0, u_1, \ldots \mid x_0) &= \\ &= \mu_C(u_0 \mid x_o) \wedge \mu_G(x_1) \wedge \mu_C(u_1 \mid x_1) \wedge \mu_G(x_2) \wedge \ldots = \\ &= \lim_{N\to\infty} \bigwedge_{t=0}^{N} [\mu_C(u_t \mid x_t) \wedge \mu_G(x_{t+1})]\end{aligned} \tag{40}$$

and the problem is to find an optimal stationary strategy $a^*_\infty = (a^*, a^*, \ldots)$ such that

$$\begin{aligned}\mu_D(a^*_\infty \mid x_0) &= \max_{a_\infty} \mu_D(a_\infty \mid x_0) = \\ &= \max_{a_\infty} \lim_{N\to\infty} \bigwedge_{t=0}^{N} [\mu_C(a(x_t) \mid x_t) \wedge \mu_G(x_{t+1})]\end{aligned} \tag{41}$$

As shown in Kacprzyk and Staniewski (1983), problem (41) may be solved in a finite number of steps by using a policy iteration algorithm whose essence is a step-by-step improvement of stationary policies.

A policy iteration type algorithm was also proposed for the stochastic system (the most challenging case!) by Kacprzyk, Safteruk, and Staniewski (1981), and for a fuzzy system by Kacprzyk and Staniewski (1982).

7 Stochastic multistage decision making under fuzzy criteria

7.1 Fuzzy criterion sets and fuzzy dynamic programming

This new and potent dimension of fuzzy decision making, specifically fuzzy dynamic programming, was first introduced in Liu and Esogbue (1996) with extensions given by Esogbue and Liu (1996). Additional studies and applications may be found in Esogbue and Liu (1997a, b, c). Here, we present the framework for fuzzy criterion set and fuzzy criterion dynamic programming that is a general tool for dealing with many decision and control situations exemplified by the stochastic reservoir operation and stochastic inventory control models of operations research and engineering.

In fuzzy criterion dynamic programming the objective is expressed as the maximization of the expected fuzzy criterion function of the product of fuzzy criterion sets. Because of the central role played by this concept, we will define it in the sequel.

Fuzzy criterion sets and fuzzy criterion functions Let X be a collection of elements denoted generally by x with the fuzzy set A in X the set of ordered pairs, defined as

$$A = \{(x, \mu_A(x)) | x \in X\} \tag{42}$$

where $\mu_A(x)$ is called the membership function of x in A. We say that A is a *fuzzy criterion set* if A is the set of all *satisfactory* elements and $\mu_A(x)$ is the *satisfactory degree* of x; we call $\mu_A(x)$ the *fuzzy criterion function.*

We define an *α-level set* as the subset of elements that belong to the fuzzy criterion set A at least to the degree α, i.e. $A_\alpha = \{x \in X | \mu_A(x) \geq \alpha\}$.

A fuzzy criterion set A is said to be *unimodal* if its fuzzy criterion function $\mu_A(x)$ is unimodal. For more detail, see Liu and Esogbue (1996).

Fuzzy criterion dynamic programming Suppose that we have an inventory system. If the demand for goods in this system must be satisfied regardless of the physical constraints of the warehouse or reservoir, then the state of the system can be described by an *imaginary* inventory level. When this imaginary inventory level is less than the *dead inventory level* (dead storage), then we cannot fulfill demand. In this case the difference represents the *shortage quantity.* When the imaginary inventory level is greater than the largest physical storage, the amount exceeds the capacity of the warehouse or reservoir, and the difference represents the degree of exceeding the level or, for the reservoir problem, when flooding would result. Usually, there exists a best state at which we define the value of fuzzy criterion to be 1. When the inventory level deviates from the best state, the fuzzy criterion value decreases. Thus, the set of all satisfactory states is a *fuzzy criterion set* whose fuzzy criterion function is the *satisfactory degree of elements.*

For a given N-stage decision process, let us define $A_1, A_2, \ldots, A_N$ as the fuzzy criterion sets of satisfactory states with fuzzy criterion functions $\mu_1, \mu_2, \ldots, \mu_N$ at stages $1, 2, \ldots, N$, respectively, on the real line R. Assume that $\lambda_1, \lambda_2, \ldots, \lambda_N$ are coefficients of convex combination representing the relative importance among $A_1, A_2, \ldots, A_N$. Let x_i, d_i and ξ_i be the state, decision and stochastic variable respectively at stage i, then the state transition equation has the following form:

$$x_{i+1} = x_i + d_i + \xi_i, \qquad i = 1, 2, \ldots, N. \tag{43}$$

The problem is then to control this system such that the states over all stages be satisfactory, i.e. at the stage n, the objective is to maximize the expected fuzzy criterion function of the product $A_n \otimes A_{n+1} \otimes \ldots \otimes A_N$.

Based on the fuzzy criterion set operations, the expected fuzzy criterion function J_n of product $A_n \otimes A_{n+1} \otimes \ldots \otimes A_N$ is

$$J_n(\mathbf{x}; \mathbf{d}) = \sum_{i=n}^{N} \gamma_i^{(n)} \int_R \mu_i(x_i + d_i + \xi_i) d\Phi_i(\xi_i) \tag{44}$$

where $\mathbf{x}$ is a state vector, $\mathbf{d}$ is a decision vector, and

$$\gamma_i^{(n)} = \lambda_i / \sum_{j=n}^{N} \lambda_j \tag{45}$$

For d_i and ξ_i, the positivity implies that it is an input, and the negativity implies that it is an output. Also, $\gamma_n^{(n)} : \gamma_{n+1}^{(n)} : \cdots : \gamma_N^{(n)}$ are simply coefficients of the convex combination and $\gamma_n^{(n)} : \gamma_{n+1}^{(n)} : \cdots : \gamma_N^{(n)} = \lambda_n : \lambda_{n+1} : \cdots : \lambda_N$.

We introduce the fuzzy criterion dynamic programming model associated with problem (44) as follows:

$$
\begin{aligned}
f_N(x) &= \sup_{d \in D_N} L_N(x+d) \\
f_n(x) &= \sup_{d \in D_n} \Big\{ \theta_n L_n(x+d) \\
&\qquad + (1-\theta_n) \int_R f_{n+1}(x+d+\xi) d\Phi_n(\xi) \Big\} \\
n &\le N-1
\end{aligned}
\tag{46}
$$

where

$$
L_n(y) = \int_R \mu_n(y+\xi) d\Phi_n(\xi), \tag{47}
$$

and $\theta_n = \gamma_n^{(n)}$; $D_n = [q_n, Q_n]$ is a set of feasible policies, and q_n and Q_n are not necessarily finite and positive.

We also assume that:

(A_1) the quantities $\xi_1, \xi_2, \ldots, \xi_N$ are independent stochastic variables with distributions $\Phi_1, \Phi_2, \ldots, \Phi_N$, respectively, and $E|\xi_i| < +\infty$, where E denotes the expectation operator;

(A_2) the fuzzy criterion functions $\mu_i(x)$ of fuzzy criterion sets A_i: $R \to [0,1]$ are continuous almost everywhere for all i, and $\lim_{x \to \pm\infty} \mu_i(x) = 0$;

(A_3) at least one of the following conditions holds:

1. μ_i are continuous functions for all i,
2. Φ_i are continuous distributions for all i.

Additionally:

1. When $D_n = R^+$ and the support of the distribution Φ_n is R^-, the equation (46) is a standard inventory model. In this case, the control is to order commodities from outside and the stochastic variables are quantities of demand.
2. When D_n is a closed interval on R^- and the support of the distribution Φ_n is R^+, the equation (46) is a reservoir operation model. Meanwhile, the control is to release water from the reservoir and the stochastic variables are quantities of inflow.
3. $f_n(x)$ is the expected fuzzy criterion function of the product $A_n \otimes A_{n+1} \otimes \cdots \times A_N$ in Euclidean space R^{N-n+1} for any n.

Basic theorem Suppose that we have the following convolution operator,

$$H(y) = \int_R h(y + \xi) d\Phi(\xi) \tag{48}$$

where h is an integrable and bounded functional. Usually, the functional $H(y)$ is not necessarily continuous, but we have the following result.

Lemma 1 *If h is a measurable bounded functional which can have at most a countable number of discontinuities, then so is H. In particular, H is a continuous functional if at least one of the following conditions holds:*

1. *h is a continuous functional;*
2. *Φ is a continuous distribution.*

Liu and Esogbue (1996) established and proved the following fundamental theorem.

Theorem 1 *Assume (A_1), (A_2) and (A_3) for all stages, then the dynamic programming equation (46) defines a sequence of continuous functions. Moreover, there exists a Borel measurable function $\widehat{d}_n(x)$ such that the supremum in (46) is attained for any x if D_n can be restricted to a compact set for any n.*

Liu and Esogbue (1996) consider the infinite horizon problem to maximize

$$J_n(\mathbf{x}; \mathbf{d}) = \sum_{i=n}^{\infty} \gamma_i^{(n)} \int_R \mu_i(x_i + d_i + \xi_i) d\Phi_i(\xi_i) \tag{49}$$

where $\gamma_i^{(n)} = \lambda_i / (\lambda_n + \lambda_{n+1} + \cdots)$ and $\lambda_1 + \lambda_2 + \cdots = 1$, and develop the dynamic programming equation associated with problem (49) as follows:

$$\begin{aligned} f_n(x) = \sup_{d \in D_n} \Big\{ & \theta_n L_n(x + d) \\ & + (1 - \theta_n) \int_R f_{n+1}(x + d + \xi) d\Phi_n(\xi) \Big\} \end{aligned} \tag{50}$$

where $\theta_n = \gamma_n^{(n)}$. We will suppose here that all $\lambda_i > 0$ which implies that

$$0 < \theta_n < 1, \qquad \text{for all } n. \tag{51}$$

Liu and Esogbue (1996) provide the proofs of the following lemmas useful in establishing the existence and uniqueness theorems for the solution to (50):

Lemma 2 *Assume (A_1), (A_2) and (A_3) for all stages, then the relations*

$$\begin{aligned} W_n(x) = {} & \theta_n L_n(x + d_n) \\ & + (1 - \theta_n) \int_R W_{n+1}(x + d_n + \xi) d\Phi_n(\xi) \end{aligned} \tag{52}$$

define a bounded sequence of continuous functions. Moreover, W_n is explicitly defined by

$$W_n(x) = \sum_{i=n}^{\infty} \gamma_i^{(n)} L_{n,i}(x + d_n + \cdots + d_i) \tag{53}$$

where

$$L_{n,i}(y) = \int_R \cdots \int_R \mu_i(y + \xi_n + \cdots + \xi_i) d\Phi_n(\xi_n) \cdots d\Phi_i(\xi_i) \tag{54}$$

and d_n are any given feasible policies in D_n, respectively.

Lemma 3 *Consider*

$$t(p) = \sup_{d \in D} \left\{ \theta h(p,d) + (1-\theta) \int_R f(p,d,r) d\Phi(r) \right\} \tag{55}$$

and

$$T(p) = \sup_{d \in D} \left\{ \theta H(p,d) + (1-\theta) \int_R F(p,d,r) d\Phi(r) \right\} \tag{56}$$

where Φ is a probability measure, h, H, f and F are integrable and bounded and $0 \le \theta \le 1$. Then, for any given p and $\epsilon > 0$, there exists a point $d^0 \in D$ such that

$$\begin{aligned} |t(p) - T(p)| \le \theta |h(p,d^0) - H(p,d^0)| \\ +(1-\theta) \int_R [|f(p,d^0,r) \\ -F(p,d^0,r)| d\Phi(r)] + \epsilon \end{aligned} \tag{57}$$

Then, Liu and Esogbue (1996) prove the following existence and uniqueness theorems associated with solutions to their fuzzy dynamic programming functional equation.

Theorem 2 [Existence Theorem] *We consider*

$$W_n^0(x) = W_n(x)$$

$$\begin{aligned} W_n^{k+1}(x) = \sup_{d \in D_n} \Big\{ \theta_n L_n(x+d) \\ +(1-\theta_n) \int_R W_{n+1}^k (x+d+\xi) d\Phi_n(\xi) \Big\} \end{aligned} \tag{58}$$

Then we have

$$W_n^{k+1} \ge W_n^k, \quad k = 0, 1, 2, \ldots \tag{59}$$

and

$$W_n^k \uparrow W_n^* \tag{60}$$

Moreover, the limit $W_n^*(x)$ is a continuous bounded solution to (50) if we assume (A_1), (A_2) and (A_3).

Theorem 3 [Uniqueness Theorem] *Assume (A_1), (A_2) and (A_3) for all stages, then there is one, and only one, bounded solution to (50).*

7.2 Optimal control policy and other aspects of fuzzy criterion dynamic programming

Operating characteristics and various specific applications to open inventory networks and systems, multidimensional versions, and stochastic joint reservoir operations were developed in Esogbue and Liu (1997a, b, c).

8 Computational complexity of fuzzy dynamic programs

The development of efficient algorithms for processing various aspects of fuzzy dynamic programs is an important research area in dynamic programming which is hardly addressed in works of most authors. A notable exeption is here the work of, e.g., Esogbue (1997). In this section, we will summarize main results of the computational complexity analysis provided by (1997) Esogbue using the two algorithms of Kacprzyk (1977) and Stein (1980) for the fuzzy termination time discussed earlier in this paper.

We now examine the space and the computational complexities of the algorithm proposed by Kacprzyk (1977). For storage complexity S, we assume that each variable (computer word) takes a unit of storage space. We may then calculate the demand for the storage tables during computations ignoring all input tables and intermediate variables created during the course of processing.

For a performance profile of an algorithm, we consider the computational complexity T, as a function of the basic operations. Apparently, comparison, mod operation, assignment and arithmetic operations may be considered as such basic operations. We further assume that the total number of all above operations performed is roughly proportional to the number of comparisons. Hence the comparison constitutes the basic operation and T of an algorithm is approximated by the number of comparisons.

Using the above framework, Esogbue (1997) showed that the dynamic programming approach presented by Kacprzyk (1977) requires $N(N+1)/2$ iterations while the one proposed by Stein (1980) requires only N and hence it is computationally more efficient. Let us focus here on the time and space complexity analysis for both.

In this model consisting of n equations and u_{N-1} controls each assuming m values, and time $t = N-1, \ldots, K.$, the total number of operations involved is

$$n(2mt - 2mK - 2m - t + K) + n(N - K + 1) + (K-1)n(2m-1) \qquad (61)$$

If we let $m = K = t$, we can see that this is of the order $O(2K^3)$.

The basic dynamic programming formulation of the problem as proposed by Stein (1980) is the same except for the structure of the recurrence equations that require N only iterations of the optimizing process as opposed to $N(N+1)/2$ required in Kacprzyk's algorithm.

For this model, the space and the time complexities are of order $O(n)$ and $O(mn)$, respectively. Essentially, the time complexity is of order $O((2m-1)(N-K))$. This is of order $O(K^2)$. The total storage demand is $n(N-K+1)(N-K+2)/2 + 2n + n(K-1)$. This is of order $O(K)$.

It was pointed out that the difference between the earliest and the latest possible termination times is an important factor in the computational burden of this optimization process.

So, the later model proposed by Stein (1980) is computationally more efficient, taking up $O(K)$ memory spaces in $O(K^2)$ operations, as opposed to $O(K^2)$ memory spaces in $O(2K^3)$ operations in Kacprzyk's (1977) model. Thus the superiority is exhibited both from the space and time complexity considerations.

In the case of a stochastic system, it was shown that the computational burden and storage requirements are identical for both algorithms if, in the dynamic programming formulation, the objective is to maximize the probability of attainment of the fuzzy goal G subject to non fuzzy constraints.

9 A brief review of applications

We will mention some of more relevant applications of fuzzy dynamic programming that basically fall into two main categories:

- applications related to more general (standard) problems,
- applications related to more specific problems;

referring the reader for more detail to Kacprzyk's (1997) book.

In the first group, we should first mention a pioneering work on a general resource allocation problem with fuzzy goals and constraints by Esogbue and Ramesh (1970). This represents the first reported effort detailing the computational schema and algorithms for fuzzy dynamic programs. Another problem class of a universal relevance is data clustering, and the application of fuzzy dynamic programming was proposed here by Esogbue (1986), and Esogbue and Bellman (1981). These applications involve environmental and water pollution control modeling. There exist several applications which are directed at some mathematical programming problems. For example, Hussein and Abo-Sinna (1993) apply a hybrid fuzzy dynamic programming approach to determine a set of efficient solutions of the multiobjective mathematical programming problem. Narshima Sastry, Tiwari, and Sastry (1993), on the other hand, solved a generalized multiple goal fuzzy control (optimization) problem by using fuzzy dynamic programming.

In the second group, we should first mention Esogbue's (1983) work on a general research and development (R&D) control problem in which some limited funds are to be optimally used to attain certain goals distributed over time. This problem may be a prototype for a much wider class of applications. Second, in a series of papers, Kacprzyk and Straszak (1981, 1982a, b, 1984) proposed a fuzzy dynamic programming model for determining socioeconomic regional development strategies which take into account limited resources, requirements on the effectiveness and stability of development, some objective and subjective aspects, etc.

Relevant medical applications have been proposed, and one should mention here Esogbue and Elder's (1977) work on a fuzzy dynamic programming model of medical diagnosis and Esogbue's (1985) approach to intra-operative anesthesia administrations which is useful for planning and control. In fact, Esogbue's (1983) work on R&D is much concerned with the cancer research appropriation process which seeks an optimal resource allocation strategy such that the probability/possibility of attaining a breakthrough in cancer containment is maximized.

A fruitful area of research is energy systems. Among more relevant works there, we should first of all mention Su and Hsu (1991) who applied fuzzy dynamic programming to the unit commitment of a power system, and practically implemented the results obtained for Taiwan's power system. Huang, Lin and Huang (1992) presented a fuzzy dynamic programming model for the determination of an optimal schedule for the outage starting times of power generators for maintenance over the one year planning horizon for a Taiwanese power company. Sugianto and Mielczarski (1995a, b, 1996) consider the optimization of a spare parts inventory in a power generation plant by balancing requirements on power availability and reduction of spare parts' costs.

Water resources systems comprise an important field in which fuzzy dynamic programming models have found applications. One of the earliest applications in this involve the work of Esogbue and Bellman (1981) where an application to the analysis of water resources related data was presented. Esogbue and Ahipo (1982a, b) utilize fuzzy DP tools in developing some effectiveness measures in water resources planning. Esogbue, Theologidu, and Guo (1992) presented an application to an extremely relevant problem of flood control, while Esogbue (1996) generalizes the models to disaster control planning. An application of fuzzy dynamic programming to the open inventory problem is reported in Esogbue and Liu (1997c) while its application to the multi-reservoir operation problem, with both fuzzy and stochastic parameters, is discussed by Esogbue and Liu (1997b).

In chemical engineering we cite the work of Krasławski, Górak and Vogenpohl (1989) who proposed an application of fuzzy dynamic programming to the determination of distillation sequence (sequence of distillation columns) for a mixture of some number of components. An important problem involving the determination of a best itinerary for the transportation of hazardous waste loads in a given road structure was considered by Klein (1991) taking into account the safety of the road segments and intersection, distance, driving difficulty, dangers related to population density, etc.

Yuan and Wu (1991) proposed an application of fuzzy dynamic programming to real-time control of a transportation system in a flexible manufacturing environment, more particularly involving the so-called autonomous guided vehicles (AGVs) which are driverless, programmable vehicles that can move around the factory.

10 Concluding remarks

We have presented a brief exposition of main aspects of fuzzy dynamic programming, inlcuding main problem classes and major applications in a variety of fields.

However, because of space limitations and the scope of this short review, we have not discussed an extremely important problem of computational issues of fuzzy dynamic programming models. It must be noted however that these models, analogous to their nonfuzzy counterparts, exhibit the so-called but over-publicized "curse of dimensionality". This may prohibit their brute force use in large-scale real-world problems without first ensuring adroit formulation and employing recent computational devices including parallel computing. For discussion of these issues, we refer the interested reader to Esogbue (1991a, b, 1997), and to some "trickery" to overcome this difficulties – to Kacprzyk's (1997) book.

For other surveys of fuzzy dynamic programming and its applications, we refer the reader to Esogbue and Bellman (1984), a follow up study by Kacprzyk and Esogbue (1996), and then the fundamental presentation by Kacprzyk (1983a, 1997).

Literature

Baldwin J.F. and B.W. Pilsworth (1982) Dynamic programming for fuzzy systems with fuzzy environment, J. Math. Anal. and Appls., 85, 1–23.

Bellman R.E. (1957) Dynamic Programming. Princeton Univ. Press, Princeton, NJ.

Bellman R.E. and L.A. Zadeh (1970) Decision-making in a fuzzy environment. Management Sci., 17, 141–164.

Chang S.S.L. (1969b) Fuzzy dynamic programming and the decision making process. Proc. 3rd Princeton Conf. on Inf. Sci. and Syst. (Princeton, NJ, USA), 200–203.

Esogbue A.O. (1983) Dynamic programming, fuzzy sets and the modelling of R&D management control systems. IEEE Trans. on Systems, Man, and Cybernetics, SMC-13, 18–30.

Esogbue A.O. (1984) Some novel applications of fuzzy dynamic programming. *Proceedings of IEEE Systems, Man, and Cybernetics Conference* (Bombay, India).

Esogbue A.O. (1985) A fuzzy dynamic programming model of intra-operative anesthesia administration, In J. Kacprzyk and R.R. Yager (Eds.): Management Decision Support Systems using Fuzzy Sets and Possibility Theory. Verlag TÜV Rheinland, Cologne, 155–161.

Esogbue A.O. (1986) Optimal clustering of fuzzy data via fuzzy dynamic programming. Fuzzy Sets and Systems, 18, 283–298.

Esogbue A.O. (1989) Dynamic Programming for Optimal Water Resources Systems Analysis. Prentice-Hall, Englewood Cliffs, NJ.

Esogbue A.O. (1991a) Computational and data acquisition issues in fuzzy dynamic programming. Proceedings of ORSA/TIMS Conference (Anaheim, CA).

Esogbue A.O. (1991b) Computational aspects and applications of a branch and bound algorithm for fuzzy multistage decision processes. Computers and Mathematics with Applications, 21, 117–127.

Esogbue, A.O. (1995) On the computational complexity of fuzzy dynamic programs. Proc. 6th International Association World Congress, Sao Paolo, Brazil, 217–220.

Esogbue A.O. and Z.M. Ahipo (1982a) Fuzzy sets in water resources planning, In R.R. Yager (Eds.): Recent Developments in Fuzzy Sets and Possibility Theory, Pergamon Press, New York, 450–465.

Esogbue A.O. and Z.M. Ahipo (1982b) A fuzzy sets model for measuring the effectiveness of public participation in water resources planning, Water Resources Bulletin, 18, 451–456.

Esogbue A.O. and R.E. Bellman (1981) A fuzzy dynamic programming algorithm for clustering non-quantitative data arising in water pollution control planning. Proceedings of Third International Conference on Mathematical Modelling (Los Angeles, CA).

Esogbue A.O. and R.E. Bellman (1984) Fuzzy dynamic programming and its extensions. TIMS/Studies in the Management Sciences, 20, 147–167.

Esogbue A.O. and R.C. Elder (1983) Measurement and valuation of a fuzzy mathematical model for medical diagnosis. Fuzzy Sets and Systems, 10, 223–242.

Esogbue A.O., M. Fedrizzi and J. Kacprzyk (1988) Fuzzy dynamic programming with stochastic systems, In J. Kacprzyk and M. Fedrizzi (Eds.): Combining Fuzzy Imprecision with Probabilistic Uncertainty in Decision Making. Springer–Verlag, Berlin/New York, 266–285.

Esogbue A.O. and J. Kacprzyk (1996) Fuzzy dynamic programming: a survey of main developments and applications, Archives of Control Sciences, 5(XLI), 39–59.

Esogbue A.O. and J. Kacprzyk (1998) Fuzzy dynamic programming, In R. Słowińki (Ed.): Fuzzy Sets in Decision Analysis, Operations Reserach and Statistics, Kluwer, Boston, 281–307.

Esogbue A.O. and B. Liu (1996) On fuzzy criterion set dynamic programming. Proc. 1996 Biennial Conference of the North American Fuzzy Information Processing Society (Berkeley, CA), 70–74.

Esogbue A.O. and B. Liu (1997a) On stochastic multistage decision making under fuzzy criteria. Proc. International Conference on Fuzzy Logic and Applications (Zichron-Ya'akov, Israel).

Esogbue A.O. and B. Liu (1997b) Stochastic multi-joint reservior operation via fuzzy criterion dynamic programming. Proc. 7th International Fuzzy Systems Association (IFSA) World Congress (Pragie, Czech Republic).

Esogbue A.O. and B. Liu (1997c) Fuzzy criterion dynamic programming and optimal control of multi-dimensional open inventory networks. Proc. Sixth IEEE International Conference on Fuzzy Systems (Barcelona, Spain).

Esogbue A.O. and V. Ramesh (1970) Dynamic programming and fuzzy allocation processes. Technical Memo No. 202, Dept. of Operations Research, Case Western University, Cleveland, OH.

Esogbue A.O., M. Theologidu and K. Guo (1992) On the application of fuzzy sets theory to the optimal flood control problem arising in water resources systems. Fuzzy Sets and Systems, 48, 155–172.

Fung L.W. and K.S. Fu (1977) Characterization of a class of fuzzy optimal control problems, In M.M. Gupta, G.N. Saridis and B.R. Gaines (Eds.): Fuzzy Automata and Decision Processes. North-Holland, Amsterdam, 205–220.

Huang C.J., C.E. Lin and C.L. Huang (1992) Fuzzy approach for generator maintenance scheduling. Electric Power Systems Research, 24, 31–38.

Hussein M.L. and M.A. Abo-Sinna (1993) Decomposition of multiobjective programming problems by hybrid fuzzy dynamic programming. Fuzzy Sets and Systems, 60, 25–32.

Kacprzyk J. (1977) Control of a nonfuzzy system in a fuzzy environment with fuzzy termination time. Systems Science, 3, 325–341.

Kacprzyk J. (1878a) A branch-and-bound algorithm for the multistage control of a nonfuzzy system in a fuzzy environment. Control and Cybernetics, 7, 51–64.

Kacprzyk J. (1978b) Control of a stochastic system in a fuzzy environment with fuzzy termination time. Systems Science, 4, 291–300.

Kacprzyk J. (1978c) Decision making in a fuzzy environment with fuzzy termination time. Fuzzy Sets and Systems, 1, 169–179.

Kacprzyk J. (1979) A branch-and-bound algorithm for the multistage control of a fuzzy system in a fuzzy environment. Kybernetes, 8, 139–147.

Kacprzyk J. (1983a) A generalization of fuzzy multistage decision making and control via linguistic quantifiers. Int. J. of Control, 38, 1249–1270.

Kacprzyk J. (1983b) Multistage Decision-Making under Fuzziness. Verlag TÜV Rheinland, Cologne.

Kacprzyk J. (1993) Interpolative reasoning in optimal fuzzy control, Proc. of Second IEEE International Conference on Fuzzy Systems (FUZZ–IEEE '93), Vol. II, 1259–1263.

Kacprzyk J. (1994a) Fuzzy dynamic programming – basic issues, In M. Delgado, J. Kacprzyk, J.-L. Verdegay and M.A. Vila (Eds.): Fuzzy Optimization: Recent Advances, Physica-Verlag, Heidelberg, 321–331.

Kacprzyk J. (1994b) Prescriptive approaches to fuzzy control: yet-to-be rediscovered old jewels?, Controle and Automa¸ao, 4, 141–154.

Kacprzyk J. (1996) Fuzzy dynamic programming: a new quality through fuzy sets, In Da Ruan (Ed.): Fuzzy Sets Theory and Advanced Mathematical Applications, Kluwer, Dordrecht, 137–154.

Kacprzyk J. (1997) Multistage Fuzzy Control: A Model-Based Approach to Control and Decision Making. Wiley, Chichester.

Kacprzyk, J. (1998) Multistage control of a stochastic system in a fuzzy environment using a genetic algorithm, Int. J. of Intelligent Systems, 13, 1011–1023.

Kacprzyk J. and A.O. Esogbue (1996) Fuzzy dynamic programming: main developments and applications. Fuzzy Sets and Systems, 81, 31–45.

Kacprzyk J., K. Safteruk and P. Staniewski (1981) On the control of stochastic systems in a fuzzy environment over infinite horizon. Systems Science, 7, 121–131.

Kacprzyk J. and P. Staniewski (1980) A new approach to the control of stochastic systems in a fuzzy environment, Arch. Automat. i Telemech., XXV, 443–444.

Kacprzyk J. and P. Staniewski (1982) Long-term inventory policy-making through fuzzy decision-making models. Fuzzy Sets and Systems, 8, 117–132.

Kacprzyk J. and P. Staniewski (1983). Control of a deterministic system in a fuzzy environment over an infinite planning horizon, Fuzzy Sets and Systems, 10, 291–298.

Kacprzyk J. and A. Straszak (1981) Application of fuzzy decision -making models for determining optimal policies in 'stable' integrated regional development. In P.P. Wang and S.K. Chang (Eds.): Fuzzy Sets Theory and Applications to Policy Analysis and Information Systems, Plenum Press, New York, 321–328.

Kacprzyk J. and A. Straszak (1982a) A fuzzy approach to the stability of integrated regional development. In G.E. Lasker (Ed.): Applied Systems and Cybernetics, Vol. 6, Pergamon Press, New York, 2997–3004.

Kacprzyk J. and A. Straszak (1982b) Determination of 'stable' regional development trajectories via a fuzzy decision-making model. In R.R. Yager (Ed.): Recent Developments in Fuzzy Sets and Possibility Theory, Pergamon Press, New York, 531–541

Kacprzyk J. and A. Straszak (1984) Determination of stable trajectories for integrated regional development using fuzzy decision models. IEEE Transactions on Systems, Man and Cybernetics, SMC-14, 310–313.

Klein C.M. (1991) A model for the transportation of hazardous waste. Decision Sciences, 22, 1091–1108.

Komolov S.V. et al. (1979) On the problem of optimal control of a finite automaton with fuzzy constraints and fuzzy goal (in Russian), Kybernetika (Kiev), 6, 30–34.

Krasławski A., A. Górak and A. Vogelpohl (1989) Fuzzy dynamic programming in the synthesis of distillation column systems. Computers and Chemical Engineering, 13, 611–618.

Liu B. and A.O. Esogbue (1996) Fuzzy criterion set and fuzzy criterion dynamic programming. J. of Math. Anal. and Appls., 1991, 293–311.

Narshima Sastry V., R.N. Tiwari and K.S. Sastry (1993) Dynamic programming approach to multiple objective control problems having deterministic or fuzzy goals. Fuzzy Sets and Systems, 57, 195–202.

Stein W.E. (1980) Optimal stopping in a fuzzy environment. Fuzzy Sets and Systems, 3, 252–259.

Sugianto L.F. and W. Mielczarski (1995a) A fuzzy logic approach to optimize inventory. In G.F. Forsyth and M. Ali (Eds.): Proceedings of Eighth International Conference on Industrial and Engineering Applications of Artificial Intelligence and Expert Systems, Gordon and Breach (Australia), 419–424.

Sugianto L.F. and W. Mielczarski (1995b) Control of power station inventory by optimal allocation process with fuzzy logic approach. Proceedings of Control '95 Conference (Australia), Vol. 2, 529–533.

Yuan Y. and Z. Wu (1991) Algorithm of fuzzy dynamic programming in AGV scheduling. Proceedings of the International Conference on Computer Integrated Manufacturing (ICCIM'91), 405–408.

Zadeh L.A. (1968) Probability measures of fuzzy events, J. of Math. Anal. and Appls., 23, 421–427.

Zimmermann H.-J. (1987) Fuzzy Sets, Decision Making, and Expert Systems. Kluwer, Dordrecht.

Fuzzy Dynamic Programming in the Stochastic Environment

Seiichi Iwamoto

Department of Economic Engineering, Graduate School of Economics, Kyushu University 27, Hakozaki 6-19-1, Higashiku, Fukuoka 812-8581, JAPAN

Abstract. From a viewpoint of stochastic dynamic programming, we develop "De-cision-making in a fuzzy environment" in Bellman and Zadeh's seminal paper (1970). We present three dynamic programming approaches — (1) membership-parametric method, (2) history-parametric method and (3) multi-stage stochastic decision tree-table method —, which yield a common optimal solution. We also introduce a dynamic programming approach to both fuzzy system and an a posteriori conditional decision process. We show that their stochastic decision process is the a posteriori conditional decision process.

1 Introduction

Since Bellman and Zadeh's seminal paper [3], a study on fuzzy theory of mathematical programming has been making extensive progress. Also in dynamic programming methods, some interesting approaches have been proposed ([1],[4],[16],[17],[18],[19],[20],[25]).

In this paper, from *the* dynamic programming viewpoint, we reconsider their "Decision-making in a fuzzy environment" on three —deterministic, stochastic and fuzzy — systems. As is well-known, dynamic programming is based upon both separability and monotonicity [2],[7],[23]. It gives an optimal solution to any original problem — whether it has a sequential structure or not— by successively solving a recursive equation. That is, dynamic programming has to assure that any *sequential* solution is a *simultaneous* solution to the original problem. In this viewpoint, Bellman and Zadeh's discussion on deterministic system assures that a dynamic programming solution yields a simultaneous optimal solution to the deterministic multistage decision process [3, §4]. However, their treatment on stochastic system follows by analogy the deterministic dynamic programming approach, which does not generate a simultaneous optimal solution for the stochastic multistage decision process [3, §5]. This is due to a nonadditive (minimum) criterion on stochastic system. Such a stochastic problem does not expose separability and/or monotonicity in an explicit form. In the case, the first task for application of dynamic programming is to find or impose somehow both properties somewhere. Further, though they have mainly discussed both deterministic and stochastic systems, they have just given only a definition of fuzzy system [3, p.151]. The dynamic programming treatment on the fuzzy system has not discussed in detail.

From these viewpoints we consider some dynamic programming treatments on three systems for "Decision-making in a fuzzy environment."

In section 2 we review Bellman and Zadeh's discussion of deterministic system. This gives a regular dynamic programming treatment of minimum criterion.

In section 3, on stochastic system, we introduce three types— expanded Markov, general and primitive — of policies. An interrelation between three policy classes are discussed. We show that a common optimal general policy for minimum criterion has been obtained through three — membership-parametric, history-parametric and multi-stage stochastic decision tree-table — methods. Further we illustrate that Markov class is not enough for stochastic system with minimum criterion. We see that an invariant imbedding method [21],[24] takes an important part in deriving a recursive formula for stochastic system with nonadditive criterion.

In section 4, on fuzzy system, a recursive formula is derived through a dynamic programming, where the fuzzy expected value is taken through minimization-maximization operator.

In section 5 we propose an a posteriori conditional decision process. We show that the a posteriori process is the process Bellman and Zadeh [3] have proposed on stochastic system.

2 Deterministic System

A fuzzy decision process on a deterministic system is the following multi-stage decision process with minimum criterion (Bellman and Zadeh [3]) :

$$\begin{array}{lll} \text{Max.} & \mu_1(x_1,u_1) \wedge \mu_2(x_2,u_2) \wedge \cdots \wedge \mu_N(x_N,u_N) \wedge \mu_G(x_{N+1}) & \\ \text{s.t.} & \text{(i)} \quad x_{n+1} = f(x_n,u_n) & \\ & & n = 1,2,\ldots,N \\ & \text{(ii)} \quad u_n \in U & \end{array} \tag{1}$$

On the deterministic system, an action $u_n \in U$ at state $x_n \in X$ determines uniquely a next state $x_{n+1} = f(x_n, u_n)$, where $f : X \times U \to X$ is a state-transformation. $\mu_n : X \times U \to [0,1]$ is a membership function on a fuzzy set R_n on $X \times U$:

$$\mu_n(x,u) = \mu_{R_n}(x,u).$$

$\mu_G : X \to [0,1]$ is a membership function on a fuzzy goal (fuzzy set) G on X. Then the multi-stage decision process maximizes the membership function

$$\begin{aligned} &\mu_{R_1 \cap R_2 \cap \cdots \cap R_N \cap G}(x_1,u_1,x_2,u_2,\cdots,x_N,u_N,x_{N+1}) \\ &= \mu_1(x_1,u_1) \wedge \mu_2(x_2,u_2) \wedge \cdots \wedge \mu_N(x_N,u_N) \wedge \mu_G(x_{N+1}) \end{aligned}$$

of intersection $R_1 \cap R_2 \cap \cdots \cap R_N \cap G$.

We consider a class of policies. A mapping $\pi_n : X \to U$ is called *n-th Markov decision function*. A sequence of Markov decision functions $\pi =$

$\{\pi_1, \pi_2, \ldots, \pi_N\}$ is called *Markov policy.* We denote the set of all Markov policies by Π, which is called *Markov class.*

Then we have the backward recursive formula ([23]) :

Theorem 1. *(Bellman and Zadeh[3])*

$$\begin{aligned} v_n(x) &= \operatorname*{Max}_{u \in U}[\mu_n(x,u) \wedge v_{n+1}(f_n(x,u))] \quad 1 \leq n \leq N \\ & \qquad\qquad\qquad\qquad\qquad\qquad\qquad x \in X. \\ v_{N+1}(x) &= \mu_G(x) \end{aligned} \tag{2}$$

This is a fuzzy dynamic programming for the deterministic system.

Now let us solve a 3-state 2-action 2-stage (3-2-2) model ([3]) :

$$\begin{aligned} &\text{Max.} \;\; \mu_1(u_1) \wedge \mu_2(u_2) \wedge \mu_G(x_3) \\ &\text{s.t.} \;\; x_{n+1} = f(x_n, u_n), \;\; u_n \in U \quad n = 1, 2 \end{aligned}$$

where the data is Table 1 :

$\mu_t(u_t) \backslash u_t$	a_1	a_2
$\mu_1(u_1)$	0.7	1.0
$\mu_2(u_2)$	1.0	0.6

x_3	$\mu_G(x_3)$
s_1	0.3
s_2	1.0
s_3	0.8

$x_t \backslash u_t$	a_1	a_2
s_1	s_1	s_2
s_2	s_3	s_1
s_3	s_1	s_3

Table 1. $\{\mu_1, \mu_2\}$ μ_G $f(x_t, u_t)$

We solve the recursive equation :

$$\begin{aligned} v_3(x_3) &= \mu_G(x_3) \qquad x_3 \in X \\ v_2(x_2) &= \operatorname*{Max}_{u_2 \in U} [\mu_2(u_2) \wedge v_3(f(x_2, u_2))] \quad x_2 \in X \\ v_1(x_1) &= \operatorname*{Max}_{u_1 \in U} [\mu_1(u_1) \wedge v_2(f(x_1, u_1))] \quad x_1 \in X. \end{aligned}$$

Then the dynamic programming solution, which consists of a pair of sequence of optimal membership functions $\{v_1, v_2, v_3\}$ and optimal policy $\pi^* = \{\pi_1^*, \pi_2^*\}$, is shown in Table 2:

x_n	$v_1(x_1)$	$\pi_1^*(x_1)$	$v_2(x_2)$	$\pi_2^*(x_2)$	$v_3(x_3)$
s_1	0.8	a_2	0.6	a_2	0.3
s_2	0.6	a_1, a_2	0.8	a_1	1.0
s_3	0.6	a_1, a_2	0.6	a_2	0.8

Table 2. $\{v_1, v_2, v_3\}$ $\pi^* = \{\pi_1^*, \pi_2^*\}$

3 Stochastic System

Second we consider a fuzzy dynamic programming on stochastic system. The fuzzy decision process Bellman and Zadeh [3] have proposed is the following maximization problem of expected value of minimum criterion [8][11] :

$$\begin{array}{lll} \text{Max.} & E^{\sigma}_{x_1}[\mu_1 \wedge \mu_2 \wedge \cdots \wedge \mu_N \wedge \mu_G] & \\ \text{s.t.} & \text{(i)} \;\; x_{n+1} \sim p(\cdot|x_n, u_n) & \\ & \text{(ii)} \;\; u_n \in U & n = 1, 2, \ldots, N \end{array} \tag{3}$$

Now let us introduce a large class of policies, which depend not only on today's state but also on state-to-date. We define $X^n := X \times X \times \cdots \times X$ by direct product of n state spaces X. A mapping $\sigma_n : X^n \to U$ is called *n-th general decision function*, whose sequence $\sigma = \{\sigma_1, \sigma_2, \ldots, \sigma_N\}$ is a *general policy*. The set of all general policies Π_g is called *general class*. When each general decision function σ_n depends only on the last state, the general policy reduces to a Markov policy $\pi = \{\pi_1, \pi_2, \ldots, \pi_N\}$. Thus we have an inclusion relation : $\Pi \subset \Pi_g$.

The objective value in (3) is an expected value of minimum function through the (discrete) probability measure $P^{\sigma}_{x_1}(\cdot)$ defined by a general policy σ, an initial state x_1 and the transition law p :

$$\begin{aligned} & E^{\sigma}_{x_1}[\mu_1 \wedge \mu_2 \wedge \cdots \wedge \mu_N \wedge \mu_G] \\ &= \sum_{(x_2,\ldots,x_{N+1}) \in X \times \cdots \times X} \sum \cdots \sum [\mu_1(x_1, u_1) \wedge \cdots \wedge \mu_N(x_N, u_N) \wedge \mu_G(x_{N+1})] \\ & \qquad \times p(x_2|x_1, u_1) \cdots p(x_{N+1}|x_N, u_N) \end{aligned} \tag{4}$$

where

$$u_1 = \sigma_1(x_1), \; u_2 = \sigma_2(x_1, x_2), \; \ldots, \; u_N = \sigma_N(x_1, \ldots, x_N).$$

It is very important to note that (after-today expected value) for minimum criterion is not separated into (today's value) and (after-tomorrow expected value). This nonseparation property is different from separability for additive criterion [6],[22]. Thus we do not apply the expected utility theory for additive criterion. Here we must develop a dynamic programming method which admits the expected utility theory of nonadditive or minimum criterion. Such a dynamic programming is expected to be a fuzzy dynamic programming. In this sense, we consider the fuzzy dynamic programming in this chapter. Fortunately we see that taking into account of membership values in the unit interval $[0, 1]$, the following fact is true. That is, even if we add the *special* value 1.0 in front of the minimum function, the expected value is invariant :

$$E^{\sigma}_{x_1}[\mu_1 \wedge \cdots \wedge \mu_N \wedge \mu_G] = E^{\sigma}_{x_1}[1.0 \wedge \mu_1 \wedge \cdots \wedge \mu_N \wedge \mu_G] \tag{5}$$

Here is the beginning of an invariant imbedding method [21],[24].

Let $v_1(x_1)$ denote the maximum value of expected values over general class Π_g. Introducing a new real-parameter λ_n $(0 \le \lambda_n \le 1)$, we imbed (3) into the family of subproblems :

$$\begin{aligned} &\text{Max.} \quad E^{\sigma}_{x_n}[\lambda_n \wedge \mu_n \wedge \cdots \wedge \mu_N \wedge \mu_G] \\ &\text{s.t.} \quad \text{(i)} \ \ x_{m+1} \sim p(\cdot|x_m, u_m) \qquad m = n, n+1, \ldots, N \\ &\qquad\ \ \text{(ii)} \ \ u_m \in U \end{aligned} \tag{6}$$

Let $v_n(x_n; \lambda_n)$ denote the maximum value of (6) over $\Pi_g(n)$, where $\Pi_g(n)$ is the set of all general policies from n-th stage on : $\sigma = \{\sigma_n, \sigma_{n+1}, \ldots, \sigma_N\}$. Then we have the following recursive formula

Theorem 2. *(Iwamoto and Fujita[11])*

$$\begin{aligned} v_n(x;\lambda) &= \underset{u \in U}{\text{Max}} \sum_{y \in X} v_{n+1}(y; \lambda \wedge \mu_n(x,u))p(y|x,u) \qquad 1 \le n \le N \\ v_{N+1}(x;\lambda) &= \lambda \wedge \mu_G(x) \qquad\qquad x \in X, \quad 0 \le \lambda \le 1. \end{aligned} \tag{7}$$

By backward solving (7) from $v_{N+1} = v_{N+1}(x_{N+1}; \lambda_{N+1})$ we have $v_1 = v_1(x_1; \lambda_1)$. A substitution of $\lambda_1 = 1.0$ yields the desired maximum value $v_1(x_1)$:

$$v_1(x_1) = v_1(x_1; 1.0). \tag{8}$$

On the other hand, we consider the following policy. Let for each (n, x, λ) $\gamma^*_n(x, \lambda)$ be a maximizer for recursive equation (7). Then we have *n-th expanded Markov decision function* $\gamma^*_n : X \times [0,1] \to U$, which constitutes an *expanded Markov policy* $\gamma^* = \{\gamma^*_1, \gamma^*_2, \ldots, \gamma^*_N\}$. We denote the set of all expanded Markov policies by $\tilde{\Pi}$, which is called *expanded Markov class.* Now by defining

$$\begin{array}{lll} \text{initial state} & (x_1, \lambda_1); \ \lambda_1 := 1.0 & \\ \text{state space} & X \times [0,1] & \\ \text{action space} & U & \\ \text{state transformation} & \begin{cases} X_{n+1} \sim p(\cdot|x_n, u_n) \\ \lambda_{n+1} = \lambda_n \wedge \mu(x_n, u_n) \end{cases} & 1 \le n \le N \\ \text{reward function} & \begin{cases} n\text{-th stage } R_n(x,\lambda,u) = 0 \quad 1 \le n \le N \\ \text{terminal} \quad \Psi(x,\lambda) = \lambda \wedge r_G(x) \end{cases} & \end{array} \tag{9}$$

we have an N-stage decision process with terminal criterion:

$$\sum_{n=1}^{N} R_n(x_n, \lambda_n, u_n) + \Psi(x_{N+1}, \lambda_{N+1}) = \lambda_{N+1} \wedge r_G(x_{N+1}).$$

The terminal criterion is a special form of additive criterion. Therefore the conventional dynamic programming theory shows that the Markov policy γ^* is optimal over the expanded Markov class.

In general, any expanded Markov policy $\gamma = \{\gamma_1, \gamma_2, \ldots, \gamma_N\} \in \tilde{\Pi}$ generates an equivalent (in the sense that both yield a same expected value) general policy $\sigma = \{\sigma_1, \sigma_2, \ldots, \sigma_N\} \in \Pi_g$ through the following transformation (10) (see [15]). Given any state-sequence $(x_1, x_2, \ldots, x_n)$, generating an intermediate parameter-sequence, we define $\sigma_n(x_1, x_2, \ldots, x_n)$ as follows :

$$\begin{aligned}
&\lambda_1 := 1.0 \\
&u_1 := \gamma_1(x_1; \lambda_1), \quad \lambda_2 := \lambda_1 \wedge r(x_1, u_1) \\
&u_2 := \gamma_2(x_2; \lambda_2), \quad \lambda_3 := \lambda_2 \wedge r(x_2, u_2) \\
&\qquad\vdots \\
&u_{n-1} := \gamma_{n-1}(y_{n-1}), \quad \lambda_n := \lambda_{n-1} \wedge r(x_{n-1}, u_{n-1}) \\
&\sigma_n(x_1, x_2, \ldots, x_n) := \gamma_n(x_n; \lambda_n).
\end{aligned} \tag{10}$$

Then both expected values are equal :

$$E^{\sigma}_{x_1}[1.0 \wedge \mu_1 \wedge \cdots \wedge \mu_G] = E^{\gamma}_{x_1,1.0}[1.0 \wedge \mu_1 \wedge \cdots \wedge \mu_G]. \tag{11}$$

Thus an optimal expanded Markov policy γ^* together with transformation (10) yields an optimal general policy σ^* in general class Π_g.

We have taken the new parameter λ ranging over the closed unit interval $[0, 1]$. This is a *continuous imbedding.* On the other hand, we can consider a *discrete imbedding* approach by restricting the λ ranging over a *finite discrete set* up to date. This imbedding is computationally effective. It is a *minimal embedding.* In the following we describe the discrete imbedding [15] :

First we define the sequence of *past-value sets up to date* $\{\Lambda_n\}_1^{N+1}$:

$$\begin{aligned}
\Lambda_1 &:= \{1.0\} \\
\Lambda_{n+1} &:= \left\{ \lambda_{n+1} \;\middle|\; \begin{array}{r} \lambda_{n+1} = \mu_1(x_1, u_1) \wedge \mu_2(x_2, u_2) \wedge \cdots \wedge \mu_n(x_n, u_n) \\ (x_m, u_m) \in X \times U \quad 1 \le m \le n \end{array} \right\} \\
&\qquad\qquad\qquad\qquad 1 \le n \le N
\end{aligned} \tag{12}$$

Then they satisfy the forward recursive formula

Lemma 1.

$$\begin{aligned}
\Lambda_1 &= \{1.0\} \\
\Lambda_{n+1} &= \{\lambda_n \wedge \mu_n(x_n, u_n) \mid \lambda_n \in \Lambda_n, \ (x_n, u_n) \in X \times U\} \\
&\qquad\qquad\qquad\qquad 1 \le n \le N.
\end{aligned} \tag{13}$$

Further, the parameter λ in recursive formula (7) is restricted on the past-value set :

Theorem 3.

$$\begin{aligned}
v_n(x; \lambda) &= \operatorname*{Max}_{u \in U} \sum_{y \in X} v_{n+1}(y; \lambda \wedge \mu_n(x, u)) p(y|x, u) \\
&\qquad\qquad x \in X, \ \lambda \in \Lambda_n, \ 1 \le n \le N \\
v_{N+1}(x; \lambda) &= \lambda \wedge \mu_G(x) \quad x \in X, \ \lambda \in \Lambda_{N+1}.
\end{aligned} \tag{14}$$

Now we solve the 3-2-2 model on stochastic system Bellman and Zadeh have proposed. Their fuzzy decision model is expressed as follows ([3]):

$$\begin{aligned} &\text{Max.} \ \ E^{\sigma}_{x_1}[\,\mu_1 \wedge \mu_2 \wedge \mu_G\,] \\ &\text{s.t.} \ \ X_{n+1} \sim p(\,\cdot\,|x_n, u_n), \ \ u_n \in U \quad n = 1, 2 \end{aligned}$$

where the numerical data is the same as Bellman and Zadeh's [3] (Tables 3,4) :

$\mu_t(u_t)\backslash u_t$	a_1	a_2
$\mu_1(u_1)$	0.7	1.0
$\mu_2(u_2)$	1.0	0.6

x_3	$\mu_G(x_3)$
s_1	0.3
s_2	1.0
s_3	0.8

Table 3. $\{\mu_1, \mu_2\}$ μ_G

$u_t = a_1$

$x_t\backslash x_{t+1}$	s_1	s_2	s_3
s_1	*0.8*	*0.1*	*0.1*
s_2	*0.0*	*0.1*	*0.9*
s_3	*0.8*	*0.1*	*0.1*

$u_t = a_2$

$x_t\backslash x_{t+1}$	s_1	s_2	s_3
s_1	*0.1*	*0.9*	*0.0*
s_2	*0.8*	*0.1*	*0.1*
s_3	*0.1*	*0.0*	*0.9*

Table 4. $p(x_{t+1}|x_t, u_t)$

3.1 Expanded Markov policies

We see that the past-value sets

$$\begin{aligned} \Lambda_1 &:= \{1.0\} \\ \Lambda_2 &:= \{\lambda_1 \,|\, \lambda_2 = \mu_1(u_1), \ u_1 \in U\} \\ \Lambda_3 &:= \{\lambda_3 \,|\, \lambda_3 = \mu_1(u_1) \wedge \mu_2(u_2), \ u_1, u_2 \in U\}. \end{aligned} \tag{15}$$

takes the form :

$$\begin{aligned} \Lambda_1 &= \{0\} \\ \Lambda_2 &= \{0.7, 1.0\} \\ \Lambda_3 &= \{0.6, 0.7, 1.0\}. \end{aligned} \tag{16}$$

We solve the recursive formula

$$v^3(x_3;\lambda_3) = \lambda_3 \wedge \mu_G(x_3) \qquad x_3 \in X,\ \lambda_3 \in \Lambda_3 \tag{17}$$

$$v^2(x_2;\lambda_2) = \operatorname*{Max}_{u_2} \sum_{x_3} v^3(x_3;\lambda_2 \wedge \mu_2(u_2))p(x_3|x_2,u_2) \tag{18}$$
$$x_2 \in X,\ \lambda_2 \in \Lambda_2$$

$$v^1(x_1;\lambda_1) = \operatorname*{Max}_{u_1} \sum_{x_2} v^2(x_2;\lambda_1 \wedge \mu_1(u_1))p(x_2|x_1,u_1) \tag{19}$$
$$x_1 \in X,\ \lambda_1 \in \Lambda_1.$$

First we calculate $v^3(x_3;\lambda_3)$ through (17). On state s_1 we have

$$v^3(s_1;0.6) = 0.6 \wedge 0.3 = 0.3$$

$$v^3(s_1;0.7) = 0.7 \wedge 0.3 = 0.3$$

$$v^3(s_1;1.0) = 1.0 \wedge 0.3 = 0.3$$

Similar calculations yield Table 5 :

$x_3\backslash\lambda_3$	0.6	0.7	1.0
s_1	0.3	0.3	0.3
s_2	0.6	0.7	1.0
s_3	0.6	0.7	0.8

Table 5. $v^3(x_3;\lambda_3)$

Second Eq.(18) gives the second optimal value function $v^2(x_2;\lambda_2)$. By use of Table 5, we calculate $v^2(s_1;0.7)$ as follows :

$$\begin{aligned}
v^2(s_1;0.7) &= [v^3(s_1;0.7 \wedge 1.0)0.8 + v^3(s_2;0.7 \wedge 1.0)0.1 + v^3(s_3;0.7 \wedge 1.0)0.1] \\
&\quad \vee\ [v^3(s_1;0.7 \wedge 0.6)0.1 + v^3(s_2;0.7 \wedge 0.6)0.9 + v^3(s_3;0.7 \wedge 0.6)0.0] \\
&= [v^3(s_1;0.7)0.8 + v^3(s_2;0.7)0.1 + v^3(s_3;0.7)0.1] \\
&\quad \vee [v^3(s_1;0.6)0.1 + v^3(s_2;0.6)0.9 + v^3(s_3;0.6)0.0] \\
&= [0.3 \times 0.8 + 0.7 \times 0.1 + 0.7 \times 0.1] \\
&\quad \vee [0.3 \times 0.1 + 0.6 \times 0.9 + 0.6 \times 0.0] \\
&= 0.38 \vee 0.57 \\
&= 0.57 \qquad \gamma_1^*(s_1;0.7) = a_2
\end{aligned} \tag{20}$$

Similar calculations yield the second optimal value function v^2 and the second optimal decision function γ_2^*, which are shown in 6 :

Finally Eq.(19) yields the first optimal value function $v^1(x_1;\lambda_1)$. In fact, Table 6 yields $v^1(s_1;0.7)$ as follows :

$$v^1(s_1;0) = [v^2(s_1;0.7)0.8 + v^2(s_2;0.7)0.1 + v^2(s_3;0.7)0.1]$$

$x_2\backslash\lambda_2$	0.7		1.0	
s_1	0.57	a_2	0.57	a_2
s_2	0.7	a_1	0.82	a_1
s_3	0.57	a_2	0.57	a_2

Table 6. $v^2(x_2;\lambda_2)\quad \gamma_2^*(x_2;\lambda_2)$

$$\begin{aligned}
&\vee[v^2(s_1;1.0)0.1 + v^2(s_2;1.0)0.9 + v^2(s_3;1.0)0.0]\\
&= [0.57 \times 0.8 + 0.7 \times 0.1 + 0.57 \times 0.1]\\
&\quad \vee[0.57 \times 0.1 + 0.82 \times 0.9 + 0.57 \times 0.0]\\
&= 0.583 \vee 0.795\\
&= 0.795 \qquad \gamma_0^*(s_1;1.0) = a_2
\end{aligned} \tag{21}$$

Similarly we have the first optimal value function v^1 and the first optimal decision function γ_1^* , as shown in Table 7 :

x_1	$v^1(x_1;1.0)$	$\gamma_1^*(x_1;1.0)$
s_1	0.795	a_2
s_2	0.595	a_2
s_3	0.583	a_1

Table 7. $v^1(x_1;1.0)\quad \gamma_1^*(x_1;1.0)$

As a summary we obtain an optimal solution in Table 8 :

	$v^3(x_3;\lambda_3)$	$v^2(x_2;\lambda_2)$		$\gamma_2^*(x_2;\lambda_2)$		$v^1(x_1;1.0)$	$\gamma_1^*(x_1;1.0)$
$x_n\backslash\lambda_n$	0.6 0.7 1.0	0.7		1.0		1.0	
s_1	0.3 0.3 0.3	0.57	a_2	0.57	a_2	0.795	a_2
s_2	0.6 0.7 1.0	0.7	a_1	0.82	a_1	0.595	a_2
s_3	0.6 0.7 0.8	0.57	a_2	0.57	a_2	0.583	a_1

Table 8. Optimal Solution

Now we show that the transformation

$$\hat{\sigma}_1(x_1) := \gamma_1^*(x_1;1.0) \tag{22}$$

$$u_1 := \gamma_1^*(x_1;1.0), \qquad \lambda_2 := \mu_1(u_1)$$

$$\hat{\sigma}_2(x_1,x_2) := \gamma_2^*(x_2;\lambda_2) \tag{23}$$

reduces the optimal (expanded Markov) policy $\gamma^* = \{\gamma_1^*, \gamma_2^*\}$ for the imbedded problem to an optimal (general) policy $\hat{\sigma} = \{\hat{\sigma}_1, \hat{\sigma}_2\}$ on the general state space $X = \{s_1, s_2, s_3\}$. We have the first decision function

$$\begin{aligned} \hat{\sigma}_1(s_1) &= \gamma_1^*(s_1; 1.0) = a_2 \\ \hat{\sigma}_1(s_2) &= \gamma_1^*(s_2; 1.0) = a_2 \\ \hat{\sigma}_1(s_3) &= \gamma_1^*(s_3; 1.0) = a_1. \end{aligned} \tag{24}$$

The second decision function is

$$\begin{aligned} \hat{\sigma}_2(s_1, s_1) &= \gamma_2^*(s_1; 1.0) = a_2 \\ \hat{\sigma}_2(s_1, s_2) &= \gamma_2^*(s_2; 1.0) = a_1 \\ \hat{\sigma}_2(s_1, s_3) &= \gamma_2^*(s_3; 1.0) = a_2 \end{aligned} \tag{25}$$

$$\begin{aligned} \hat{\sigma}_2(s_2, s_1) &= \gamma_2^*(s_1; 1.0) = a_2 \\ \hat{\sigma}_2(s_2, s_2) &= \gamma_2^*(s_2; 1.0) = a_1 \\ \hat{\sigma}_2(s_2, s_3) &= \gamma_2^*(s_3; 1.0) = a_2 \end{aligned} \tag{26}$$

$$\begin{aligned} \hat{\sigma}_2(s_3, s_1) &= \gamma_2^*(s_1; 0.7) = a_2 \\ \hat{\sigma}_2(s_3, s_2) &= \gamma_2^*(s_2; 0.7) = a_1 \\ \hat{\sigma}_2(s_3, s_3) &= \gamma_2^*(s_3; 0.7) = a_2. \end{aligned} \tag{27}$$

Thus we have obtained an optimal policy $\hat{\sigma}$ through an invariant imbedding. (This Bellman and Zadeh's 3-2-2 model *happens to* have an optimal policy *in Markov class.*) Of course, the optimal policy $\hat{\sigma}$ is identical to the optimal policy σ^*, which will be obtained through a multi-stage stochastic decision tree-table method — an enumeration method.

3.2 Primitive policies

Now we introduce a *more* general policy depending on the total history up to date. Let a direct product $H_n := X \times U \times X \times U \times \cdots X \times U \times X$((2$n$ − 1)factors) denote a *history space* up to n-th stage, $n = 1, 2, \ldots, N$. A mapping $\nu_n : H_n \to U$ is called *n-th primitive decision function*, whose sequence $\nu = \{\nu_1, \nu_2, \ldots, \nu_N\}$ is a *primitive policy.* A *primitive class* Π_p is the set of all primitive policies. It includes the set of all general policies $\Pi_g : \Pi_g \subset \Pi_p$. Although any primitive policy imposes more information on history than general policy, primitive class Π_p applies to any criterion. We obtain a recursive formula for stochastic optimization of any objective function. Actually any primitive yields the same expected value through a general policy. We show this.

Now let any criterion function $g : H_{N+1} \to [0, 1]$ be given. Then we consider the following stochastic optimization problem [11]:

$$\begin{aligned} \text{Max.} \quad & E_{x_1}^{\nu}[g] \\ \text{s.t.} \quad & \text{(i)} \quad x_{n+1} \sim p(\cdot|x_n, u_n) \qquad n = 1, 2, \ldots, N \\ & \text{(ii)} \quad u_n \in U \end{aligned} \tag{28}$$

where the expected value is calculated through a primitive policy ν :

$$E_{x_1}^{\nu}[g] = \sum_{(x_2,\ldots,x_{N+1})\in X\times\cdots\times X}\sum\cdots\sum g(x_1,u_1,\ldots,x_N,u_N,x_{N+1}) \times p(x_2|x_1,u_1)\cdots p(x_{N+1}|x_N,u_N) \tag{29}$$

$$(u_1 = \nu_1(x_1),\ u_2 = \nu_2(x_1,u_1,x_2),\ \ldots,\ u_N = \nu_N(x_1,u_1,\ldots,u_{N-1},x_N)).$$

Now we imbed this problem as follows. Given any n $(1 \le n \le N+1)$, $h_n = (x_1,u_1,x_2,u_2,\ldots,x_n) \in H_n$ we consider the subproblem :

$$v^n(h_n) = \underset{\nu}{\mathrm{Max}}\, E_{h_n}^{\nu} g(h_n,U_n,X_{n+1},\ldots,X_N,U_N,X_{N+1}) \tag{30}$$

$$h_n \in H_n,\quad 1 \le n \le N$$

$$v^{N+1}(h_{N+1}) = g(h_{N+1}) \quad h_{N+1} \in H_{N+1} \tag{31}$$

where an *intial* state h_n and a primitive policy

$$\nu = \{\nu_n,\nu_{n+1},\ldots,\nu_N\};\quad \nu_m : H_m \to U \quad n \le m \le N$$

from here determines the resulting alternating sequence of decision and state $(u_n,x_{n+1},u_{n+1},\ldots,u_N,x_{N+1})$ in stochastic sense. Then we have the recursive formula :

Theorem 4. *(Iwamoto, Tsurusaki and Fujita[12])*

$$v^n(h) = \underset{u\in U}{\mathrm{Max}} \sum_{y\in X} v^{n+1}(h,u,y)p(y|x,u) \qquad h \in H_n,\quad 1 \le n \le N$$

$$v^{N+1}(h) = g(h) \qquad h \in H_{N+1}. \tag{32}$$

Letting $\nu_n^*(h)$ $(h \in H_n)$ denote the set of maximizers in (32), we have an optimal policy $\nu^* = \{\nu_1^*,\nu_2^*,\ldots,\nu_N^*\}$ in primitive class Π_p.

In general, any primitive policy $\nu = \{\nu_1,\nu_2,\ldots,\nu_N\}$ generates an *equivalent* (in the sense that both expected values are identical) general policy $\sigma = \{\sigma_1,\sigma_2,\ldots,\sigma_N\}$ through the transformation (33). That is, for any state sequence $(x_1,x_2,\ldots,x_n)$, generating a sequence of intermediate decisions $\{u_m\}_{1\le m\le n}$, we define $\sigma_n(x_1,x_2,\ldots,x_n)$ as follows :

$$\begin{aligned} u_1 &:= \nu_1(x_1),\quad h_2 := (x_1,u_1,x_2) \\ u_2 &:= \nu_2(h_2),\quad h_3 := (h_2,u_2,x_3) \\ &\vdots \\ u_{n-1} &:= \nu_{n-1}(h_{n-1}),\quad h_n := (h_{n-1},u_{n-1},x_n) \\ \sigma_n(x_1,x_2,\ldots,x_n) &:= \nu_n(h_n). \end{aligned} \tag{33}$$

Then both expected values are equal :

$$E_{x_1}^{\sigma}[g] = E_{x_1}^{\nu}[g] \tag{34}$$

Thus, transliterating the optimal primitive policy ν^* by (33), we obtain an optimal general policy σ^* in general class Π_g.

Now let us solve Bellman and Zadeh's 3-2-2 stochastic model by the above method. On this model we have the recursive formula

$$v^3(h_3) = \mu_1(u_1) \wedge \mu_2(u_2) \wedge \mu_G(x_3) \qquad h_3 = (x_1, u_1, x_1, x_2, u_2, x_3) \tag{35}$$

$$v^2(h_2) = \underset{u_2 \in U}{\text{Max}} \sum_{x_3 \in X} v^3(h_2, u_2, x_3) p(x_3 | x_2, u_2) \qquad h_2 = (x_1, u_1, x_1, x_2) \tag{36}$$

$$v^1(x_1) = \underset{u_1 \in U}{\text{Max}} \sum_{x_2 \in X} v^2(x_1, u_1, x_2) p(x_2 | x_1, u_1). \tag{37}$$

First, the terminal function v^3 :

$$v^3(x_0, u_0, x_1, u_1, x_2) = \mu_1(u_1) \wedge \mu_2(u_2) \wedge \mu_G(x_3) \tag{38}$$

is independent of x_1, x_2. It is shown in Table 9 :

u_1	a_1		a_2	
$x_3 \backslash u_2$	a_1	a_2	a_1	a_2
s_1	0.3	0.3	0.3	0.3
s_2	0.7	0.6	1.0	0.6
s_3	0.7	0.6	0.8	0.6

Table 9. $v^3(\underline{x_1}, u_1, \underline{x_2}, u_2, x_3)$

Second, by use of Table 9, we calculate the second optimal value function v^2 as follows :

$$v^2(x_1, u_1, x_2) = \underset{u_2}{\text{Max}} \sum_{x_3} v^3(x_1, u_1, x_2, u_2, x_3) p(x_3 | x_2, u_2). \tag{39}$$

$v^2(x_1, u_1, x_2)$ is independent of the first component x_1. It is

$$\begin{aligned} v^2(x_1, a_1, s_1) = & [v^3(x_1, a_1, s_1, a_1, s_1) p(s_1 | s_1, a_1) \\ & + v^3(x_1, a_1, s_1, a_1, s_2) p(s_2 | s_1, a_1) \\ & + v^3(x_1, a_1, s_1, a_1, s_3) p(s_3 | s_1, a_1)] \\ & \vee [v^3(x_1, a_1, s_1, a_2, s_1) p(s_1 | s_1, a_2) \\ & + v^3(x_0, a_1, s_1, a_2, s_2) p(s_2 | s_1, a_2) \\ & + v^3(x_1, a_1, s_1, a_2, s_3) p(s_3 | s_1, a_2)] \\ = & [0.3 \times 0.8 + 0.7 \times 0.1 + 0.7 \times 0.1] \\ & \vee [0.3 \times 0.1 + 0.6 \times 0.9 + 0.6 \times 0.0] \\ = & 0.38 \vee 0.57 \\ = & 0.57 \quad \mu_1^*(x_1, a_1, s_1) = a_2. \end{aligned} \tag{40}$$

A similar calculation yields a pair of the second optimal value function v^2 and the second optimal decision function μ_2^*, as shown in Table 10.

x_2	$v^2(x_1, a_1, x_2)$	$\mu_2^*(x_1, a_1, x_2)$	$v^2(x_1, a_2, x_2)$	$\mu_2^*(x_1, a_2, x_2)$
s_1	0.57	a_2	0.57	a_2
s_2	0.7	a_1	0.82	a_1
s_3	0.57	a_2	0.57	a_2

Table 10. $v^2(x_1, u_1, x_2) \quad \mu_2^*(x_1, u_1, x_2)$

Finally the first optimal value function

$$v^1(x_1) = \operatorname*{Max}_{u_1} \sum_{x_1} v^2(x_1, u_1, x_2) p(x_2|x_1, u_1) \tag{41}$$

is calculated as follows. We have for $v^1(s_1)$

$$\begin{aligned} v^1(s_1) &= [v^2(s_1, a_1, s_1)p(s_1|s_1, a_1) + v^2(s_1, a_1, s_2)p(s_2|s_1, a_1) \\ &\qquad + v^2(s_1, a_1, s_3)p(s_3|s_1, a_1)] \\ &\quad \vee [v^2(s_1, a_2, s_1)p(s_1|s_1, a_2) + v^2(s_1, a_2, s_2)p(s_2|s_1, a_2) \\ &\qquad + v^2(s_1, a_2, s_3)p(s_3|s_1, a_2)] \\ &= [0.57 \times 0.8 + 0.7 \times 0.1 + 0.57 \times 0.1] \\ &\quad \vee [0.57 \times 0.1 + 0.82 \times 0.9 + 0.57 \times 0.0] \\ &= 0.583 \vee 0.795 \\ &= 0.795 \qquad \mu_0^*(s_1) = a_2. \end{aligned} \tag{42}$$

Similarly, we have (v^1, μ_1^*) in Table 11.

x_0	$v^1(x_1)$	$\mu_1^*(x_1)$
s_1	0.785	a_2
s_2	0.595	a_2
s_3	0.583	a_1

Table 11. $v^1(x_1) \quad \mu_1^*(x_1)$

Now, we show that the optimal primitive policy $\mu^* = \{\mu_1^*, \mu_2^*\}$ generate a general policy $\sigma^* = \{\sigma_1^*, \sigma_2^*\}$ through the transformation

$$\sigma_1^*(x_1) := \nu_1^*(x_1) \tag{43}$$

$$\sigma_2^*(x_1, x_2) := \nu_2^*(x_1, u_1, x_2) \quad \text{where } u_1 = \sigma_1^*(x_1). \tag{44}$$

Then we have σ^* as follows :

$$\sigma_1^*(s_1) = a_2, \quad \sigma_1^*(s_2) = a_2, \quad \sigma_1^*(s_3) = a_1 \tag{45}$$

$$\begin{array}{lll} \sigma_2^*(s_1, s_1) = a_2, & \sigma_2^*(s_1, s_2) = a_1, & \sigma_2^*(s_1, s_3) = a_2 \\ \sigma_2^*(s_2, s_1) = a_2, & \sigma_2^*(s_2, s_2) = a_1, & \sigma_2^*(s_2, s_3) = a_2 \\ \sigma_2^*(s_3, s_1) = a_2, & \sigma_2^*(s_3, s_2) = a_1, & \sigma_2^*(s_3, s_3) = a_2 \end{array} \tag{46}$$

This is a Markov policy. We note that σ^* is identical to $\hat{\sigma}$ obtained through the optimal expanded Markov policy γ^*.

3.3 Multi-stage stochastic decision tree-table

A *multistage stochastic decision tree-table* consists of a pair of decision tree and decision table for multistage stochastic decision processes. It contains in a sheet from problem-statement to solution-specification via backward-calculation process, which is based upon a total enumeration method. According to progression of processes, it allocates the problem-data. It also tabulates the intermediate recursive computational results. Thus all possible histories to the final stage are evaluated by accumulated membership together with its probability. It gives an optimal decision on each subhistory. In this sense, the tree-table method is totally enumerative. From the tree-table we see that how optimal primitive policy is constructed and that in some situation it happens to be general or Markov. The tree-table method applies to any stochastic optimization problem—it is objective function free.

Now, let us solve the Bellman and Zadeh's 3-2-2 stochastic model by multi-stage stochastic decision tree-table method. First we express one-stage decision process from an initial state x_2 :

$$\begin{array}{ll} \text{Max.} & E^{\nu}_{x_2}[\,\mu_2 \wedge \mu_G\,] \\ \text{s.t.} & X_3 \sim (\,\cdot\,|x_2, u_2), \quad u_2 \in U \end{array}$$

by tree-table, where $\nu = \{\nu_2\}$ is a primitive policy.

In Tree-table 1 we have the following simplified notations :

history $= x_2 \quad \mu_2\backslash u_2 \quad p_2 \quad x_3 \quad \mu_G$

where $\mu_2 = \mu_2(u_2), \quad p_2 = p(x_3|x_2, u_2), \quad \mu_G = \mu_G(x_3)$

min = minimum value $= \mu_2(u_2) \wedge \mu_G(x_3)$

path = *path probability* $= p(x_3|x_2, u_2)$

m $\times\, p$ = min $\times$ *path*, Exp = Expected value.

Tree-table 1 consists of three parts—upper, middle and lower —. The upper part shows the following. The decision maker can choose one of decisions a_1, a_2 at the starting state $x_2 = s_1$. When he/she chooses one, he will go to three states with the specified probabilities, and he/she will get a terminal membership to the state. The columm 'Exp' tells that the choice of up-decision (a_1) (resp. down-decision (a_2)) yields an expected value 0.42 (resp. 0.57). A **bold 0.57** shows that a selection of the larger 0.57 is better than the smaller 0.42. This is reflected in the down-arrow, which becomes not a dotted line but a solid line.

Similarly, the middle and lower parts show that the processes starting at $x_2 = s_2$ and $x_2 = s_3$ yield computational results and optimal selections, respectively.

Tree-table 1 : one-stage stochastic decision tree-table from s_1, s_2, s_3

x_2	$\mu_2 \backslash u_2$	history	p_2	x_3	μ_G	min	*path*	m×p	Exp
s_1	1.0 a_1		*0.8*	s_1	0.3	0.3	*0.8*	0.24	0.42
			0.1	s_2	1.0	1.0	*0.1*	0.1	
			0.1	s_3	0.8	0.8	*0.1*	0.08	
	0.6 a_2		*0.1*	s_1	0.3	0.3	*0.1*	0.03	**0.57**
			0.9	s_2	1.0	0.6	*0.9*	0.54	
			0.0	s_3	0.8	0.6	*0.0*	0.0	
s_2	1.0 a_1		*0.0*	s_1	0.3	0.3	*0.0*	0.0	**0.82**
			0.1	s_2	1.0	1.0	*0.1*	0.1	
			0.9	s_3	0.8	0.8	*0.9*	0.72	
	0.6 a_2		*0.8*	s_1	0.3	0.3	*0.8*	0.24	0.36
			0.1	s_2	1.0	0.6	*0.1*	0.06	
			0.1	s_3	0.8	0.6	*0.1*	0.06	
s_3	1.0 a_1		*0.8*	s_1	0.3	0.3	*0.8*	0.24	0.42
			0.1	s_2	1.0	1.0	*0.1*	0.1	
			0.1	s_3	0.8	0.8	*0.1*	0.08	
	0.6 a_2		*0.1*	s_1	0.3	0.3	*0.1*	0.03	**0.57**
			0.0	s_2	1.0	0.6	*0.0*	0.0	
			0.9	s_3	0.8	0.6	*0.9*	0.54	

Second we solve the two-stage process from x_1 :

$$\begin{aligned}&\text{Max.}\ \ E^{\nu}_{x_1}[\,\mu_1 \wedge \mu_2 \wedge \mu_G\,]\\ &\text{s.t.}\ \ X_{n+1} \sim (\,\cdot\,|x_n, u_n),\ \ u_n \in U \quad n = 1, 2\end{aligned}$$

where $\nu = \{\nu_1, \nu_2\}$ is a primitive policy.

In the following Tree-tables 2, 3, 4, we use the simple notations :

$$\text{history} = x_1 \quad \mu_1\backslash u_1 \quad p_2 \quad x_2 \quad \mu_2\backslash u_2 \quad p_2 \quad x_3 \quad \mu_G$$

$$\text{where } \mu_1 = \mu_1(u_1),\ \ p_1 = p(x_2|x_1, u_1),\ \ \mu_2 = \mu_2(u_2),$$
$$p_2 = p(x_3|x_2, u_2),\ \ \mu_G = \mu_G(x_3)$$

$$\text{min} = \text{minimum value} = \mu_1(u_1) \wedge \mu_2(u_2) \wedge \mu_G(x_3)$$

$$\textit{path} = \textit{path probability} = p(x_2|x_1, u_1)p(x_3|x_2, u_2)$$

$$\text{m} \times p \ = \text{min} \times \textit{path}$$

Tree-table 2 generates optimal decisions from state s_1 as follows. First, the column 'Sub' tells that when the process experiences $x_1 = s_1 \to u_1 \to x_2$, a better primitive decision is to select one of $\{a_1, a_2\}$ which yields a larger sub-expected value than the other, as shown in **bold** numerals :

$$\mu_2(s_1, a_1, s_1) = a_2, \quad \mu_2(s_1, a_1, s_2) = a_1, \quad \mu_2(s_1, a_1, s_3) = a_2$$

$$\mu_2(s_1, a_2, s_1) = a_2, \quad \mu_2(s_1, a_2, s_2) = a_1, \quad \mu_2(s_1, a_2, s_3) = a_1, a_2.$$

Second, the column 'Ttl' tells that a comparison between the upper total expected value and the lower yields the first optimal decision $\mu_1(s_1) = a_2$ together with the resulting optimal value $V_1(s_1) = \mathbf{0.795}$. Thus we have the following optimal general decisions from s_1

$$\sigma_1(s_1) = a_2; \qquad \sigma_2(s_1, s_1) = a_2, \quad \sigma_2(s_1, s_2) = a_1, \quad \sigma_2(s_1, s_3) = a_1, a_2.$$

Similarly, Tree-tables 2 and 3 generate primitive optimal decisions from s_2 and s_3, respectively. A triplet of Tree-table 1, 2 and 3 yields an *optimal* primitive policy $\mu = \{\mu_1, \mu_2\}$. Thus we have optimal solution :

$$\sigma_1(s_2) = a_2; \qquad \sigma_2(s_2, s_1) = a_2, \quad \sigma_2(s_2, s_2) = a_1, \quad \sigma_2(s_2, s_3) = a_2$$

$$\sigma_1(s_3) = a_1; \qquad \sigma_2(s_3, s_1) = a_2, \quad \sigma_2(s_2, s_2) = a_1, \quad \sigma_2(s_3, s_3) = a_2$$

$$V_1(s_2) = \mathbf{0.595}, \qquad V_1(s_3) = \mathbf{0.583}$$

The optimal general policy $\sigma = \{\sigma_1, \sigma_2\}$ happens also to reduce to a Markov policy $\pi = \{\pi_1, \pi_2\}$:

$$\pi_1(s_1) = a_2, \quad \pi_1(s_2) = a_2, \quad \pi_1(s_3) = a_1$$

$$\pi_2(s_1) = a_2, \quad \pi_2(s_2) = a_1, \quad \pi_2(s_3) = a_2.$$

Tree-table 2 : two-stage stochastic decision tree-table from state s_1

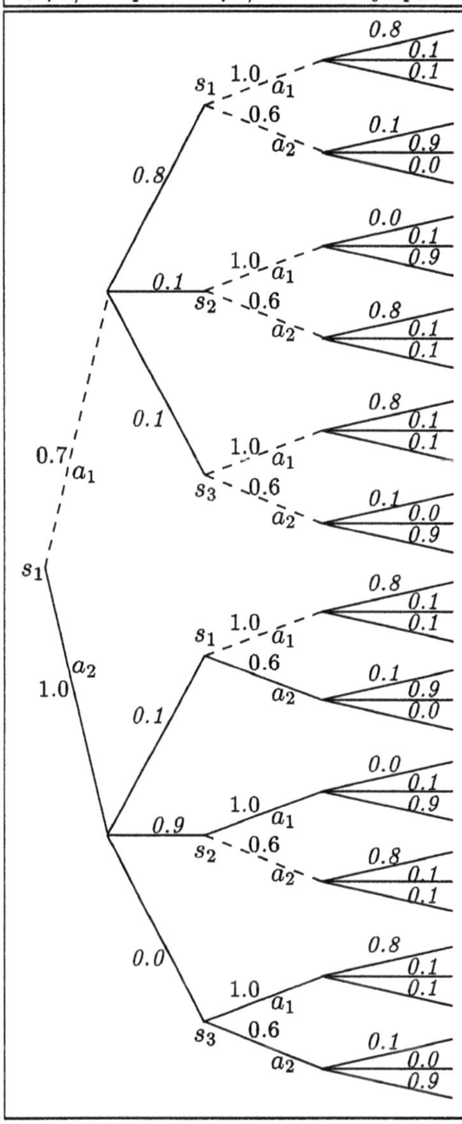

x_3	μ_G	min	*path*	m×p	Sub	Ttl
s_1	0.3	0.3	*0.64*	0.192		
s_2	1.0	0.7	*0.08*	0.056	0.304	
s_3	0.8	0.7	*0.08*	0.056		
s_1	0.3	0.3	*0.08*	0.024		
s_2	1.0	0.6	*0.72*	0.432	**0.456**	
s_3	0.8	0.6	*0.0*	0		
s_1	0.3	0.3	*0.0*	0		
s_2	1.0	0.7	*0.01*	0.007	**0.070**	
s_3	0.8	0.7	*0.09*	0.063		0.583
s_1	0.3	0.3	*0.08*	0.024		
s_2	1.0	0.6	*0.01*	0.006	0.036	
s_3	0.8	0.6	*0.01*	0.006		
s_1	0.3	0.3	*0.08*	0.024		
s_2	1.0	0.7	*0.01*	0.007	0.038	
s_3	0.8	0.7	*0.01*	0.007		
s_1	0.3	0.3	*0.01*	0.003		
s_2	1.0	0.6	*0.0*	0	**0.057**	
s_3	0.8	0.6	*0.09*	0.054		
s_1	0.3	0.3	*0.08*	0.024		
s_2	1.0	1.0	*0.01*	0.01	0.042	
s_3	0.8	0.8	*0.01*	0.008		
s_1	0.3	0.3	*0.01*	0.003		
s_2	1.0	0.6	*0.09*	0.054	**0.057**	
s_3	0.8	0.6	*0.0*	0		
s_1	0.3	0.3	*0.0*	0		
s_2	1.0	1.0	*0.09*	0.09	**0.738**	
s_3	0.8	0.8	*0.81*	0.648		**0.795**
s_1	0.3	0.3	*0.72*	0.216		
s_2	1.0	0.6	*0.09*	0.054	0.324	
s_3	0.8	0.6	*0.09*	0.065		
s_1	0.3	0.3	*0.0*	0		
s_2	1.0	1.0	*0.0*	0	**0**	
s_3	0.8	0.8	*0.0*	0		
s_1	0.3	0.3	*0.0*	0		
s_2	1.0	0.6	*0.0*	0	**0**	
s_3	0.8	0.6	*0.0*	0		

Sub = Sub expected value

$$= \sum_{x_2} [\mu_1(u_1) \wedge \mu_2(u_2) \wedge \mu_G(x_3)] p(x_2|x_1, u_1) p(x_3|x_2, u_2).$$

Tree-table 3 : two-stage stochastic decision tree-table from state s_2

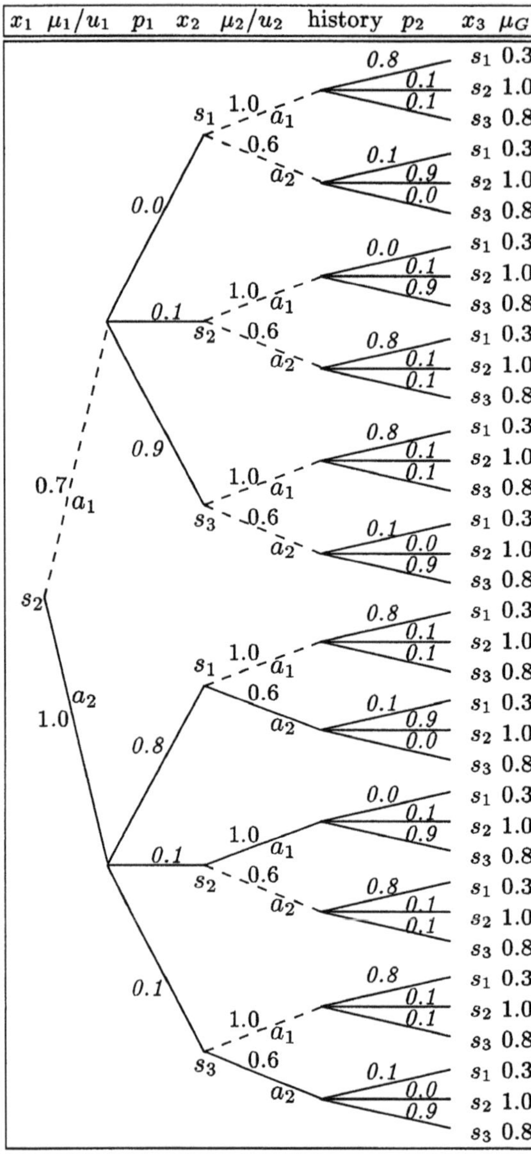

x_3	μ_G	min	*path*	m×p	Sub	Ttl
s_1	0.3	0.3	*0.0*	0		
s_2	1.0	0.7	*0.0*	0	**0.0**	
s_3	0.8	0.7	*0.0*	0		
s_1	0.3	0.3	*0.0*	0		
s_2	1.0	0.6	*0.0*	0	**0.0**	
s_3	0.8	0.6	*0.0*	0		
s_1	0.3	0.3	*0.0*	0		
s_2	1.0	0.7	*0.01*	0.007	**0.070**	
s_3	0.8	0.7	*0.09*	0.063		0.583
s_1	0.3	0.3	*0.08*	0.024		
s_2	1.0	0.6	*0.01*	0.006	0.036	
s_3	0.8	0.6	*0.01*	0.006		
s_1	0.3	0.3	*0.72*	0.216		
s_2	1.0	0.7	*0.09*	0.063	0.342	
s_3	0.8	0.7	*0.09*	0.063		
s_1	0.3	0.3	*0.09*	0.027		
s_2	1.0	0.6	*0.0*	0	**0.513**	
s_3	0.8	0.6	*0.81*	0.486		
s_1	0.3	0.3	*0.64*	0.192		
s_2	1.0	1.0	*0.08*	0.08	0.336	
s_3	0.8	0.8	*0.08*	0.064		
s_1	0.3	0.3	*0.08*	0.024		
s_2	1.0	0.6	*0.72*	0.432	**0.456**	
s_3	0.8	0.6	*0.0*	0		
s_1	0.3	0.3	*0.0*	0		
s_2	1.0	1.0	*0.01*	0.01	**0.082**	
s_3	0.8	0.8	*0.09*	0.072		**0.595**
s_1	0.3	0.3	*0.08*	0.024		
s_2	1.0	0.6	*0.01*	0.006	0.036	
s_3	0.8	0.6	*0.01*	0.006		
s_1	0.3	0.3	*0.08*	0.024		
s_2	1.0	1.0	*0.01*	0.01	0.042	
s_3	0.8	0.8	*0.01*	0.008		
s_1	0.3	0.3	*0.01*	0.003		
s_2	1.0	0.6	*0.0*	0	**0.057**	
s_3	0.8	0.6	*0.09*	0.054		

Ttl = Total expected value

$$= \sum_{x_1} \sum_{x_2} [\mu_1(u_1) \wedge \mu_2(u_2) \wedge \mu_G(x_3)] p(x_2|x_1, u_1) p(x_3|x_2, u_2).$$

Tree-table 4 : two-stage stochastic decision tree-table from state s_3

x_1	μ_1/u_1	p_1	x_2	μ_2/u_2	history	p_2	x_3	μ_G	min	*path*	m×p	Sub	Ttl
s_3	0.7 / a_1	*0.8*	s_1	1.0 / a_1		*0.8*	s_1	0.3	0.3	*0.64*	0.192		
						0.1	s_2	1.0	0.7	*0.08*	0.056	0.304	
						0.1	s_3	0.8	0.7	*0.08*	0.056		
				0.6 / a_2		*0.1*	s_1	0.3	0.3	*0.08*	0.024		
						0.9	s_2	1.0	0.6	*0.72*	0.432	**0.456**	
						0.0	s_3	0.8	0.6	*0.0*	0		
		0.1	s_2	1.0 / a_1		*0.0*	s_1	0.3	0.3	*0.0*	0		
						0.1	s_2	1.0	0.7	*0.01*	0.007	**0.070**	
						0.9	s_3	0.8	0.7	*0.09*	0.063		**0.583**
				0.6 / a_2		*0.8*	s_1	0.3	0.3	*0.08*	0.024		
						0.1	s_2	1.0	0.6	*0.01*	0.006	0.036	
						0.1	s_3	0.8	0.6	*0.01*	0.006		
		0.1	s_3	1.0 / a_1		*0.8*	s_1	0.3	0.3	*0.08*	0.024		
						0.1	s_2	1.0	0.7	*0.01*	0.007	0.038	
						0.1	s_3	0.8	0.7	*0.01*	0.007		
				0.6 / a_2		*0.1*	s_1	0.3	0.3	*0.01*	0.003		
						0.0	s_2	1.0	0.6	*0.0*	0	**0.057**	
						0.9	s_3	0.8	0.6	*0.09*	0.054		
	1.0 / a_2	*0.1*	s_1	1.0 / a_1		*0.8*	s_1	0.3	0.3	*0.08*	0.024		
						0.1	s_2	1.0	1.0	*0.01*	0.01	0.042	
						0.1	s_3	0.8	0.8	*0.01*	0.008		
				0.6 / a_2		*0.1*	s_1	0.3	0.3	*0.01*	0.003		
						0.9	s_2	1.0	0.6	*0.09*	0.054	**0.057**	
						0.0	s_3	0.8	0.6	*0.0*	0		
		0.0	s_2	1.0 / a_1		*0.0*	s_1	0.3	0.3	*0.0*	0		
						0.1	s_2	1.0	1.0	*0.0*	0	**0.0**	
						0.9	s_3	0.8	0.8	*0.0*	0		0.570
				0.6 / a_2		*0.8*	s_1	0.3	0.3	*0.0*	0		
						0.1	s_2	1.0	0.6	*0.0*	0	**0.0**	
						0.1	s_3	0.8	0.6	*0.0*	0		
		0.9	s_3	1.0 / a_1		*0.8*	s_1	0.3	0.3	*0.72*	0.216		
						0.1	s_2	1.0	1.0	*0.09*	0.09	0.378	
						0.1	s_3	0.8	0.8	*0.09*	0.072		
				0.6 / a_2		*0.1*	s_1	0.3	0.3	*0.09*	0.027		
						0.0	s_2	1.0	0.6	*0.0*	0	**0.513**	
						0.9	s_3	0.8	0.6	*0.81*	0.486		

The *italic* means probabilities, and **bold** denotes a selection of the larger of the two; the upper expected value and the lower.

Threefore we have reconfirmed that three *general* optimal policy $\hat{\sigma}$ (via an optimal expanded Markov policy in subsection **3.1**) and σ^* (via an optimal primitive policy in **3.2**) and σ (via an optimal primitive policy by multi-stage stochastic decision tree-table method in this **3.3**) are identical.

3.4 Nonoptimality of Markov policy

As we have seen, it happens that an Markov policy is optimal in 3-2-2 model with Bellman and Zadeh's data. However, the following data (Tables 12,13) does show that Markov class is not enough. The optimal policy is general policy and that there does not exist in Markov class (Iwamoto, Tsurusaki and Fujita [13]).

$\mu_t(u_t)\backslash u_t$	a_1	a_2
$\mu_1(u_1)$	0.9	0.6
$\mu_2(u_2)$	1.0	0.8

x_3	$\mu_G(x_3)$
s_1	0.5
s_2	0.2
s_3	0.8

Table 12. $\{\mu_1, \mu_2\}$ μ_G

$u_t = a_1$

$x_t\backslash x_{t+1}$	s_1	s_2	s_3
s_1	0.4	0.5	0.1
s_2	0.2	0.6	0.2
s_3	0.3	0.1	0.6

$u_t = a_2$

$x_t\backslash x_{t+1}$	s_1	s_2	s_3
s_1	0.1	0.6	0.3
s_2	0.7	0.2	0.1
s_3	0.3	0.3	0.4

Table 13. $p(x_{t+1}|x_t, u_t)$

This data yields an optimal policy $\tilde{\sigma} = \{\tilde{\sigma}_1, \tilde{\sigma}_2\}$:

$$\tilde{\sigma}_1(s_1) = a_2, \quad \tilde{\sigma}_1(s_2) = a_1, \quad \tilde{\sigma}_1(s_3) = a_1$$

$$\begin{aligned} &\tilde{\sigma}_2(s_1, s_1) = a_1, \quad \tilde{\sigma}_2(s_2, s_1) = a_2, \quad \tilde{\sigma}_2(s_3, s_1) = a_2 \\ &\tilde{\sigma}_2(s_1, s_2) = a_2, \quad \tilde{\sigma}_2(s_2, s_2) = a_2, \quad \tilde{\sigma}_2(s_3, s_2) = a_2 \\ &\tilde{\sigma}_2(s_1, s_3) = a_1, \quad \tilde{\sigma}_2(s_2, s_3) = a_1, \quad \tilde{\sigma}_2(s_3, s_3) = a_1. \end{aligned}$$

Since $\tilde{\sigma}_2(s_1, s_1) \neq \tilde{\sigma}_2(s_1, s_1)$, the optimal policy $\tilde{\sigma}$ is not Markov.

4 Fuzzy System

In general, fuzzy system has been extensively investigated. As far as multi-stage decision process, it is a very controversy. In this section we focus on Bellman and Zadeh's *fuzzy system* [3, p.151]. We propose a dynamic programming method on the fuzzy system through minimization-maximization expectation. Let us consider a maximization problem of fuzzy expected value of minimum criterion :

$$\begin{aligned} \text{Max.} \quad & F^{\pi}_{x_1}[\,\mu_1 \wedge \mu_2 \wedge \cdots \wedge \mu_N \wedge \mu_G\,] \\ \text{s.t.} \quad & \text{(i)} \quad X_{n+1} \simeq \mu(\cdot|x_n, u_n) \qquad n = 1, 2, \ldots, N \\ & \text{(ii)} \quad u_n \in U \end{aligned} \tag{47}$$

Here $\mu = \{\mu(y|x, u)\}$ is a fuzzy transition law which controls a fuzzy state on X for a pair of current realized state x and applied control u. That is, for any given $(x, u) \in X \times U$, $\mu(\cdot|x, u)$ is a membership function of fuzzy set $X(x, u)$ on X. A membership degree of moving to next state x_{n+1} from state x_n under decision u_n on the n-th stage is $\mu(x_{n+1}|x_n, u_n)$ $(0 \leq \mu(x_{n+1}|x_n, u_n) \leq 1)$. Thus the degree that the fuzzy state variable X_{n+1} belongs to the fuzzy set $X(x, u)$ is represented by $\mu(x_{n+1}|x_n, u_n)$. We write this fuzzy transition as $X_{n+1} \simeq \mu(\cdot|x_n, u_n)$. Further, instead of the so called expectation $E[\cdots]$ by multiplication-addition operation through probability measure, we take a fuzzy expectation $F[\cdots]$ by minimization-maximization operation through fuzzy measure [3][5][10]. Let $f_1(x_1)$ denote the maximum of the fuzzy expected value over Markov class Π. Then we have a backward recursive formula – similar to one in stochastic system — as follows :

Theorem 5. *(Iwamoto and Sniedovich[14])*

$$\begin{aligned} f_n(x) &= \operatorname*{Max}_{u \in U} \bigvee_{y \in X} [\mu_n(x, u) \wedge (f_{n+1}(y) \wedge \mu(y|x, u))] \quad 1 \leq n \leq N \\ & \qquad\qquad x \in X. \\ f_{N+1}(x) &= \mu_G(x) \end{aligned} \tag{48}$$

Now we solve a 3-2-2 model on fuzzy system. The decision process is expressed as follows :

$$\begin{aligned} \text{Max.} \quad & F^{\pi}_{x_1}[\,\mu_1 \wedge \mu_2 \wedge \mu_G\,] \\ \text{s.t.} \quad & X_{n+1} \simeq \mu(\cdot|x_n, u_n), \quad u_n \in U \quad n = 1, 2 \end{aligned}$$

where the numerical data is given in Tables 14,15 :

Then, solving the resulting recursive formula

$$\begin{aligned} f_3(x_3) &= \mu_G(x_3) \qquad x_3 \in X \\ f_2(x_1) &= \operatorname*{Max}_{u_1 \in U} \bigvee_{x_3 \in X} [\mu_2(u_2) \wedge (f_3(x_3) \wedge \mu(x_3|x_2, u_2))] \quad x_2 \in X \\ f_1(x_1) &= \operatorname*{Max}_{u_1 \in U} \bigvee_{x_2 \in X} [\mu_1(u_1) \wedge (f_2(x_2) \wedge \mu(x_2|x_1, u_1))] \quad x_1 \in X \end{aligned}$$

$\mu_t(u_t)\backslash u_t$	a_1	a_2
$\mu_1(u_1)$	0.6	0.9
$\mu_2(u_2)$	0.9	0.7

x_3	$\mu_G(x_3)$
s_1	0.6
s_2	1.0
s_3	0.8

Table 14. $\{\mu_1, \mu_2\}$ μ_G

$u_t = a_1$

$x_t\backslash x_{t+1}$	s_1	s_2	s_3
s_1	0.6	0.9	0.7
s_2	0.5	0.8	1.0
s_3	0.3	0.4	1.0

$u_t = a_2$

$x_t\backslash x_{t+1}$	s_1	s_2	s_3
s_1	0.4	0.9	0.8
s_2	0.8	0.6	0.5
s_3	1.0	0.8	0.7

Table 15. $\mu(x_{t+1}|x_t, u_t)$

we have the optimal solution (a pair of sequence of optimal membership-functions $\{f_1, f_2, f_3\}$ and optimal policy $\pi^* = \{\pi_1^*, \pi_2^*\}$) as shown in Table 16 :

x_n	$f_1(x_1)$	$\pi_1^*(x_1)$	$f_2(x_2)$	$\pi_2^*(x_2)$	$f_3(x_3)$
s_1	0.8	a_2	0.9	a_1	0.6
s_2	0.8	a_2	0.8	a_1	1.0
s_3	0.9	a_2	0.8	a_1	0.8

Table 16. $\{f_1, f_2, f_3\}$ $\pi^* = \{\pi_1^*, \pi_2^*\}$

5 A Posterior Conditional Decision Process

In this section, we propose a conditional optimization problems subject to the successive constraint. We take, at each stage, backward conditional expectation of remaining process *after* performing take-action for the regular stochastic decision process (3). This generates an *a posteriori conditional decision process* (cdp) as follows :

$$\begin{aligned} \text{Max.} \quad & \mu_1(x_1, u_1) \wedge E_{x_1}^{u_1}[\mu_2(x_2, u_2) \wedge \cdots \wedge E_{x_{N-1}}^{u_{N-1}}[\mu_N(x_N, u_N) \\ & \qquad\qquad\qquad\qquad\qquad\qquad\qquad \wedge E_{x_N}^{u_N} \mu_G] \cdots] \\ \text{s.t.} \quad & \text{(i)} \quad X_{n+1} \sim p(\cdot|x_n, u_n) \qquad n = 1, 2, \ldots, N \\ & \text{(ii)} \quad u_n \in U \end{aligned} \tag{49}$$

where $E_x^u \mu$ is a conditional expected value of function $\mu = \mu(\cdot)$ through probability distribution $p(\cdot|x, u)$ together with n-th Markov decision function π_n :

$$E_x^u \mu = \sum_{y \in X} \mu(y) p(y|x, u) \qquad u = \pi_n(x). \tag{50}$$

Let $w_1(x_1)$ denote the maximum value in (49) over Markov class Π. Then we have the backward recursive equation :

Theorem 6. *(Bellman and Zadeh[3], Iwamoto, Tsurusaki and Fujita[12])*

$$\begin{aligned} w_n(x) &= \operatorname*{Max}_{u \in U} \left[\mu_n(x,u) \wedge \left(\sum_{y \in X} w_{n+1}(y) p(y|x,u) \right) \right] \qquad 1 \le n \le N \\ & \qquad\qquad x \in X. \\ w_{N+1}(x) &= \mu_G(x) \end{aligned} \tag{51}$$

This is *the* recursive formula Bellman and Zadeh have proposed on stochastic system [3].

We solve their (3,2,2) model

$$\begin{aligned} &\text{Max.} \quad [\,\mu_1(u_1) \wedge E_{x_1}^{u_1} [\mu_2(u_2) \wedge E_{x_2}^{u_2} \mu_G\,]] \\ &\text{s.t.} \quad X_{n+1} \sim p(\cdot|x_n, u_n), \; u_n \in \{a_1, a_2\} \quad n = 1, 2 \end{aligned} \tag{52}$$

with data ([3, pp. B154]) Tables 3,4. Then the maximization in Eq.(51) reduces to

$$\begin{aligned} &\operatorname*{Max}_{\pi} [\,\mu_1(u_1) \wedge E_{x_2}^{u_1} [\mu_1(u_1) \wedge E_{x_2}^{u_2} \mu_G\,]] \\ &= \operatorname*{Max}_{\pi_1} [\,\mu_1(u_1) \wedge E_{x_1}^{u_1} \operatorname*{Max}_{\pi_2} [\mu_2(u_2) \wedge E_{x_2}^{u_2} \mu_G\,]] \\ &\qquad (u_n = \pi_n(x_n) \quad n = 1, 2). \end{aligned} \tag{53}$$

This is equivalent to

$$\begin{aligned} w_3(x_3) &= \mu_G(x_3) \\ w_2(x_2) &= \operatorname*{Max}_{u_2} [\,\mu_2(u_2) \wedge \sum_{x_3} w_3(x_3) p(x_3|x_2, u_2)\,] \\ w_1(x_1) &= \operatorname*{Max}_{u_1} [\,\mu_1(u_1) \wedge \sum_{x_2} w_2(x_2) p(x_2|x_1, u_1)\,]. \end{aligned} \tag{54}$$

First we have

$$w_3(s_1) = 0.3, \quad w_3(s_2) = 1.0, \quad w_3(s_3) = 0.8. \tag{55}$$

By solving the recursive equation, Bellman and Zadeh [3, pp. B154] gives

$$w_2(s_1) = 0.6, \quad w_2(s_2) = 0.82, \quad w_2(s_3) = 0.6 \tag{56}$$

$$\pi_2^*(s_1) = a_1, \quad \pi_2^*(s_2) = a_1, \quad \pi_2^*(s_3) = a_2, \tag{57}$$

$$w_1(s_1) = 0.8, \quad w_1(s_2) = 0.62, \quad w_1(s_3) = 0.62 \tag{58}$$

$$\pi_1^*(s_1) = a_1, \quad \pi_1^*(s_2) = a_1 \text{ or } a_2, \quad \pi_1^*(s_3) = a_1. \tag{59}$$

However, Iwamoto and Fujita [11] gives the exact values as follows :

$$w_1(s_1) = 0.798, \quad w_1(s_2) = 0.622, \quad w_1(s_3) = 0.622 \tag{60}$$

$$\pi_1^*(s_1) = a_2, \quad \pi_1^*(s_2) = a_1 \text{ or } a_2, \quad \pi_1^*(s_3) = a_1. \tag{61}$$

As a summary we have Table 17:

x_n	$w_1(x_1)$	$\pi_1^*(x_1)$	$w_2(x_2)$	$\pi_2^*(x_2)$	$w_3(x_3)$
s_1	0.798	a_2	0.6	a_1	0.3
s_2	0.622	a_1, a_2	0.82	a_1	1.0
s_3	0.622	a_1	0.6	a_2	0.8

Table 17. $\{w_1, w_2, w_3\}$ $\pi = \{\pi_1^*, \pi_2^*\}$

This solution is also obtained through a multistage stochastic a posteriori decision tree-table [12]. An a priori conditional decision process is also discussed in [9],[12].

References

1. Baldwin, J. F. Pilsworth, B. W. (1982) Dynamic programming for fuzzy systems with fuzzy environment. J. Math. Anal. Appl. **85**, 1–23
2. Bellman, R. E. (1957) Dynamic Programming. Princeton Univ. Press, NJ
3. Bellman, R. E., Zadeh, L. A. (1970) Decision–making in a fuzzy environment. Manag. Sci. B **17**, 141–164
4. Esogbue, A. O. Bellman, R. E. (1984) Fuzzy dynamic programming and its extensions, *TIMS/Studies in the Management Sciences.* **20**, 147–167
5. Fujita, T., Iwamoto S. (2000) An optimistic decision-making in fuzzy environment. Ed. J.L. Casti, Proceedings of International Workshop on Computation, Optimization and Control (The Seventh Bellman Continuum), The Santa Fe Institute, USA, 1999; *Applied Mathematics and Computation*, to appear
6. Howard, R. (1960) Dynamic Programming and Markov Processes. MIT Press, Mass
7. Iwamoto, S. (1987) Theory of Dynamic Program (in Japanese). Kyushu Univ. Press, Fukuoka
8. Iwamoto, S. (1998) Decision-making in fuzzy environment: A survey from stochastic decision process. Ed. L.C. Jain and R.K. Jain, *Proceedings of The Second International Conference on Knowledge-based Intelligent Electronics Systems (KES '98), Adelaide*, 542–546

9. Iwamoto, S. (1999) Conditional decision processes with recursive reward function. J. Math. Anal. Appl. **230**, 193–210
10. Iwamoto, S. (2000) A class of dual fuzzy dynamic programs. Ed. J.L. Casti, *Proceedings of The Seventh Bellman Continuum Workshop*, The Santa Fe Institute, USA, 1999;*Applied Mathematics and Computation*, to appear
11. Iwamoto, S., Fujita, T. (1995) Stochastic decision–making in a fuzzy environment. J. Operations Res. Soc. Japan **38**, 467–482
12. Iwamoto, S., Tsurusaki, K., Fujita, T. (1999) Conditional decision–making in a fuzzy environment. J. Operations Res. Soc. Japan **42**, 198–218
13. Iwamoto, S., Tsurusaki, K., Fujita, T. (2000) On Markov policies for minimax decision processes. J. Math. Anal. Appl. to appear
14. Iwamoto, S., Sniedovich, M. (1998) Sequential decision making in fuzzy environment. J. Math. Anal. Appl. **222**, 208–224
15. Iwamoto, S., Ueno, T., Fujita, T. (1999) Controlled Markov chains with utility functions. International Workshop on Markov Processes and Controlled Markov Chains, Changsha, Hunan, China, August
16. Kacprzyk, J. (1977) Multistage control of a stochastic system under fuzzy goals and constraints using a generic algorithm. Seventh IFSA World Congress, Prague, **2**, 306–311
17. Kacprzyk, J. (1978) Decision-making in a fuzzy environment with fuzzy termination time. Fuzzy Sets and Systems **1**, 169–179
18. Kacprzyk, J. (1992) Fuzzy optimal control revisited: Toward a new generation of fuzzy control. Proceedings of the 2nd International Conference on Fuzzy Logic & Neural Networks (Iizuka, Japan), 429–432
19. Kacprzyk, J., Esogbue, A. O. (1996) Fuzzy dynamic programming: Main developments and applications. Fuzzy Sets and Systems **81**, 31–45
20. Kacprzyk, J., Staniewski, P. (1980) A new approach to the control of stochastic systems in a fuzzy environment. Archiwum Automatyki i Telemechaniki **25**, 443–444
21. Lee, E. S. (1968) Quasilinearization and Invariant Imbedding. Academic Press, NY
22. Puterman, M. (1994) Markov Decision Processes : discrete stochastic dynamic programming. Wiley & Sons, NY
23. Sniedovich, M. (1992) Dynamic Programming, Marcel Dekker,Inc., NY
24. Scott, M. R. (1973) Invariant Imbedding and its Applications to Ordinary Differential Equations : An introduction. Addison-Wesly, London
25. Stein, W. E. (1980) Optimal stopping in a fuzzy environment. Fuzzy Sets and Systems **3**, 253–259

Management of Data Uncertainty in Dynamic Programming

Ly Fie Sugianto

School of Business Systems, Monash University 3800, Victoria, Australia

Email: lyfie.sugianto@infotech.monash.edu.au

Summary:
This chapter introduces an innovative approach to Dynamic Programming optimization to deal with data uncertainty problem. The proposed approach incorporates confidence measure to quantify the data uncertainty. The concept of confidence level enables the utilization of alternative data sources for estimating uncertain data. This algorithm of fuzzy optimization has been applied to optimize the availability of unique spare parts of a power station. In particular, the paper describes two types of confidence level propagation: confidence level at the component level and confidence level at the power station level. Simulated case studies have been included to show the characteristics of the fuzzy aggregators and their suitability in propagating the confidence level. Empirical research on fuzzy aggregators is useful because it allows different approaches (from conservative to risky) to optimum decision making. This notion of dynamic decision making is addressed in this chapter. Although the study implements Dynamic Programming in optimizing the spare parts inventory of an electrical power plant, the proposed technique is generally applicable to optimize similar categories of objective functions when fuzzy aggregators can be determined by empirical research.

Keywords: *Data uncertainty, Dynamic Programming, Empirical research, Fuzzy operators.*

1 Introduction

A common problem in power systems reliability engineering is the problem of data uncertainty and/or data unavailability. For example, the Mean Time To Failure (MTTF) data of some plant items is often unknown because of low frequency of breakdown and preventive maintenance strategy. Some attempts to cope with the problems of data uncertainty include the Interval Mathematics [2], Sensitivity Analysis [4] and Bayesian Statistics [3]. Assumptions, which are used in these approaches, are not necessarily justifiable in other circumstances.

Intuitively, in the event of data unavailability, unknown data can be approximated by intelligent estimates or with the assistance of external reliability databases. Nonetheless, the appropriateness of the approximation should be questioned since the data accuracy has a significant influence on the optimized result.

In quantifying the degree of uncertainty, a novel approach of Fuzzy Optimization [6] has been proposed in which the concept of Confidence Level (CL) in the Probability Theory has been expanded to cope with problems of weak statistical basis. CL in fuzzy optimization is a means to measure the degree of similarity or accuracy of an estimated datum. In the attempt to approximate an unknown datum, given that the characteristic of the object associated with the data can be expressed in terms of a mathematical model, CL indicates a resemblance factor and may be used to quantify the degree of compatibility between the object under investigation with the object within affinity whose data is readily available.

Figure 1.1 illustrates the fuzzy optimization method that quantifies data uncertainty and optimizes decision using the Dynamic Programming technique. It is composed of three stages:

1. Determination of confidence level
2. Determination of fuzzy aggregator
3. Interpretation of confidence level using Multi Attribute Transformation (MAT) scheme.

This chapter concerns with the second stage of the overall approach: in relation to the use of fuzzy aggregators for CL propagation. Distinctive techniques of CL determination have been documented in [6]: statistic-based CL, similarity-based CL and subjective-based CL, while the methodology and case studies of the MAT scheme have also been established [7, 8].

Aiming to determine fuzzy aggregator for the fuzzy optimization, the content of this chapter has been organised in three sections:

- The formulation of the objective function of the optimization
- Uncertainty propagation type 1 - which is subdivided into subheadings: sensitivity analysis, approximation equations of parameter variation and fuzzy aggregator as parameterized conjunction operator
- Uncertainty propagation type 2 - which is subdivided into subheadings: plant items forming "components in series", case studies (components in

series), plant items with spare parts as "components in parallel" and case studies (components in parallel).

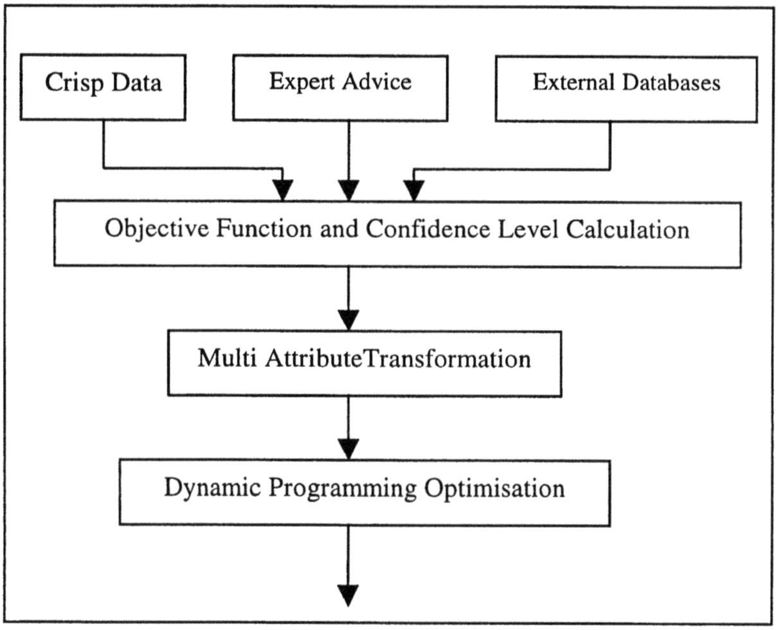

Fig.1.1. Dynamic Programming optimization with uncertain data [6]

The application of Dynamic Programming in this chapter has been defined as a multistage allocation process which searches for an optimum solution by partitioning the overall case into a series of stages. In a dynamic type problem, the division is performed based on the time factor, whereas in a static type problem, the allocation process is time independent. In this application, the formulation of the inventory problem falls into the static type.

Given that there are N stages, the resource for stage i is x_i while the return function for that stage is $g_i(x_i)$. The return of each stage is directly determined by the resource allocated for that particular stage. However, allocating more resources for a particular stage implies fewer resources are available for the remaining stages.

The objective function of the availability calculation is given by Equation (1) while Equation (2) shows the constraint function or limitation.

$$F_N(x) = g_1(x_1) * g_2(x_2) * \ldots * g_N(x_N) \tag{1}$$

$$\sum_{i=1}^{N} x_i \leq X_{Total}, \text{ where } x_i = C_i * n_i \tag{2}$$

where x_i - resources for stage i

X_{Total} - total resources

C_i - cost of spare parts i

n_i - number of spare parts purchased

$g_i(x_i)$ - return function using x_i as resources for stage i (the availability of a single item)

$F_N(x)$ - total return function; the product of return functions from all stages (the availability of the complete system).

The availability of a single item i is given by $g_i(x_i)$. It depends on the availability of the spare parts held in stock. It is clear that the availability level of the plant item increases with the inventory of the spare parts. Keeping some spare parts in stock is analogous to a redundancy in an electrical circuit, that is, having a parallel connection to provide an alternative path for the current to flow through the circuit (see Fig.1.2).

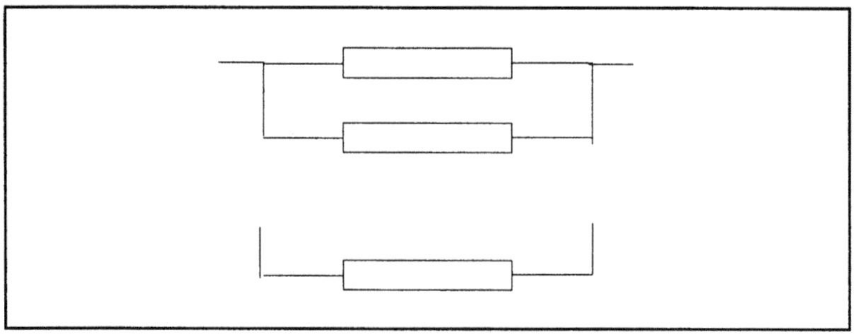

Fig.1.2. Dynamic Programming optimization with uncertain data [6]

The availability of the complete system is given by $F_N(x)$. The operation of the complete system requires all N components to work successfully (or to be available for operation). In an electrical circuit, this is analogous to a series arrangement of the N components. Therefore, the availability of the complete system is given by the product of the availability of each component.

The optimization procedure at each stage is given by the following:

- For stage 1-

$$f_1(x) = \max[g_1(x)] \tag{3}$$

- For stage 2-

$$f_2(x) = \max[f_1(x_1) * g_2(x-x_1)] \tag{4}$$

- For stage N-

$$f_N(x) = \max[f_{N-1}(x_{N-1}) * g_N(x-x_{N-1})] \quad (5)$$

where $f_i(x)$ = optimized return function for stage i.

When the optimization process has completely allocated the whole of the resources, the next step in the procedure is to execute a backward iteration. This calculates the resources used at each stage and the optimized number of spare parts for each component.

The backward iteration process starts from Equation (5). Knowing that $x - x_{N-1}$ is the resources allocated for stage N, x_{N-1} is the resources allocated to optimize stage N-1. In the same way, substituting N with N-1 to Equation (5), the resources allocated for stage N-1 can be found. Thus, the remaining resources are to be distributed for component 1 to component N-2. This iteration is repeated until the optimized numbers of spare parts for all N components are found.

2 The Formulation of the Objective Function

The objective of the optimization has been defined as the maximum availability of the power plant. The availability of a plant item belonging to a base-load power station is commonly modelled as:

$$A = MTTF/(MTTF+MTTR) \quad (6)$$

where A – plant item availability
MTTF – Mean Time To Failure of a plant item
MTTR – Mean Time To Repair of a plant item.

The availability of the whole power plant is the (simultaneous) availability of all critical plant items for the generation of electrical power. Hence, the power plant availability is the product of the individual plant item availability, as shown in Equation (7):

$$A_{TOTAL} = \prod_{i=1}^{N} A_i \quad (7)$$

where A_{TOTAL} – power plant availability
A_i – plant item availability
N – total number of critical plant items in the power plant.

The data structure in the optimization method represents an approximated datum using two elements: the data itself and the associated CL. As the uncertain data is used in the computational of the optimum objective, CL of the uncertain data must also be propagated. It is assumed that CL occupies a range of [0,1] and it is analogous to the membership value in the fuzzy sets theory. This leads to the use of fuzzy aggregators to propagate CL in the optimization procedure.

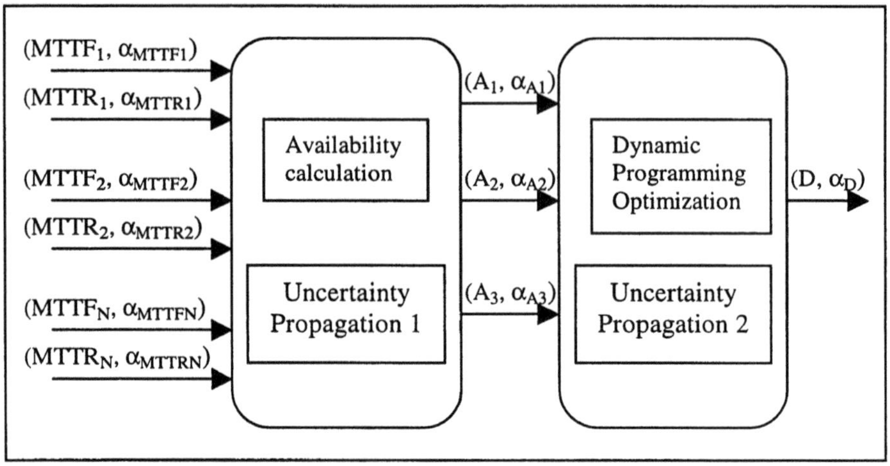

Fig. 2.1. The propagation of the confidence level [6].

In identifying different types of uncertainty propagation, the path of propagation undergone by the approximate data in the Dynamic Programming method must be examined. As can be seen in Figure 2.1, there are two types of CL diffusions in the optimization procedure:

1. Resolution of CL of the availability function from its parameters or

$$\alpha_A = f(\alpha_{MTTF}, \alpha_{MTTR})$$

where α_A – CL of the availability of a plant item
α_{MTTF} – CL of the MTTF of the plant item
α_{MTTR} – CL of the MTTR of the plant item.

2. Resolution of CL of the optimized objective function from the availability function or

$$\alpha_D = \alpha_{A\ \text{optimized}} = f(\alpha_{A_1}, \alpha_{A_2} \dots \alpha_{A_N})$$

where α_D – CL of the decision (optimized availability)
α_{A_N} – CL of the availability of plant item "N".

3 Uncertainty Propagation 1

Figure 3.1 shows the diagram of the procedure to conduct the empirical research for determining the fuzzy aggregator. In uncertainty propagation 1, the inference of α_A from α_{MTTF} and α_{MTTR} can be viewed as the problem to determine a change in an availability level resulting from changes in MTTF and MTTR. Sensitivity Analysis has been conducted in order to examine how the perturbation on the parameters affects the objective function. Upon finding the effect of the perturbation, the uncertainty propagation can be modelled using fuzzy conjunction operator. Approximation equations of the extreme functions produced by the analysis (referred to as approximation equations of parameter variation) are useful to simplify the modelling of the uncertainty propagation.

3.1 Sensitivity Analysis

Having defined the range of the perturbation of the parameters to be:

$$MTTF = [1, 10] \text{ years and } MTTR = [1, 10] \text{ days},$$

the sensitivity analysis technique has been used to determine the worst case scenario which causes the maximum deviation in the final result.

Consider the following:

$$\forall x, y, z \exists x, y, z \in A,$$

where $A \subset R$,

$x \in (x_{min}, x_{max})$, $y \in (y_{min}, y_{max})$, $z = f(x,y)$,

where $x_{min} = \mu - \sigma$ & $x_{max} = \mu + \sigma$;

y_{min} and y_{max} are calculated similarly

x – MTTF

y – MTTR

f – the availability formulation for a base load power station.

For this particular function "f" and typical x and y values, it can be deduced that

$$z_{min} = f(x_{min}, y_{max}) \text{ and } z_{max} = f(x_{max}, y_{min})$$

and that the deviation is such that $(z - z_{min}) > (z_{max} - z)$

Since the data uncertainty problem concerns with the largest deviation, only the expression $z_{min} = f(x_{min}, y_{max})$ is of concern.

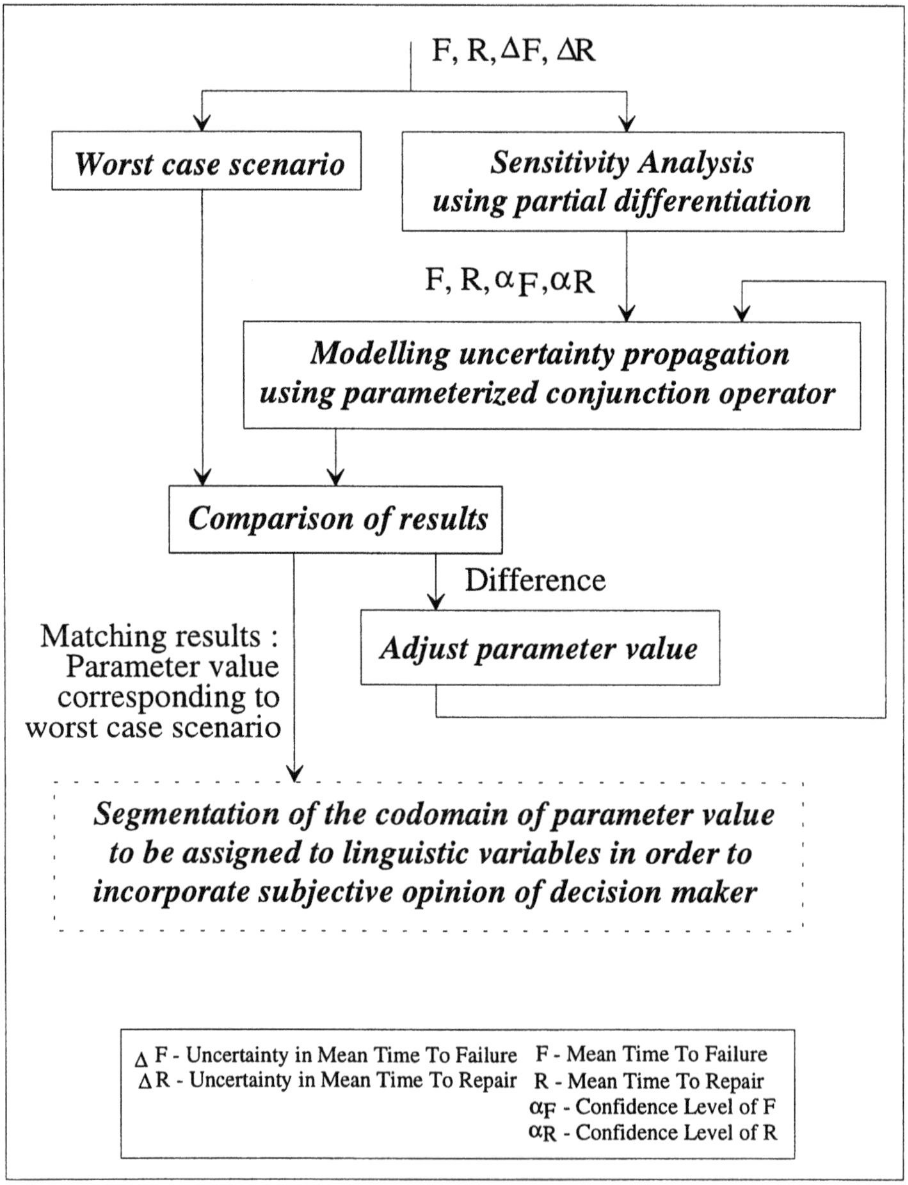

Fig. 3.1. Uncertainty Propagation 1.

Upon differentiating Equation (6) with a limitation to linear parts, the following equation is obtained:

$$\delta A = (\delta A/\delta MTTF)^* \alpha_{MTTF} + (\delta A/\delta MTTR)^* \alpha_{MTTR} \quad (8)$$

where $\delta A/\delta MTTF = MTTR/(MTTF+MTTR)^2$ (9)

and $\delta A/\delta MTTR = -MTTF/(MTTF+MTTR)^2$ (10)

A change in MTTF alters the availability value exponentially in the order of 10^{-6}. When the parameter MTTR is assigned to the other extreme value of 10 (days), the change in the overall availability becomes more significant. Perturbation of the parameter MTTR alters the availability value in the order of 10^{-3}, and this change is merely constant as MTTR increases from 1 to 10 days. Therefore, the perturbation of either parameter causes negligible effect on the final availability. However, it should be emphasized that this analysis is conducted on the availability of a single plant item. When this approach is applied to a power station, which consists of numerous plant items, a slight variation in each plant item availability may well accumulate to a significant change in the overall availability (refer to Equation (7)).

3.2 Approximation Equations of Parameter Variation

The above partial differentiation equations can be approximated by parameterized equations. The approximation is to simplify the partial differentiation components in Equation (8), namely δA/δMTTF and δA/δMTTR. It is possible to parameterize Equations (9) and (10) since their characteristics are apparent: exponential and linear for the respective equations. The approximation may be done in a number of ways, such as using the polynomial function or the piece-wise approximation. The characteristics of Equations (9) and (10) enforce the appropriateness of the polynomial function for the approximation. The coefficients for the polynomial approximation can be found using computer simulations, for example, using "Matlab".

δA/δMTTF can be approximated using an equation involving the inverse of a quadratic variable:

$$y = (k_0(z)+k_1)/x^2 \quad (11)$$

where y – δA/δMTTF
x – $1/MTTF^2$
z – MTTR

k_0 – coefficient of the polynomial = $9.4202 * 10^{-1}$

k_1 – coefficient of the polynomial = $1.1454 * 10^{-1}$

The approximation of δA/δMTTR is proportional to MTTR, thus

$$y = l_0 (x) + l_1 \tag{12}$$

where y – δA/δMTTR
x – 1/MTTF (with the assumption that x represents the inverse of MTTF)
l_0, l_1 – coefficient of the polynomial: $-9.7114 * 10^{-1}$ & $-1.1709 * 10^{-5}$

3.3 Fuzzy Aggregator as Parameterized Conjunction Operator

In this proposed method of uncertainty propagation, the approximation equations of parameter variation are regarded as the basis for propagating the data uncertainty, that is from the uncertainty in the parameter MTTF and MTTR to the uncertainty in the availability level.

It should be noted that in the sensitivity analysis, the overall approximation equation for δA has been defined as a straight forward addition between δA/δ MTTF and δA/δMTTR (see Equation (8)). However, the summation operation is not flexible enough to be used as the fuzzy aggregator in the uncertainty propagation. For instance, when CL of MTTF and CL of MTTR are specified by an expert, CL of the availability cannot be obtained using the summation operation. This signifies the need for an empirical research on parameterized conjunction operators to find fuzzy aggregators which can produce comparable results as that predicted by the sensitivity analysis (the worst case scenario).

The empirical research on fuzzy aggregators is concerned with the suitability of the aggregators to infer CL based on their compensatory characteristics. Researchers have formulated a number of fuzzy operators classified into t-norms, t-conorms and averaging operators. Parameterized t-norms, t-conorms and averaging operators are suitable for fuzzy aggregation (type) 1 because their degree of compensatory can be adjusted through the parameter value.

Figure 3.2 portrays the characteristics of these operators in aggregating CL of MTTF and CL of MTTR. The characteristics shown in the figure facilitates the selection of the appropriate aggregator to model the uncertainty propagation. The plots in Figure 3.2 have been produced by setting the parameters to the lowest boundary, namely :

- $\chi = 0.1$ for Hamacher's intersection (AND) operator [11], (to avoid the modification of the aggregator to Hamacher product, if χ is set to 0),
- $\chi = -1$ for Hamacher's union (OR) operator [11]
- $p = 1$ for Yager's intersection and union operators [10]
- $\chi = 0.1$ for Werners' both intersection and union operators [9].

In Figure 3.2, it can be observed that Yager's parameterized conjunction operators are either non-compensatory (Yager's AND) or full compensatory (Yager's OR), whereas those of Werners' have the characteristic of averaging operators: the plot of CL values lies within α_{MTTF} and α_{MTTR}. Further, it should be noted that the trend of Yager's operators opposes that of Hamacher's. As α_{MTTF} increases, Yager's union operator produces a declining plot of CL while Hamacher's union operator generates a series of increasing CL values.

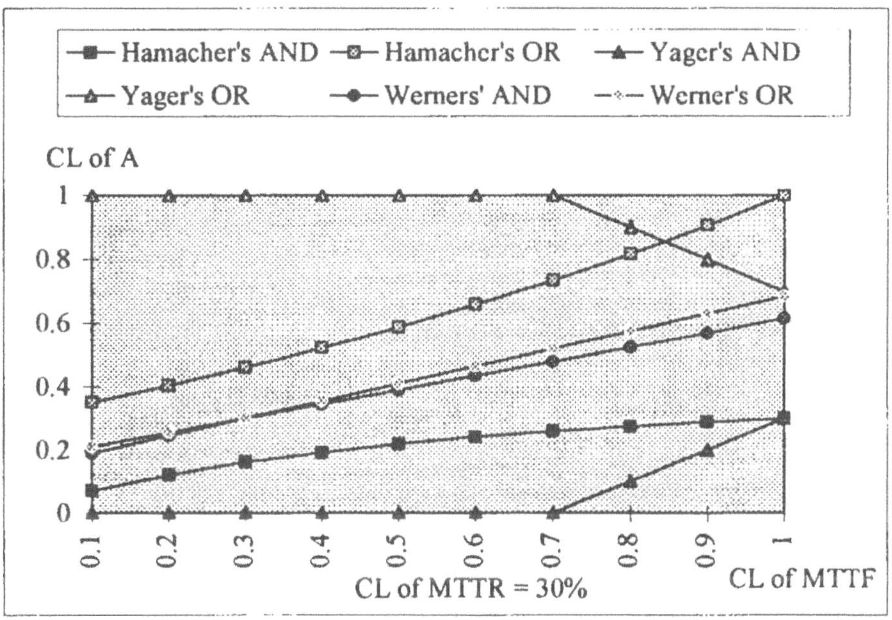

Fig. 3.2. Comparison of aggregated CL produced by parameterized conjunction operators [6].

The behaviour of each aggregator with different parameter values has been investigated. Without an upper limit, Hamacher's operators allow more flexibility in the degree of compensatory of the aggregation. Likewise, Yager's conjunction operators also allow some flexibility since the parameter "p" does not have an upper limit. Due to the boundary for the parameter values, that is $\chi \in [0,1]$, Werners' conjunction operators are least flexible compared to Yager's and Hamacher's operators. A distinctive feature of Werners' conjunctive operators is its averaging nature; the aggregated CL lies between the CL of MTTF and the CL of MTTR.

An empirical research on fuzzy aggregators has been conducted to determine the suitability of the operators for CL propagation. The determination of the most appropriate fuzzy aggregator is based on the following hypothesis:

1. The utilization of Werners' "fuzzy AND" and "fuzzy OR" operators in uncertainty propagation cannot be justified due to their degree of compensatory. The "averaging" character of Werners' operators are not suitable to propagate CL, as concluded from the sensitivity analysis that uncertainty in the parameters MTTF and MTTR only have little impact on the objective function.
2. Hamacher's intersection operator is also not suitable to aggregate CL since the plot of the resulting CL is bounded by the lower CL value. This is due to the non-compensatory characteristic of the operator.
3. Likewise, the trend of Yager's union operator opposes the characteristic of the uncertainty propagation: as CL of MTTF increases, the aggregated CL decreases.
4. Hamacher's union and Yager's intersection operators show similar trend as the characteristic of the propagated CL, which has been predicted using extreme cases and sensitivity analysis. Thus, the suitability of these two operators is studied more carefully.

Various cases of different α_{MTTF} and α_{MTTR} values have been simulated and the results have been graphed and compared. It has been concluded Yager's intersection operator with "p" set to 5.6 can induce CL of the extreme case (worst case scenario) more closely compared to Hamacher's operator with "χ" set to 33. Hence, Yager's intersection operator is the most appropriate fuzzy operator to aggregate CL of MTTF and MTTR in fuzzy aggregation 1.

4 Uncertainty Propagation 2

Uncertainty propagation (type) 2 is the diffusion of CL of the individual plant item availability. The two combinations in uncertainty propagation type 2 are (see Figure 4.1):

1. When the plant items are in "series" arrangement - which is analogous to the availability of the plant items required for electrical power generation
2. When the plant items are in "parallel" arrangement - which is analogous to a plant item with spare component(s).

The empirical research on fuzzy aggregators for these combinations are distinguishable due to their different practical implications.

4.1 Plant Items Forming "Components in Series"

The inferred CL of the objective function when components are in "series" arrangement is as follows:

$$\alpha_{Aseries} = \overset{N}{\underset{i=1}{\circ}} \alpha_{Ai} \tag{13}$$

where o – fuzzy aggregator
α_{Ai} – CL of the availability of plant item "i"
$\alpha_{Aseries}$ – CL of the availability of the system.

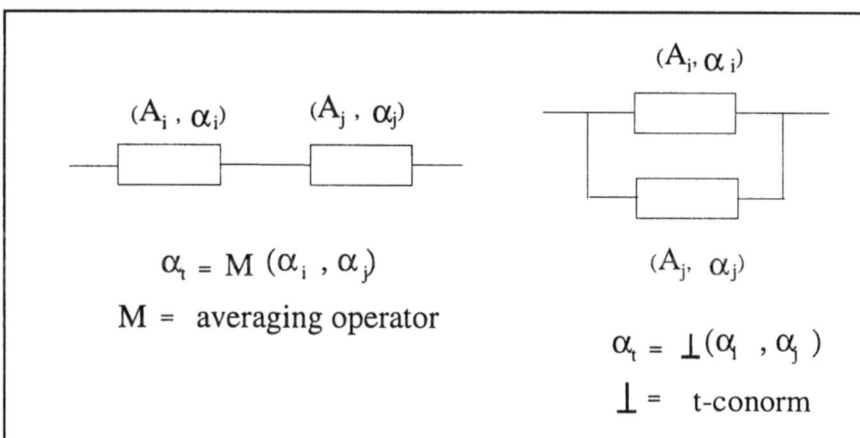

Fig. 4.1. Uncertainty propagation type 1 ("in series") and type 2 ("in parallel") [6].

The criteria for selecting the suitable operator should consider the extreme case where the number of plant items included in the modelling of the power station (denoted by "N") is substantially large. The inferred CL of the availability of such a model should still relate to the physical interpretation of any real life problems (regardless the value of N) if appropriate fuzzy aggregators are employed.

- For example, in a situation where N = 10 and α_i = 90%, if the algebraic product, which is a t-norm, is used to aggregate CL of the availability of the plant items, CL of the availability of the whole system would be 34.9%. When thirty critical plant items are included in the availability modelling of the power plant (N = 30), CL of the availability of the power plant drops significantly to 4.24%.
- If the algebraic sum, which is a t-conorm, is used to operate the CL of the availability of the "components in series", the resulting CL would be equally unrealistic. For instance, in the above situation when N = 10, the resulting CL is 99.99999999% (note that there is N number of 9).

Thus, t-norm falls inadequate for propagating "component in series" since the propagated CL of components with individual CL of 90% drops significantly to 34.9%, which is rather unrealistic. On the other hand, when t-conorm is utilized, the resulting CL saturates as it reaches 100% rapidly. In conclusion, a vital aspect to selecting the most appropriate fuzzy aggregator is the degree of compensatory of the fuzzy aggregator.

Further, the degree of compensatory of the fuzzy aggregators exhibits a bigger impact in cases involving unsymmetrical CL. For instance, when the CL of one parameter is significantly lower than the other, the resulting CL may also be unrealistic. For example, a situation where α_{A1} = 0.9 and α_{A2} = 0.2, $\alpha_{Aseries}$ = 18% (if a t-norm such as the algebraic product is applied) and 92% (if a t-conorm such as the algebraic sum is used).

From the foregoing, it can be concluded that an operator, whose degree of compensatory lies between t-norm and t-conorm, is most suitable for aggregating the confidence levels of "components in series". In both symmetrical and unsymmetrical cases of confidence levels, such an operator seems to be appropriate since it does not compensate its operands as much as a t-norm would, nor does it elevate the resulting CL above the operand values, like when a t-conorm is applied.

The Sugianto 1 and the Sugianto 2 fuzzy operators have been introduced in this case study as alternative fuzzy aggregators whose degree of compensatory allows the inferred CL value to match closer to the worst case scenario:

- Sugianto 1 "fuzzy AND" [6] expressed as

$$\mu_{\text{and}(\mu_{\tilde{A}}(x),\, \mu_{\tilde{B}}(x))} = \chi\,(\min\{\mu_{\tilde{A}}(x), \mu_{\tilde{B}}(x)\}) + (1-\chi)\frac{2\,\mu_{\tilde{A}}(x)\,\mu_{\tilde{B}}(x)}{\mu_{\tilde{A}}(x) + \mu_{\tilde{B}}(x)}$$

- Sugianto 1 "fuzzy OR" [6] is expressed as

$$\mu_{\text{or}(\mu_{\tilde{A}}(x),\, \mu_{\tilde{B}}(x))} = \chi\,(\max\{\mu_{\tilde{A}}(x), \mu_{\tilde{B}}(x)\}) + (1-\chi)\frac{2\,\mu_{\tilde{A}}(x)\,\mu_{\tilde{B}}(x)}{\mu_{\tilde{A}}(x) + \mu_{\tilde{B}}(x)}$$

- Sugianto 2 "fuzzy AND" [6] is expressed as

$$\mu_{\text{and}(\mu_{\tilde{A}}(x),\, \mu_{\tilde{B}}(x))} = \chi\,(\min\{\mu_{\tilde{A}}(x), \mu_{\tilde{B}}(x)\}) + (1-\chi)\sqrt{\mu_{\tilde{A}}(x)\,\mu_{\tilde{B}}(x)}$$

- Sugianto 2 "fuzzy OR" [6] is expressed as

$$\mu_{\text{or}(\mu_{\tilde{A}}(x),\, \mu_{\tilde{B}}(x))} = \chi\,(\max\{\mu_{\tilde{A}}(x), \mu_{\tilde{B}}(x)\}) + (1-\chi)\sqrt{\mu_{\tilde{A}}(x)\,\mu_{\tilde{B}}(x)}$$

where $x \in X$, $\chi \in [0, 1]$.

The Sugianto 1 "AND" operator is a modification of the Werners' operator, in which a weighted harmonic mean is used instead of the arithmetic mean. Since the degree of compensatory of the harmonic mean is "softer" than that of arithmetic mean, the overall degree of compensatory of the Sugianto 1 "AND" operator is "softer" than that of Werners' "fuzzy AND".

Likewise, the Sugianto 2 operator is a parameterized operator whose degree of compensatory lies between the Sugianto 1 and the Werners' fuzzy operators. It employs the weighted geometric mean as the second element of its expression.

Such parameterized operators are beneficial for this case as it allows flexibility in applying the fuzzy aggregator to real problems. When a more "averaging" character is desired, "χ" can be set closer to 1 and in other circumstances, a slightly stronger degree of compensatory is desired, "χ" can be set to a number close to 0.

4.2 Case Studies - "Components in Series"

The case example discussed in this section is drawn from a major section of a gas turbine power station [1, 5], namely the Heat Recovery Steam Generators (HRSG). The HRSG plant consists of six unique plant items. Table 4.1 lists the reliability data of the HRSG components. Artificial data uncertainty is introduced to the data in the table: CL_{MTBF} = 70% and the CL_{MTTR} = 70%. Table 4.2 shows the approximate data derived from the information contained in Table 4.1.

Table 4.1: The reliability data of the HRSG plant items.

No.	COMPONENT NAME	MTBF	MTTR
1	Feedwater System	3113.8	15.4
2	Afterburners	4776.9	12.6
3	Valves	9553.8	9.7
4	Evaporator	6369.2	31.9
5	Economizer	6092.3	40.4
6	Dampers and Ductwork	10008.7	43.7

Table 4.2: The approximate data of the availability level of the HRSG plant items (with α_{MTTF} = 70% and α_{MTTR} = 70%)

No.	MTTF	MTTF (min)	MTTR	MTTR (max)	A	A (min)	αA
1	3098	2168.88	15.4	20.02	0.9951	0.9909	0.9958
2	4764	3335.01	12.6	16.38	0.9974	0.9951	0.9977
3	9544	6680.87	9.7	12.61	0.9990	0.9981	0.9991
4	6337	4436.11	31.9	41.47	0.9950	0.9907	0.9957
5	6052	4236.33	40.4	52.52	0.9934	0.9878	0.9943
6	9965	6975.5	43.7	56.81	0.9956	0.9919	0.9963

The resulting propagated CL of the availability of the HRSG plant items are listed below:

- Arithmetic Mean: 0.995931699
- Sugianto 2 "AND": 0.994510400

- Geometric Mean: 0.995930980
- Harmonic Mean: 0.995930262
- Werners' "AND": 0.994519467
- Sugianto 1 "AND": 0.994519333
- Worst case scenario: 0.979174305.

These values are compared with the possible deviation produced in worst case situation:

- The HRSG availability level = 0.9757
- The percentage deviation of these two figures is 97.93%
- The worst case availability level = 0.9553.

As can be observed from Figure 4.2, the parameterized averaging operators can vary (or "soften") the degree of compensatory. The "softening" effect enables the control of the impact of CL on influencing the decision variable. In this case study, "χ" has been set to 0.9 for the Werner's, the Sugianto 1 and the Sugianto 2 operations. This is in order to attain the highest degree of compensatory whilst preserving the "averaging" nature of the operation. A similar trend that can be observed in Figure 4.2 is that the harmonic mean, the arithmetic mean and the geometric mean operators produce nearly similar results due to their degree of compensatory. Comparing these propagated CL values with the worst case scenario, it is obvious that the fuzzy aggregators produce rather optimistic results.

Case examples modelling other subsections of the gas turbine, namely Balance of Plant (BP), Combustion Turbine Components (CTC) and Combined Cycle Steam Turbines (CCST) have been simulated. The results are compared in Figure 4.3. Conclusions drawn from the case studies are:

- The reason for the low availability level of the CTC plant is due to the number of plant items included in the model, ie. number of operands aggregated by the algebraic product.
- The increase in the number of plant items does not affect the propagated CL substantially. The worst possible scenario shows a CL of 97.09%.
- The propagated CL of a more reliable subsection is higher compared to that of a less reliable subsection.
- Cases involving the application of Hamacher product to aggregate the CL values are also simulated. From the simulations, it is concluded that imposing algebraic product to infer the CL of the objective function does not affect the characteristic of the fuzzy aggregators.

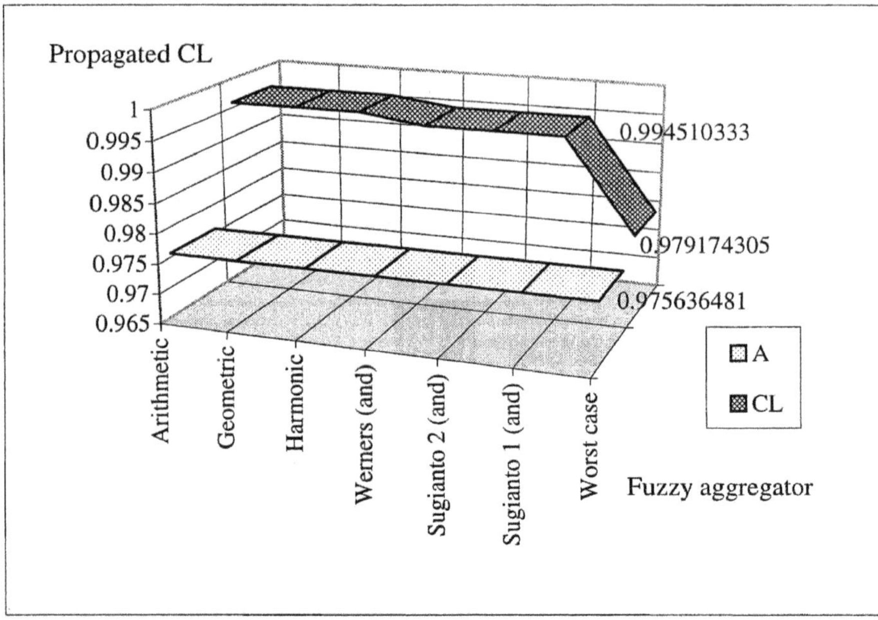

Fig. 4.2. The propagated CL of the availability of the HRSG plant items [6].

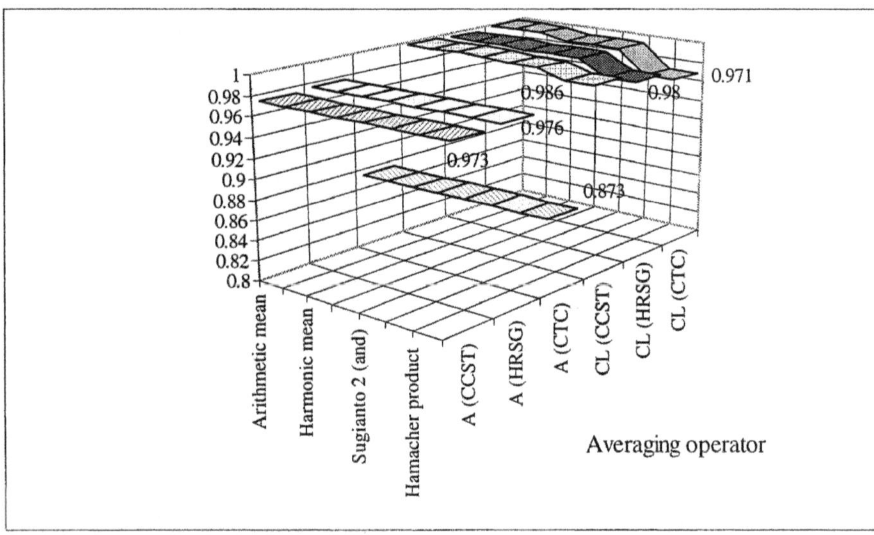

Fig 4.3. The propagated CL of the Combustion System availability [6].

In all cases, the propagated CL indicates a trend that follows the order of the degree of compensatory of the fuzzy aggregator. The ordering of the aggregators would enable the formation of continuous path of degree of compensatory from a risk-oriented (optimistic) approach to a very conservative (or pessimistic) approach, such as in the worst case scenario.

4.3 Plant Items with Spare Parts as "Components in Parallel"

Referring to Figure 4.1, the aggregation of CL of components in "parallel" must be done prior to aggregating the confidence levels of components in "series". The inferred CL of the objective function when components are in "parallel" arrangement is given in the following:

$$\alpha_{\text{Aparallel}} = \mathop{\circ}_{i=1}^{N} \alpha_{\text{Ai}} \tag{14}$$

where o – fuzzy aggregator

N – number of similar components or components in "parallel"

(the number of spare parts in stock = N-1)

α_{Ai} – CL of the availability of the plant item "i" which is operation

$\alpha_{Aparallel}$ – CL of the availability of the plant item, taking into account its spare parts in stock.

The selection of the most appropriate fuzzy operator for aggregating "components in parallel" concerns with the degree of compensatory of the fuzzy operator. The characteristics of aggregating CL of the availability of "components in parallel" should confer to the calculation of the availability of "components in parallel". When a plant item has one or more spare(s), the availability level of that particular component becomes higher. The implication of component with spares is that when the installed component fails, it can be replaced immediately by its spare part. Accordingly, the duration of the inoperable time of the power plant is shorter, compared to the case when there is no spare part in stock and the component must be repaired or a new component must be ordered.

The aggregation of α_A of the "components in parallel" is rather symmetrical in nature, since α_A of the spare parts of any plant item is the same. Two important remarks on propagating α_A of plant items with spare parts are:

1. Averaging operator is also not suitable for this aggregation because it merely calculates the mean of the CL values.

2. The selection of the fuzzy aggregator should then consider t-conorm for the above aggregation procedure. In fact, t-conorm is suitable for such an aggregation due to its degree of compensation; as the number of the operands increases, the resulting CL value also increases.

4.4 Case Studies - "Components in Parallel"

The following case studies investigate the effect of the fuzzy aggregator in propagating α_A of the spare parts component. They concern with the components of the Combustion Turbine (CT) plant: the turbine section and the combustion system. Both plants are critical components of the combustion turbine that frequently fail, as indicated by the relatively low MTTF value; thus the spare parts are kept in stock.

The reliability information of the turbine section is as follows:

- (MTTF, CL of MTTF) = (11111 hours, 60%)
- (MTTR, CL of MTTR) = (488 hours, 40%)
- Availability = 0.9579
- (Mean Time To Restore, CL of MTTRestore) = (335 hours, 40%).

These imprecise data has been used to deduce the approximate data for the availability of the spare part component. Using the formulation of the availability of a plant item installed in a base load operating mode, the approximate data for the spare part availability is calculated to be 0.9706 with CL of 95.26%.

Having the availability levels of the working component and its spare part, the overall plant item availability is calculated according to the "parallel" arrangement using algebraic sum. Such an operation implies that the availability of the plant item is secured unless both the plant item and its spare parts fail. Table 4.3 contains the summary of the availability calculation with and without spare parts in stock. As can be seen in the table, the spare part components improve the availability of the turbine section significantly.

Figure 4.4 illustrates the CL inferred by various t-conorms and parameterized averaging operators. There is an apparent trend in the behaviour of these operators: the CL which is propagated by the averaging operators, is lower than those propagated by t-conorms. Although the parameter χ has been set to 0.9, the CL produced by the averaging operators differs significantly from the CL in the worst case scenario. Comparing the characteristics of the four t-conorms used in this case study, the algebraic sum produces a CL which is closest to the CL in the worst case scenario. The Hamacher's sum operator exhibits a softer degree of compensation, allowing some flexibility for pessimistic decision maker.

The reliability data of the combustion system is as follows:

- (MTTF, CL of MTTF) = (2071 hours, 60%)
- (MTTR, CL of MTTR) = (75 hours, 40%)
- Availability = 0.9651
- (Mean Time To Restore, CL of MTTRestore) = (30 hours, 50%).

The approximate data for the spare part availability based on the above information is 0.9764 with CL of 98.84%.

The results of the availability calculation with and without spare parts in stock are contained in Table 4.3. As can be seen from the table, the spare part components improve the availability of the combustion section significantly.

Table 4.3. Availability level of the Turbine Section and the Combustion System.

TURBINE SECTION			
Spare part(s)	**A (Availability)**	**A minimum**	α_A
0	0.957927408	0.90704509	94.68%
1	0.998765057	0.993070578	99.43%
2	0.999963751	0.999483439	99.95%
3	0.999998936	0.999961492	100.00%
4	0.999999969	0.999997129	100.00%
COMBUSTION SYSTEM			
Spare part(s)	**A (Availability)**	**A minimum**	α_A
0	0.96509623	0.965051258	95.6%
1	0.999177186	0.997280272	99.81%
2	0.999975848	0.999904949	99.99%
3	0.999999291	0.999996678	100.00%
4	0.999999979	0.999999884	100.00%

Figure 4.5 displays the plots of α_A propagated using t-conorms and parameterized averaging operators. As in the previous case study, the CL propagated using algebraic sum is slightly higher than the worst case scenario. This is because the same operator (algebraic sum) has been used in modelling the overall availability of the component with spare part(s).

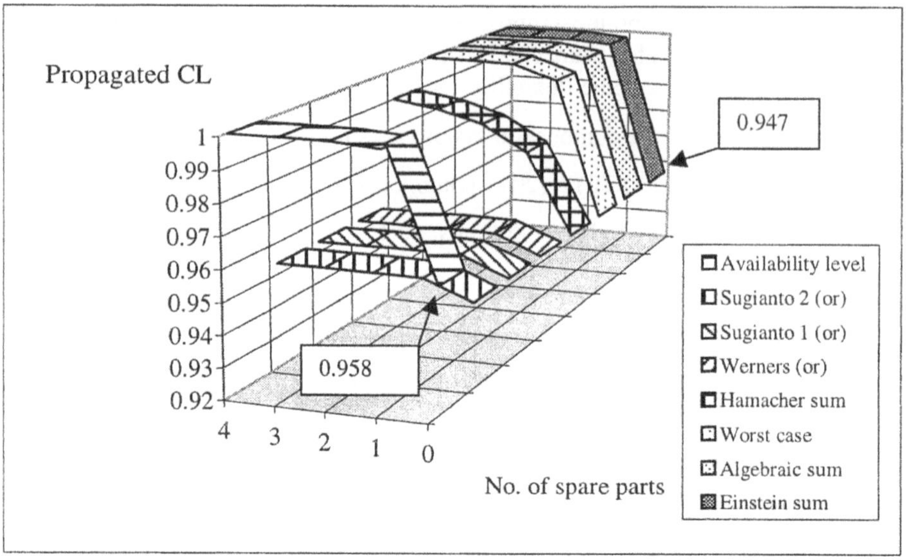

Fig.4.4. The propagated CLs of the Turbine Section availability [6].

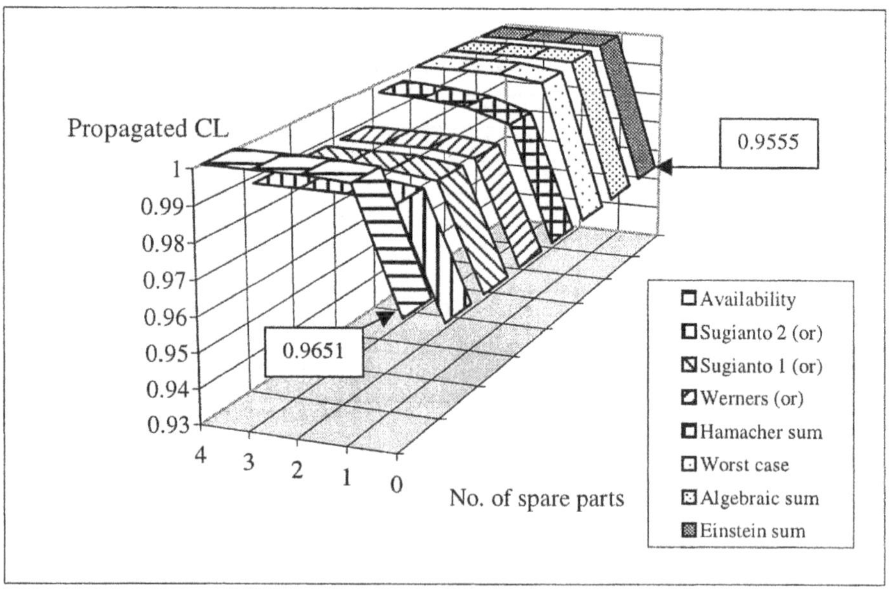

Fig.4.5. The propagated CLs of the Combustion System availability [6].

Comparing the results shown in Figure 4.4 and Figure 4.5, it can be seen that the CL inferred by the parameterized averaging operators in the later figure is generally higher compared to the CL in the former. Some explanations for such a characteristic are:

- For the "working" component - the availability level of the working combustion system (0.9651) is slightly higher than the availability level of the turbine section (0.9579)
- α_A of the combustion system is higher than α_A of the turbine section (95.6% in contrast to 94.68%)
- For the spare part components - although the availability levels in both systems are almost identical, their CL values are different: $\alpha_{A\text{spare part}}$ of the combustion system is 3.28% higher than $\alpha_{A\text{spare part}}$ of the turbine section.

Hence, the average value of α_A of the CT is slightly higher than that of the TB plant. As the CL values are propagated further (with increasing number of spare part components), the effect of the degree of compensatory of fuzzy aggregators become more evident.

5 Summary

The development of the Fuzzy Optimization method to propagate CL of approximate data is feasible by employing fuzzy aggregators. Two types of CL diffusion have been distinguished, namely uncertainty propagation type 1 - in which CL of the parameters in the availability function are aggregated together (to form CL of the availability of the plant item); and uncertainty propagation type 2 - whereby CL of the availability of the individual and spare part components are aggregated as the objective function undergoes optimization process.

The suitability of CL measure to represent the degree of uncertainty in the data and how they affect the objective function have been examined by conducting sensitivity analysis on the objective function. The analysis indicates that the uncertainties in the input parameters: Mean Time To Failure (MTTF) and Mean Time To Repair (MTTR) do not effect the final availability significantly. This is due to the modelling of the plant item availability belonging to a base load power station, the plant item is either working or being repaired, as well as the nature of the data uncertainty problem (data unavailability is frequently encountered on the cases of critical plant items). Due to their importance to the operation of the power plant, they often undergo overhaul prior to being worn out. Thus, they appear to be highly reliable.

Further, the empirical research on uncertainty propagation has drawn an assumption that the worst case scenario is determined by the extreme values of the uncertain data. The worst possible condition is adopted as the pessimistic approach (lowest boundary) for the prediction of the outcome decision.

For the uncertainty propagation 1, the empirical research on parameterized conjunction operators indicates that the Yager's parameterized "fuzzy AND" operator is the most suitable aggregator for propagating CL of MTTF and MTTR. An alternative would be the Hamacher's parameterized "fuzzy OR" operator.

Further, the CL diffusion in the uncertainty propagation 2 are classified into CL aggregations:

- where the plant items are "arranged in series" (in the power plant availability model)
- where the plant items and the spare parts are modelled as "components in parallel".

From the case studies, it is concluded that the worst case scenario can be well estimated when algebraic product and algebraic sum are employed in propagating CL type 1 and type 2 respectively. For decisions involving some risk factors, parameterized averaging operators might be used instead of the algebraic operator.

6 Conclusion

All of us have had to make important decisions where we were uncertain about factors that were relevant to the decisions. Decision models are helpful in such cases because they can assist in the analysis and understanding of the problem and its uncertainty factors. Obviously, in developing the decision model, one should abstract the important aspects from the reality, draws certain assumptions and delineates the boundaries of interest. The relevant system or model, thus, is that part of reality which is of major consequence to the decision maker.

In this chapter, the author has presented an innovative approach to Dynamic Programming optimization to deal with data uncertainty problem. In illustrating the dynamic aspect of the fuzzy decision making, the chapter features the common problem of spare parts inventory optimization. The methodology proposed in this chapter is a submodule of an attempt to find an optimized solution with data uncertainty. The empirical research on the fuzzy aggregators is advantageous as it enables different approaches, from conservative to risky, in optimizing a decision. A subjective approach to optimization with data uncertainty can be taken into account by interpreting the linguistic expression of confidence level on numerical value, which in turn serves as an input parameter to the aggregation operation.

References

1. Budenaers, D. (1984) Gas Turbine-Outage Data Gathering and Analysis, EPRI AP-3520, Systems Control Inc., Palo Alto, California
2. Kutscher, S., Schultze, J. (1992) Some Aspects of Uncertain Modelling Experiences in Applying Interval Mathematics to Practical Problems. In: Bandemar, H. (Ed.) Modelling Uncertain Data, Akademie Verlag Mathematical Research, Germany, Vol.68, 62-68
3. Pilz, J. (1992) Some Thoughts on the Present Position in Bayesian Statistics, Modelling Uncertain Data In: Bandemar, H. (Ed.) Modelling Uncertain Data, Akademie Verlag Mathematical Research, Germany, Vol.68, 70-82
4. Rubenstein, R.Y., Shapiro, A. (1993) Discrete Event Systems: Sensitivity Analysis and Stochastic Optimization by the Score Function Method, John Wiley & Sons, England
5. Shimko, G., Carlton, J., Hornady, D. (1988) Reliability and Availability Data for Gas Turbine Generator Procurement, EPRI AP-5974, Houston, Texas
6. Sugianto, L.F. (1997) Optimization of Spare Parts Inventory in Power Stations with Uncertain Data, PhD. Thesis, Monash University, Australia
7. Sugianto, L.F., Khan, M.E., Mielczarski, W. (1997) Optimizing Decision using Multi Attribute Transformation Technique, Proceedings of the IASTED International Conference Modelling, Simulation and Optimization, 241-244.
8. Sugianto, L.F., Mielczarski, W., Khan, E. (1997) Fuzzy Approach to deal with Uncertain Data in Spare Parts Management, in: W. Mielczarski, Ed.,

Fuzzy Logic Techniques in Power Systems, Heidelberg: Springer-Verlag, 421-461

9. Werners, B. (1988) Aggregation Models in Mathematical Programming, Mitra, 295-319

10. Yager, R.R. (1979) On a General Class of Fuzzy Connectives, Fuzzy Sets and Systems 4, 235-242

11. Zimmermann, H.J. (1991) Fuzzy Set Theory - and Its Applications, Kluwer Academic Publishers, Massachusetts

Discrete Multi-Level Programming in a Dynamic Environment

Hsu-Shih Shih [1]
Dept. of Industrial Engineering & Management
I-Shou University, Kaohsiung 84008, Taiwan, R.O.C.
Tel: (886) 7-657-7711 ext. 5519; Fax: (886) 7-657-8536
E-mail: hshih@isu.edu.tw

E. Stanley Lee
Dept. of Industrial & Manufacturing Systems Engineering
Kansas State University, Manhattan, Kansas 66506, U.S.A.
Tel: 785-532-3730; Fax: 785-532-7810
E-mail: eslee@ksu.edu

Summary: *This study aims to develop a multi-stage process of the discrete multi-level programming (MLP). To simulate the actual decision-making process of the hierarchical structure of an organization, MLP is a practical and useful approach which is applied to the decentralized planning problems. Because of the complexity of the problems, there is no traditional technique which is efficient enough to obtain the numerical solution of a reasonable size problem. Shih et al. (1996) proposed a fuzzy approach for the MLP, a supervised search procedure to simplify the complex structure. And that approach had been proven to be feasible and efficient. However, while the process is extended over time, a new multi-level dynamic programming problem occurred, within which decisions will change over various stages. On account of such decisions of interrelated stages, we will take advantage of recursive formulation in the dynamic programming for simplifying the process. The overall satisfaction of decision making will be evaluated through a stage-wise max-min operation and via hierarchical structure as well. Furthermore, the application of resource allocation is developed and a solution procedure is illustrated step by step. Discrete multi-objective and discrete multi-level dynamic programming problems are also compared with each other through examples in detail. Finally, the compensatory operation that is considered as a managerial decision is examined in this study.*

Keywords: *dynamic programming, multi-level programming, resource allocation.*

---

1. The corresponding author.

1 INTRODUCTION

Discrete multi-level programming in a dynamic environment is reformed as a discrete multi-level programming (MLP) with changing decisions over various stages. The traditional MLP concerns with decentralized planning problems with multiple decision makers (DMs) in a multi-level or hierarchical organization where decisions have interacted with each other (Wen & Hsu 1991). Its characteristics are fitted for the activities of democratic society, and is especially suitable for conflict resolution (Anandalingam & Friesz 1992). Motivated by the concept of dynamic programming (DP) and the operation of fuzzy dynamic programming (Bellman 1957, Kacprzyk 1983), we try to extend the decentralized planning problems over time. Hence, the new multi-level dynamic programming (MLDP) problem occurs where the hierarchical decisions could be made stage by stage.

The mathematical structure of MLP in a dynamic environment is similar to traditional multi-objective dynamic programming (MODP), but each DM independently maximizes his or her net benefits and is affected by actions of other DMs through externalities. As both problems are imbedded in a constructed DP structure, the contents of MODP and fuzzy MLP might offer some clues to attack the new problem. Hence, we will first review related literature of MODP for directing our development.

The MODP is developed to manage the conflicting objectives over time, and it is characterized as a sequential decision making problem with multiple objectives (Hussein & Abo-Sinna 1993). The solving procedure for MODP will include: (1) obtaining an efficient solution under multiple objectives, and (2) processing its recursive equations in a fuzzy environment. Fundamentally, its computation will rely on the principle of optimality in DP. Based on the principle, an original MODP problem can be converted into a family of single-stage multi-objective problems. In most cases, this sequence of sub-problems is easier to solve than the original problem. Yu and Seiford (1981) had investigated the principle in a more general setting of MODP. After the roles of separability, monotonicity and non-dominant boundedness are studied, a MODP formulation is offered in which the return functions are calculated in its multi-objective form at each stage. Furthermore, Carraway et al. (1990) develop a generalized DP for multi-criteria optimization, which is created on the absence of monotonicity, and claims that its optimality is guaranteed. Therefore, the concept of vector optimization directs a way to handle the problems of multiple objectives in each stage. Hence, MODP problems could be processed by some simple methodologies.

In the first category, a MODP problem can be transformed into a corresponding scalar-objective DP problem if DMs' preference is given. Mitten (1974) first proposes a method for solving finite-stage problems where the preference structure over the policies can be represented by a complete weak ordering. Under a monotonicity assumption, the solution method is an interactive approach in which there is a dialogue between DMs and analysts. In addition, Levary (1984) applied the concepts of goal programming to some MODP problems. By setting pre-assigned goal levels and values of targets for the relevant criteria of the concerned problem, the MODP problem will be a scalar-objective DP at each priority level. Moreover, Daellenbach and de Kluyver (1980) considered a discrete MODP problem with additive objectives. After the set of non-inferior solutions has been generated, DMs will specify a weighting vector and solutions are sought. Salukvadze (1982) deliberated an idea-point method of the vector optimization problem of dynamic systems. After identifying the ideal point of problem, the vector optimization problem is converted into a scalar-objective problem. DP is then used to find the compromise solution. In short, this category tries to obtain the preferred solution with simplicity. However, DMs usually cannot offer preference information in a complex system (Li & Haimes 1989).

In the second category, generating methods try to identify the set of non-inferior solutions for DMs, and DMs will make post-preference assignment among the members of the solution set to select the preferred solution. Tauxe et al.(1979) propose a MODP technique through ε-constraint method which transforms multi-objective problems into one objective with additional ε-constraints from the rest objectives. However, the approach is inefficient, because the number of state variables will increase with the number of objectives. In addition, Villarreal and Karwan (1982) consider a general stage-wise separable class of MODP framework with discrete states and control variables. The imbedded-state recursive equation developed in a scalar-objective DP has been extended to multi-objective discrete mathematical programming problems. Furthermore, Li and Haimes (1987) develop an envelope approach to find a set of non-inferior solutions which is equivalent to finding the envelope of this family. A parametric decomposition scheme, which is a direct application of the envelope approach, is proposed for multi-objective optimization problems. This method will lead to an efficient new version of MODP that can deal with general classes of multi-objective multi-stage decision problems. Recently, Abo-Sinna et al. (1995) propose a new algorithm for generating efficient solution based on the constrained method which decomposes the parametric space in general multi-objective non-linear programming problems. In summary, the major benefit of generating methods is that DMs can acquire full knowledge and better understanding of the system, impelling themselves to select a preferred solution from the set of non-inferior solutions.

For fuzzy decision making, Bellman and Zadeh (1970) have shown the fuzzy decisions to be the confluence or intersection of goals and constraints, and they futher apply the decisions to a dynamic environment. Afterwards, Esogbue and Bellman (1984) make some extensions and introduced many applications. At the same time, Kacprzyk (1983) offers a general view about multi-stage decision-making under fuzziness, and derived a general structure for solving fuzzy DP problems. Its max-min and other operators for fuzzy DP become a general view for the dynamic environment. Afterwards, Kacprzyk and Esogbue (1996) make a main survey of major developments and applications of fuzzy DP. However, the breadth of theory and applications of fuzzy MODP is still limited, even that none of them tries to make an extension to the field of decentralized planning.

In dealing with decentralized planning, there is no efficient traditional techniques for obtaining the numerical solution of a reasonable size problem because of the complexity of the MLP problem. Thus, Shih et al. (1996) suggest a fuzzy approach for MLP to simplify the complex structure, and it is proven to be feasible and efficient. In addition, the suggested supervised search procedure can be easily extended to a k-level hierarchical system, and it is also a flexible structures for further expansion. Consequently, we like to examine the possibility of unifying the level-wise (hierarchical) operation and stage-wise operation for MLDP in a fuzzy environment. The new structure would be simplified following an extension of the structure of Kacprzyk (1983).

In the next section, we will first introduce the concept of resource allocation (RA) and how fuzzy decisions can work for dynamic programming. Then, the concepts of fuzzy DP and MODM are involved to solve fuzzy MODP and fuzzy MLDP problems. A fuzzy compensatory operation is also taken into account for MLDP to meet the requirements of managerial decision making. In the final part, we will draw some conclusions and remarks.

2 DYNAMIC PROGRAMMING FOR RESOURCE ALLOCATION

In general, dynamic programming (or sequential decision processes, recursive optimization) is an effective algorithm for solving multi-stage decision problems. It utilizes a functional equation to circumvent the dimensional explosion for multi-stage processes with enumeration (Bellman & Lee 1984). Since the functional equation is rather flexible, its applications have been introduced to many real world problems, such as optimal control, inventory control, advertising campaign, production planning, equipment replacement, and resource allocation (Denardo 1982). In this study, we only focus on resource allocation problems.

2.1 Resource Allocation Problems

Resource allocation problems consider the allocation of limited resources among competing activities (Klein et al. 1992). Although many techniques could meet the requirement, this problem is ideally suitable for the DP approach (Bellman

& Lee 1978). Assume that there is a N-stage process from stage 1 to stage N. The total amount of resources B are given in the beginning, and we can then set the initial state s^0 equal to the total resources available B for allocation. The process will consume some amount of resources at each stage, i.e. s^{l-1}-s^l and $l = 1, 2, ..., N$. These consumed resources will make a contribution to the system as an isolated return function R^l at each stage. Furthermore, the state variable s^j will represent the amount of resources remaining at stage j, and it is ready for the allocation from stage j to stage N (the last stage). We use B^j as the consumed budget before stage j usually; thus, $0 \le s^j \le B - B^j$. In practice, we can leave some resources unallocated, but we cannot utilize more than the initial amount of resources at any single stage. In addition, the state variable equation at each stage is kept as the same as in a DP structure. Meanwhile, the different policy control (variables) at each stage form a feasible space in the DP structure. Following the computational procedure, the consumed resources at any stage will yield a contribution for its objective, and these contribution will be accumulated to the total return (i.e. return function $g^l(s^{l-1})$ with the stage $l = 1, 2, ..., N$) in the end. Consequently, the DP formulation for a RA problem will be carried out by accumulated resource returns R^l through various stages:

$$g^l(s^{l-1}) = \underset{kl}{\mathrm{Max}} \; [\, R^l + g^{l+1}(s^l) \,] \,, \; l = 1, 2, ..., N\text{-}1 \text{ and}$$

$$g^N(s^{N-1}) = \underset{kN}{\mathrm{Max}} \; [\, R^N \,] \,,$$

s.t.

$u^l(k^l) = s^{l-1}$-s^l, $l = 1, 2, ..., N$ (state variable equation),
$k^l \in \boldsymbol{F}$ (feasible region for policy control variables),
$s^l \in \boldsymbol{S}$ (resource availability constraint),
$s^0 = B$ (initial resource restriction),
s^0 and s^l are positive integers, $l = 1, 2, ..., N$,

where $\boldsymbol{F} = \{F^l, l = 1, 2, ..., N\}$ is a feasible region for all possible policy control variables in all stages, and $\boldsymbol{S}$ is a resource availability set which includes budget, capacity and other constraints throughout the stages, i.e. $\boldsymbol{S} = \{(0 \le s^l \le B - B^l), l = 1, 2, ..., N\}$. In addition, the objective function $g^l(s^{l-1})$ is a recursive expression at each stage except the last stage N.

Furthermore, if the types of resources are more than one, we need more than one state variables to describe the resource utilization. However, we frequently take a budget as the only one type of resources for simplicity. Moreover, it is a discrete RA problem if the resource is discrete or integer (Rao 1991). Since the number of stage is finite, it can be categorized as a discrete (time) or a finite-stage deterministic DP problem.

2.2 Fuzzy Multi-Objective Dynamic Programming

In a dynamic programming structure, the state variable equation will implicitly transfer a policy control variable and an input state to an output state at each stage, where the constraint is imposed on policy control variable and the goal is imposed on the output state. For a specific stage j, an input state s^{j-1} will be applied to a policy control variable k^j, which is subjected to a fuzzy constraint $\mu_{Cj}(k^j)$, and proceeded to an output state s^j, on which fuzzy goal $\mu_{Gj}(s)$ is imposed, through some known cause/effect relationship as shown in Figure 1. Fuzzy decision will become an aggregation of the fuzzy constraint and fuzzy goal at a particular stage; however, the decision will be affected by the decisions of other stages. The optimality of fuzzy multi-stage decision making will express how well the subsequent fuzzy constraints and fuzzy goals are satisfied by the policy controls and states, respectively. Mathematically, the fuzzy decision in the dynamic environment can be represented as the following expression (Kacprzyk 1983).

$$\mu_D(k^1, \ldots, k^{(N-1)} \mid s^0) = \mu_{C1}(k^1) \otimes \ldots \otimes \mu_{CN}(k^N) \otimes \mu_{GN}(s^N),$$

where $\otimes$ is a fuzzy operator.

The problem is to find an optimal sequence of control variables $k^1*, \ldots, k^{N-1}*$, such as

$$\mu_D(k^1*, \ldots, k^{(N-1)*} \mid s^0) = \max_{k1, \ldots, kN} [\mu_{C1}(k^1) \otimes \ldots \otimes \mu_{CN}(k^N) \otimes \mu_{GN}(s^N)]$$

Moreover, a group of recursive equations can be obtained for the backward iteration

$$\begin{cases} \mu_{Gj}(s^{(j-1)}) = \max_{kj} [\mu_{Cj}(k^j) \otimes \mu_{G(j+1)}(s^j)] \text{ and} \\ s^j = g(s^{(j-1)}, k^j), j = 1, \ldots, N, \end{cases}$$

where $\mu_{Gj}(s^{(j-1)})$ can be regarded as the fuzzy goal at stage j induced by the fuzzy goal at stage $j+1$.

After the structure is defined, an imbedded MODM problem will be processed in a fuzzy domain. The multi-objective RA problem is defined as follows: Q units of resources are to be distributed among T activities to maximize M objectives. There are also given $T \times M$ data tables $f_{tm}(x)$ ($t = 1, 2, \ldots, T$; $m = 1, 2, \ldots, M$) representing the return which is realized by the jth objective from an allocation of x units of resources to the tth activity ($x = 0, 1, 2, \ldots, Q$). The problem is to allocate Q units of resources to the T activities, such that the returns of M

objectives from the activities are maximized simultaneously (Lai & Li 1999).

Most of the fuzzy approaches for multi-objective RA problems will be classified as scalar-objective and generating methods which are the same categories of the approaches for MODP. Hussein and Abo-Sinna (1995) present an approach for scalarizing the multiple objectives to be a synthetic objective so that the RA problem can be solved in a DP structure. Lai and Li (1999) propose a method which makes marginal evaluation for each single objective and the method then works for global evaluation for multiple objectives by their relative important in DM's mind. It seems that the former is difficult to catch the decision information and the latter involves too much computation so far. It is worthy of making further development.

According to Salukvadze's consideration of ideal point (1982) and the comment of Li and Haimes (1989), we introduce the concept of (positive) ideal solution (PIS) and negative ideal solution (NIS) (Hwang & Yoon 1981) to overcome the drawback. The PIS and NIS are used for defining the possible optimistic outcome and pessimistic outcome, respectively. Then the degree of satisfaction of DMs can be established in terms of fuzzy membership functions. The imbedded MODM problem at each stage is to seek a maximum degree of satisfaction through fuzzy operation under each control. Afterwards, these temporal results are accumulated in the structure of multi-stage decision-making process under fuzziness (Kacprzyk 1983).

The process to solve the imbedded MODM problem is analogous to the concept of global criterion in MODM (see Hwang & Masud 1979), but the decision space of the former is discrete. Nevertheless, we can obtain the sufficient information in an efficient way so that the solution will be much meaningful and the procedure is straightforward.

It is noted that we consider Bellman and Zadeh's max-min operation for the imbedded fuzzy MODM problems as well as the stage-wise DP problem here. There are many degree of satisfactions at each stage represent the compromise of MODM when the input state will be applied to the policy control variable, which is subjected to some fuzzy constraints at that stage. Since it is unknown for the exact amount budget at any specific stage, the backward procedure of DP will help us enumerate all temporary optimal cases under available budget at each intermediate stage. When the process is reached to the first stage, the optimum of global evaluation is obtained. Then we will trace forward from stage 1 to stage N to pick up the optimal policy controls among stages and their correspondent optimal decisions among levels. These results will be the global optimum because all temporary optimal solutions are checked on the stage-wise and level-wise operations. Consequently, the MODM over various stages could be manipulated in the designed way.

In summary, the solution procedure of fuzzy approach for MODM over various stages for RA problems is proposed as the following steps:

Step 0. (Pre-process)

0a) Construct a payoff table for each objective of the DM at each stage (*N* stages totally) based on the possible budgets allocated under policy control (variables).

0b) Establish the degree of satisfaction for each DM in terms of fuzzy membership function through the distance between his/her PIS and NIS at each stage.

Step 1. Seek compromise solutions among multiple objectives for possible budgets allocated at each stage.

Take minimum operation of the degree of satisfaction of multiple objectives as DM's decisions for possible budgets allocated at each stage.

Step 2. Choose optimal decisions of MODM.

Take maximum operation of the possible outcomes, from Step 1, given by each specified budget at each stage as its optimal decision of MODM.

Step 3. Process of the last stage *N*th problem.

Record all possible non-inferior outcomes under available budgets at the last stage as the current results from Step 2 and, for further backward calculation.

Step 4. Process the previous stage (N-1)th problem.

The degree of satisfaction of stage N is aggregated together with the previous stage (N-1)'s as a current accumulated degree of satisfaction. Take minimum operation of the results from stage N and the recorded results from stage N-1 (obtained from Step 2) under available budgets for these two successive stages. Then, take maximum operator of the possible outcomes for the combinations under policy control (variables) for these two stages. And the maximum degree of satisfaction is utilized as a current accumulated optimal decisions. Set $N = N$-1.

Step 5. (Termination)

Under the condition of $N = 1$, the process is located at the beginning and terminated. Check the optimal solution for each stage under a specified policy, which is suggested as the group of best policies for the MODM problem in the dynamic environment. Otherwise, go to Step 4.

Observe that the forward process in DP structure can also be applicable to the above procedure.

Let us illustrate the proposed procedure through an example.

Example 1. A bi-objective dynamic programming problem for allocating a budget of 10 discrete units under the policy control (variables) of two DMs among three stages, $l = 1, 2$, and 3.

There is exactly a budget of \$10 millions (10 discrete units) available for Glamour Corporation in the future. The decisions of the corporation are controlled by the plant manager and the president of the corporation with different objectives. The whole decision process will last for three periods, and shall be executed at three stages. For a given stage l, the total budget s^{l-1} is allocated for investing stage l and the rest of stages. However, only B^l amount of budgets is available for the imbedded bi-objective problem. The DMs can leave some units of the resources unallocated, but they cannot spend more than the given budget at any stage. The investments will yield the objective increases as $f_1^l(\boldsymbol{x}^l)$ and $f_2^l(\boldsymbol{x}^l)$ as the performance measures at each stage, $l = 1, 2$, and 3. Therefore, the imbedded bi-objective problem will maximize its objectives at each stage, and is expressed as the following mathematical programming under the initial state s^0:

For stage 1,

$$\text{Max } f_1^1 = 2.5\, x_1 - 1.5\, x_2 \text{, and}$$
$$\text{Max } f_2^1 = 1.5\, x_1 + 2.5\, x_2 \text{;}$$

For stage 2,

$$f_1^2 = 3\, x_1 - 2\, x_2 \text{, and } f_2^2 = 2\, x_1 + 3\, x_2 \text{;}$$

For stage 3,

$$f_1^3 = 2\, x_1 - x_2 \text{, and } f_2^3 = x_1 + 2\, x_2 \text{;}$$

s.t.

$B^l = x_1 + x_2 \leq 10,\ l = 1, 2, \text{ and } 3$, (budget constraints)

x_1 and x_2 are positive integers, (non-negative constraints)

where at each stage the imbedded bi-objective function $\boldsymbol{f}^l = (f_1^l, f_2^l)$ is to give the optimal returns (or goals) in DP structure under the input state and the control variable. In addition, the available budget B^l is allocated to the imbedded two objective problems only at stage l, where $B^l = s^{l-1} - s^l$, $l = 1, 2$, and 3, under DP structure. Note that all the above constraints can be represented by $\boldsymbol{Y}$.

All decision information is listed in Tables 1 to 3 for three different stages, and the constraint for the possible policies is also implicitly represented. Now we solve the problem through the proposed procedure:

Step 0. According to the basic information in these tables, we will set up the degree of satisfaction by fuzzifying the objectives through their PIS and NIS of the possible budgets allocated at each stage.

Step 1. The satisfactory solution of the imbedded bi-objective problem at each stage can be obtained through max-min operation, which means minimizing the satisfactory degree of two objectives, and then go to **Step 2** for maximizing the satisfactory degree among all possible cases of combinations under different inputs and states, and yet the given budget remains a constant constraint. Therefore, the individual degree of satisfaction corresponding to the spending budgets at three different stages are listed in Tables 1 to 3 as well. This max-min operation search for an optimal solution is similar to the traditional fuzzy MODM. Note that the fuzzy constraint for the budget allocation in each stage has been incorporated into the outside policy control and the inside goal, thus the term of fuzzy constraint in Step 1 will be implicitly expressed in the corresponding tables.

Step 3. After all individual problems are solved, i.e. single stage problems, we will establish the backward relationship among stages through DP structure. To trace the budget allocation, we start from the last stage, stage 3, with the resources remaining after the previous stage, stage 2, then go back to the second stage, and to the first stage. In the manipulation, two maximum satisfactions under the input states are defined for backward accumulation of the degree of satisfaction so far, i.e. $\mu^{2\prime *} = \min(\mu^{3*}, \mu^{2*})$ at stage 2 and $\mu^{1\prime *} = \min(\mu^{2\prime *}, \mu^{1*})$ at stage 1, as described in **Step 4** and **Step 5**. The overall optimal solution for satisfaction of the problem will be achieved after all, i.e. $\mu^{1\prime *}$, then the corresponding policy at each stage is optimal solution.

The calculation are shown in Tables 4 to 6 stage by stage backward. The result indicates that optimal degree of satisfaction for the given problem is 0.26, which is accumulated by 0.26 at stage 3, 0.28 at stage 2, and 0.30 at stage 1, respectively. The optimal proposal for RA are 3 units with $(x_1, x_2) = (1, 2)$ or $(0, 3)$ to the third stage, 3 units with $(x_1, x_2) = (0, 3)$ to the second stage, and 4 units with $(x_1, x_2) = (2, 2)$ or $(1, 3)$, to the first stage. Furthermore, the procedure of fuzzy DP will eliminate unpromising cases, i.e. keep DMs at any stage satisfactory, the suggested proposal is conducted stage-wise in a well-balanced way.

2.3 Fuzzy Multi-Level Dynamic Programming

Multi-level mathematical programming is used to solve decentralized planning problems with multiple executors in a multi-level system or hierarchical organization. The system explicitly assigns each decision unit a unique objective, a set of decision variables, and a set of common constraints which will affect all decision units (Anandalingam & Friesz 1992). The basic concept of multi-level programming technique is that an upper-level DM sets his or her goal and/or decisions and then asks each subordinate level of the organization for its optimum which is calculated independently. Lower-level DM's decisions are then submitted and modified by the upper-level DM with consideration of the overall benefits for the organization. The process is continued until a satisfactory solution is reached. This decision-making process is extremely practical for such decentralized systems as agriculture, government policy, economic systems, finance, warfare, transportation and network designs, and is suitable for conflict resolution (Anandalingam & Friesz 1992, Ben-Ayed 1993, Wen & Hsu 1991).

The simplest case of MLP is the bi-level programming (BLP), which are usually viewed of as two DMs at two different hierarchical levels, and is similar to a static Stackelberg game – a special case of a two-person, non-zero sum, non-cooperative game, with full information. It is a nested optimization model involving two problems, an upper one and a lower one (Ben-Ayed 1993). In discussing BLP, let two vectors of decision variables ($\boldsymbol{x}_1$, $\boldsymbol{x}_2$) be partitioned into two planners where the top level DM has controlled over vector $\boldsymbol{x}_1$ while the bottom level DM has controlled over vector $\boldsymbol{x}_2$, and let the performance functions of f_1 and f_2 for the two planners be linear and bounded. Among various representations of BLP, the representation of Wen and Hsu (1991) is stated as follows:

$$\max_{x1} \ f_1(\boldsymbol{x}_1, \boldsymbol{x}_2) = \boldsymbol{c}_{11}{}^{\mathrm{T}} \boldsymbol{x}_1 + \boldsymbol{c}_{12}{}^{\mathrm{T}} \boldsymbol{x}_2 \qquad \text{(upper level)}$$

where $\boldsymbol{x}_2$ solves

$$\max_{x2} \ f_2(\boldsymbol{x}_1, \boldsymbol{x}_2) = \boldsymbol{c}_{21}{}^{\mathrm{T}} \boldsymbol{x}_1 + \boldsymbol{c}_{22}{}^{\mathrm{T}} \boldsymbol{x}_2 \qquad \text{(lower level)}$$

s.t.

$$(\boldsymbol{x}_1, \boldsymbol{x}_2) \in \boldsymbol{X} = \{(\boldsymbol{x}_1, \boldsymbol{x}_2) \mid \boldsymbol{A}_1 \boldsymbol{x}_1 + \boldsymbol{A}_2 \boldsymbol{x}_2 \le \boldsymbol{b}, \text{ and } \boldsymbol{x}_1, \boldsymbol{x}_2 \ge \boldsymbol{0}\},$$

where $\boldsymbol{c}_{11}$, $\boldsymbol{c}_{12}$, $\boldsymbol{c}_{21}$, $\boldsymbol{c}_{22}$, and $\boldsymbol{b}$ are linear vectors, $\boldsymbol{A}_1$ and $\boldsymbol{A}_2$ are linear matrices, as well as $\boldsymbol{X}$ denotes the constraint region.

There are many approaches to solving MLP or hierarchical optimization problems. Traditional programming tools, such as decomposition principle (in linear programming), goal programming, multi-objective programming, or game theory, cannot meet the common features of multi-level systems. Thus, many heuristic methodologies have been proposed to solve MLP during the last three decades. Most methods for linear cases are based on concepts of extreme point search and transformation approach. The former is to search for a compromise vertex by simplex algorithm based on adjusting higher level control variables, but it is rather inefficient, especially for large size problems. The transformation approach involves transforming lower-level programming problems to be the constraints of the higher level by Karush-Kuhn-Tucker (KKT) conditions or other functions (Wen & Hsu 1991). Because non-linear terms will appear in constraints, auxiliary problems become complicated and sometimes unmanageable. Since most existing methods are computationally inefficient, Shih et al. (1996) use the concepts of tolerance membership functions and multi-objective optimization to develop a fuzzy approach for solving MLP.

An auxiliary problem for the imbedded BLP will be expressed as follows:

$$\begin{aligned}
&\text{Max} \quad \lambda \\
&\text{s.t.} \\
&\qquad \boldsymbol{A}_1 \boldsymbol{x}_1 + \boldsymbol{A}_2 \boldsymbol{x}_2 \le \boldsymbol{b}, \\
&\qquad [f_1(\boldsymbol{x}) - f_1^-] / [f_1^+ - f_1^-] \ge \lambda, \\
&\qquad [(\boldsymbol{x}_1^{\mathrm{U}} + \boldsymbol{p}_1) - \boldsymbol{x}_1)] / \boldsymbol{p}_1 \ge \lambda \mathbf{I}, \\
&\qquad [\boldsymbol{x}_1 - (\boldsymbol{x}_1^{\mathrm{U}} - \boldsymbol{p}_2)] / \boldsymbol{p}_2 \ge \lambda \mathbf{I}, \\
&\qquad [f_2(\boldsymbol{x}) - f_2^-] / [f_2^+ - f_2^-] \ge \lambda, \\
&\qquad \lambda \in [0, 1], \\
&\qquad \boldsymbol{x}_1, \boldsymbol{x}_2 \ge 0,
\end{aligned}$$

where $\mathbf{I}$ is a column vector with the same dimension as $\boldsymbol{x}_1$ and all its elements are 1. f_1^+ and f_1^- represent the PIS and NIS of f_1, respectively, so as the f_2. In addition, $\boldsymbol{p}_1$ and $\boldsymbol{p}_2$ are the tolerances of LHS and RHS of $\boldsymbol{x}_1$, respectively.

The above expression can be solved by any mathematical programming code and the procedure, a supervised search procedure, which has been proven to be efficient. Besides, it will not increase the complexity of the original problem and is flexible for extension (Shih et al. 1996).

The MLP over time is defined as a general form of MLP in which decisions may be changed over various stages. The central part of the problem is an imbedded MLP problem under a DP structure, so that the resources may be allocated over time. Note that most problems will concentrate on discrete (time) RA processes for easy comprehension, thus the term of "stages" will replace the term of "time" for a clear definition. In fuzzy MODM for resource allocation, Esogbue and Bellman (1984) have offered a fuzzy mathematical model of the resultant fuzzy allocation process by decomposing the system into three levels, and process these hierarchical levels by the concept of stage of DP. However, we consider the stage as time horizon instead of this simple approach for dealing with a more complex system. Moreover, MLP over various stages is suitable for long range planning, especially good for production planning, inventory control, social-economic policy development, and resource allocation in planning, programming and budget system.

In RA problems, the state variables are related to budget, and the budget constraints will be implicit in DP. In practice, the total available budgets will be the initial state, and the available budgets for the rest stages will be the input state for any specific stage. In addition, the other constraints, e.g. other resources or capacities, will be implicitly imbedded at each stage. The return or objective function could vary at any duration in which the return is under the input state and policy control at any given stage. The central idea for the extension is to keep available budgets at each stage as the state variables of DP, so that the budget will be consumed as the stage passes by, and the states change at the same time. This consumed budgets at any stage will be given to each level of the hierarchical system inside. Therefore, the structure of imbedded MLP problem will be similar to the previous MODP problem, and the decision may be changed over various stages. However, the execution of decisions is sequential top-down, the imbedded MLP problem will search for its optimum first, and then merge into the DP structure. Since the decisions under controls are reflected in its restricted decision space, their compromise solutions might be inferior to the MODP's solutions.

The solving procedure for MLDP is similar to the MODP's, but the difference only exists in its imbedded system. Compared to the procedure of MODP, we make some modifications as follows:

Step 0. (Pre-process)

0b) Establish the degree of satisfaction of each DM in terms of fuzzy membership function by the distance between his/her PIS and NIS at each stage. The establishment will search for a restricted decision space controlled by the multiple level DMs.

Step 1. Seek compromise solutions among multiple levels for possible budgets allocated at each stage.

Take minimum operation of the multiple levels' objectives and controlled decisions as their modified decision for possible budgets allocated at each stage.

Step 2. Choose optimal decisions of MLP.

Take maximum operation of the possible outcomes from Step 1 given by each specified budget at each stage as the optimal decision of MLP. The establishment will search for a restricted decision space controlled by the multiple level DMs.

The rest steps are the same as described in Section 2.1, and a satisfactory solution is obtained.

Now, we shall see that through an example.

Example 2. A bi-level dynamic programming problem for allocating a budget for two decision units among three stages which are similar to Example 1.

The imbedded BLP can be illustrated as a three-stage problem in the following expression:

For stage 1,

$$\max_{x1} \; f_1^{\,1} = 2.5\,x_1 - 1.5\,x_2\,, \qquad \text{(upper level)}$$

where x_2 solves,

$$\max_{x2} \; f_2^{\,1} = 1.5\,x_1 + 2.5\,x_2\,; \qquad \text{(lower level)}$$

For stage 2,

$$f_1^{\,2} = 3\,x_1 - 2\,x_2 \text{ and } f_2^{\,2} = 2\,x_1 + 3\,x_2\,;$$

For stage 3,

$$f_1^{\,3} = 2\,x_1 - x_2 \text{ and } f_2^{\,3} = x_1 + 2\,x_2\,;$$

s.t.

$(x_1\,,\,x_2) \in \boldsymbol{Y}$, where $\boldsymbol{Y}$ is defined as in Example 1.

Similar to the procedure shown in Example 1, we first establish payoff tables, then the decision information is transformed in terms of fuzzy membership function. And these data are joined into the DP structure. Here the upper level DM asks for more resources than the lower level DM's, i.e. $x_1 \geq x_2$, which represents the interactions between two level DMs.

The result indicates that optimal degree of satisfaction for the given problem is 0.23, that is accumulated of 0.27 at stage 3, 0.24 at stage 2, and 0.23 at stage 1, respectively. The optimal proposal for RA are 4 units with $(x_1, x_2) = (4, 0)$ to the third stage, 3 units with $(x_1, x_2) = (3, 0)$ to the second stage, and 3 units with $(x_1, x_2) = (3,0)$ to the first stage. Furthermore, the procedure of fuzzy DP will eliminate unpromising cases, i.e. keep DMs at any stage satisfactory.

3 COMPENSATORY CONSIDERATION IN FUZZY DYNAMIC PROGRAMMING

One crucial problem in fuzzy sets is to aggregate fuzzy information through an operation. The information aggregation is carried out through the framework of the fuzzy set theory and is the foundation of decision making in fuzzy environment (Klir & Folger 1988). For manipulation, fuzzy decision will be the operation of several fuzzy membership functions, in which each of them depicts the characteristic of an alternative. According to Zimmermann's suggestion for selecting an appropriate aggregation operator (1991), there are eight criteria, including axiomatic strength, empirical fit, adaptability, numerical efficiency, compensation, range of compensation, aggregating behavior, and required scale level of membership functions. These are the guidelines for choosing a suitable fuzzy operator.

Due to ease of calculation, Bellman and Zadeh's max-min operation (1970) has been accepted as a general tool for processing fuzzy decision-making problems. However, the min-type decision is a representation of a pessimistic attitude (Kacprzyk 1983). The interpretation of a decision as an intersection (logical and) or union (logical or) will result in no compensation (under-achievement) or full compensation (over-achievement). Managerial decisions always have some kind of compensation between either different degrees of goal achievement or decision restrictions (Zimmermann & Zysno 1980, 1983). Hence, under the above criteria, they propose a compensatory operator γ, which is a combination of the product and the algebraic sum with parameter γ, and a proven empirical fit. For a pair set (μ_A, μ_B), the γ operation is defined as:

$$\mu_{A\gamma B} = [(\mu_{A\cap B})^{1-\gamma}][(\mu_{A\cup B})^{\gamma}], \text{ or}$$
$$= [(\mu_A)(\mu_B)]^{1-\gamma}\,[1-(1-\mu_A)(1-\mu_B)]^{\gamma},$$

where $\gamma \in [0, 1]$ and is interpreted as grade of compensation which represents a tendency for non-compensation to fully compensation by 0 to 1, respectively.

Note that Shih and Lee (2000) has recommended compensatory multi-level decision making by taking Werners' "fuzzy and" operator (1988) in a continuous space.

By introducing the γ operator, we can process the MLDP problems with compensation. On the other hand, since MLP problem has a hierarchical structure, the binary operation will be processed from the upper level to the one lower level, then to the next lower level, and so on. And the calculation procedure is the same as previous section, i.e. max-min operation. Compared to the procedure of solving

MLDP, some modifications are made as follows:

Step 1. Seek compromise solutions among multiple levels for possible budgets allocated at each stage.
Take γ operator of the multiple levels' objectives and controlled decisions as their modified decision for possible budgets allocated at each stage.

Step 4. Process the previous stage, (N-1)th problem.
The decision information of stage N is aggregated with the previous stage (N-1)'s by γ operator as a current accumulated degree of satisfaction.

The rest of steps are the same as described in Section 2.3, and a satisfactory solution can be picked up.

Again, let us illustrate the modified process through an example.

Example 3. The same case as Example 2 with compensatory operation.

According to the basic information from Example 2, we make use of Zimmermann and Zysno's γ-operator (1983) with the degree of compensation $\gamma = 0.5$. This max-γ operation is similar to the fuzzy BLP, but extra more sub-problems are needed as the number of the stages or the distributed budget combinations within the BLP problem increase.

The result indicates that the optimal degree of satisfaction for the given problem is 0.10, which is accumulated by 0.09 at stage 3, 0.18 at stage 2, and 0.36 at stage 1, respectively. The optimal proposal for RA are 2 units with $(x_1, x_2) = (2, 0)$ to the third stage, 3 units with $(x_1, x_2) = (3, 0)$ to the second stage, and 5 units with $(x_1, x_2) = (5,0)$ to the first stage.

4 CONCLUSIONS AND REMARKS

In this study, we try to investigate a discrete multi-level programming in a dynamic environment. An efficient algorithm is developed, and a solution procedure has been proposed through Microsoft Excel as well. Although the size of the examples under scrutinizing are small, large size problems are expected to be solved through the same procedure.

Since different decision variables can be controlled by separated different decision units (or DMs) in a multi-level system, its decision space will be more restricted than that of the MODM problems'. In general, its solution will no better than that of the MODM's. However, both are efficient solutions.

Notwithstanding only bi-level problems are illustrated, multiple-level dynamic programming problems can be solved through the same algorithm. Please see the details of the search algorithm in Shih et al. (1996) for simplifying multiple level structures.

Compensatory operators are common for managerial decision making. In this context, only Zimmermann and Zyno's γ operator (1983) is considered, because the operator has been tested for fitting human judgment. In addition, its parameter γ can be adjusted from 0 to 1 so that the operator is more flexible than many traditional operators, such as min, product, etc. The chosen value for γ will depend upon an empirical data from a specified decision making problem. Furthermore, for m number of elements to be connected, we have the following general expression.

$$\mu_\gamma = \left(\prod_{i=1}^{m} \mu_i\right)^{1-\gamma} \left[1 - \prod_{i=1}^{m} (1-\mu_i)\right]^\gamma,\ 0 \leq \mu, \gamma \leq 1.$$

This generalized operator can be easily applied to MODP and MLDP problems, but extra more works are needed for processing their imbedded problems.

ACKNOWLEDGEMENT

We like to thank Chia-Jung Hsu for her help in calculation. We are also thankful to anonymous reviewers for their valuable comments.

REFERENCES

Abo-Sinna, M.A. and M.L. Hussein (1995), An algorithm for generating efficient solutions of multi objective dynamic programming problems. *European J. Operational Research* **80(1)**, 156-165.

Anandalingam, G. and T.L. Friesz (eds.) (1992), Hierarchical Optimization. *Annals of Operational Research* **34**.

Bellman, R.E. (1957), *Dynamic Programming*. Princeton University Press, Princeton, NJ.

Bellman, R.E. and E.S. Lee (1978), Functional equations in dynamic programming. *Aequationes Mathematicae* **17(1)**, 1-18.

Bellman, R.E. and E.S. Lee (1984), History and development of dynamic programming. *Control Systems Magazine* **14(4)**, 24-28.

Bellman, R.E. and L.A. Zadeh (1970), Decision making in a fuzzy environment.

Management Science **17**, B141-164.

Ben-Ayed, O., Bilevel linear programming. *Computers and Operations Research* **20**, 485-501 (1993).

Carraway, R.L., T.L. Morin and H. Moskowitz (1990), Generalized dynamic programming for multicriteria optimization. *European J. of Operational Research* **44(1)**, 95-104.

Daellenbach, H.G. and C.A. Kluyver (1980), Note on multiple objective dynamic programming. *J. of Operational Research Society* **31(7)**, 591-594.

Denardo, E.V. (1982), *Dynamic Programming: models and applications.* Prentice Hall, Englewood Cliffs, New Jersey.

Esogbue, A.O. and R.E. Bellman (1984), Fuzzy dynamic programming and its extensions. in *TIMS Studies in the Management Sciences* (eds. by H.-J. Zimmermann, L.A. Zadeh and B.R. Gaines) **20**, 147-167.

Hussein, M.L. and M.A. Abo-Sinna (1993), Decomposition of multiobjective programming problems by hybrid fuzzy-dynamic programming. *Fuzzy Sets and Systems* **60**, 25-32.

Hussein, M.L. and M.A. Abo-Sinna (1995), A fuzzy dynamic approach to the multicriterion resource allocation problem. *Fuzzy Sets and Systems* **69(2)**, 115-124.

Hwang, C.L. and A.S.M. Masud (1979), *Multiple Objectives Decision Making: methods and applications.* Springer-Verlag, Berlin.

Hwang, C.L. and K. Yoon (1981), *Multiple Attribute Decision Making: Methods and Applications.* Springer-Verlag, Berlin.

Kacprzyk, J. (1983), *Multistage Decision-making under Fuzziness: theory and applications.* Verlag TUV Rheinland, Koln.

Kacprzyk, J. and A.O. Esogbue (1996), Fuzzy dynamic programming: main development and applications. *Fuzzy Sets and Systems* **81(1)**, 31-45.

Klein, R.S., H. Luss and D.R. Smith (1992), A lexicographic minimax algorithm for multiperiod resource allocation. *Mathematical Programming* **55**, 213-234.

Klir, G.J. and T.A. Folger (1988), *Fuzzy Sets, Uncertainty, and Information.* Prentice-Hall, Englewood, NJ.

Levary, R.R. (1984), Dynamic programming models with goal objectives. *International J. of Systems Science* **15(3)**, 309-314.

Lai, K.K. and Lushu Li (1999), A dynamic approach to multi-objective resource allocation. *European J. of Operational Research* **117(2)**, 293-309.

Li, D. and Y.Y. Haimes (1987), The envelope approach for multiobjective optimization problems. *IEEE Transactions on Systems, Man, and Cybernetics* **17(6)**, 1026-1038.

Li, D. and Y.Y. Haimes (1989), Multiobjective dynamic programming: the state of the art. *Control-Theory and Advanced Technology* **5(4)**, 471-483.

Mitten, L.G. (1974), Preference order dynamic programming. *Management Science* **21(1)**, 43-46.

Rao, H.R. (1991), An information and preference theory approach to a discrete resource allocation problem. *Automatica* **27(5)**, 837-843.

Salukvadze, M.E. (1982), An approach to the solution of the vector optimization problem of dynamic systems. *J. of Optimization Theory and Applications* **38(3)**, 409-422.

Sastry, V.N., R.N. Tiwari and K.S. Sastri (1993), Dynamic programming approach to multiple objective control problem having deterministic or fuzzy goal. *Fuzzy Sets and Systems* **57(2)**, 195-202.

Shih, H.S., Y.J. Lai and E.S. Lee (1996), Fuzzy approach for multi-level mathematical programming problems. *Computers and Operations Research* **23(1)**, 73-91.

Shih, H.S. and E.S. Lee (2000), Compensatory multi-level decision making. *Fuzzy Sets and Systems* **114(1)**, 71-87.

Tauxe, G.W., R.R. Inman and D.M. Mades (1979), Multiobjective dynamic programming: a classic problem redressed. *Water Resource Research* **15(6)**, 1398-1402.

Thomas, M.E. (1976), A survey of the state of the art in dynamic programming. *AIIE Transactions* **8(1)**, 59-69.

Trzaskalik, T. (1992), Hierarchical approach to multi-criteria dynamic programming. *INFOR* **30(2)**, 138-147.

Villarreal, B. and M.H. Karwan (1982), Multicriteria dynamic programming with an application to the integer case. *J. of Optimization Theory and Applications* **38(1)**, 43-69.

Werners, B.M. (1988), Aggregation models in mathematical programming. in *Mathematical Models for Decision Support* (ed. by G. Mitra), 295-305, Springer-Verlag: Berlin.

Wen, U.P. and S.T. Hsu (1991), Linear bi-level programming problems - a review. *J. of Operational Research Society* **42**, 125-133.

Yu, P.L. and L. Seiford (1981), Multistage decision problems with multiple criteria. in *Multiple Criteria Analysis* (eds. by P. Nijkamp and J. Spronk), Gower, Hampshire, England, 235-244.

Zimmermann, H.-J. (1991), *Fuzzy Set Theory and Its Applications.* Kluwer Academic Publishers, Boston, 2nd ed.

Zimmermann, H.-J. and P. Zysno (1980), Latent connectives in human decision making. *Fuzzy Sets and Systems* **4(1)**, 37-51.

Zimmermann, H.-J. and P. Zysno (1983), Decision and evaluations by hierarchical aggregation of information. *Fuzzy Sets and Systems* **10**, 243-260.

Interactive Fuzzy Programming for Multi-Level Nonconvex Nonlinear Programming Problems Through Genetic Algorithms

Masatoshi Sakawa and Ichiro Nishizaki

Department of Industrial and Systems Engineering, Faculty of Engineering, Hiroshima University, Higashi-Hiroshima, 739-8527, Japan

Abstract. In this paper, we present interactive fuzzy programming through genetic algorithms, which are reported their effectiveness to solving nonconvex nonlinear programming problems, for multi-level nonconvex nonlinear programming problems. In the proposed method, fuzzy goals for objective function of each decision maker and a ratio of satisfactory degrees of decision makers at adjacent two levels are introduced to take the vague or fuzzy nature of human judgments into account, and mathematical programming problems for obtaining satisfactory solutions concerned in some groups within all the decision makers are successively solved to lead to a global satisfactory solution such that the decision makers at relatively upper levels are esteemed and the satisfactory degree of each decision maker balances with those of the others. Finally, a numerical example is given to illustrate an interactive process in the proposed method for deriving a satisfactory solution.
Keyword: Multi - level nonconvex nonlinear programming problem, interactive method, fuzzy programming, fuzzy goal, genetic algorithm

1 Introduction

In this paper, we consider interactive fuzzy programming for multi-level nonconvex nonlinear programming problems. A noncooperative solution concept, the Stackelberg solution, has been usually employed to multi-level programming problems [26,7,3,2,28,1,4,5,27]. To describe the concept of the Stackelberg solution, consider a two-level programming problem. There are two decision makers (DMs); each DM completely knows objective functions and constraints of the two DMs, and the DM at the upper level first makes a decision and then the DM at the lower level specifies a decision so as to optimize the objective function with full knowledge of the decision of the DM at the upper level. According to the rule, the DM at the upper level also makes a decision so as to optimize the objective function of the DM at the upper level. Then a solution defined as the above mentioned procedure is called the Stackelberg solution.

When the Stackelberg solution is employed, it is assumed that there is no communication between the two DMs, or they do not make any binding agreement even if there exists such communication. However, the above assumption is not always reasonable when we model decision making problems in a decentralized firm as a two-level programming problem in which top management is a DM at the upper level and an operation division of the firm is a DM at the lower level because it is supposed that there exists cooperative relationship between them.

In 1996, for two-level linear programming problems, Lai [11] and Shih, Lai and Lee [25] have proposed a solution concept which is different from the Stackelberg solution such that decisions of DMs at both levels are sequential and all of the DMs essentially cooperate with each other. Their method is based on the idea that the DM at the lower level optimizes a objective function, taking a goal or preference of the DM at the upper level into consideration. The DMs elicit membership functions of fuzzy goals for their objective functions, and especially, the DM at the upper level also specifies those of fuzzy goals for decision variables. The DM at the lower level solves a fuzzy programming problem with a constraint on a satisfactory degree of the DM at the upper level. Unfortunately, however, there is a possibility that their method leads a final solution to an undesirable one because of inconsistency between the fuzzy goals of the objective functions and the decision variables.

For avoiding such problems in the methods of Lai et al., by eliminating the fuzzy goals for the decision variables, Sakawa, Nishizaki and Uemura have developed interactive fuzzy programming for two-level linear programming problems [19]. Moreover, from the viewpoint of experts' imprecise or fuzzy understanding of the nature of parameters in a problem-formulation process [15], they have extended it to interactive fuzzy programming for two-level linear programming problems with fuzzy parameters [20]. These results have been extended so as to deal with two-level linear fractional programming problems both without and with fuzzy parameters [16,21]. Furthermore, Sakawa et al. have also investigated the interactive fuzzy programming for multi-level zero-one programming problems [17,18].

In the interactive fuzzy programming methods [25,11,17,20,16] proposed before, after all the DMs identify the fuzzy goals for their objective functions and the DMs except for the DM at the lowest level specify the minimal satisfactory levels, the DMs taking account of overall satisfactory balance among all the levels, a satisfactory solution is derived under the condition that the satisfactory degrees of the DMs are larger than or equal to their minimal satisfactory levels.

However, the following two difficulties in the previous methods are pointed out. First, one of the termination conditions in these methods is that the ratio of the satisfactory degrees of DMs at adjacent two levels with respect to an obtained solution lies in an interval representing the upper and the lower bounds specified the DM at the upper level of the adjacent two levels. It is difficult for the DMs to specify the bounds so as to reflect their preferences precisely.

Second, because the DMs must specify the minimal satisfactory levels individually and they may update the levels at the same time, it is difficult to find a solution such that all of the satisfactory degrees of the DMs are larger than or equal to their minimal satisfactory levels.

To overcome the first problem in the methods, we introduce a fuzzy goal for the ratio of the satisfactory degrees from the viewpoint of the vague or fuzzy nature of human judgments. For the second problem, we propose a new interactive procedure in which mathematical programming problems for obtaining solutions concerned in some groups within all the DMs are successively solved to lead to a global satisfactory solution.

Because we deal with multi-level nonlinear programming problems with nonconvex objective functions and constraints, conventional nonlinear programming methods such as the generalized reduced gradient method, the recursive quadratic programming method, etc. are not always effective in solving such problems. In this paper, we solve the nonconvex nonlinear programming problems through genetic algorithms (GAs), which were proposed by Holland [10] and have recently attracted considerable attention as promising methods for complex function optimization [9,12].

In section 2, multi-level nonconvex nonlinear programming problems are formulated. In section 3, we present an interactive fuzzy programming method for multi-level nonconvex nonlinear programming problems. In section 4, we describe some techniques for applying the coevolutionary genetic algorithm, called the revised GENOCOP III proposed by Sakawa and Yauchi [23,24], to the multi-level nonconvex nonlinear programming problems. In section 5, an illustrative numerical example demonstrates an interactive process in the proposed method for deriving a satisfactory solution.

2 Problem formulation

Let the number of levels be t, and then a multi-level nonconvex nonlinear programming problem is formally formulated as

$$\underset{\text{level } 1}{\text{minimize}} \quad f_1(\boldsymbol{x}_1, \dots, \boldsymbol{x}_t) \tag{1a}$$

$$\cdots\cdots\cdots\cdots\cdots$$

$$\underset{\text{level } t}{\text{minimize}} \quad f_t(\boldsymbol{x}_1, \dots, \boldsymbol{x}_t) \tag{1b}$$

$$\text{subject to} \quad g_j(\boldsymbol{x}_1, \dots, \boldsymbol{x}_t) \leq 0, \ j = 1, \dots, q \tag{1c}$$

$$h_j(\boldsymbol{x}_1, \dots, \boldsymbol{x}_t) = 0, \ j = q+1, \dots, m \tag{1d}$$

$$\boldsymbol{l}_i \leq \boldsymbol{x}_i \leq \boldsymbol{u}_i, \ i = 1, \dots, t, \tag{1e}$$

where $\boldsymbol{x}_i = (x_{i1}, \dots, x_{in_i})^T$, $i = 1, \dots, t$ is an n_i-dimensional decision variable vector of the DM at level i; T denotes transposition; $f_i(\boldsymbol{x}_1, \dots, \boldsymbol{x}_t)$, $i = 1, \dots, t$, $g_j(\boldsymbol{x}_1, \dots, \boldsymbol{x}_t)$, $j = 1, \dots, q$, $h_j(\boldsymbol{x}_1, \dots, \boldsymbol{x}_t)$, $j = q+1, \dots, m$

are $(\sum_{i=1}^{t} n_i)$-dimensional real-valued functions. Especially, $f_i(\boldsymbol{x}_1, \ldots, \boldsymbol{x}_t)$ is the objective function of the DM at level i. Moreover, $\boldsymbol{l}_i = (l_{i1}, \ldots, l_{in_i})$, $\boldsymbol{u}_i = (u_{i1}, \ldots, u_{in_i})$, $i = 1, \ldots, t$ are the lower and the upper bounds of the decision variable vector $\boldsymbol{x}_i$, respectively. Naturally, in problem (1), the convexity conditions of the objective functions and/or the feasible region are not satisfied.

In the following, for compact notation, we sometimes use $\boldsymbol{x} = (\boldsymbol{x}_1, \ldots, \boldsymbol{x}_t) \in R^{n_1+\cdots+n_t}$, and denote the feasible region satisfying all of the constraints of problem (1) by X. Also, for notational convenience, let DM1 denote the DM at the highest level, level 1, and DMi denote the DM at level i.

In general, for problem (1), an optimal solution which simultaneously minimizes the t objective functions does not always exist when the objective functions conflict with each other. Thus, if all the DMs can communicate and make decisions cooperatively, it is possible and desirable to derive a satisfactory solution by coordinating their satisfactory degrees of the fuzzy goals for the objective functions. From the above viewpoint, interactive fuzzy programming methods for multi-level programming problems have been proposed [25,11,17,20,16]. Let us review the setting of the interactive fuzzy programming briefly.

For problem (1), considering the vague or fuzzy nature of human judgments, it is quite natural to assume that the DMs at all levels may have fuzzy goals for the objective functions $f_i(\boldsymbol{x})$ [15,29]. In a minimization problem, the fuzzy goal stated by the DM may be to achieve "substantially less than or equal to some value p_i." This type of statement can be quantified by eliciting a corresponding membership function $\mu_i(f_i(\boldsymbol{x}))$ which is a strictly monotone decreasing function with respect to $f_i(\boldsymbol{x})$.

To elicit a membership function $\mu_i(f_i(\boldsymbol{x}))$ from DMi for the objective function $f_i(\boldsymbol{x})$ in problem (1), we first calculate the individual minimum and maximum of each objective function under the given constraints X. By taking account of the calculated individual minimum and maximum of each objective function together with the rate of increase of membership satisfaction, DMi may be able to determine a membership function $\mu_i(f_i(\boldsymbol{x}))$ in a subjective manner which is a strictly monotone decreasing function with respect to $f_i(\boldsymbol{x})$ [15]. Observe that the domain of the membership function is the closed interval $[f_i^{\min}, f_i^{\max}]$ and DMi specifies the value f_i^0 of the objective function for which the degree of satisfaction is 0 and the value f_i^1 of the objective function for which the degree of satisfaction is 1. For the value undesired (larger) than f_i^0, it is defined that $\mu_i(f_i(\boldsymbol{x})) = 0$, and for the value desired (smaller) than f_i^1, it is defined that $\mu_i(f_i(\boldsymbol{x})) = 1$.

After eliciting the membership functions $\mu_i(f_i(\boldsymbol{x}))$, $i = 1, \ldots, t$ of all the DMs for the objective functions $f_i(\boldsymbol{x})$, $i = 1, \ldots, t$, problem (1) can be converted into the membership function maximization problem represented by

$$\underset{\text{level 1}}{\text{maximize}} \ \mu_1(f_1(\boldsymbol{x})) \tag{2a}$$

$$\cdots\cdots\cdots\cdots$$

$$\underset{\text{level } t}{\text{maximize}} \ \mu_t(f_t(\boldsymbol{x})) \tag{2b}$$

$$\text{subject to} \ \ \boldsymbol{x} \in X. \tag{2c}$$

For problem (2), in the interactive fuzzy programming proposed before [25,11,17,20], a satisfactory solution is derived by updating the minimal satisfactory levels to the fuzzy goals for the objective functions with considerations of overall satisfactory balance among all the DMs.

Unfortunately, however, the following two difficulties are pointed out: (a) It is difficult for DMs to specify the bounds for the ratio of the satisfactory degrees so as to reflect their preferences precisely; (b) It is not always easy to find a solution in which all of the satisfactory degrees of the DMs are larger than or equal to their minimal satisfactory levels to the fuzzy goals for the objective functions.

To overcome the first problem (a), we introduce a fuzzy goal for the ratio of the satisfactory degrees from the viewpoint of the vague or fuzzy nature of human judgments. For avoiding the second problem (b), we propose a new interactive procedure in which mathematical programming problems for obtaining solutions concerned in some groups within all the DMs are successively solved to lead to a global satisfactory solution.

3 Interactive fuzzy programming

To derive a satisfactory solution to the formulated problem (2), we first find the maximizing decision of the fuzzy decision proposed by Bellman and Zadeh [6]. Namely, we solve the following problem for obtaining an optimal solution which maximizes the smallest degree of satisfaction among those of the t DMs:

$$\underset{\boldsymbol{x} \in X}{\text{maximize}} \min\{\mu_1(f_1(\boldsymbol{x})), \dots, \mu_t(f_t(\boldsymbol{x}))\}. \tag{3}$$

By introducing the auxiliary variable λ, this problem can be transformed into the following equivalent maximization problem:

$$\underset{\boldsymbol{x}, \lambda}{\text{maximize}} \ \lambda \tag{4a}$$

$$\text{subject to} \ \ \boldsymbol{x} \in X \tag{4b}$$

$$\mu_i(f_i(\boldsymbol{x})) \geq \lambda, \ i = 1, \dots, t \tag{4c}$$

$$0 \leq \lambda \leq 1. \tag{4d}$$

In order to take account of the satisfactory balance between adjacent two levels, the following ratio of the satisfactory degrees of the DMs at the adjacent two levels is computed:

$$\Delta_i(\boldsymbol{x}) = \frac{\mu_{i+1}(f_{i+1}(\boldsymbol{x}))}{\mu_i(f_i(\boldsymbol{x}))}, \; i = 1, \ldots, t-1. \tag{5}$$

DMi determines the minimal satisfactory level $\hat{\delta}_i$ to the fuzzy goals for the objective functions $f_i(\boldsymbol{x})$, consulting the optimal solution to problem (4). Moreover, DMi identifies a fuzzy goal for the ratio $\Delta_i(\boldsymbol{x})$ of the satisfactory degree of DMi to that of DM$(i+1)$ and specifies the minimal satisfactory level $\hat{\delta}_{\Delta_i}$ to the fuzzy goal for the ratio $\Delta_i(\boldsymbol{x})$.

The methods developed before are to derive a solution in which the ratio $\Delta_i(\boldsymbol{x})$, $i = 1, \ldots, t$ of the satisfactory degrees lies in the interval $[\Delta_i^{\min}, \Delta_i^{\max}]$ representing the upper and the lower bounds specified by DMi. If all of DMi, $i = 1, \ldots, t-1$ are satisfied with a certain solution, it becomes a satisfactory solution. Otherwise, the DMs must find another candidate of the satisfactory solution through the interactive process [25,11,17,20,16].

However, it is difficult to find such a satisfactory solution if the interval is narrow. If the interval is wide, it is easy to find a solution satisfying the conditions but the DMs could not be always satisfied with the solution. This may imply that it is hard for the DMs to express their preferences by using the intervals representing the bounds of the satisfactory degree. In this paper, to express the preferences of the DMs suitably, we introduce a fuzzy goal for the ratio of the satisfactory degrees expressed in words such as "$\Delta_i(\boldsymbol{x})$ should be in the vicinity of some value Δ_i^M" in place of the interval. Suppose that DMi identifies the membership function $\mu_{\Delta_i}(\Delta_i(\boldsymbol{x}))$ of the fuzzy goal and specifies the minimal satisfactory level $\hat{\delta}_{\Delta_i}$. Concerning the membership function $\mu_{\Delta_i}(\Delta_i(\boldsymbol{x}))$, it is obvious that a strictly monotone increasing function and a strictly monotone decreasing function corresponding to the left and the right sides of Δ_i^M must be determined through interaction with DMi. We give the following linear membership function as an example and it is depicted in Figure 1.

$$\mu_{\Delta_i}(\Delta_i(\boldsymbol{x})) = \begin{cases} 0 & ; \Delta_i(\boldsymbol{x}) < \Delta_i^{\mathrm{L}} \\ \dfrac{\Delta_i(\boldsymbol{x}) - \Delta_i^{\mathrm{L}}}{\Delta_i^{\mathrm{M}} - \Delta_i^{\mathrm{L}}} & ; \Delta_i^{\mathrm{L}} \leq \Delta_i(\boldsymbol{x}) < \Delta_i^{\mathrm{M}} \\ \dfrac{\Delta_i(\boldsymbol{x}) - \Delta_i^{\mathrm{R}}}{\Delta_i^{\mathrm{M}} - \Delta_i^{\mathrm{R}}} & ; \Delta_i^{\mathrm{M}} \leq \Delta_i(\boldsymbol{x}) < \Delta_i^{\mathrm{R}} \\ 0 & ; \Delta_i(\boldsymbol{x}) \geq \Delta_i^{\mathrm{R}} \end{cases} \tag{6}$$

In the methods proposed before [25,11,17,20,16], the DMs subjectively specify the minimal satisfactory levels $\hat{\delta}_i$, $i = 1, \ldots, t-1$ for the membership function $\mu_i(f_i(\boldsymbol{x}))$, $i = 1, \ldots, t-1$ and the following problem in which the minimal satisfactory degree among those of DMt and from DM1 to DM$(q -$

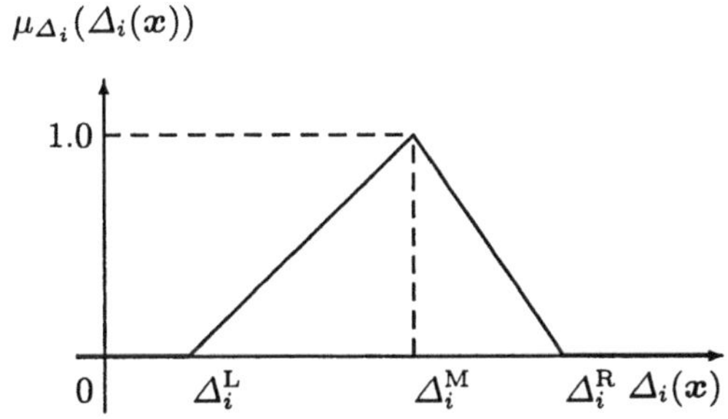

Fig. 1. Linear membership function of the fuzzy goal for the ratio of the satisfactory degrees

1) is maximized under the conditions $\mu_i(f_i(\boldsymbol{x})) \geq \hat{\delta}_i$, $i = q, \ldots, t-1$ is formulated:

$$\begin{aligned}
&\underset{\boldsymbol{x},\lambda}{\text{maximize}} \quad \lambda && \text{(7a)}\\
&\text{subject to} \quad \boldsymbol{x} \in X && \text{(7b)}\\
&\qquad \mu_i(f_i(\boldsymbol{x})) \geq \lambda, \; i = 1, \ldots, q-1 && \text{(7c)}\\
&\qquad \mu_i(f_i(\boldsymbol{x})) \geq \hat{\delta}_i, \; i = q, \ldots, t-1 && \text{(7d)}\\
&\qquad \mu_t(f_t(\boldsymbol{x})) \geq \lambda. && \text{(7e)}
\end{aligned}$$

After updating the minimal satisfactory levels $\hat{\delta}_i$, $i = 1, \ldots, t-1$, problem (7) is iteratively solved until $q = 1$. There are some cases where multiple DMs must update their minimal satisfactory levels simultaneously, and then the feasible region of problem (7) would be empty. Obtaining a satisfactory solution depends on how to update the minimal satisfactory levels, avoiding conflict with each other, and efficient devices for updating them are not provided in the previous methods.

To overcome such difficulties, in this paper, we propose a method in which mathematical programming problems for obtaining tentative satisfactory solutions concerned in some groups within all the DMs are successively solved to lead to a final satisfactory solution. We formulate a problem for DM$(t-1)$ and DMt and derive a satisfactory solution of them first, and then formulate a problem including DM$(t-2)$. In this manner, a DM at an upper level is added into the sphere of the problem step by step. To obtain consistent solutions in relevant DMs, we formulate problems yielding solutions preserving the ratios of the satisfactory degrees of adjacent two levels.

At first, the problem of DM$(t-1)$ and DMt

$$
\begin{aligned}
\underset{\boldsymbol{x},\lambda}{\text{maximize}} \quad & \lambda && \text{(8a)}\\
\text{subject to} \quad & \boldsymbol{x} \in X && \text{(8b)}\\
& 0 \le \lambda \le 1 && \text{(8c)}\\
& \mu_{t-1}(f_{t-1}(\boldsymbol{x})) \ge \hat{\delta}_{t-1} && \text{(8d)}\\
& \mu_{\Delta_{t-1}}(\Delta_{t-1}(\boldsymbol{x})) \ge \hat{\delta}_{\Delta_{t-1}} && \text{(8e)}\\
& \mu_t(f_t(\boldsymbol{x})) \ge \lambda && \text{(8f)}
\end{aligned}
$$

is solved. Inequality (8d) is DM$(t-1)$'s required condition for solutions and inequality (8e) is provided in order to balance the satisfactory degree of DM$(t-1)$ with that of DMt. Adjusting $\hat{\delta}_{t-1}$ and $\hat{\delta}_{\Delta_{t-1}}$, DM$(t-1)$ at the upper level of the two levels derives a satisfactory solution of DM$(t-1)$ and DMt by iteratively solving problem (8). Let $\hat{\Delta}_{t-1}$ be the ration of the satisfactory degrees of DM$(t-1)$ and DMt with respect to the obtained satisfactory solution of them.

After obtaining the satisfactory solution of DM$(t-1)$ and DMt, the following problem for from DM$(t-2)$ to DMt is solved:

$$
\begin{aligned}
\underset{\boldsymbol{x},\lambda}{\text{maximize}} \quad & \lambda && \text{(9a)}\\
\text{subject to} \quad & \boldsymbol{x} \in X && \text{(9b)}\\
& 0 \le \lambda \le 1 && \text{(9c)}\\
& \mu_{t-2}(f_{t-2}(\boldsymbol{x})) \ge \hat{\delta}_{t-2} && \text{(9d)}\\
& \mu_{\Delta_{t-2}}(\Delta_{t-2}(\boldsymbol{x})) \ge \hat{\delta}_{\Delta_{t-2}} && \text{(9e)}\\
& \hat{\Delta}_{t-1}\mu_{t-1}(f_{t-1}(\boldsymbol{x})) \ge \lambda && \text{(9f)}\\
& \mu_t(f_t(\boldsymbol{x})) \ge \lambda. && \text{(9g)}
\end{aligned}
$$

In problem (9), inequality (9f) is introduced in order to preserve the ratio $\hat{\Delta}_{t-1}$ of the satisfactory degrees of DM$(t-1)$ and DMt.

In general, a problem for from DMq to DMt is represented by:

$$
\begin{aligned}
&\underset{\boldsymbol{x},\lambda}{\text{maximize}} && \lambda && \text{(10a)}\\
&\text{subject to} && \boldsymbol{x} \in X && \text{(10b)}\\
& && 0 \le \lambda \le 1 && \text{(10c)}\\
& && \mu_q(f_q(\boldsymbol{x})) \ge \hat{\delta}_q && \text{(10d)}\\
& && \mu_{\Delta_q}(\Delta_q(\boldsymbol{x})) \ge \hat{\delta}_{\Delta_q} && \text{(10e)}\\
& && \prod_{i=q+1}^{t-1} \hat{\Delta}_i \ \mu_{q+1}(f_{q+1}(\boldsymbol{x})) \ge \lambda && \text{(10f)}\\
& && \cdots\cdots\cdots\cdots\cdots\cdots && \\
& && \hat{\Delta}_{t-1}\hat{\Delta}_{t-2}\ \mu_{t-2}(f_{t-2}(\boldsymbol{x})) \ge \lambda && \text{(10g)}\\
& && \hat{\Delta}_{t-1}\ \mu_{t-1}(f_{t-1}(\boldsymbol{x})) \ge \lambda && \text{(10h)}\\
& && \mu_t(f_t(\boldsymbol{x})) \ge \lambda. && \text{(10i)}
\end{aligned}
$$

From inequalities (10f)–(10h), the ratio of the satisfactory degrees of DMi and DM$(i+1)$, $i = q+1, \ldots, t-1$ is prone to become $\hat{\Delta}_i$. Although it is difficult for DMq to specify the minimal satisfactory level $\hat{\delta}_q$ taking the satisfactory degrees of from DM$(q+1)$ to DMt into account, in problem (10) of the proposed method, taking the satisfactory degrees of only DM$(q+1)$ into account, DMq specifies $\hat{\delta}_q$.

For an optimal solution to problem (10), from the relation between inequalities (10d) and (10e), there are some cases where the satisfactory degree of DM$(q+1)$ is smaller than an expected value. On that occasion, after DMq updates $\hat{\delta}_q$ and $\hat{\delta}_{\Delta_q}$, problem (10) is solved again. Moreover, there is a possibility that the satisfactory degree of a certain DM, DMr, may become large. Because such a phenomenon happens when the constraint corresponding to DMr is not active, by giving the upper bound $\hat{\lambda}_r^u \in [0,1]$ to the constraint, we prevent the satisfactory degree of DMr from increasing too much. We can obtain a final satisfactory solution by solving the following problem with the upper bound:

$$
\begin{aligned}
\underset{\boldsymbol{x},\lambda}{\text{maximize}}\quad & \lambda && \text{(11a)}\\
\text{subject to}\quad & \boldsymbol{x} \in X && \text{(11b)}\\
& 0 \le \lambda \le 1 && \text{(11c)}\\
& \mu_q(f_q(\boldsymbol{x})) \ge \hat{\delta}_q && \text{(11d)}\\
& \mu_{\Delta_q}(\Delta_q(\boldsymbol{x})) \ge \hat{\delta}_{\Delta_q} && \text{(11e)}\\
& \prod_{i=q+1}^{t-1} \hat{\Delta}_i \; \mu_{q+1}(f_{q+1}(\boldsymbol{x})) \ge \lambda && \text{(11f)}\\
& \cdots\cdots\cdots\cdots\cdots\cdots && \\
& \hat{\lambda}_r^u \ge \prod_{i=r}^{t-1} \hat{\Delta}_i \; \mu_r(f_r(\boldsymbol{x})) \ge \lambda && \text{(11g)}\\
& \cdots\cdots\cdots\cdots\cdots\cdots && \\
& \hat{\Delta}_{t-1}\hat{\Delta}_{t-2} \; \mu_{t-2}(f_{t-2}(\boldsymbol{x})) \ge \lambda && \text{(11h)}\\
& \hat{\Delta}_{t-1} \; \mu_{t-1}(f_{t-1}(\boldsymbol{x})) \ge \lambda && \text{(11i)}\\
& \mu_t(f_t(\boldsymbol{x})) \ge \lambda. && \text{(11j)}
\end{aligned}
$$

We are now ready to present an interactive algorithm for deriving a satisfactory solution to problem (1), which is summarized as follows:

Algorithm of the interactive fuzzy programming

Step 1 Let $\ell := 1$. After identifying the membership functions $\mu_i(f_i(\boldsymbol{x}))$, $i = 1, \ldots, t$ of the fuzzy goals of DMi, solve problem (4).

Step 2 Ask DM$(t-\ell)$ to specify the minimal satisfactory level $\hat{\delta}_{t-\ell}$ by consulting the optimal solutions to problems (4), (10) and (11). Furthermore, ask DM$(t-\ell)$ to identify the membership function $\mu_{\Delta_{t-\ell}}(\Delta_{t-\ell}(\boldsymbol{x}))$ of the fuzzy goal for the ratio of the satisfactory degrees and to specify the corresponding minimal satisfactory level $\hat{\delta}_{\Delta_{t-\ell}}$.

Step 3 Solve problem (10) for from DM$t-\ell$ to DMt.

Step 4 If DM$(t-\ell)$ is satisfied with the solution obtained from problem (10) or (11) and $t-\ell = 1$, the algorithm stops and the DMs obtain a final satisfactory solution. If $t-\ell > 1$, it follows that a satisfactory solution of from DM$(t-\ell)$ to DMt is derived. Let $\hat{\Delta}_{t-\ell}$ be the ratio of the satisfactory degrees of DM$(t-\ell)$ and DM$(t-\ell+1)$ and $\ell := \ell + 1$. Return to step 2. If DM$(t-\ell)$ is not satisfied with the solution, return to step 3 after updating $\hat{\delta}_{t-\ell}$ and $\hat{\delta}_{\Delta_{t-\ell}}$. If the satisfactory degree of a certain DM, DMr, becomes large excessively, go to step 5.

Step 5 Solve problem (11) with the upper bound and then return to Step 4.

We assume that the proposed method is applied to multi-level decision making problems in a stratified society such as a large-scale firm. In such multi-level organizations, because it is supposed that DMs at adjacent two levels discuss and negotiate for the decision making problems, we have proposed the interactive fuzzy programming method following such fashion.

4 Revised GENOCOP III

Because we deal with multi-level nonlinear programming problems with nonconvex objective functions and constraints, conventional nonlinear programming methods such as the generalized reduced gradient method, the recursive quadratic programming method, etc. are not always effective in solving the problems. In our method, we solve the nonconvex nonlinear programming problems (4), (10) and (11) through the revised GENOCOP III.

The GENOCOP III proposed by Michalewicz et al. [13,14] for solving general nonlinear programming problems. It has two separate populations, where a development in one population influences evaluations of individuals in the other population. The first population consists of so-called search points which satisfy linear constraints of the problem, and the second population consists of so-called reference points which satisfy all constraints of the problem.

Sakawa and Yauchi [23,24] have recently proposed the coevolutionary genetic algorithm, called the revised GENOCOP III, which improves in generating an initial reference point and in effectiveness and speed of search by minimizing the sum of squares of violated nonlinear constraints and introducing a bisection method for generating a new feasible point on the line segment between a search point and a reference point efficiently.

The algorithm of the revised GENOCOP III for solving the nonconvex nonlinear programming problems (4), (10) and (11) can be summarized as follows:

Step 1 Generate two separate initial populations. An initial population of search points is created randomly from individuals satisfying the lower and the upper bounds determined by both the linear constraints and the original lower and upper bounds. An initial reference point is generated by minimizing the sum of squares of violated nonlinear constraints. Then an initial population of reference points is created via multiple copies of the initial reference point obtained in this way.

Step 2 Apply the crossover and the mutation operators to the population of search points.

Step 3 Create a new point on a segment between a search point and a reference point using a bisection method, and perform the replacement procedure.

Step 4 After evaluating the individuals, apply the selection operator for generating individuals of the next generation.

Step 5 If termination conditions are satisfied, stop. Otherwise, return to Step 2.

The details of the revised GENOCOP III can be found in Sakawa and Yauchi [23,24].

5 Numerical example

To illustrate an interactive process in the proposed fuzzy programming method, consider the following three-level nonconvex programming problem in which DM1 has four decision variables, each of the other DMs has three decision variables, each of the decision variables has the upper and the lower bounds, and there are three linear and fives nonlinear constraints.

$$
\begin{aligned}
\underset{\text{level 1}}{\text{minimize}}\ f_1(\boldsymbol{x}) &= 7x_{11}^2 - x_{12}^2 + x_{11}x_{12} - 14x_{11} - 16x_{12} + 8(x_{13}-10)^2 \\
&\quad + 4(x_{14}-5)^2 + (x_{21}-3)^2 + 2(x_{22}-1)^2 + 5x_{23}^2 \\
&\quad + 7(x_{31}-11)^2 + 2(x_{32}-10)^2 + x_{33}^2 + 45 \\
\underset{\text{level 2}}{\text{minimize}}\ f_2(\boldsymbol{x}) &= (x_{11}-5)^2 + 5(x_{12}-12)^2 + 0.5x_{13}^4 + 3(x_{14}-11)^2 \\
&\quad + 0.2x_{21}^5 + 7x_{22}^2 + 0.1x_{23}^4 - 4x_{22}x_{23} - 10x_{22} - 8x_{23} \\
&\quad + x_{31}^2 + 3(x_{32}-5)^2 + (x_{33}-5)^2 \\
\underset{\text{level 3}}{\text{minimize}}\ f_3(\boldsymbol{x}) &= x_{11}^3 + (x_{12}-5)^2 + 3(x_{13}-9)^2 - 12x_{13} + 2x_{14}^3 \\
&\quad + 4x_{21}^2 + (x_{22}-5)^2 + 6x_{23}^2 + 3(x_{23}-2)^2x_{31}^2 \\
&\quad - 9x_{32}x_{33} + 4x_{32}^3 + 5x_{11} - 8x_{11}x_{23} \\
\text{subject to}\ & -3(x_{11}-2)^2 - 4(x_{12}-3)^2 - 2x_{13}^2 + 7x_{14} - 2x_{21}x_{22}x_{31} \\
& \quad +120 \geq 0 \\
& -5x_{11}^2 - 8x_{12} - (x_{13}-6)^2 + 2x_{14} + 40 \geq 0 \\
& -x_{11}^2 - 2(x_{12}-2)^2 + 2x_{11}x_{12} - 14x_{21} - 6x_{21}x_{22} \geq 0 \\
& -0.5(x_{11}-8)^2 - 2(x_{12}-4)^2 - 3x_{21}^2 + x_{21}x_{31} + 30 \geq 0 \\
& 3x_{11} - 6x_{12} - 12(x_{32}-8)^2 + 7x_{33} \geq 0 \\
& 4x_{11} + 5x_{12} - 3x_{23} + 9x_{31} \leq 105 \\
& 10x_{11} - 8x_{12} - 17x_{23} + 2x_{31} \leq 0 \\
& -8x_{11} + 2x_{12} + 5x_{32} - 2x_{33} \leq 0 \\
& -5.0 \leq x_{1k} \leq 10.0,\ k = 1, \ldots, 4 \\
& -5.0 \leq x_{ik} \leq 10.0,\ i = 2, 3,\ k = 1, 2, 3,
\end{aligned}
$$

where $\boldsymbol{x} = (\boldsymbol{x}_1^T, \boldsymbol{x}_2^T, \boldsymbol{x}_3^T)^T$, $\boldsymbol{x}_1 = (x_{11}, \ldots, x_{14})^T$, $\boldsymbol{x}_2 = (x_{21}, x_{22}, x_{23})^T$, $\boldsymbol{x}_3 = (x_{31}, x_{32}, x_{33})^T$. Let X denote the feasible region of the numerical example.

For this numerical example, parameter values of the revised GENOCOP III are set as follows: the population size is 70, the replacement probability is $p_r = 0.2$ and the number of generations is 5000.

To elicit the membership functions from the DMs, we compute optimal solutions $\boldsymbol{x}^{io}$ to individual minimization problems formulated as $\min_{\boldsymbol{x} \in X} f_i(\boldsymbol{x})$,

$i = 1, 2, 3$ through the revised GENOCOP III, and let $f_i^{\min} = f_i(\boldsymbol{x}^{io})$ and $f_i^{\mathrm{m}} = \max_{j \neq i} f_i(\boldsymbol{x}^{jo})$, $i = 1, 2, 3$.

In this numerical example, for simplicity, following the method by Zimmermann [29], it is assumed that the DMs determine the linear membership functions by choosing $f_i^1 = f_i^{\min}$, $f_i^0 = f_i^{\mathrm{m}}$, $i = 1, 2, 3$. The calculated optimal solution $\boldsymbol{x}^{io}$ and the corresponding individual minimum $f_i^{\min}$ and f_i^{m} are shown in Table 1.

Table 1. Parameter values for membership functions

$\boldsymbol{x}_1^{1o}$	1.767 3.450 8.815 5.565		
$\boldsymbol{x}_2^{1o}$	0.288 0.486 0.821		
$\boldsymbol{x}_3^{1o}$	9.239 6.426 6.447		
$\boldsymbol{x}_1^{2o}$	1.679 4.226 2.523 10.000		
$\boldsymbol{x}_2^{2o}$	−2.832 1.663 3.321		
$\boldsymbol{x}_3^{2o}$	−4.993 6.368 7.468		
$\boldsymbol{x}_1^{3o}$	2.244 1.551 8.037 0.886		
$\boldsymbol{x}_2^{3o}$	−0.311 5.055 1.932		
$\boldsymbol{x}_3^{3o}$	3.673 5.630 10.000		
$f_1^{\min}$	93.718	$f_1^{\mathrm{m}} = f_1(\boldsymbol{x}^{2o})$	2472.588
$f_2^{\min}$	302.867	$f_2^{\mathrm{m}} = f_2(\boldsymbol{x}^{1o})$	3565.523
$f_3^{\min}$	587.801	$f_3^{\mathrm{m}} = f_3(\boldsymbol{x}^{2o})$	3289.967

Problem (4) for this numerical example, which maximizes the smallest degree of satisfaction among the three DMs, is formulated and is solved through the revised GENOCOP III. The result is shown in Table 2, and a superscript indicates the number of iteration.

Table 2. Iteration 1

λ^1	0.859202				
$\boldsymbol{x}_1^1$	1.867 3.448 4.285 3.977				
$\boldsymbol{x}_2^1$	0.233 1.364 1.915				
$\boldsymbol{x}_3^1$	8.665 5.980 9.153				
f_1^1	428.658	$\mu_1(f_1^1)$	0.859202	Δ_1^1	1.000000
f_2^1	762.242	$\mu_2(f_2^1)$	0.859202	Δ_2^1	1.000001
f_3^1	968.259	$\mu_3(f_3^1)$	0.859203		

Suppose that DM2 is not satisfied with the current optimal solution. Therefore, problem (8) of DM2 and DM3 must be formulated to derive a tentative satisfactory solution. Suppose that DM2 specifies the minimal satisfactory level to the fuzzy goal for the objective function as $\hat{\delta}_2 = 0.90$, identifies the membership function $\mu_{\Delta_2}(\Delta_2(\boldsymbol{x}))$ with the parameters $(\Delta_2^{\mathrm{L}}, \Delta_2^{\mathrm{M}}, \Delta_2^{\mathrm{R}}) = (0.20, 0.95, 1.30)$ of the fuzzy goal for the ratio of the satisfactory degrees of

DM2 and DM3, and specifies the corresponding minimal satisfactory level to the fuzzy goal for the ratio of satisfactory degrees as $\hat{\delta}_{\Delta_2} = 0.90$. Problem (8) with the above parameters is solved through the revised GENOCOP III. The result is shown in Table 3.

Table 3. Iteration 2

x_1^2	1.732	3.090	3.263	3.611
x_2^2	0.003	1.827	2.171	
x_3^2	0.001	5.827	10.000	
f_1^2	1374.560	$\mu_1(f_1^2)$	0.461575	
f_2^2	629.132	$\mu_2(f_2^2)$	0.900000	
f_3^2	912.788	$\mu_3(f_3^2)$	0.879731	
Δ_1^2	1.949844			
Δ_2^2	0.977479	$\mu_{\Delta_2}(\Delta_2^2)$	0.921488	

As can be seen from Table 3, the satisfactory degrees of DM2 are $\mu_2(f_2^2) = 0.900000$ and $\mu_{\Delta_2}(\Delta_2^2) = 0.921488$. Suppose that DM2 judges that it is desirable for self to increase his or her satisfactory degree at the sacrifice of that of DM3. Consulting the result of Iteration 2, suppose that DM2 specifies the minimal satisfactory level as $\hat{\delta}_2 = 0.93$. The corresponding problem (8) is formulated and is solved through the revised GENOCOP III. The result is shown in Table 4.

Table 4. Iteration 3

x_1^3	1.547	3.739	3.287	4.618
x_2^3	0.004	1.672	2.496	
x_3^3	0.003	5.914	10.000	
f_1^3	1354.163	$\mu_1(f_1^3)$	0.470150	
f_2^3	531.252	$\mu_2(f_2^3)$	0.930000	
f_3^3	1054.348	$\mu_3(f_3^3)$	0.827344	
Δ_1^3	1.978093			
Δ_2^3	0.889617	$\mu_{\Delta_2}(\Delta_2^3)$	0.919489	

For the obtained solution, the satisfactory degrees of DM2 are $\mu_2(f_2^3) = 0.930000$ and $\mu_{\Delta_2}(\Delta_2^3) = 0.919489$. Supposing DM2 is satisfied with the solution, the ratio of the satisfactory degrees of DM2 and DM3 becomes $\hat{\Delta}_2 = 0.889617$.

Next, to obtain a global satisfactory solution, suppose that DM1 specifies the minimal satisfactory level to the fuzzy goal for the objective function as $\hat{\delta}_1 = 0.90$, identifies the membership function $\mu_{\Delta_1}(\Delta_1(\boldsymbol{x}))$ with the parameters $(\Delta_1^{\mathrm{L}}, \Delta_1^{\mathrm{M}}, \Delta_1^{\mathrm{R}}) = (0.20, 0.95, 1.30)$ of the fuzzy goal for the ratio of the satisfactory degrees of DM1 and DM2, and specifies the minimal satisfactory level to the fuzzy goal for the ratio of satisfactory degrees as $\hat{\delta}_{\Delta_1} = 0.90$. The corresponding problem (9) is formulated and is solved through the revised GENOCOP III. The result is shown in Table 5.

Table 5. Iteration 4

λ^4	0.757117		
x_1^4	1.766 4.220 5.032 5.303		
x_2^4	0.089 1.252 1.972		
x_3^4	8.341 6.267 8.009		
f_1^4	331.605	$\mu_1(f_1^4)$	0.900000
f_2^4	788.810	$\mu_2(f_2^4)$	0.851059
f_3^4	1244.108	$\mu_3(f_3^4)$	0.757118
Δ_1^4	0.945621	$\mu_{\Delta_1}(\Delta_1^4)$	0.994162
Δ_2^4	0.889691	$\mu_{\Delta_2}(\Delta_2^4)$	0.919492

For the obtained solution, the satisfactory degrees of DM1 are $\mu_1(f_1^4) = 0.900000$ and $\mu_{\Delta_1}(\Delta_1^4) = 0.994162$. Suppose that DM1 judges that it is desirable for self to increase his or her satisfactory degree at the sacrifice of those of DM2 and DM3. Consulting the result of Iteration 4, suppose that DM1 specifies the minimal satisfactory level as $\hat{\delta}_1 = 0.92$. The corresponding problem (9) is formulated and is solved through the revised GENOCOP III. The result is shown in Table 6.

Table 6. Iteration 5

λ^5	0.605330		
x_1^5	2.337 3.085 5.335 6.214		
x_2^5	0.310 1.212 1.633		
x_3^5	8.643 6.641 4.809		
f_1^5	284.028	$\mu_1(f_1^5)$	0.920000
f_2^5	939.083	$\mu_2(f_2^5)$	0.805000
f_3^5	1654.263	$\mu_3(f_3^5)$	0.605331
Δ_1^5	0.875000	$\mu_{\Delta_1}(\Delta_1^5)$	0.900001
Δ_2^5	0.751963	$\mu_{\Delta_2}(\Delta_2^5)$	0.735951

For the obtained solution, the satisfactory degrees of DM1 are $\mu_1(f_1^5) = 0.920000$ and $\mu_{\Delta_1}(\Delta_1^5) = 0.900001$. Suppose that DM1 is satisfied with these values but DM1 is not satisfied with $\mu_{\Delta_2}(\Delta_2^5) = 0.735951$ because DM1 recognizes that there is a large gap between $\Delta_2^5 = 0.751963$ and $\hat{\Delta}_2 = 0.889617$. Suppose that DM1 decreases the minimal satisfactory level as $\hat{\delta}_1 = 0.91$. The corresponding problem (9) is formulated and is solved through the revised GENOCOP III. The result is shown in Table 7.

As can be seen from Table 7, the satisfactory degrees of DM1 are $\mu_1(f_1^6) = 0.910000$ and $\mu_{\Delta_1}(\Delta_1^6) = 0.900000$. $\Delta_2^6 = 0.884073$ is in the neighborhood of

Table 7. Iteration 6

λ^6	0.703943		
x_1^6	2.269 3.001 5.330 5.102		
x_2^6	0.297 1.297 1.921		
x_3^6	8.062 6.598 4.970		
f_1^6	307.816	$\mu_1(f_1^6)$	0.910000
f_2^6	967.633	$\mu_2(f_2^6)$	0.796250
f_3^6	1387.797	$\mu_3(f_3^6)$	0.703943
Δ_1^6	0.875000	$\mu_{\Delta_1}(\Delta_1^6)$	0.900000
Δ_2^6	0.884073	$\mu_{\Delta_2}(\Delta_2^6)$	0.912097

$\hat{\Delta}_2 = 0.889617$ and we have $\mu_{\Delta_2}(\Delta_2^6) = 0.912097$. In this example, it is assumed that, at Iteration 6, DM1 concludes that the obtained solution is a global satisfactory solution and the interactive procedure stops.

6 Conclusions

In this paper, for multi-level nonconvex programming problems with the essentially cooperative DMs, we have proposed an interactive fuzzy programming method through the revised GENOCOP III. In our interactive method, after having determined the fuzzy goals of the DMs at all levels and the ratio of satisfactory degrees of DMs at adjacent two levels, by solving mathematical programming problems for obtaining satisfactory solutions concerned in some groups within all the DMs, an satisfactory solution has been efficiently derived through the revised GENOCOP III. By using the method, we can derive a satisfactory solution such that the DMs at relatively upper levels are esteemed and the satisfactory degree of each DM balances with those of the others. An illustrative numerical example for three-level nonconvex programming problems has demonstrated an interactive procedure of the proposed method. Applications of the proposed method to the real-world decision making situations would be desired in the near future.

References

1. G. Anandalingam, R. Mathieu, C.L. Pittard and N. Sinha, Artificial intelligence based approaches for solving hierarchical optimization problems, in: Sharda, Golden, Wasil, Balci and Stewart (eds.), Impacts of Recent Computer Advances on Operations Research, North-Holland (1989) 289–301.
2. J.F. Bard, An efficient point algorithm for a linear two-stage optimization problem, Operations Research 38 (1983) 556-560.
3. J.F. Bard and J.E. Falk, An explicit solution to the multi-level programming problem, Computers and Operations Research 9 (1982) 77-100.
4. J. Bard and J. Moore, The mixed integer linear bilevel programming problem, Operations Research 38 (1990) 911–921.

5. J. Bard and J. Moore, An algorithm for the discrete bilevel programming problem, Naval Research Logistics 39 (1992) 419–435.
6. R.E. Bellman and L.A. Zadeh, Decision making in a fuzzy environment, Management Science 17 (1970) 141-164.
7. W.F. Bialas and M.H. Karwan, Two-level linear programming, Management Science 30 (1984) 1004-1020.
8. M. Gen and R. Cheng, Genetic Algorithms and Engineering Design, (John Wiley & Sons, New York, 1997).
9. D.E. Goldberg, Genetic Algorithms in Search, Optimization, and Machine Learning, (Addision Wesley, Massachusetts, 1989).
10. J.H. Holland, Adaptation in Natural and Artificial Systems, (University of Michigan Press, 1975; MIT Press, Cambridge, 1992).
11. Y.J. Lai, Hierarchical optimization: a satisfactory solution, Fuzzy Sets and Systems 77 (1996) 321–335.
12. Z. Michalewicz, Genetic Algorithms + Data Structures = Evolution Programs, Third, revised and extended edition, (Springer-Verlag, Berlin, 1996).
13. Z. Michalewicz and G. Nazhiyath: Genocop III : a co-evolutionary algorithm for numerical optimization problems with nonlinear constrains, in: Proceedings of the Second IEEE International Conference Evolutionary Computation (1995) 647–651.
14. Z. Michalewicz and M. Schoenauer, Evolutionary algorithms for constrained parameter optimization problems, Evolutionary Computation 4 (1996) 1-32.
15. M. Sakawa, Fuzzy Sets and Interactive Multiobjective Optimization, (Plenum Press , New York, 1993).
16. M. Sakawa and I. Nishizaki, Interactive fuzzy programming for two-level linear fractional programming problems, Fuzzy Sets and Systems (in press).
17. M. Sakawa, I. Nishizaki and M. Hitaka, Interactive fuzzy programming for multi-level 0-1 programming problems through genetic algorithms, European Journal of Operational Research 114 (1999) 580–588.
18. M. Sakawa, I. Nishizaki and M. Hitaka, Interactive fuzzy programming for multi-level 0-1 programming problems with fuzzy parameters through genetic algorithms, Fuzzy Sets and Systems (in press).
19. M. Sakawa, I. Nishizaki and Y. Uemura, Interactive fuzzy programming for multi-level linear programming problems, Computers & Mathematics with Applications 36 (1998) 71–86.
20. M. Sakawa, I. Nishizaki and Y. Uemura, Interactive fuzzy programming for multi-level linear programming problems with fuzzy parameters, Fuzzy Sets and Systems 109 (2000) 3–19.
21. M. Sakawa, I. Nishizaki and Y. Uemura, Interactive fuzzy programming for multi-level linear fractional programming problems with fuzzy parameters, Fuzzy Sets and Systems 115 (2000) 90–103.
22. M. Sakawa and H. Yano, An interactive fuzzy satisfyicing method for generalized multiobjective linear programming problems with fuzzuy parameters, Fuzzy Sets and Systems 35 (1990) 125–142.
23. M. Sakawa and K. Yauchi, Coevolutionary genetic algorithms for nonconvex nonlinear programming problems: Revised GENOCOP III, Cybernetics and Systems: An International Journal 29 (1998) 885–899.
24. M. Sakawa and K. Yauchi, An interactive fuzzy satisficing method for multiobjective nonconvex programming problems through floating point genetic algorithms, European Journal of Operational Research 117 (1999) 113–124.

25. H.S. Shih, Y.J. Lai and E.S. Lee, Fuzzy approach for multi-level programming problems, Computers and Operations Research 23 (1996) 73–91.
26. M. Simaan and J.B. Cruz, Jr., On the Stackelberg strategy in nonzero-sum games, Journal of Optimization Theory and Applications 11 (1973) 533–555.
27. U.P. Wen and Y.H. Yang, Algorithms for solving the mixed integer two-level linear programming problem, Computers and Operations Research 17 (1990) 133–142.
28. D.J. White and G. Anandalingam, A penalty function approach for solving bi-level linear programs, Journal of Global Optimization 3 (1993) 397-419.
29. H.-J. Zimmermann, Fuzzy programming and linear programming with several objective functions, Fuzzy Sets and Systems 1 (1978) 45–55.

Two-Stage Linear Recourse Problems under Non-Probabilistic Uncertainty

Masahiro Inuiguchi[1] and Tetsuzo Tanino[1]

Osaka University, 2-1, Yamadaoka, Suita, Osaka 565-0871, Japan

Abstract. In this paper, we apply two-stage recourse programming approach to linear programming problems with uncertain parameters. It is assumed that the set of possible realizations of parameters are known as a polytope. A two-stage recourse problem is formulated in the pessimistic viewpoint. It is shown that this problem is a convex programming problem with respect to the first stage variable vector and a large-scale linear programming problem when all vertices of the polytope representing possible realizations of uncertain parameters are given. A solution algorithm based on a relaxation procedure is proposed. Generally, we need to solve max-min problems or bilinear programming problems during the solution process. Some special cases are discussed in order to solve the max-min problems efficiently.

1 Introduction

Possibilistic programming has recently developed to treat non-probabilistic, more exactly possibilistic uncertainty involved in programming problems such as production planning problems[1], network problems[2], scheduling problems[3,4], portfolio selection problems[5–7] and so on. The idea of formulation of possibilistic programming problems is quite similar to that of stochastic programming problems (see [6,8–11]). The previous research results demonstrated the advantage of the possibilistic programming over the stochastic programming in tractability of the reduced problems (see, for example, [6]).

In stochastic programming, three different approaches, chance constrained programming, two-stage programming and distribution problems have been proposed. On the other hand, in possibilistic programming, the ones corresponding to chance constrained programming and distribution problems have mainly treated in the literature and quite a few attempts [12] on two-stage programming under possibilistic uncertainty have been made. Considering the tractability of the reduced problems by the possibilistic programming approaches, two-stage programming problems under possibilistic uncertainty may be reduced to easier problems than those under probabilistic uncertainty.

In this paper, we treat the two-stage programming problems with complete recourse under non-graded possibilistic uncertainty. Non-graded possibilistic uncertainty means that possible ranges of parameters are given by crisp sets. Two-stage programming problems with simple recourse under graded possibilistic uncertainty have been treated based on a possibility measure by Itoh and Ishii [12]. Graded possibilistic uncertainty means that possible ranges of parameters are given by fuzzy sets. Possibility measures are used to evaluate the results optimistically. Thus, their approach is suitable neither for risk averse decision maker nor in a situation required the safety. Moreover, they assumed that only the right-hand side values are uncertain and non-interactive one another.

Under non-graded possibilistic uncertainty, we propose a treatment of the problems suitable for risk averse decision maker and in the situation required the safety. Parameters of objective function coefficients, right-hand side values and technical matrix are uncertain and interactive so that the possible range of parameters is expressed by a polytope. We show that the reduced problem obtained by the proposed treatment is a convex programming with respect to the decision variable vector. It is also shown that the problem can be reduced to a large-scale linear programming problem when all vertices of the polytope which represents the possible range of uncertainty parameters are known. A solution algorithm based on relaxation procedure is proposed. Since the solution algorithm requires to solve max-min problems or equivalently, bilinear programming problems, we discuss how to solve the max-min problems in some special cases.

2 Problem Statement and Previous Approaches

In this paper, we treat the following linear programming problem with uncertain parameters:

$$\begin{array}{ll} \underset{\boldsymbol{x}}{\text{minimize}} & \boldsymbol{c}^{\mathrm{T}}\boldsymbol{x}, \\ \text{subject to} & A_0\boldsymbol{x} = \boldsymbol{b}_0, \\ & A_1\boldsymbol{x} = \boldsymbol{b}_1, \\ & A_2\boldsymbol{x} \leq \boldsymbol{b}_2, \\ & \boldsymbol{x} \geq \boldsymbol{0}, \end{array} \qquad \begin{pmatrix} \boldsymbol{c}^{\mathrm{T}} & 0 \\ A_1 & \boldsymbol{b}_1 \\ A_2 & \boldsymbol{b}_2 \end{pmatrix} \in \Theta \tag{1}$$

where A_0, A_1 and A_2 are $m_0 \times n$, $m_1 \times n$ and $m_2 \times n$ matrices and $\boldsymbol{c}$, $\boldsymbol{b}_0$, $\boldsymbol{b}_1$ and $\boldsymbol{b}_2$ are n-, m_0-, m_1- and m_2-dimensional column vectors. $\boldsymbol{x}$ is an n-dimensional decision variable vector. While components of the matrix A_0 and the vector $\boldsymbol{b}_0$ are known exactly, components of the matrices A_1 and A_2 and vectors $\boldsymbol{c}$, $\boldsymbol{b}_1$ and $\boldsymbol{b}_2$ are not know exactly but the possible realizations of the $(m_1 + m_2 + 1) \times (n + 1)$ matrix,

$$\begin{pmatrix} \boldsymbol{c}^{\mathrm{T}} & 0 \\ A_1 & \boldsymbol{b}_1 \\ A_2 & \boldsymbol{b}_2 \end{pmatrix}$$

is known as a set of $(m_1 + m_2 + 1) \times (n + 1)$ matrices, Θ.

To such linear programming problems with uncertain parameters have been treated in possibilistic programming. In the previous approaches, the objective function and constrains are treated in optimistic and/or pessimistic ways. In optimistic way, Problem (1) is formulated as

$$\begin{aligned}
\underset{\boldsymbol{x},A_1,A_2,\boldsymbol{b}_1,\boldsymbol{b}_2,\boldsymbol{c}}{\text{minimize}} \quad & \boldsymbol{c}^{\mathrm{T}}\boldsymbol{x}, \\
\text{subject to} \quad & A_0\boldsymbol{x} = \boldsymbol{b}_0, \\
& A_1\boldsymbol{x} = \boldsymbol{b}_1, \\
& A_2\boldsymbol{x} \leq \boldsymbol{b}_2, \\
& \boldsymbol{x} \geq \boldsymbol{0}, \\
& \begin{pmatrix} \boldsymbol{c}^{\mathrm{T}} & 0 \\ A_1 & \boldsymbol{b}_1 \\ A_2 & \boldsymbol{b}_2 \end{pmatrix} \in \Theta.
\end{aligned} \tag{2}$$

On the other hand, in the pessimistic way, Problem (1) is formulated as

$$\begin{aligned}
\underset{\boldsymbol{x}}{\text{minimize}} \ \underset{\boldsymbol{c}\in\Theta_{\boldsymbol{c}}}{\text{maximize}} \quad & \boldsymbol{c}^{\mathrm{T}}\boldsymbol{x}, \\
\text{subject to} \quad & A_0\boldsymbol{x} = \boldsymbol{b}_0, \\
& \begin{cases} A_1\boldsymbol{x} = \boldsymbol{b}_1, \\ A_2\boldsymbol{x} \leq \boldsymbol{b}_2, \end{cases} \quad \forall \begin{pmatrix} A_1 & \boldsymbol{b}_1 \\ A_2 & \boldsymbol{b}_2 \end{pmatrix} \in \Theta_{(A_1,A_2,\boldsymbol{b}_1,\boldsymbol{b}_2)}, \\
& \boldsymbol{x} \geq \boldsymbol{0}.
\end{aligned} \tag{3}$$

where $\Theta_{\boldsymbol{c}}$ and $\Theta_{(A_1,A_2,\boldsymbol{b}_1,\boldsymbol{b}_2)}$ are projected areas of Θ to the space of vectors $\boldsymbol{c}$ and to the space of matrices $(A_2, \boldsymbol{b}_2)$, i.e.,

$$\Theta_{\boldsymbol{c}} = \left\{ \boldsymbol{c} \;\middle|\; \exists(A_1, A_2, \boldsymbol{b}_1, \boldsymbol{b}_2) \text{ such that } \begin{pmatrix} \boldsymbol{c}^{\mathrm{T}} & \boldsymbol{0} \\ A_1 & \boldsymbol{b}_1 \\ A_2 & \boldsymbol{b}_2 \end{pmatrix} \in \Theta \right\}, \tag{4}$$

$$\Theta_{(A_1,A_2,\boldsymbol{b}_1,\boldsymbol{b}_2)} = \left\{ \begin{pmatrix} A_1 & \boldsymbol{b}_1 \\ A_2 & \boldsymbol{b}_2 \end{pmatrix} \;\middle|\; \exists\boldsymbol{c} \text{ such that } \begin{pmatrix} \boldsymbol{c}^{\mathrm{T}} & \boldsymbol{0} \\ A_1 & \boldsymbol{b}_1 \\ A_2 & \boldsymbol{b}_2 \end{pmatrix} \in \Theta \right\}, \tag{5}$$

Generally, there is no guarantee of the existence of a feasible solution of Problem (3). However, when $m_1 = 0$, in other words, when Problem (1) has only inequality constraints except $A_0\boldsymbol{x} = \boldsymbol{b}_0$, it is more often that there exists a feasible solution of Problem (3).

As an intermediate approach, we can consider the following formulation:

$$\begin{aligned}
\underset{\boldsymbol{x},\boldsymbol{c}\in\Theta_{\boldsymbol{c}}}{\text{minimize}} \quad & \boldsymbol{c}^{\mathrm{T}}\boldsymbol{x}, \\
\text{subject to} \quad & A_0\boldsymbol{x} = \boldsymbol{b}_0, \\
& \begin{cases} A_1\boldsymbol{x} = \boldsymbol{b}_1, \\ A_2\boldsymbol{x} \leq \boldsymbol{b}_2, \end{cases} \quad \forall \begin{pmatrix} A_1 & \boldsymbol{b}_1 \\ A_2 & \boldsymbol{b}_2 \end{pmatrix} \in \Theta_{(A_1,A_2,\boldsymbol{b}_1,\boldsymbol{b}_2|\boldsymbol{c})}, \\
& \boldsymbol{x} \geq \boldsymbol{0},
\end{aligned} \tag{6}$$

where we define

$$\Theta_{(A_1,A_2,\boldsymbol{b}_1,\boldsymbol{b}_2|\boldsymbol{c})} = \left\{ \begin{pmatrix} A_1 & \boldsymbol{b}_1 \\ A_2 & \boldsymbol{b}_2 \end{pmatrix} \;\middle|\; \begin{pmatrix} \boldsymbol{c}^{\mathrm{T}} & \boldsymbol{0} \\ A_1 & \boldsymbol{b}_1 \\ A_2 & \boldsymbol{b}_2 \end{pmatrix} \in \Theta \right\}. \tag{7}$$

The approaches by Problems (2), (3) and (6) have been treated (see [13–15]) under the assumption that all uncertain parameters are possibilistically independent one another but Θ may be a fuzzy set. Under possibilistic independence, Θ can be represented as

$$\Theta = \left\{ \begin{pmatrix} \boldsymbol{c}^{\mathrm{T}} & 0 \\ A_1 & \boldsymbol{b}_1 \\ A_2 & \boldsymbol{b}_2 \end{pmatrix} \middle| \, \boldsymbol{c}^{\mathrm{L}} \le \boldsymbol{c} \le \boldsymbol{c}^{\mathrm{R}},\ A_1^{\mathrm{L}} \le A_i \le A_i^{\mathrm{R}},\ \boldsymbol{b}_i^{\mathrm{L}} \le \boldsymbol{b}_i \le \boldsymbol{b}_i^{\mathrm{R}},\ i = 1, 2 \right\}. \tag{8}$$

Under assumptions of possibilistic independence and $m_1 = 0$, Problems (2), (3) and (6) are reduced to the following linear programming problems:

$$\begin{aligned} \underset{\boldsymbol{x}}{\text{minimize}} \quad & {\boldsymbol{c}^{\mathrm{L}}}^{\mathrm{T}} \boldsymbol{x}, \\ \text{subject to} \quad & A_0 \boldsymbol{x} = \boldsymbol{b}_0, \\ & A_2^{\mathrm{L}} \boldsymbol{x} \le \boldsymbol{b}_2^{\mathrm{R}}, \\ & \boldsymbol{x} \ge \boldsymbol{0}, \end{aligned} \tag{9}$$

$$\begin{aligned} \underset{\boldsymbol{x}}{\text{minimize}} \quad & {\boldsymbol{c}^{\mathrm{R}}}^{\mathrm{T}} \boldsymbol{x}, \\ \text{subject to} \quad & A_0 \boldsymbol{x} = \boldsymbol{b}_0, \\ & A_2^{\mathrm{R}} \boldsymbol{x} \le \boldsymbol{b}_2^{\mathrm{L}}, \\ & \boldsymbol{x} \ge \boldsymbol{0}, \end{aligned} \tag{10}$$

$$\begin{aligned} \underset{\boldsymbol{x}}{\text{minimize}} \quad & {\boldsymbol{c}^{\mathrm{L}}}^{\mathrm{T}} \boldsymbol{x}, \\ \text{subject to} \quad & A_0 \boldsymbol{x} = \boldsymbol{b}_0, \\ & A_2^{\mathrm{R}} \boldsymbol{x} \le \boldsymbol{b}_2^{\mathrm{L}}, \\ & \boldsymbol{x} \ge \boldsymbol{0}. \end{aligned} \tag{11}$$

3 Two-Stage Recourse Programming Approach

The previous approaches described above are corresponding to chance constrained programming approaches [16,17] in stochastic programming problems. In stochastic programming problems, two-stage recourse programming approaches also proposed and shown that chance constrained programming approaches are special cases of two-stage recourse programming approaches. On the other hand, two-stage recourse programming approaches have not yet introduced to programming problems under non-probabilistic uncertainty considerably.

In this section, we introduce two-stage recourse programming approaches to linear programming problems with uncertain parameters represented by Problem (1). In the previous approaches, the constraints of Problem (1) has been treated so as to satisfy for at least one possible realization of $(\boldsymbol{c}, A_1, A_2, \boldsymbol{b}_1, \boldsymbol{b}_2)$ (in case of (2)) or for all possible realizations of $(\boldsymbol{c}, A_1, A_2, \boldsymbol{b}_1, \boldsymbol{b}_2)$ (in case of (3)). Those treatments are sometimes too extreme. In two-stage recourse programming approaches, we approve the violation of constraints by paying penalties (recourse). Thus, the treatment of constraints is more moderate than the previous approaches. If the right-hand sides represent resources, the penalties can be understood as costs for emergency purchase of resources when left-hand side values exceed right-hand values and clearance costs of the remaining resources when left-hand side values are smaller than right-hand side values.

From the pessimistic viewpoint, the two-stage recourse programming problem corresponding to Problem (1) is formulated as follows:

$$\begin{aligned}
\underset{\boldsymbol{x}}{\text{minimize}} \ \underset{A_1,A_2,\boldsymbol{b}_1,\boldsymbol{b}_2,\boldsymbol{c}}{\text{maximize}} \ \underset{\boldsymbol{y}}{\text{minimize}} \ & \boldsymbol{c}^{\mathrm{T}}\boldsymbol{x} + \boldsymbol{q}^{\mathrm{T}}\boldsymbol{y}, \\
\text{subject to } & A_0\boldsymbol{x} = \boldsymbol{b}_0, \\
& A_1\boldsymbol{x} + W_1\boldsymbol{y} = \boldsymbol{b}_1, \\
& A_2\boldsymbol{x} + W_2\boldsymbol{y} \leq \boldsymbol{b}_2, \\
& \boldsymbol{x} \geq \boldsymbol{0}, \ \boldsymbol{y} \geq \boldsymbol{0}, \\
& \begin{pmatrix} \boldsymbol{c}^{\mathrm{T}} & 0 \\ A_1 & \boldsymbol{b}_1 \\ A_2 & \boldsymbol{b}_2 \end{pmatrix} \in \Theta.
\end{aligned} \tag{12}$$

where W_1 and W_2 are $m_1 \times p$ and $m_2 \times p$ matrices and $\boldsymbol{q} > \boldsymbol{0}$ is a p-dimensional column vector. $\boldsymbol{y}$ is a p-dimensional decision variable vector. W_1 and W_2 are called recourse matrices. We assume that for all $\boldsymbol{x}$ and for all

$$\begin{pmatrix} \boldsymbol{c}^{\mathrm{T}} & 0 \\ A_1 & \boldsymbol{b}_1 \\ A_2 & \boldsymbol{b}_2 \end{pmatrix} \in \Theta,$$

there exists $\boldsymbol{y}$ such that

$$\begin{cases} A_1\boldsymbol{x} + W_1\boldsymbol{y} = \boldsymbol{b}_1, \\ A_2\boldsymbol{x} + W_2\boldsymbol{y} \leq \boldsymbol{b}_2. \end{cases}$$

The recourse matrices W_1 and W_2 which satisfy this assumption are said to be complete (see [17]). Thus, in this paper, we treat two-stage recourse programming problems with complete recourse matrices.

In the previously proposed pessimistic approach, i.e., Problem (3), there is no guarantee that there exists a feasible solution. If no feasible solution exists, neither an optimal solution does. Thus, Problem (3) is not always useful. On the other hand, Problem (12) always has a feasible solution whenever there exists $\boldsymbol{x} \geq \boldsymbol{0}$ which satisfies $A_0\boldsymbol{x} = \boldsymbol{b}_0$. Thus, it is much more often to have an optimal solution to Problem (12) than to Problem (3).

The terminology, two-stage recourse programming problem comes from the following observation. At the first stage, the variable vector $\boldsymbol{x}$ is decided, and after all uncertain parameters A_1, A_2, $\boldsymbol{b}_1$, $\boldsymbol{b}_2$ and $\boldsymbol{c}$ are known, the variable vector $\boldsymbol{y}$ is decided to satisfy the constraints (see Fig. 1). In this sense, $\boldsymbol{x}$ is called the first stage decision variable vector and $\boldsymbol{y}$ is called the second stage decision variable vector. In Problem (12), in order to cope with the uncertainty of parameters, the first stage decision variable vector is selected

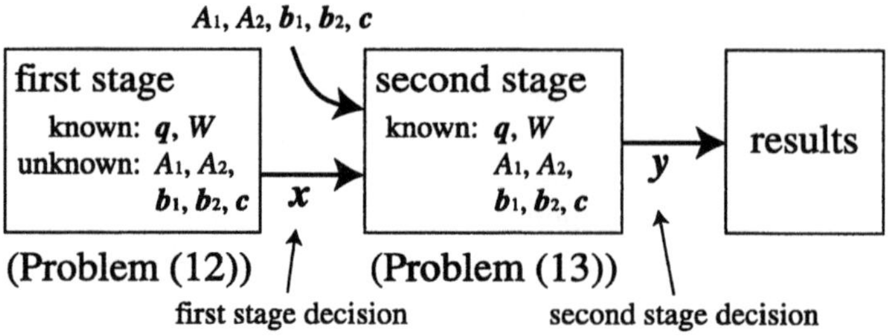

Fig. 1. Two-Stage Recourse Programming Problem

as $\boldsymbol{x} = \bar{\boldsymbol{x}}$ so as to minimize the worst case objective function value. Then, after all uncertain parameters are known, $\boldsymbol{y}$ is decided by solving the following linear programming problem:

$$\begin{array}{rl} \underset{\boldsymbol{y}}{\text{minimize}} & \boldsymbol{q}^{\mathrm{T}}\boldsymbol{y}, \\ \text{subject to} & W_1\boldsymbol{y} = \boldsymbol{b}_1 - A_1\bar{\boldsymbol{x}}, \\ & W_2\boldsymbol{y} \leq \boldsymbol{b}_2 - A_2\bar{\boldsymbol{x}}, \\ & \boldsymbol{y} \geq \boldsymbol{0}. \end{array} \tag{13}$$

In two-stage recourse programming problem (12), we concentrate to make the first stage decision.

Problem (12) corresponds to Problem (3). We can formulate two-stage recourse programming problems corresponding to Problems (2) and (6). Namely, from the optimistic viewpoint, we have

$$\begin{array}{rl} \underset{\boldsymbol{x},A_1,A_2,\boldsymbol{b}_1,\boldsymbol{b}_2,\boldsymbol{c},\boldsymbol{y}}{\text{minimize}} & \boldsymbol{c}^{\mathrm{T}}\boldsymbol{x} + \boldsymbol{q}^{\mathrm{T}}\boldsymbol{y}, \\ \text{subject to} & A_0\boldsymbol{x} = \boldsymbol{b}_0, \\ & A_1\boldsymbol{x} + W_1\boldsymbol{y} = \boldsymbol{b}_1, \\ & A_2\boldsymbol{x} + W_2\boldsymbol{y} \leq \boldsymbol{b}_2, \\ & \boldsymbol{x} \geq \boldsymbol{0},\ \boldsymbol{y} \geq \boldsymbol{0}, \\ & \begin{pmatrix} \boldsymbol{c}^{\mathrm{T}} & 0 \\ A_1 & \boldsymbol{b}_1 \\ A_2 & \boldsymbol{b}_2 \end{pmatrix} \in \Theta, \end{array} \tag{14}$$

and as an intermediate problem between Problems (12) and (14), we have

$$\begin{array}{rl} \underset{\boldsymbol{x},\boldsymbol{c}}{\text{minimize}} \ \underset{A_1,A_2,\boldsymbol{b}_1,\boldsymbol{b}_2}{\text{maximize}} \ \underset{\boldsymbol{y}}{\text{minimize}} & \boldsymbol{c}^{\mathrm{T}}\boldsymbol{x} + \boldsymbol{q}^{\mathrm{T}}\boldsymbol{y}, \\ \text{subject to} & A_0\boldsymbol{x} = \boldsymbol{b}_0, \\ & A_1\boldsymbol{x} + W_1\boldsymbol{y} = \boldsymbol{b}_1, \\ & A_2\boldsymbol{x} + W_2\boldsymbol{y} \leq \boldsymbol{b}_2, \\ & \boldsymbol{x} \geq \boldsymbol{0},\ \boldsymbol{y} \geq \boldsymbol{0}, \\ & \begin{pmatrix} \boldsymbol{c}^{\mathrm{T}} & 0 \\ A_1 & \boldsymbol{b}_1 \\ A_2 & \boldsymbol{b}_2 \end{pmatrix} \in \Theta. \end{array} \tag{15}$$

We obtain the following relationships between previous approaches and two-stage recourse programming approaches.

Theorem 1. *When $\boldsymbol{q}$ is positive and sufficiently large, two-stage recourse programming problem (14) is reduced to Problem (2). Moreover, as $\boldsymbol{q}$ increases, Problems (12) and (15) approach to Problems (3) and (6), respectively, when Problems (3) and (6) have feasible solutions.*

Proof. It is obvious. □

In what follows, we concentrate on Problem (12) since the pessimistic treatment is useful for a safe and robust decision. We mainly discuss the solution algorithm for Problem (12) when Θ is a polytope so that Θ can be expressed as

$$\Theta = \{Q \mid FQ\boldsymbol{k} \leq \boldsymbol{g}\}, \tag{16}$$

where Q is an $(m_1 + m_2 + 1) \times (n + 1)$ variable matrix with zero component at the right-upper corner. and F is a $q \times (m_1 + m_2 + 1)$ constant matrix. $\boldsymbol{k}$ and $\boldsymbol{g}$ are $(n + 1)$- and q-dimensional constant vectors, respectively.

We can prove that Problem (12) is a convex programming problem with respect to $\boldsymbol{x}$.

Theorem 2. *Problem (12) is a convex programming problem with respect to $\boldsymbol{x}$.*

Proof. The dual problem of Problem (13) is obtained as

$$\begin{aligned} \underset{\boldsymbol{u}_1,\boldsymbol{u}_2}{\text{maximize}}\ & (\boldsymbol{b}_1 - A_1\bar{\boldsymbol{x}})^{\mathrm{T}}\boldsymbol{u}_1 - (\boldsymbol{b}_2 - A_2\bar{\boldsymbol{x}})^{\mathrm{T}}\boldsymbol{u}_2, \\ \text{subject to}\ & W_1^{\mathrm{T}}\boldsymbol{u}_1 - W_2^{\mathrm{T}}\boldsymbol{u}_2 \leq \boldsymbol{q}, \\ & \boldsymbol{u}_2 \geq \boldsymbol{0}. \end{aligned} \tag{17}$$

Because of the completeness of W_1 and W_2, we have

$$f(\bar{\boldsymbol{x}} : A_1, A_2, \boldsymbol{b}_1, \boldsymbol{b}_2) = \text{optimal value of (13)} = \text{optimal value of (17)}$$

Given $(A_1, A_2, \boldsymbol{b}_1, \boldsymbol{b}_2)$, let $(\boldsymbol{u}_1^j, \boldsymbol{u}_2^j)$ be an optimal solution of (17) with respect to $\boldsymbol{x}^j$ for $j = 1, 2$. Let $\boldsymbol{x}(\lambda) = \lambda\boldsymbol{x}^1 + (1-\lambda)\boldsymbol{x}^2$, $\lambda \in [0, 1]$. Then, for any feasible solution $(\boldsymbol{u}_1, \boldsymbol{u}_2)$ of (17), we have

$$\begin{aligned} f(\boldsymbol{x}(\lambda) : A_1, A_2, \boldsymbol{b}_1, \boldsymbol{b}_2) &= (\boldsymbol{b}_1 - A_1\boldsymbol{x}(\lambda))\boldsymbol{u}_1 - (\boldsymbol{b}_2 - A_2\boldsymbol{x}(\lambda))\boldsymbol{u}_2 \\ &\leq \lambda(\boldsymbol{b}_1 - A_1\boldsymbol{x}^1)\boldsymbol{u}_1^1 - \lambda(\boldsymbol{b}_2 - A_2\boldsymbol{x}^1)\boldsymbol{u}_2^1 \\ &\quad +(1-\lambda)(\boldsymbol{b}_1 - A_1\boldsymbol{x}^2)\boldsymbol{u}_1^2 - (1-\lambda)(\boldsymbol{b}_2 - A_2\boldsymbol{x}^2)\boldsymbol{u}_2^2 \\ &= \lambda f(\boldsymbol{x}^1 : A_1, A_2, \boldsymbol{b}_1, \boldsymbol{b}_2) \\ &\quad +(1-\lambda) f(\boldsymbol{x}^2 : A_1, A_2, \boldsymbol{b}_1, \boldsymbol{b}_2) \end{aligned}$$

Hence, $f(\boldsymbol{x} : A_1, A_2, \boldsymbol{b}_1, \boldsymbol{b}_2)$ is a convex function with respect to $\boldsymbol{x}$. Let

$$F(\boldsymbol{x}) = \max\left\{ \boldsymbol{c}^{\mathrm{T}}\boldsymbol{x} + f(\boldsymbol{x} : A_1, A_2, \boldsymbol{b}_1, \boldsymbol{b}_2) \;\middle|\; \begin{pmatrix} \boldsymbol{c}^{\mathrm{T}} & 0 \\ A_1 & \boldsymbol{b}_1 \\ A_2 & \boldsymbol{b}_2 \end{pmatrix} \in \Theta \right\}. \tag{18}$$

Since $c^{\mathrm{T}}x + f(x : A_1, A_2, b_1, b_2)$ is a convex function for any (A_1, A_2, b_1, b_2, c), $F(x)$ is a convex function of x. Hence, Problem (12) is nothing but a minimization problem of a convex function $F(x)$ under convex constraints $\{x \mid A_0 x = b_0,\ x \geq 0\}$. □

From Theorem 2, we can solve Problem (12) by a descent method. However, generally $F(x)$ is not differentiable. Thus, as is discussed in nondifferentiable optimization [18], application of a descent method does not always as simple as in differentiable case.

Let $V(\Theta)$ be a set of vertices of Θ. Then we have the following theorem.

Theorem 3. *Problem (12) is equivalent to*

$$\begin{aligned}
\underset{x}{\text{minimize}}\ \underset{A_1,A_2,b_1,b_2,c}{\text{maximize}}\ \underset{y}{\text{minimize}}\ & c^{\mathrm{T}}x + q^{\mathrm{T}}y, \\
\text{subject to}\ & A_0 x = b_0, \\
& A_1 x + W_1 y = b_1, \\
& A_2 x + W_2 y \leq b_2, \\
& x \geq 0,\ y \geq 0, \\
& \begin{pmatrix} c^{\mathrm{T}} & 0 \\ A_1 & b_1 \\ A_2 & b_2 \end{pmatrix} \in V(\Theta).
\end{aligned} \tag{19}$$

Proof. First let us prove $f(x : A_1, A_2, b_1, b_2)$ is a convex function with respect to (A_1, A_2, b_1, b_2). Given $\bar{x}$, let $(\bar{u}_1^j, \bar{u}_2^j)$ be an optimal solution to (17) with respect to $(\bar{A}_1^j, \bar{A}_2^j, \bar{b}_1^j, \bar{b}_2^j)$ for $j = 1, 2$. Let $(\bar{A}_1(\lambda), \bar{A}_2(\lambda), \bar{b}_1(\lambda), \bar{b}_2(\lambda)) = \lambda(\bar{A}_1^1, \bar{A}_2^1, \bar{b}_1^1, \bar{b}_2^1) + (1-\lambda)(\bar{A}_1^2, \bar{A}_2^2, \bar{b}_1^2, \bar{b}_2^2)$, $\lambda \in [0, 1]$. Then, for any feasible solution (u_1, u_2) of (17), we have

$$\begin{aligned}
f(\bar{x} &: \bar{A}_1(\lambda), \bar{A}_2(\lambda), \bar{b}_1(\lambda), \bar{b}_2(\lambda)) \\
&= (\bar{b}_1(\lambda) - \bar{A}_1(\lambda)\bar{x})u_1 - (\bar{b}_2(\lambda) - \bar{A}_2(\lambda)\bar{x})u_2 \\
&\leq \lambda(\bar{b}_1^1 - \bar{A}_1^1\bar{x})u_1^1 - \lambda(\bar{b}_2^1 - \bar{A}_2^1\bar{x})u_2^1 \\
&\quad + (1-\lambda)(\bar{b}_1^2 - \bar{A}_1^2\bar{x})u_1^2 - (1-\lambda)(\bar{b}_2^2 - \bar{A}_2^2\bar{x})u_2^2 \\
&= \lambda f(\bar{x} : \bar{A}_1^1, \bar{A}_2^1, \bar{b}_1^1, \bar{b}_2^1) + (1-\lambda) f(\bar{x} : \bar{A}_1^2, \bar{A}_2^2, \bar{b}_1^2, \bar{b}_2^2)
\end{aligned}$$

Thus, $f(x : A_1, A_2, b_1, b_2)$ is a convex function with respect to (A_1, A_2, b_1, b_2). This implies that the left-hand side problem in (18) is a convex maximization problem. As is known in the literature [19], an optimal solution of a convex maximization problem exists in the set of extreme points of feasible set. $F(x)$ is attained at an extreme point of Θ, i.e., a vertex of Θ. From this fact, the theorem is obvious. □

We have the following corollary.

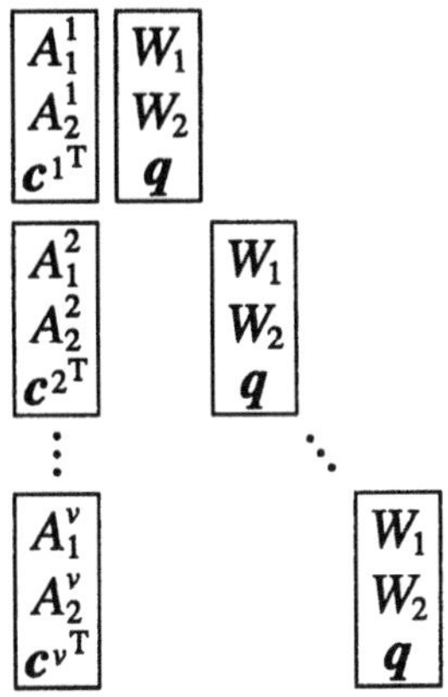

Fig. 2. Block structure of Problem (23)

Corollary 1. *Consider* Δ *such that* $V(\Theta) \subseteq \Delta \subseteq \Theta$. *Problems (12) and (19) and the following problem are equivalent one another:*

$$\begin{array}{llll} \underset{\boldsymbol{x}}{\text{minimize}} & \underset{A_1,A_2,\boldsymbol{b}_1,\boldsymbol{b}_2,\boldsymbol{c}}{\text{maximize}} & \underset{\boldsymbol{y}}{\text{minimize}} & \boldsymbol{c}^{\mathrm{T}}\boldsymbol{x} + \boldsymbol{q}^{\mathrm{T}}\boldsymbol{y}, \\ & & \text{subject to} & A_0\boldsymbol{x} = \boldsymbol{b}_0, \\ & & & A_1\boldsymbol{x} + W_1\boldsymbol{y} = \boldsymbol{b}_1, \\ & & & A_2\boldsymbol{x} + W_2\boldsymbol{y} \leq \boldsymbol{b}_2, \\ & & & \boldsymbol{x} \geq \boldsymbol{0},\ \boldsymbol{y} \geq \boldsymbol{0}, \\ & & & \begin{pmatrix} \boldsymbol{c}^{\mathrm{T}} & 0 \\ A_1 & \boldsymbol{b}_1 \\ A_2 & \boldsymbol{b}_2 \end{pmatrix} \in \Delta. \end{array} \tag{20}$$

Proof. Let $Opt_V(\mathrm{P}(\chi))$ be the optimal value of Problem (χ). From $V(\Theta) \subseteq \Delta \subseteq \Theta$, we have $Opt_V(\mathrm{P}(19)) \leq Opt_V(\mathrm{P}(20)) \leq Opt_V(\mathrm{P}(12))$. From Theorem 3, we obtain $Opt_V(\mathrm{P}(19)) = Opt_V(\mathrm{P}(12))$. Hence, Problems (12), (19) and (20) are equivalent one another. □

From Theorem 3, we know that Θ can be replaced with a finite set $V(\Theta)$. Corollary 1 extends the implication of Theorem 3. Namely, from Corollary 1, not only Θ but also Δ such that $V(\Theta) \subseteq \Delta \subseteq \Theta$ are replaced with $V(\Theta)$. Moreover, when a set Γ of possible realizations of parameters is given as

$$\Gamma = \left\{ \begin{pmatrix} \bar{\boldsymbol{c}}^{j\mathrm{T}} & 0 \\ \bar{A}_1^j & \bar{\boldsymbol{b}}_1^j \\ \bar{A}_2^j & \bar{\boldsymbol{b}}_2^j \end{pmatrix} \,\middle|\, j = 1, 2, \ldots, t \right\},$$

Corollary 1 implies that we may use the convex hull of Γ denoted as $\mathrm{co}(\Gamma)$ or the vertex set, $V(\mathrm{co}(\Gamma))$ instead of Γ.

Let $\hat{\boldsymbol{y}}(A_1, A_2, \boldsymbol{b}_1, \boldsymbol{b}_2)$ be an optimal solution to Problem (13). Then, Problem (12) can be rewritten as

$$
\begin{aligned}
&\underset{\boldsymbol{x},z,\boldsymbol{y}(A_1,A_2,\boldsymbol{b}_1,\boldsymbol{b}_2)}{\text{minimize}} \quad z, \\
&\text{subject to} \\
&\quad A_0\boldsymbol{x} = \boldsymbol{b}_0, \\
&\quad \left\{\begin{array}{l} A_1\boldsymbol{x} + W_1\boldsymbol{y}(A_1, A_2, \boldsymbol{b}_1, \boldsymbol{b}_2) = \boldsymbol{b}_1, \\ A_2\boldsymbol{x} + W_2\boldsymbol{y}(A_1, A_2, \boldsymbol{b}_1, \boldsymbol{b}_2) \leq \boldsymbol{b}_2, \\ \boldsymbol{c}^{\mathrm{T}}\boldsymbol{x} + \boldsymbol{q}^{\mathrm{T}}\boldsymbol{y}(A_1, A_2, \boldsymbol{b}_1, \boldsymbol{b}_2) \leq z, \\ \boldsymbol{y}(A_1, A_2, \boldsymbol{b}_1, \boldsymbol{b}_2) \geq \boldsymbol{0} \end{array}\right. \quad \forall \begin{pmatrix} \boldsymbol{c}^{\mathrm{T}} & 0 \\ A_1 & \boldsymbol{b}_1 \\ A_2 & \boldsymbol{b}_2 \end{pmatrix} \in \Theta, \\
&\quad \boldsymbol{x} \geq \boldsymbol{0}.
\end{aligned} \tag{21}
$$

$V(\Theta)$ has a finite number of elements, thus we denotes

$$
V(\Theta) = \left\{ \begin{pmatrix} \boldsymbol{c}^{j\mathrm{T}} & 0 \\ A_1^j & \boldsymbol{b}_1^j \\ A_2^j & \boldsymbol{b}_2^j \end{pmatrix} \;\middle|\; j = 1, 2, \ldots, v \right\}. \tag{22}
$$

From Theorem 3, Problem (12) is reduced to the following large scale linear programming problem:

$$
\begin{aligned}
\underset{\boldsymbol{x},z,\boldsymbol{y}_1,\ldots,\boldsymbol{y}_v}{\text{minimize}} \quad & z, \\
\text{subject to} \quad & A_0\boldsymbol{x} = \boldsymbol{b}_0, \\
& A_1^j\boldsymbol{x} + W_1\boldsymbol{y}_j = \boldsymbol{b}_1^j, \ j = 1, 2, \ldots, v, \\
& A_2^j\boldsymbol{x} + W_2\boldsymbol{y}_j \leq \boldsymbol{b}_2^j, \ j = 1, 2, \ldots, v, \\
& \boldsymbol{c}^{j\mathrm{T}}\boldsymbol{x} + \boldsymbol{q}^{\mathrm{T}}\boldsymbol{y}_j \leq z, \ j = 1, 2, \ldots, v, \\
& \boldsymbol{x} \geq \boldsymbol{0}, \quad \boldsymbol{y}_j \geq \boldsymbol{0}, \ j = 1, 2, \ldots, v.
\end{aligned} \tag{23}
$$

This linear programming problem has a block structure (see Fig. 2) so that this problem can be solved by a decomposition technique, e.g., Dantzig-Wolfe decomposition, Benders decomposition (see [20]). However, in general, $V(\Theta)$ is not given directly but Θ is. To obtain $V(\Theta)$, we should apply an enumeration method. This is not always computationally efficient. In this paper, we discuss a solution algorithm based on a relaxation procedure.

4 A Solution Algorithm Based on a Relaxation Procedure

Based on a relaxation procedure, a solution algorithm for Problem (12) is given as follows.

[Algorithm based on a relaxation procedure]

Step 1. Set $k = 1$. Select an arbitrary parameter matrix,

$$\begin{pmatrix} \boldsymbol{c}(0)^{\mathrm{T}} & 0 \\ A_1(0) & \boldsymbol{b}_1(0) \\ A_2(0) & \boldsymbol{b}_2(0) \end{pmatrix} \in \Theta.$$

Solve the following linear programming problem and let $(\boldsymbol{x}^0, \boldsymbol{y}^0)$ be the obtained optimal solution and z^0 the optimal value:

$$\begin{aligned} \underset{\boldsymbol{x},\boldsymbol{y}}{\text{minimize}} \quad & \boldsymbol{c}(0)^{\mathrm{T}}\boldsymbol{x} + \boldsymbol{q}^{\mathrm{T}}\boldsymbol{y}, \\ \text{subject to} \quad & A_0\boldsymbol{x} = \boldsymbol{b}_0, \\ & A_1(0)\boldsymbol{x} + W_1\boldsymbol{y} = \boldsymbol{b}_1(0), \\ & A_2(0)\boldsymbol{x} + W_2\boldsymbol{y} \leq \boldsymbol{b}_2(0), \\ & \boldsymbol{x} \geq \boldsymbol{0}, \ \boldsymbol{y} \geq \boldsymbol{0}. \end{aligned} \tag{24}$$

Step 2. Solve the following max-min problem:

$$\begin{aligned} \underset{A_1,A_2,\boldsymbol{b}_1,\boldsymbol{b}_2,\boldsymbol{c}}{\text{maximize}} \ \underset{\boldsymbol{y}}{\text{minimize}} \quad & \boldsymbol{c}^{\mathrm{T}}\boldsymbol{x}^{k-1} + \boldsymbol{q}^{\mathrm{T}}\boldsymbol{y}, \\ \text{subject to} \quad & A_1\boldsymbol{x}^{k-1} + W_1\boldsymbol{y} = \boldsymbol{b}_1, \\ & A_2\boldsymbol{x}^{k-1} + W_2\boldsymbol{y} \leq \boldsymbol{b}_2, \\ & \boldsymbol{y} \geq \boldsymbol{0}, \\ & \begin{pmatrix} \boldsymbol{c}^{\mathrm{T}} & 0 \\ A_1 & \boldsymbol{b}_1 \\ A_2 & \boldsymbol{b}_2 \end{pmatrix} \in \Theta. \end{aligned} \tag{25}$$

Let z' and $(A_1(k), A_2(k), \boldsymbol{b}_1(k), \boldsymbol{b}_2(k), \boldsymbol{c}(k), \boldsymbol{y}')$ be the optimal value and an optimal solution of Problem (25), respectively.

Step 3. If $z' \leq z^{k-1}$ then terminate the algorithm. In this case, the optimal value and an optimal solution are obtained as z^{k-1} and $\boldsymbol{x}^{k-1}$, respectively.

Step 4 Solve the following linear programming problem:

$$\begin{aligned} \underset{\boldsymbol{x},z,\boldsymbol{y}_1,\dots,\boldsymbol{y}_k}{\text{minimize}} \quad & z, \\ \text{subject to} \quad & A_0\boldsymbol{x} = \boldsymbol{b}_0, \\ & A_1(j)\boldsymbol{x} + W_1\boldsymbol{y}_j = \boldsymbol{b}_1(j), \ j = 0, 1, \dots, k, \\ & A_2(j)\boldsymbol{x} + W_2\boldsymbol{y}_j \leq \boldsymbol{b}_2(j), \ j = 0, 1, \dots, k, \\ & \boldsymbol{c}(j)^{\mathrm{T}}\boldsymbol{x} + \boldsymbol{q}^{\mathrm{T}}\boldsymbol{y}_j \leq z, \ j = 0, 1, \dots, k, \\ & \boldsymbol{x} \geq \boldsymbol{0}, \ \ \boldsymbol{y}_j \geq \boldsymbol{0}, \ j = 0, 1, \dots, k. \end{aligned} \tag{26}$$

Let z^k and $(\boldsymbol{x}^k, \hat{\boldsymbol{y}}_1, \hat{\boldsymbol{y}}_2, \dots, \hat{\boldsymbol{y}}_k)$ be the optimal value and an optimal solution of Problem (26), respectively. Update $k = k + 1$ and return to Step 2.

The following two theorems ensure the validity of the termination criterion of the algorithm.

Theorem 4. *Assume that* $(\boldsymbol{x}^{k-1}, z^{k-1})$ *satisfies* $F(\boldsymbol{x}^{k-1}) \leq z^{k-1}$. *Then we have* $z' \leq z^{k-1}$ *at Step 3.*

Proof. It is obvious from $z' = F(\boldsymbol{x}^{k-1})$. □

Theorem 5. *At Step 4, we always have* $z^k \leq F(\boldsymbol{x}^k)$.

Proof. Let $\hat{\boldsymbol{x}}$ be an optimal solution to Problem (12). Since Problem (26) is a relaxed problem of Problem (23) which is equivalent to Problem (12). Thus, we have $z^k \leq F(\hat{\boldsymbol{x}}) \leq F(\boldsymbol{x}^k)$. □

Since a new vertex $(A_1^j, A_2^j, \boldsymbol{b}_1^j, \boldsymbol{b}_2^j, \boldsymbol{c}^j)$ of Θ is always produced at Step 2 of every iteration whenever $z' > z^{k-1}$ and there exist finite number of $(A_1^j, A_2^j, \boldsymbol{b}_1^j, \boldsymbol{b}_2^j, \boldsymbol{c}^j)$'s, this algorithm terminates in finite number of iterations.

In the above solution algorithm, the most difficulty is in solving Problem (25) at Step 2. Using (16) and the dual problem (17) of Problem (13), Problem (25) is reduced to the following bilinear programming problem:

$$\begin{array}{ll} \underset{A_1, A_2, \boldsymbol{b}_1, \boldsymbol{b}_2, \boldsymbol{c}, \boldsymbol{u}_1, \boldsymbol{u}_2}{\text{maximize}} & \boldsymbol{c}^{\mathrm{T}} \boldsymbol{x}^{k-1} + (\boldsymbol{b}_1 - A_1 \boldsymbol{x}^{k-1})^{\mathrm{T}} \boldsymbol{u}_1 - (\boldsymbol{b}_2 - A_2 \boldsymbol{x}^{k-1})^{\mathrm{T}} \boldsymbol{u}_2, \\ \text{subject to} & W_1^{\mathrm{T}} \boldsymbol{u}_1 - W_2^{\mathrm{T}} \boldsymbol{u}_2 \leq \boldsymbol{q}, \\ & \boldsymbol{u}_2 \geq \boldsymbol{0}, \\ & F \begin{pmatrix} \boldsymbol{c}^{\mathrm{T}} & 0 \\ A_1 & \boldsymbol{b}_1 \\ A_2 & \boldsymbol{b}_2 \end{pmatrix} \boldsymbol{k} \leq \boldsymbol{g}. \end{array} \tag{27}$$

Generally, such problem can be solved by global optimization techniques [19], e.g., cutting hyperplane method, outer approximation, inner approximation and so on. Moreover, when a feasible solution $(A_1, A_2, \boldsymbol{b}_1, \boldsymbol{b}_2, \boldsymbol{c}, \boldsymbol{y})$ of Problem (25) such that $\boldsymbol{c}^{\mathrm{T}} \boldsymbol{x}^{k-1} + \boldsymbol{q}^{\mathrm{T}} \boldsymbol{y} > z^{k-1}$, we can go to Step 4. This is because the purpose of Steps 3 and 4 is to check the existence of such a solution.

In the next section, we show some special cases where Problem (25) or Problem (27) can be solved easily.

5 Special Cases

5.1 Finite possible realizations

When all vertices of Θ is known as in (22) or all possible realizations of parameters are known as a finite set, Step 2 is performed in the following way.

Step 2. For $j = 1, \ldots, v$, solve the following linear programming problem:

$$\begin{array}{ll} \underset{\boldsymbol{y}}{\text{minimize}} & \boldsymbol{c}^{j\mathrm{T}} \boldsymbol{x}^{k-1} + \boldsymbol{q}^{\mathrm{T}} \boldsymbol{y}, \\ \text{subject to} & A_1^j \boldsymbol{x}^{k-1} + W_1 \boldsymbol{y} = \boldsymbol{b}_1^j, \\ & A_2^j \boldsymbol{x}^{k-1} + W_2 \boldsymbol{y} \leq \boldsymbol{b}_2^j, \\ & \boldsymbol{y} \geq \boldsymbol{0}. \end{array} \tag{28}$$

Let z_j^k and $\boldsymbol{y}^j$ be the optimal value and an optimal solution to Problem (28). Let $\hat{j} = \arg\max_j z_j^k$. Set $z^k = z_{\hat{j}}^k$ and $(A_1(k), A_2(k), \boldsymbol{b}_1(k), \boldsymbol{b}_2(k), \boldsymbol{c}(k), \boldsymbol{y}') = (A_1^{\hat{j}}, A_2^{\hat{j}}, \boldsymbol{b}_1^{\hat{j}}, \boldsymbol{b}_2^{\hat{j}}, \boldsymbol{c}^{\hat{j}}, \boldsymbol{y}^{\hat{j}})$.

As shown above, in this case, Step 2 can be performed by solving v linear programming problems.

5.2 Special structure of Θ

Consider a case when $m_1 = 0$ (A_1 and $\boldsymbol{b}_1$ are empty) and Θ is given as

$$\Theta = \left\{ \begin{pmatrix} \boldsymbol{c}^{\mathrm{T}} & \boldsymbol{0} \\ A_1 & \boldsymbol{b}_1 \\ A_2 & \boldsymbol{b}_2 \end{pmatrix} \middle| \, \boldsymbol{c}^{\mathrm{L}} \le D^{\mathrm{T}}\boldsymbol{c} \le \boldsymbol{c}^{\mathrm{R}},\ A_i^{\mathrm{L}} \le A_i D \le A_i^{\mathrm{R}}, \right.$$

$$\left. \boldsymbol{b}_i^{\mathrm{L}} \le \boldsymbol{b}_i \le \boldsymbol{b}_i^{\mathrm{R}},\ i = 1, 2 \right\}, \tag{29}$$

where D is a non-singular matrix. When $D = I_n$ (I_n: an identity matrix of dimension n), Θ of (29) coincides with that of (8).

In this case, we have the following theorem.

Theorem 6. *The possible range of $\boldsymbol{c}^{\mathrm{T}}\boldsymbol{x}$ is given as*

$$\left[\boldsymbol{c}^{\mathrm{C}^{\mathrm{T}}} D^{-1}\boldsymbol{x} - \boldsymbol{c}^{\mathrm{W}^{\mathrm{T}}} |D^{-1}\boldsymbol{x}|,\ \boldsymbol{c}^{\mathrm{C}^{\mathrm{T}}} D^{-1}\boldsymbol{x} + \boldsymbol{c}^{\mathrm{W}^{\mathrm{T}}} |D^{-1}\boldsymbol{x}| \right], \tag{30}$$

where $|(r_1, r_2, \ldots, r_n)^{\mathrm{T}}| = (|r_1|, |r_2|, \ldots, |r_n|)^{\mathrm{T}}$. $\boldsymbol{c}^{\mathrm{C}}$ and $\boldsymbol{c}^{\mathrm{W}}$ are defined as

$$\boldsymbol{c}^{\mathrm{C}} = \frac{1}{2}(\boldsymbol{c}^{\mathrm{L}} + \boldsymbol{c}^{\mathrm{R}}), \tag{31}$$

$$\boldsymbol{c}^{\mathrm{W}} = \frac{1}{2}(\boldsymbol{c}^{\mathrm{R}} - \boldsymbol{c}^{\mathrm{L}}). \tag{32}$$

Similarly, the possible range of $A_i\boldsymbol{x}$ ($i = 1, 2$) is given as

$$\{\ \boldsymbol{d} \mid A_i^{\mathrm{C}} D^{-1}\boldsymbol{x} - A_i^{\mathrm{W}} |D^{-1}\boldsymbol{x}| \le \boldsymbol{d} \le A_i^{\mathrm{C}} D^{-1}\boldsymbol{x} + A_i^{\mathrm{W}} |D^{-1}\boldsymbol{x}|\ \}, \tag{33}$$

where A_i^{C} and A_i^{W} ($i = 1, 2$) are defined as

$$A_i^{\mathrm{C}} = \frac{1}{2}(A_i^{\mathrm{L}} + A_i^{\mathrm{R}}), \tag{34}$$

$$A_i^{\mathrm{W}} = \frac{1}{2}(A_i^{\mathrm{R}} - A_i^{\mathrm{L}}). \tag{35}$$

Proof. We only prove (30). (33) can be obtained in the same way. By the definition, the range of $\boldsymbol{c}^{\mathrm{T}}\boldsymbol{x}$ is represented as

$$Range(\boldsymbol{c}^{\mathrm{T}}\boldsymbol{x}) = \{\boldsymbol{c}^{\mathrm{T}}\boldsymbol{x} \mid \boldsymbol{c}^{\mathrm{L}} \le D^{\mathrm{T}}\boldsymbol{c} \le \boldsymbol{c}^{\mathrm{R}}\}.$$

Let $\boldsymbol{d} = D^{\mathrm{T}}\boldsymbol{c}$. Then we have $\boldsymbol{c} = (D^{\mathrm{T}})^{-1}\boldsymbol{d}$. Thus,

$$Range(\boldsymbol{c}^{\mathrm{T}}\boldsymbol{x}) = \{\boldsymbol{d}^{\mathrm{T}}D^{-1}\boldsymbol{x} \mid \boldsymbol{c}^{\mathrm{L}} \leq \boldsymbol{d} \leq \boldsymbol{c}^{\mathrm{R}}\} = \left[\boldsymbol{c}^{\mathrm{L}^{\mathrm{T}}},\ \boldsymbol{c}^{\mathrm{R}^{\mathrm{T}}}\right] D^{-1}\boldsymbol{x}.$$

By the interval arithmetic [21], we have

$$Range(\boldsymbol{c}^{\mathrm{T}}\boldsymbol{x}) = \left[\ \boldsymbol{c}^{\mathrm{C}^{\mathrm{T}}}D^{-1}\boldsymbol{x} - \boldsymbol{c}^{\mathrm{W}^{\mathrm{T}}}|D^{-1}\boldsymbol{x}|,\ \boldsymbol{c}^{\mathrm{C}^{\mathrm{T}}}D^{-1}\boldsymbol{x} + \boldsymbol{c}^{\mathrm{W}^{\mathrm{T}}}|D^{-1}\boldsymbol{x}|\ \right].$$

□

From Theorem 6, Problem (25) is reduced to the following linear programming problem:

$$\begin{array}{ll} \underset{\boldsymbol{y}}{\text{minimize}} & \boldsymbol{c}^{\mathrm{C}^{\mathrm{T}}}D^{-1}\boldsymbol{x}^{k-1} + \boldsymbol{c}^{\mathrm{W}^{\mathrm{T}}}|D^{-1}\boldsymbol{x}^{k-1}| + \boldsymbol{q}^{\mathrm{T}}\boldsymbol{y}, \\ \text{subject to} & A_2^{\mathrm{C}}D^{-1}\boldsymbol{x}^{k-1} + A_2^{\mathrm{W}}|D^{-1}\boldsymbol{x}^{k-1}| + W_2\boldsymbol{y} \leq \boldsymbol{b}_2^{\mathrm{L}}, \\ & \boldsymbol{y} \geq \boldsymbol{0}. \end{array} \tag{36}$$

Moreover, from Theorem 6, Problem (12) is reduced to

$$\begin{array}{ll} \underset{\boldsymbol{x},\boldsymbol{y}}{\text{minimize}} & \boldsymbol{c}^{\mathrm{C}^{\mathrm{T}}}D^{-1}\boldsymbol{x} + \boldsymbol{c}^{\mathrm{W}^{\mathrm{T}}}|D^{-1}\boldsymbol{x}| + \boldsymbol{q}^{\mathrm{T}}\boldsymbol{y}, \\ \text{subject to} & A_0\boldsymbol{x} = \boldsymbol{b}_0, \\ & A_2^{\mathrm{C}}D^{-1}\boldsymbol{x} + A_2^{\mathrm{W}}|D^{-1}\boldsymbol{x}| + W_2\boldsymbol{y} \leq \boldsymbol{b}_2^{\mathrm{L}}, \\ & \boldsymbol{x} \geq \boldsymbol{0},\ \boldsymbol{y} \geq \boldsymbol{0}. \end{array} \tag{37}$$

The next theorem shows that Problem (37) can be reduced to a linear programming problem.

Theorem 7. *Problem (37) is equivalent to the following linear programming problem:*

$$\begin{array}{ll} \underset{\boldsymbol{x},\boldsymbol{y}}{\text{minimize}} & \boldsymbol{c}^{\mathrm{C}^{\mathrm{T}}}D^{-1}\boldsymbol{x} + \boldsymbol{c}^{\mathrm{W}^{\mathrm{T}}}\boldsymbol{w} + \boldsymbol{q}^{\mathrm{T}}\boldsymbol{y}, \\ \text{subject to} & A_0\boldsymbol{x} = \boldsymbol{b}_0, \\ & A_2^{\mathrm{C}}D^{-1}\boldsymbol{x} + A_2^{\mathrm{W}}\boldsymbol{w} + W_2\boldsymbol{y} \leq \boldsymbol{b}_2^{\mathrm{L}}, \\ & D^{-1}\boldsymbol{x} \leq \boldsymbol{w},\ -D^{-1}\boldsymbol{x} \leq \boldsymbol{w}, \\ & \boldsymbol{x} \geq \boldsymbol{0},\ \boldsymbol{y} \geq \boldsymbol{0},\ \boldsymbol{w} \geq \boldsymbol{0}. \end{array} \tag{38}$$

Proof. Let $(\hat{\boldsymbol{x}}, \hat{\boldsymbol{y}})$ be an optimal solution to Problem (37). Define $\hat{\boldsymbol{w}} = |D^{-1}\hat{\boldsymbol{x}}|$. Then $(\hat{\boldsymbol{x}}, \hat{\boldsymbol{y}}, \hat{\boldsymbol{w}})$ is a feasible solution to Problem (38) whose objective function value equals to the optimal value of Problem (37). Hence, we have

$$Opt_V(\mathrm{P}(37)) \geq Opt_V(\mathrm{P}(38)).$$

On the other hand, let $(\check{\boldsymbol{x}}, \check{\boldsymbol{y}}, \check{\boldsymbol{w}})$ be an optimal solution to Problem (38). From constraints of Problem (38), $D^{-1}\check{\boldsymbol{x}} \leq \check{\boldsymbol{w}}$ and $-D^{-1}\check{\boldsymbol{x}} \leq \check{\boldsymbol{w}}$ we have $|D^{-1}\check{\boldsymbol{x}}| \leq \check{\boldsymbol{w}}$. Thus, from $\boldsymbol{c}^{\mathrm{W}} \geq \boldsymbol{0}$ and $A_2^{\mathrm{W}} \geq O$ (O: a zero matrix), we obtain

$$\begin{aligned} \boldsymbol{c}^{\mathrm{W}^{\mathrm{T}}}\check{\boldsymbol{w}} &\geq \boldsymbol{c}^{\mathrm{W}^{\mathrm{T}}}|D^{-1}\check{\boldsymbol{x}}|, \\ A_2^{\mathrm{W}}\check{\boldsymbol{w}} &\geq A_2^{\mathrm{W}}|D^{-1}\check{\boldsymbol{x}}|. \end{aligned}$$

This implies that $(\check{\boldsymbol{x}}, \check{\boldsymbol{y}})$ is a feasible solution to Problem (37) whose objective function value is not greater than the optimal value of Problem (38). Hence, we have

$$Opt_V(\mathrm{P}(37)) \leq Opt_V(\mathrm{P}(38)).$$

Therefore, Problem (37) and Problem (38) are equivalent. □

Theorem 7 implies that Problem (12) is reduced to a linear programming problem (38) when $m_1 = 0$ and Θ is defined by (29).

When $m_1 = 0$ and Θ is defined by (8), i.e., $D = I_n$, because of non-negativity of $\boldsymbol{x}$, we have

$$\boldsymbol{c}^{\mathrm{C}^{\mathrm{T}}} D^{-1}\boldsymbol{x} + \boldsymbol{c}^{\mathrm{W}^{\mathrm{T}}} |D^{-1}\boldsymbol{x}| = \boldsymbol{c}^{\mathrm{R}^{\mathrm{T}}}\boldsymbol{x} \quad \text{and} \quad A_2^{\mathrm{C}} D^{-1}\boldsymbol{x} + A_2^{\mathrm{W}} |D^{-1}\boldsymbol{x}| = A_2^{\mathrm{R}}\boldsymbol{x}.$$

Thus, Problem (37) is reduced to a simpler linear programming problem,

$$\begin{array}{ll} \underset{\boldsymbol{x},\boldsymbol{y}}{\text{minimize}} & \boldsymbol{c}^{\mathrm{R}^{\mathrm{T}}}\boldsymbol{x} + \boldsymbol{q}^{\mathrm{T}}\boldsymbol{y}, \\ \text{subject to} & A_0\boldsymbol{x} = \boldsymbol{b}_0, \\ & A_2^{\mathrm{R}}\boldsymbol{x} + W_2\boldsymbol{y} \leq \boldsymbol{b}_2^{\mathrm{L}}, \\ & \boldsymbol{x} \geq \boldsymbol{0}, \ \boldsymbol{y} \geq \boldsymbol{0}. \end{array} \tag{39}$$

This problem is an extension of Problem (10).

5.3 Special recourse matrix

Let us consider a case when $m_2 = 0$ and W_1 is given as

$$W_1 = (V \ \ -V). \tag{40}$$

In this case, $\boldsymbol{y}$ is uniquely determined by

$$\boldsymbol{y} = \begin{pmatrix} \max(\boldsymbol{0}, V^{-1}(\boldsymbol{b}_1 - A_1\boldsymbol{x}^{k-1})) \\ \max(\boldsymbol{0}, V^{-1}(A_1\boldsymbol{x}^{k-1} - \boldsymbol{b}_1)) \end{pmatrix} \tag{41}$$

where V is a non-singular $m_1 \times m_1$ matrix. max is taken in each component, i.e., $\max((r_1^1, r_2^1, \ldots, r_m^1)^{\mathrm{T}}, (r_1^2, r_2^2, \ldots, r_m^2)^{\mathrm{T}}) = (\max(r_1^1, r_1^2), \max(r_2^1, r_2^2), \ldots, \max(r_m^1, r_m^2))^{\mathrm{T}}$. When $V = I_{m_1}$ (I_{m_1}: an identity matrix of dimension m_1), the recourse matrix (40) is called a simple recourse matrix (see [17]).

Moreover, we assume that Θ is given by (29). Under this assumption, from Theorem 6, Problem (25) is reduced to

$$\begin{array}{lll} \underset{A_1,\boldsymbol{b}_1}{\text{maximize}} & \underset{\boldsymbol{y}}{\text{minimize}} & \boldsymbol{c}^{\mathrm{C}^{\mathrm{T}}} D^{-1}\boldsymbol{x}^{k-1} + \boldsymbol{c}^{\mathrm{W}^{\mathrm{T}}} |D^{-1}\boldsymbol{x}^{k-1}| + \boldsymbol{q}^{\mathrm{T}}\boldsymbol{y}, \\ & \text{subject to} & A_1\boldsymbol{x}^{k-1} + W_1\boldsymbol{y} = \boldsymbol{b}_1, \\ & & \boldsymbol{y} \geq \boldsymbol{0}, \\ & & (A_1 \ \boldsymbol{b}_1) \in \Theta_{(A_1,\boldsymbol{b}_1)}. \end{array} \tag{42}$$

Corresponding to the special structure of W_1, we divide $\boldsymbol{y}$ and $\boldsymbol{q}$ into two parts, i.e., $\boldsymbol{y} = (\boldsymbol{y}^{+\mathrm{T}}, \boldsymbol{y}^{-\mathrm{T}})^{\mathrm{T}}$ and $\boldsymbol{q} = (\boldsymbol{q}^{+\mathrm{T}}, \boldsymbol{q}^{-\mathrm{T}})^{\mathrm{T}}$. From (29), (41) and the uniqueness of $\boldsymbol{y}$, Problem (42) is rewritten as

$$\begin{aligned}
\underset{A_1, \boldsymbol{b}_1, \boldsymbol{y}^+, \boldsymbol{y}^-}{\text{maximize}} \quad & \boldsymbol{c}^{\mathrm{C}^{\mathrm{T}}} D^{-1}\boldsymbol{x}^{k-1} + \boldsymbol{c}^{\mathrm{W}^{\mathrm{T}}} |D^{-1}\boldsymbol{x}^{k-1}| + \boldsymbol{q}^{+\mathrm{T}}\boldsymbol{y}^+ + \boldsymbol{q}^{-\mathrm{T}}\boldsymbol{y}^-, \\
\text{subject to} \quad & A_1\boldsymbol{x}^{k-1} + V\boldsymbol{y}^+ - V\boldsymbol{y}^- = \boldsymbol{b}_1, \\
& \boldsymbol{y}^+ \geq \boldsymbol{0}, \ \boldsymbol{y}^- \geq \boldsymbol{0}, \ \boldsymbol{y}^{+\mathrm{T}}\boldsymbol{y}^- = 0, \\
& A_1^{\mathrm{L}} \leq A_1 D \leq A_1^{\mathrm{R}}, \ \boldsymbol{b}_1^{\mathrm{L}} \leq \boldsymbol{b}_1 \leq \boldsymbol{b}_1^{\mathrm{R}}.
\end{aligned} \tag{43}$$

Problem (43) is a linear programming problem if we discard the complementary condition $\boldsymbol{y}^{+\mathrm{T}}\boldsymbol{y}^- = 0$. Thus, it is conceivable to solve Problem (43) by a branch and bound techniques iteratively introducing a constraint $y_i^+ = 0$ or $y_i^- = 0$, where $\boldsymbol{y}^+ = (y_1^+, y_2^+, \ldots, y_{m_1}^+)^{\mathrm{T}}$ and $\boldsymbol{y}^- = (y_1^-, y_2^-, \ldots, y_{m_1}^-)^{\mathrm{T}}$. However, the relaxed linear programming problem is always unbounded as shown in the following theorem.

Theorem 8. *Let Y^+ and Y^- be arbitrary index sets of constraints $y_i^+ = 0$ and $y_i^- = 0$, respectively, such that $Y^+ \cap Y^- = \emptyset$ and $Y^+ \cup Y^- \subset \{1, 2, \ldots, m_1\}$. Then the following linear programming problem has an unbounded solution or no feasible solution:*

$$\begin{aligned}
\underset{A_1, \boldsymbol{b}_1, \boldsymbol{y}^+, \boldsymbol{y}^-}{\text{maximize}} \quad & \boldsymbol{c}^{\mathrm{C}^{\mathrm{T}}} D^{-1}\boldsymbol{x}^{k-1} + \boldsymbol{c}^{\mathrm{W}^{\mathrm{T}}} |D^{-1}\boldsymbol{x}^{k-1}| + \boldsymbol{q}^{+\mathrm{T}}\boldsymbol{y}^+ + \boldsymbol{q}^{-\mathrm{T}}\boldsymbol{y}^-, \\
\textit{subject to} \quad & A_1\boldsymbol{x}^{k-1} + V\boldsymbol{y}^+ - V\boldsymbol{y}^- = \boldsymbol{b}_1, \\
& \boldsymbol{y}^+ \geq \boldsymbol{0}, \ \boldsymbol{y}^- \geq \boldsymbol{0}, \\
& y_i^+ = 0, \ i \in Y^+, \ \ y_i^- = 0, \ i \in Y^-, \\
& A_1^{\mathrm{L}} \leq A_1 D \leq A_1^{\mathrm{R}}, \ \boldsymbol{b}_1^{\mathrm{L}} \leq \boldsymbol{b}_1 \leq \boldsymbol{b}_1^{\mathrm{R}}.
\end{aligned} \tag{44}$$

Proof. Assume that there exists a feasible solution $(\bar{A}_1, \bar{\boldsymbol{b}}_1, \bar{\boldsymbol{y}}^-, \bar{\boldsymbol{y}}^+)$ of Problem (44). Let Obj be the objective function value of this solution, i.e.,

$$Obj = \boldsymbol{c}^{\mathrm{C}^{\mathrm{T}}} D^{-1}\boldsymbol{x}^{k-1} + \boldsymbol{c}^{\mathrm{W}^{\mathrm{T}}} |D^{-1}\boldsymbol{x}^{k-1}| + \boldsymbol{q}^{+\mathrm{T}}\bar{\boldsymbol{y}}^+ + \boldsymbol{q}^{-\mathrm{T}}\bar{\boldsymbol{y}}^-.$$

Let $\boldsymbol{\delta} = (\delta_1, \delta_2, \ldots, \delta_{m_1})^{\mathrm{T}} \geq \boldsymbol{0}$ be an m_1-dimensional vector such that $\delta_i = 0$, $\forall i \in Y^+ \cup Y^-$ and $\exists i$; $\delta_i > 0$. Let $\lambda > 0$ be an arbitrary scalar. We have $V\bar{\boldsymbol{y}}^+ - V\bar{\boldsymbol{y}}^- = V(\bar{\boldsymbol{y}}^+ + \lambda\boldsymbol{\delta}) - V(\bar{\boldsymbol{y}}^- + \lambda\boldsymbol{\delta})$, $\bar{y}_i^+ + \lambda\delta_i = 0$, $\forall i \in Y^+$ and $\bar{y}_i^- + \lambda\delta_i = 0$, $\forall i \in Y^-$. Thus, $(\bar{A}_1, \bar{\boldsymbol{b}}_1, \bar{\boldsymbol{y}}^- + \lambda\boldsymbol{\delta}, \bar{\boldsymbol{y}}^+ + \lambda\boldsymbol{\delta})$ is also a feasible solution of Problem (44). The objective function value of this new feasible solution is obtained as

$$Obj + \lambda(\boldsymbol{q}^+ + \boldsymbol{q}^-)^{\mathrm{T}}\boldsymbol{\delta}.$$

The second term is positive since $\boldsymbol{q} = (\boldsymbol{q}^{+\mathrm{T}}, \boldsymbol{q}^{-\mathrm{T}})^{\mathrm{T}} > \boldsymbol{0}$ and there exists i such that $\delta_i > 0$. Since λ is arbitrary, thus the new feasible solution can take infinitely large positive objective function value. Thus, Problem (44) has an unbounded solution. □

Now, we introduce the upper bounds of $\boldsymbol{y}^-$ and $\boldsymbol{y}^+$ so that a problem equivalent to Problem (44) has no unbounded solution.

Let V^{-1^+} and V^{-1^-} be matrices defined by

$$V^{-1^+} = \max(V^{-1}, O), \tag{45}$$
$$V^{-1^-} = \min(V^{-1}, O), \tag{46}$$

where O is a zero matrix and max and min are taken by each component, i.e., the (i, j)-components v_{ij}^{-1+} and v_{ij}^{-1-} of V^{-1^+} and V^{-1^-} are defined by $v_{ij}^{-1+} = \max(0, v_{ij}^{-1})$ and $v_{ij}^{-1-} = \min(0, v_{ij}^{-1})$, respectively. Here, v_{ij}^{-1} is the (i, j)-component of V^{-1}. Then we have the following theorem.

Theorem 9. *Define $\varphi^{\mathrm{L}}(\boldsymbol{x}^{k-1})$ and $\varphi^{\mathrm{R}}(\boldsymbol{x}^{k-1})$ as*

$$\varphi^{\mathrm{L}}(\boldsymbol{x}^{k-1}) = A_1^{\mathrm{C}} D^{-1}\boldsymbol{x}^{k-1} - A_1^{\mathrm{W}}|D^{-1}\boldsymbol{x}^{k-1}|, \tag{47}$$
$$\varphi^{\mathrm{R}}(\boldsymbol{x}^{k-1}) = A_1^{\mathrm{C}} D^{-1}\boldsymbol{x}^{k-1} + A_1^{\mathrm{W}}|D^{-1}\boldsymbol{x}^{k-1}|. \tag{48}$$

For any $(A_1, \boldsymbol{b}_1) \in \Theta_{(A_1,\boldsymbol{b}_1)}$, the uniquely determined $\boldsymbol{y}^+$ and $\boldsymbol{y}^-$ by (41) satisfies

$$\boldsymbol{y}^+ \le \max\left(\boldsymbol{0},\ V^{-1^+}\left(\boldsymbol{b}_1^{\mathrm{R}} - \varphi^{\mathrm{L}}(\boldsymbol{x}^{k-1})\right) + V^{-1^-}\left(\boldsymbol{b}_1^{\mathrm{L}} - \varphi^{\mathrm{R}}(\boldsymbol{x}^{k-1})\right)\right), \tag{49}$$

$$\boldsymbol{y}^- \le \max\left(\boldsymbol{0},\ V^{-1^+}\left(\varphi^{\mathrm{R}}(\boldsymbol{x}^{k-1}) - \boldsymbol{b}_1^{\mathrm{L}}\right) + V^{-1^-}\left(\varphi^{\mathrm{L}}(\boldsymbol{x}^{k-1}) - \boldsymbol{b}_1^{\mathrm{R}}\right)\right), \tag{50}$$

$$\begin{aligned}\boldsymbol{y}^+ + \boldsymbol{y}^- \le \max\Big(&V^{-1^+}\left(\boldsymbol{b}_1^{\mathrm{R}} - \varphi^{\mathrm{L}}(\boldsymbol{x}^{k-1})\right) + V^{-1^-}\left(\boldsymbol{b}_1^{\mathrm{L}} - \varphi^{\mathrm{R}}(\boldsymbol{x}^{k-1})\right),\\ &V^{-1^+}\left(\varphi^{\mathrm{R}}(\boldsymbol{x}^{k-1}) - \boldsymbol{b}_1^{\mathrm{L}}\right) + V^{-1^-}\left(\varphi^{\mathrm{L}}(\boldsymbol{x}^{k-1}) - \boldsymbol{b}_1^{\mathrm{R}}\right)\Big),\end{aligned} \tag{51}$$

where max *is taken in each component.*

Proof. (49) and (50) are obvious from (41) and Theorem 6. To prove (51), first we show the non-negativity of the right-hand side value. We have

$$\begin{aligned}&V^{-1^+}\left(\boldsymbol{b}_1^{\mathrm{R}} - \varphi^{\mathrm{L}}(\boldsymbol{x}^{k-1})\right) + V^{-1^-}\left(\boldsymbol{b}_1^{\mathrm{L}} - \varphi^{\mathrm{R}}(\boldsymbol{x}^{k-1})\right)\\ &\quad + V^{-1^+}\left(\varphi^{\mathrm{R}}(\boldsymbol{x}^{k-1}) - \boldsymbol{b}_1^{\mathrm{L}}\right) + V^{-1^-}\left(\varphi^{\mathrm{L}}(\boldsymbol{x}^{k-1}) - \boldsymbol{b}_1^{\mathrm{R}}\right)\\ &= V^{-1^+}\left(\boldsymbol{b}_1^{\mathrm{R}} - \boldsymbol{b}_1^{\mathrm{L}} + \varphi^{\mathrm{R}}(\boldsymbol{x}^{k-1}) - \varphi^{\mathrm{L}}(\boldsymbol{x}^{k-1})\right)\\ &\quad + V^{-1^-}\left(\boldsymbol{b}_1^{\mathrm{L}} - \boldsymbol{b}_1^{\mathrm{R}} + \varphi^{\mathrm{L}}(\boldsymbol{x}^{k-1}) - \varphi^{\mathrm{R}}(\boldsymbol{x}^{k-1})\right)\\ &\ge \boldsymbol{0}.\end{aligned}$$

If the sum of two real numbers is non-negative, then at least one of the two real numbers should be non-negative. Thus, the right-hand side value of (51) is non-negative. This fact and the complementary condition ${\boldsymbol{y}^-}^{\mathrm{T}}\boldsymbol{y}^+ = 0$ implies (51). □

From Theorem 9, we can add any of inequalities (49), (50) and (51) to the constraints of Problem (44). In order to reduce the number of added constraints, we define $v_j^+(\boldsymbol{x}^{k-1})$ and $v_j^-(\boldsymbol{x}^{k-1})$ by the jth component of the right-hand side vectors of (49) and (50), respectively, i.e.,

$$\begin{aligned}
v_j^+(\boldsymbol{x}^{k-1}) &= j\text{th component of} \\
&\qquad \max\left(\boldsymbol{0},\ V^{-1^+}\left(\boldsymbol{b}_1^{\mathrm{R}} - \boldsymbol{\varphi}^{\mathrm{L}}(\boldsymbol{x}^{k-1})\right) + V^{-1^-}\left(\boldsymbol{b}_1^{\mathrm{L}} - \boldsymbol{\varphi}^{\mathrm{R}}(\boldsymbol{x}^{k-1})\right)\right), \\
v_j^-(\boldsymbol{x}^{k-1}) &= j\text{th component of} \\
&\qquad \max\left(\boldsymbol{0},\ V^{-1^+}\left(\boldsymbol{\varphi}^{\mathrm{R}}(\boldsymbol{x}^{k-1}) - \boldsymbol{b}_1^{\mathrm{L}}\right) + V^{-1^-}\left(\boldsymbol{\varphi}^{\mathrm{L}}(\boldsymbol{x}^{k-1}) - \boldsymbol{b}_1^{\mathrm{R}}\right)\right).
\end{aligned}$$

Let $J^+(\boldsymbol{x}^{k-1})$ and $J^-(\boldsymbol{x}^{k-1})$ be index sets defined by

$$J^+(\boldsymbol{x}^{k-1}) = \{j \mid v_j^+(\boldsymbol{x}^{k-1}) < v_j^-(\boldsymbol{x}^{k-1}),\ j \in \{1, 2, \ldots, m_1\}\}, \tag{52}$$
$$J^-(\boldsymbol{x}^{k-1}) = \{j \mid v_j^-(\boldsymbol{x}^{k-1}) < v_j^+(\boldsymbol{x}^{k-1})\ j \in \{1, 2, \ldots, m_1\}\}. \tag{53}$$

Then, Problem (43) is equivalent to

$$\begin{aligned}
\underset{A_1, \boldsymbol{b}_1, \boldsymbol{y}^+, \boldsymbol{y}^-}{\text{maximize}} \quad & {\boldsymbol{c}^{\mathrm{C}}}^{\mathrm{T}} D^{-1}\boldsymbol{x}^{k-1} + {\boldsymbol{c}^{\mathrm{W}}}^{\mathrm{T}}|D^{-1}\boldsymbol{x}^{k-1}| + {\boldsymbol{q}^+}^{\mathrm{T}}\boldsymbol{y}^+ + {\boldsymbol{q}^-}^{\mathrm{T}}\boldsymbol{y}^-, \\
\text{subject to} \quad & A_1\boldsymbol{x}^{k-1} + V\boldsymbol{y}^+ - V\boldsymbol{y}^- = \boldsymbol{b}_1, \\
& \boldsymbol{y}^+ \geq \boldsymbol{0},\ \boldsymbol{y}^- \geq \boldsymbol{0},\ {\boldsymbol{y}^+}^{\mathrm{T}}\boldsymbol{y}^- = 0, \\
& A_1^{\mathrm{L}} \leq A_1 D \leq A_1^{\mathrm{R}},\ \boldsymbol{b}_1^{\mathrm{L}} \leq \boldsymbol{b}_1 \leq \boldsymbol{b}_1^{\mathrm{R}}, \\
& y_j^+ \leq v_j^+(\boldsymbol{x}^{k-1}),\ j \in J^+(\boldsymbol{x}^{k-1}), \\
& y_j^- \leq v_j^-(\boldsymbol{x}^{k-1}),\ j \in J^-(\boldsymbol{x}^{k-1}), \\
& y_j^+ + y_j^- \leq v_j^+(\boldsymbol{x}^{k-1}),\ j \in \{1, 2, \ldots, m_1\} \backslash J^+(\boldsymbol{x}^{k-1}), \\
& y_j^+ + y_j^- \leq v_j^-(\boldsymbol{x}^{k-1}),\ j \in J^+(\boldsymbol{x}^{k-1}),
\end{aligned} \tag{54}$$

Problem (54) is a linear programming problem if we discard the complementary condition, ${\boldsymbol{y}^+}^{\mathrm{T}}\boldsymbol{y}^- = 0$. Thus, it is conceivable to solve Problem (54) by a branch and bound method. The sub-problem which is encountered during the solution process is the following linear programming problem:

$$
\begin{aligned}
\underset{A_1,\boldsymbol{b}_1,\boldsymbol{y}^+,\boldsymbol{y}^-}{\text{maximize}}\quad & \boldsymbol{c}^{\mathrm{C}^{\mathrm{T}}} D^{-1}\boldsymbol{x}^{k-1} + \boldsymbol{c}^{\mathrm{W}^{\mathrm{T}}}|D^{-1}\boldsymbol{x}^{k-1}| + \boldsymbol{q}^{+^{\mathrm{T}}}\boldsymbol{y}^{+} + \boldsymbol{q}^{-^{\mathrm{T}}}\boldsymbol{y}^{-},\\
\text{subject to}\quad & A_1\boldsymbol{x}^{k-1} + V\boldsymbol{y}^+ - V\boldsymbol{y}^- = \boldsymbol{b}_1,\\
& \boldsymbol{y}^+ \geq \boldsymbol{0},\ \boldsymbol{y}^- \geq \boldsymbol{0},\\
& y_i^+ = 0,\ i \in Y^+,\quad y_i^- = 0,\ i \in Y^-,\\
& A_1^{\mathrm{L}} \leq A_1 D \leq A_1^{\mathrm{R}},\ \boldsymbol{b}_1^{\mathrm{L}} \leq \boldsymbol{b}_1 \leq \boldsymbol{b}_1^{\mathrm{R}},\\
& y_j^+ \leq v_j^+(\boldsymbol{x}^{k-1}),\ j \in J^+(\boldsymbol{x}^{k-1}),\\
& y_j^- \leq v_j^-(\boldsymbol{x}^{k-1}),\ j \in J^-(\boldsymbol{x}^{k-1}),\\
& y_j^+ + y_j^- \leq v_j^+(\boldsymbol{x}^{k-1}),\ j \in \{1,2,\ldots,m_1\}\backslash J^+(\boldsymbol{x}^{k-1}),\\
& y_j^+ + y_j^- \leq v_j^-(\boldsymbol{x}^{k-1}),\ j \in J^+(\boldsymbol{x}^{k-1}),
\end{aligned}
\tag{55}
$$

This linear programming problem is obviously bounded. Hence the following solution algorithm for Problem (54) or equivalently, Problem (25) is obtained by applying a branch and bound method.

[A branch and bound algorithm for Problem (54)]

Step 1. Initialize $\tilde{z} = -\infty$ and $\mathcal{P} = \emptyset$. Let $Y^+(P_0) = Y^-(P_0) = \emptyset$.

Step 2. Obtain an optimal solution $(\hat{A}_1, \hat{\boldsymbol{b}}_1, \hat{\boldsymbol{y}}^+, \hat{\boldsymbol{y}}^-)$ and the optimal value $\check{z}$ of Problem (55) with $Y^+ = Y^+(P_0)$ and $Y^- = Y^-(P_0)$. If no feasible solution exists, terminate the algorithm. In this case, there is no feasible solution to Problem (12).

Step 3. Update $\tilde{z} = \max(\tilde{z}, \boldsymbol{c}^{\mathrm{C}^{\mathrm{T}}} D^{-1}\boldsymbol{x}^{k-1} + \boldsymbol{c}^{\mathrm{W}^{\mathrm{T}}}|D^{-1}\boldsymbol{x}^{k-1}| + \boldsymbol{q}^{+^{\mathrm{T}}}\max(\boldsymbol{0}, \hat{\boldsymbol{y}}^+ - \hat{\boldsymbol{y}}^-) + \boldsymbol{q}^{-^{\mathrm{T}}}\max(\boldsymbol{0}, \hat{\boldsymbol{y}}^- - \hat{\boldsymbol{y}}^+))$. If $\tilde{z} > z^{k-1}$, go to Step 9.

Step 4. If $\hat{\boldsymbol{y}}^{+^{\mathrm{T}}}\hat{\boldsymbol{y}}^- = 0$, go to Step 7.

Step 5. If $\check{z} \leq \tilde{z}$, go to Step 7.

Step 6. Select a j such that $\hat{y}_j^+\hat{y}_j^- > 0$. Generate two linear programming problems: Problem (P_1) with $Y^+(P_1) = Y^+(P_0) \cup \{j\}$ and $Y^-(P_1) = Y^-(P_0)$ and Problem (P_2) with $Y^+(P_2) = Y^+(P_0)$ and $Y^-(P_2) = Y^-(P_0) \cup \{j\}$. Update $\mathcal{P} = \mathcal{P} \cup \{(P_1), (P_2)\}$.

Step 7. If $\mathcal{P} = \emptyset$, terminate. The solution $(\hat{A}_1, \hat{\boldsymbol{b}}_1, \hat{\boldsymbol{y}}^+, \hat{\boldsymbol{y}}^-)$ is an optimal solution to Problem (54).

Step 8. Select one linear programming problem (P_0) from $\mathcal{P}$. Update $\mathcal{P} = \mathcal{P} - \{(P_0)\}$. Return to Step 2.

Step 9. Terminate. The solution $(\hat{A}_1, \hat{\boldsymbol{b}}_1, \max(\boldsymbol{0}, \hat{\boldsymbol{y}}^+ - \hat{\boldsymbol{y}}^-), \max(\boldsymbol{0}, \hat{\boldsymbol{y}}^- - \hat{\boldsymbol{y}}^+))$ is an feasible solution of Problem (54) whose objective function value is greater than z^{k-1}.

The second part of Step 3 and Step 9 are introduced in order to skip the remaining optimization procedure of Problem (54) and go to Step 4 of the algorithm of relaxation procedure in Section 4. This is because Step 2 of the algorithm of relaxation procedure in Section 4 is required in order to check the existence of a feasible solution of Problem (25) whose objective function value is greater than z^{k-1}. The solution described in Step 9 is such a solution since Problem (54) is equivalent to Problem (25) under the assumption of this subsection.

The above approach is applicable in some other cases. First, the same discussion is valid for the case when Θ is given by (29) and W_1 and W_2 are given by

$$\begin{pmatrix} W_1 \\ W_2 \end{pmatrix} = \begin{pmatrix} V & -V & \\ & & -I_{m_2} \end{pmatrix}. \tag{56}$$

In this case, by the virtue of Theorem 6, $\boldsymbol{y}_2$ can be determined as

$$\boldsymbol{y}_2 = \max(\boldsymbol{0}, A_2^{\mathrm{C}} D^{-1}\boldsymbol{x} + A_2^{\mathrm{W}} |D^{-1}\boldsymbol{x}| - \boldsymbol{b}_2^{\mathrm{L}}),$$

where we divide $\boldsymbol{y}$ into three parts $(\boldsymbol{y}_1^+, \boldsymbol{y}_1^-, \boldsymbol{y}_2)$ corresponding to the special structure (56) of W. Then $\boldsymbol{y}_2$ in Problem (25) is a constant vector and Problems (24) and (26) can be replaced with the following linear programming problems, respectively:

$$\begin{aligned}
\underset{\boldsymbol{x},\boldsymbol{y}}{\text{minimize}} \quad & {\boldsymbol{c}^{\mathrm{C}}}^{\mathrm{T}} D^{-1}\boldsymbol{x} + {\boldsymbol{c}^{\mathrm{W}}}^{\mathrm{T}} \boldsymbol{w} + {\boldsymbol{q}_1^+}^{\mathrm{T}} \boldsymbol{y}_1^+ + {\boldsymbol{q}_1^-}^{\mathrm{T}} \boldsymbol{y}_1^- + {\boldsymbol{q}_2}^{\mathrm{T}} \boldsymbol{y}_2, \\
\text{subject to} \quad & A_0\boldsymbol{x} = \boldsymbol{b}_0, \\
& A_1(0)\boldsymbol{x} + V\boldsymbol{y}_1^+ - V\boldsymbol{y}_1^- = \boldsymbol{b}_1(0), \\
& A_2^{\mathrm{C}} D^{-1}\boldsymbol{x} + A_2^{\mathrm{W}}\boldsymbol{w} - \boldsymbol{y}_2 \le \boldsymbol{b}_2^{\mathrm{L}}, \\
& D^{-1}\boldsymbol{x} \le \boldsymbol{w}, \ -D^{-1}\boldsymbol{x} \le \boldsymbol{w}, \\
& \boldsymbol{x}, \ \boldsymbol{y}_1^+, \ \boldsymbol{y}_1^-, \ \boldsymbol{y}_2 \ge \boldsymbol{0},
\end{aligned}$$

$$\begin{aligned}
\underset{\boldsymbol{x},z,\boldsymbol{y}_{11},\ldots,\boldsymbol{y}_{1k}}{\text{minimize}} \quad & z, \\
\text{subject to} \quad & A_0\boldsymbol{x} = \boldsymbol{b}_0, \\
& A_1(j)\boldsymbol{x} + V\boldsymbol{y}_{1j}^+ - V\boldsymbol{y}_{1j}^- = \boldsymbol{b}_1(j), \ j = 0, 1, \ldots, k, \\
& A_2^{\mathrm{C}} D^{-1}\boldsymbol{x} + A_2^{\mathrm{W}}\boldsymbol{w} - \boldsymbol{y}_2 \le \boldsymbol{b}_2^{\mathrm{L}}, \\
& {\boldsymbol{c}^{\mathrm{C}}}^{\mathrm{T}} D^{-1}\boldsymbol{x} + {\boldsymbol{c}^{\mathrm{W}}}^{\mathrm{T}} \boldsymbol{w} + {\boldsymbol{q}_1^+}^{\mathrm{T}} \boldsymbol{y}_{1j}^+ + {\boldsymbol{q}_1^-}^{\mathrm{T}} \boldsymbol{y}_{1j}^- + {\boldsymbol{q}_2}^{\mathrm{T}} \boldsymbol{y}_2 \le z, \\
& \qquad\qquad j = 0, 1, \ldots, k, \\
& D^{-1}\boldsymbol{x} \le \boldsymbol{w}, \ -D^{-1}\boldsymbol{x} \le \boldsymbol{w}, \ \boldsymbol{x} \ge \boldsymbol{0}, \\
& \boldsymbol{y}_{1j}^+, \ \boldsymbol{y}_{1j}^- \ge \boldsymbol{0}, \ j = 0, 1, \ldots, k, \ \boldsymbol{y}_2 \ge \boldsymbol{0},
\end{aligned}$$

where $\boldsymbol{q}$ is divided into three parts $(\boldsymbol{q}_1^+, \boldsymbol{q}_1^-, \boldsymbol{q}_2)$ corresponding to the special structure of W.

Moreover, when Θ is not given by (29) but by (16), the same branch and bound method is applicable. However, in this case, we should solve the following $2m_1$ linear programming problems in order to evaluate upper and lower bounds $\eta_j^+(\boldsymbol{x}^{k-1})$ and $\eta_j^-(\boldsymbol{x}^{k-1})$ of each element of $V^{-1}(\boldsymbol{b}_1 - A_1\boldsymbol{x}^{k-1})$:

$$\begin{aligned}
\underset{A_1,\boldsymbol{b}_1,\boldsymbol{c}}{\text{maximize}} \quad & V_{j\cdot}^{-1}(\boldsymbol{b}_1 - A_1\boldsymbol{x}^{k-1}), \\
\text{subject to} \quad & F\begin{pmatrix} \boldsymbol{c}^{\mathrm{T}} & 0 \\ A_1 & \boldsymbol{b}_1 \end{pmatrix}\boldsymbol{k} \le \boldsymbol{g},
\end{aligned} \qquad j = 1, 2, \ldots, m_1, \tag{57}$$

$$\begin{aligned} &\underset{A_1,\boldsymbol{b}_1,\boldsymbol{c}}{\text{minimize}} \ V_{j\cdot}^{-1}(\boldsymbol{b}_1 - A_1\boldsymbol{x}^{k-1}), \\ &\text{subject to } F\begin{pmatrix} \boldsymbol{c}^{\mathrm{T}} & 0 \\ A_1 & \boldsymbol{b}_1 \end{pmatrix}\boldsymbol{k} \le \boldsymbol{g}, \end{aligned} \qquad j = 1, 2, \ldots, m_1. \tag{58}$$

Then $\upsilon_j^+(\boldsymbol{x}^{k-1})$ and $\upsilon_j^-(\boldsymbol{x}^{k-1})$ are defined by

$$\upsilon_j^+(\boldsymbol{x}^{k-1}) = \max(0, \eta_j^+(\boldsymbol{x}^{k-1})), \quad \upsilon_j^-(\boldsymbol{x}^{k-1}) = \max(0, -\eta_j^-(\boldsymbol{x}^{k-1})). \tag{59}$$

In this case, the problem (25) is reduced to

$$\begin{aligned} &\underset{A_1,\boldsymbol{b}_1,\boldsymbol{y}^+,\boldsymbol{y}^-}{\text{maximize}} && \boldsymbol{c}^{\mathrm{T}}\boldsymbol{x}^{k-1} + \boldsymbol{q}^{+\mathrm{T}}\boldsymbol{y}^+ + \boldsymbol{q}^{-\mathrm{T}}\boldsymbol{y}^-, \\ &\text{subject to} && A_1\boldsymbol{x}^{k-1} + V\boldsymbol{y}^+ - V\boldsymbol{y}^- = \boldsymbol{b}_1, \\ &&& \boldsymbol{y}^+ \ge \boldsymbol{0},\ \boldsymbol{y}^- \ge \boldsymbol{0},\ \boldsymbol{y}^{+\mathrm{T}}\boldsymbol{y}^- = 0, \\ &&& F\begin{pmatrix} \boldsymbol{c}^{\mathrm{T}} & 0 \\ A_1 & \boldsymbol{b}_1 \end{pmatrix}\boldsymbol{k} \le \boldsymbol{g}. \end{aligned} \tag{60}$$

Using index sets $J^+(\boldsymbol{x}^{k-1})$ and $J^-(\boldsymbol{x}^{k-1})$ defined by (52) and (53), the linear programming problem corresponding to Problem (55) is as follows:

$$\begin{aligned} &\underset{A_1,\boldsymbol{b}_1,\boldsymbol{y}^+,\boldsymbol{y}^-}{\text{maximize}} && \boldsymbol{c}^{\mathrm{T}}\boldsymbol{x}^{k-1} + \boldsymbol{q}^{+\mathrm{T}}\boldsymbol{y}^+ + \boldsymbol{q}^{-\mathrm{T}}\boldsymbol{y}^-, \\ &\text{subject to} && A_1\boldsymbol{x}^{k-1} + V\boldsymbol{y}^+ - V\boldsymbol{y}^- = \boldsymbol{b}_1, \\ &&& \boldsymbol{y}^+ \ge \boldsymbol{0},\ \boldsymbol{y}^- \ge \boldsymbol{0}, \\ &&& y_i^+ = 0,\ i \in Y^+,\ y_i^- = 0,\ i \in Y^-, \\ &&& F\begin{pmatrix} \boldsymbol{c}^{\mathrm{T}} & 0 \\ A_1 & \boldsymbol{b}_1 \end{pmatrix}\boldsymbol{k} \le \boldsymbol{g}, \\ &&& y_j^+ \le \upsilon_j^+(\boldsymbol{x}^{k-1}),\ j \in J^+(\boldsymbol{x}^{k-1}), \\ &&& y_j^- \le \upsilon_j^-(\boldsymbol{x}^{k-1}),\ j \in J^-(\boldsymbol{x}^{k-1}), \\ &&& y_j^+ + y_j^- \le \upsilon_j^+(\boldsymbol{x}^{k-1}),\ j \in \{1, 2, \ldots, m_1\} \backslash J^+(\boldsymbol{x}^{k-1}), \\ &&& y_j^+ + y_j^- \le \upsilon_j^-(\boldsymbol{x}^{k-1}),\ j \in J^+(\boldsymbol{x}^{k-1}). \end{aligned} \tag{61}$$

Thus, Problem (60) can be solved by the above branch and bound algorithm replacing Problems (54) and (55) with Problem (60) and (61), respectively.

6 A Numerical Example

In order to show how the solution algorithm proceeds, let us consider the following recourse problem:

$$\begin{aligned} &\underset{x_1,x_2,x_3,y_1^+,y_2^+,y_1^-,y_2^-}{\text{maximize}} && 4x_1 + 5x_2 + 6y_1^+ + 20y_2^+ + 8y_1^- + 2y_2^-, \\ &\text{subject to} && x_1 + x_2 + x_3 = 20, \\ &&& a_{11}x_1 + a_{12}x_2 + y_1^+ + y_2^+ - y_1^- - y_2^- = 50, \\ &&& a_{21}x_1 + a_{22}x_2 + y_2^+ - y_2^- = 50, \\ &&& x_1, x_2, x_3, y_1^+, y_2^+, y_1^-, y_2^- \ge 0, \end{aligned} \tag{62}$$

where the possible range of $A = (a_{ij})$ $(i = 1, 2,\ j = 1, 2)$ is given as

$$\Theta = \left\{ A = \begin{pmatrix} a_{11} & a_{12} \\ a_{21} & a_{22} \end{pmatrix} \;\middle|\; \begin{pmatrix} -2 & 2 \\ 0 & 2 \end{pmatrix} \leq A \begin{pmatrix} 1 & 0 \\ -1 & 1 \end{pmatrix} \leq \begin{pmatrix} 0 & 4 \\ 2 & 2 \end{pmatrix} \right\}. \tag{63}$$

This is a problem of the case described in Subsection 5.3 with

$$V = \begin{pmatrix} 1 & 1 \\ 0 & 1 \end{pmatrix}, \quad D = \begin{pmatrix} 1 & 0 \\ -1 & 1 \end{pmatrix}, \quad A^{\mathrm{C}} = \begin{pmatrix} -1 & 3 \\ 1 & 2 \end{pmatrix}, \quad A^{\mathrm{W}} = \begin{pmatrix} 2 & 2 \\ 2 & 0 \end{pmatrix}.$$

We obtain

$$V^{-1} = \begin{pmatrix} 1 & -1 \\ 0 & 1 \end{pmatrix}, \quad D^{-1} = \begin{pmatrix} 1 & 0 \\ 1 & 1 \end{pmatrix}, \quad V^{-1^{+}} = \begin{pmatrix} 1 & 0 \\ 0 & 1 \end{pmatrix}, \quad V^{-1^{-}} = \begin{pmatrix} 0 & -1 \\ 0 & 0 \end{pmatrix}.$$

Applying the proposed algorithm, we obtain an optimal solution as

$$\begin{array}{l} x_1 = 19.2857,\ x_2 = 0.7143,\ x_3 = 0, \\ y_1^+ = 0,\ y_2^+ = 10,\ y_1^- = 40,\ y_2^- = 0, \end{array} \quad A = \begin{pmatrix} 4 & 4 \\ 2 & 2 \end{pmatrix}.$$

The solution process is shown in Table 1. In the solution process, we have $\boldsymbol{b}_1(j) = (50, 50)^{\mathrm{T}}$ and $\boldsymbol{c}(j) = (4, 5)^{\mathrm{T}}$ for any j.

7 Concluding Remarks

In this paper, we discuss two-stage recourse problems under non-graded possibilistic uncertainty. The problem is formulated from pessimistic viewpoint introducing min-max criterion. We assume that the set of possible realizations of uncertain parameters is given by a polytope. It is shown that the formulated problem is a convex programming problem with respect to the first stage variable vector. Moreover, we showed that the problem can be reduced to a large scale linear programming problem when all vertices of the polytope which represents the possible range of parameters are given. A solution algorithm based on a relaxation procedure is proposed. In the solution process, we should solve max-min problems or bilinear programming problems. Some special cases are discussed. It is shown that the max-min problems are reduced to simpler problems in those special cases.

In this paper, we concentrate a solution algorithm based on a relaxation procedure. The solution procedures for the max-min problems are discussed only in some special cases. The solution procedure in a general case is a topic for a future research. On the other hand, it is also conceivable to apply non-differentiable optimization techniques [18] to solve the two-stage recourse problems because as is shown in this paper, the reduced problem is a minimization problem of non-differentiable convex function under linear constraints. This would also be one of future research topics. Furthermore, we can extend the proposed approach from non-graded possibilistic uncertainty to graded one.

Table 1. The solution process

step	step (branch and bound method)	relaxation procedure
1		$k=1,\ A_1(0)=\begin{pmatrix}4&4\\4&2\end{pmatrix}\in\Theta$. Solve Problem (24): $\boldsymbol{x}^0=(12.5,0)^{\mathrm{T}}$.
2	step	branch and bound method
	0	$\varphi^{\mathrm{L}}(\boldsymbol{x}^0)=(-25,12.5)^{\mathrm{T}}$ and $\varphi^{\mathrm{R}}(\boldsymbol{x}^0)=(75,62.5)^{\mathrm{T}}$. Hence, $v_1^+(\boldsymbol{x}^0)=87.5$, $v_2^+(\boldsymbol{x}^0)=37.5$, $v_1^-(\boldsymbol{x}^0)=25$ and $v_2^-(\boldsymbol{x}^0)=12.5$.
	1	$\tilde{z}=-\infty$, $\mathcal{P}-\emptyset$ and $Y^+(P_0)=Y^-(P_0)=\emptyset$.
	2	Solve Problem (55): $a_{11}=0$, $a_{12}=3$, $a_{21}=2$, $a_{22}=2$, $y_1^+=50$, $y_2^+=31.25$, $y_1^-=25$ and $y_2^-=6.25$.
	3	$\tilde{z}=700>50=z^0$.
	9	$A_1(1)=\begin{pmatrix}0&3\\2&2\end{pmatrix}$.
4		Solve Problem (26): $z^1=351.765$ and $\boldsymbol{x}^1=(4.706,15.294)^{\mathrm{T}}$. $k=2$.
2	step	branch and bound method
	0	$\varphi^{\mathrm{L}}(\boldsymbol{x}^1)=(5.882,35.294)^{\mathrm{T}}$ and $\varphi^{\mathrm{R}}(\boldsymbol{x}^1)=(104.706,54.118)^{\mathrm{T}}$. Hence, $v_1^+(\boldsymbol{x}^1)=48.234$, $v_2^+(\boldsymbol{x}^1)=14.7059$, $v_1^-(\boldsymbol{x}^1)=69.412$ and $v_2^-(\boldsymbol{x}^1)=4.118$.
	1	$\tilde{z}=-\infty$, $\mathcal{P}-\emptyset$ and $Y^+(P_0)=Y^-(P_0)=\emptyset$.
	2	Solve Problem (55): $a_{11}=4$, $a_{12}=4$, $a_{21}=2$, $a_{22}=2$, $y_1^+=14.706$, $y_2^+=12.353$, $y_1^-=54.706$ and $y_2^-=2.353$.
	3	$\tilde{z}=615.294>351.765=z^1$.
	9	$A_1(2)=\begin{pmatrix}4&4\\2&2\end{pmatrix}$.
4		Solve Problem (26): $z^2=600$ and $\boldsymbol{x}^2=(20,0)^{\mathrm{T}}$. $k=3$.
2	step	branch and bound method
	0	$\varphi^{\mathrm{L}}(\boldsymbol{x}^2)=(-40,20)^{\mathrm{T}}$ and $\varphi^{\mathrm{R}}(\boldsymbol{x}^2)=(120,100)^{\mathrm{T}}$. Hence, $v_1^+(\boldsymbol{x}^2)=140$, $v_2^+(\boldsymbol{x}^2)=30$, $v_1^-(\boldsymbol{x}^2)=100$ and $v_2^-(\boldsymbol{x}^2)=50$.
	1	$\tilde{z}=-\infty$, $\mathcal{P}-\emptyset$ and $Y^+(P_0)=Y^-(P_0)=\emptyset$.
	2	Solve Problem (55): $a_{11}=4$, $a_{12}=4$, $a_{21}=2$, $a_{22}=2$, $y_1^+=50$, $y_2^+=30$, $y_1^-=90$ and $y_2^-=20$.
	3-5	$\tilde{z}=600\le 600=z^2$. $\hat{\boldsymbol{y}}^{+\mathrm{T}}\hat{\boldsymbol{y}}^->0$. $\check{z}=2100>600=\tilde{z}$.
	6-8	(P_1) with $Y^+(P_1)=\{1\}$ and $Y^-(P_1)=\emptyset$ and (P_2) with $Y^+(P_2)=\emptyset$ and $Y^-(P_2)=\{1\}$. $\mathcal{P}=\{(P_1),(P_2)\}$. $\mathcal{P}\neq\emptyset$. Select (P_2).
	2	Solve Problem (55): $a_{11}=0$, $a_{12}=2$, $a_{21}=2$, $a_{22}=2$, $y_1^+=40$, $y_2^+=30$, $y_1^-=0$ and $y_2^-=20$.
	3-5	$\tilde{z}=520\le 600=z^2$. $\hat{\boldsymbol{y}}^{+\mathrm{T}}\hat{\boldsymbol{y}}^->0$. $\check{z}=1320>600=\tilde{z}$.
	6-8	(P_3) with $Y^+(P_3)=\{1,2\}$ and $Y^-(P_3)=\emptyset$ and (P_4) with $Y^+(P_4)=\{2\}$ and $Y^-(P_4)=\{1\}$. $\mathcal{P}=\{(P_1),(P_3),(P_4)\}$. $\mathcal{P}\neq\emptyset$. Select (P_4).
	2	Solve Problem (55): $a_{11}=0$, $a_{12}=2$, $a_{21}=4$, $a_{22}=2$, $y_1^+=80$, $y_2^+=0$, $y_1^-=0$ and $y_2^-=30$.
	3	$\tilde{z}=620>600=z^2$.
	9	$A_1(3)=\begin{pmatrix}0&2\\4&2\end{pmatrix}$.
4		Solve Problem (26): $z^3=600.714$ and $\boldsymbol{x}^3=(19.286,0.714)^{\mathrm{T}}$. $k=4$.
		Continue. We find that $\boldsymbol{x}^3$ is optimal.

References

1. Inuiguchi, M., Sakawa, M., Kume, Y. (1994) The usefulness of possibilistic programming in production planning problems. International Journal of Pro-

duction Economics **33**, 45–52
2. Itoh, T., Ishii, H. (1997) Fuzzy sharing problem by possibility measure. European Journal of Operational Research **102**(3), 648–656
3. Han, S., Ishii, H., Fujii, S. (1994) One machine scheduling problem with fuzzy duedates. European Journal of Operational Research **79**(1), 1–12
4. Ishii, H., Tada, M. (1995) Single machine scheduling problem with fuzzy precedence relation. European Journal Of Operational Research **87**(2), 284–288
5. Tanaka, H., Guo, P. (1999) Possibilistic Data Analysis for Operations Research. Physica-Verlag, Heidelberg
6. Inuiguchi, M., Ramik, J. (2000) Possibilistic linear programming: A brief review of fuzzy mathematical programming and a comparison with stochastic programming in portfolio selection problem. Fuzzy Sets and Systems **111**(1), 3–28
7. Inuiguchi, M., Tanino, T. (2000) Portfolio selection under independent possibilistic information. Fuzzy Sets and Systems (to appear)
8. Yazenin, A. V. (1987) Fuzzy and stochastic programming. Fuzzy Sets and Systems **22** 171–180
9. Słowiński, R., Teghem, J. (1988) Fuzzy versus stochastic approaches to multicriteria linear programming under uncertainty. Naval Research Logistics **35** 673–695
10. Inuiguchi, M. (1992) Stochastic programming problems versus fuzzy mathematical programming problems. Japanese Journal of Fuzzy Theory and Systems **4**(1) 97–109
11. Inuiguchi, M., Sakawa, M. (1995) A possibilistic linear program is equivalent to a stochastic linear program in a special case. Fuzzy Sets and Systems **76** 309–318
12. Itoh, T., Ishii, H. (1997) Fuzzy two-stage problem by possibility measure. Mathematica Japonica **46** 279–288
13. Dubois D. (1987) Linear programming with fuzzy data, in: Bezdek, J. C. (Ed.), Analysis of Fuzzy Information, Vol.III: Applications in Engineering and Science, CRC Press, Boca Raton, FL, 241–263.
14. Inuiguchi, M., Ichihashi, H., Tanaka, H. (1990) Fuzzy programming: a survey of recent developments. in: Słowiński, R., Teghem, J. (Eds.) Stochastic versus Fuzzy Approaches to Multiobjective Programming under Uncertainty, Kluwer Academic Publishers, Dordrecht, 45–68
15. Inuiguchi, M., Ichihashi, H., Kume, Y. (1993) Modality constrained programming problems: A unified approach to fuzzy mathematical programming problems in the setting of possibility theory. Information Sciences **67** 93–126
16. Stancu-Minasian, I. M. (1984) Stochastic Programming with Multiple Objective Functions, D. Reidel Publishing Company, Dordrecht
17. Birge, J. R., Louveaux, F. (1997) Introduction to Stochastic Programming, Springer-Verlag, New York
18. Shor, N. Z. (1985) Minimization Methods for Non-Differentiable Functions, Springer-Verlag, Berlin
19. Horst, R., Tuy, H. (1995) Global Optimization: Deterministic Approaches, Third, Revised and Enlarged Edition, Springer-Verlag, Berlin
20. Lasdon, L. S. (1970) Optimization Theory for Large Systems, The Macmillan Company, New York
21. Moore, R. E. (1979) Methods and Applications of Interval Analysis, SIAM, Philadelphia

Fuzzy Portfolio Model for Decision Making in Investment

Junzo Watada

School of Industrial Engineering
Osaka Institute of Technology
5-16-1 Omiya, Asahi, Osaka 535-8585 JAPAN

Abstract. Financial engineering is one of the most important fields, today. Soft-computing methodologies are widely employed in financial engineering. Many problems of decision-making in investment have mainly been studied from optimizing points of view. As the investment is much influenced by the disturbance of a social and economical circumstances, optimization approach is not always the best. It is because problems used to be ill-structured under such influences. Therefore, a satisfaction approach is much better than an optimization one. In this discussion, we employ the aspiration level on the base of past experiences and knowledge possessed by a decision maker to treat a problem. That is, the aspiration level of the decision maker should be considered to solve a problem from the perspective of satisfaction strategy. It is more natural that the vague aspiration level of a decision maker is denoted as a fuzzy number.

In this chapter, the new methodologies in dealing with portfolio selection are studied. We explain the fuzzy approach to the decision making in portfolio selection problems after illustrating Bellman-Zadeh's decision-making approach under uncertain environments and the fuzzy mathematical programming formulated by H. -J. Zimmermann. Before explaining the detail of the method of fuzzy portfolio selections, we survey the various soft-computing approaches to decision-makings in financial egnineering.

First, the recent methodologies related to portfolio selection are explained, which including neural networks, genetic algorithm chaotic analysis and fuzzy approach. Then fuzzy programming method is discussed. The fuzzy portfolio method is formulated and illustrated using an example.[1]

1 Introduction

Financial engineering is one of the most important fields, today. Soft-computing methodologies are widely employed in financial engineering [41,17,43]. Many problems of decision-making in investment have mainly been studied from optimizing points of view. As the investment is much influenced by the disturbance of a social and economical circumstances, optimization approach

[1] This research was supported in part by Grant-in Aid for Scientific Research(C-2);Grant No.08680471 and Grant No.11680459 of Ministry of Education of Science, Sports and Culture.

is not always the best. It is because problems used to be ill-structured under such influences. Therefore, a satisfaction approach is much better than an optimization one. In this discussion, we employ the aspiration level on the base of past experiences and knowledge possessed by a decision maker to treat a problem. That is, the aspiration level of the decision maker should be considered to solve a problem from the perspective of satisfaction strategy. It is more natural that the vague aspiration level of a decision maker is denoted as a fuzzy number.

In this chapter, the new methodologies in dealing with portfolio selection are studied. We explain the fuzzy approach to the decision making in portfolio selection problems after illustrating Bellman-Zadeh's decision-making approach under uncertain environments [2] and the fuzzy mathematical programming formulated by H. -J. Zimmermann [53]. Before explaining the detail of the method of fuzzy portfolio selections, we survey the various soft-computing approaches to decision-makings in financial egnineering.

Fuzzy Approach

Portfolio selection has been originally proposed by H. M. Markowitz. The Markowitz' approach to the portfolio selection has several difficulties to solve it. For instance, 1) it is difficult to distinguish the portfolios on its efficient frontier, and 2) an aspiration level and utility given by a decision-maker are not taken into consideration in the portfolio selection.

Fuzzy portfolio selection is recently proposed to overcome these difficulties. The fuzzy portfolio selection enables us to obtain a solution which realizes the best within a vague aspiration level and a fuzzy goal given as fuzzy numbers. The vague aspiration, the fuzzy goal and the fuzzy numbers are obtained from the expertise of decision-makers'.

Generally speaking, the formulation of a conventional mathematical programming problem is defined using crisp values for coefficients and constant values of its objective function and constraints. In problems encountered in a real world, the complexity and scale of the objective function and constraint conditions are too large and it is hard to say that the models employed for a problem are not sophisticated saficiently for the problems.

Recently, an interval programming is proposed by G. R. Bitran [3] to deal with uncertainty and vagueness. The coefficients and constants included in a mathematical programming model are defined using a closed interval in order to treat vagueness of the problem. Since then, various methods are studied and invented to solve this interval programming.

On the other hand, the concept of a fuzzy set proposed by L.A.Zadeh [50] in 1965 is employed by H. Tanaka et al. [40] to define a fuzzy linear programming. Theoretical researches in this area has been much fertile and productive, and furthermore these results are recently used in applied researches[13]. Fuzzy sets are employed in a fuzzy mathematical programming to define the objective and constraints [2] and to formulate the fuzzy mathematical programming so that a vague aspiration level of a decision maker can be reflected on its solution [52,53]. In this formulation, the fuzzy mathematical programming is defined using real numbers for coefficients of the objective and constraint conditions. Since then under the consideration that the fuzzy aspiration level of the decision-maker should not only be considered, but also the coefficients of the objective and the constraint conditions themselves should be vague, the fuzzy mathematical programming is formulated to define coefficients as a fuzzy number [34]. Another model of the fuzzy mathematical programming is formulated to define only the coefficients of the objective and constraints using a fuzzy number without considering an aspiration level which a decision maker has. [40,41].

Portfolio selection has been originally proposed by H. M. Markowitz. The Markowitz's approach to the portfolio selection has several difficulties in solving it. It is difficult to distinguish portfolios on its efficient frontier, and an aspiration level and utility given by decision-makers are not taken into consideration in the portfolio selection. Fuzzy portfolio selection is proposed to overcome these difficulties. The fuzzy objective and fuzzy constraints are defined using a logistic membership function.

The fuzzy portfolio selection enables us to obtain a solution which realizes the best within a vague aspiration level and a fuzzy goal given as a fuzzy number, which are obtained from the expertise of decision makers.

Genetic Approaches

As described below, some portfolio selection problem results in an integer programming. A genetic algorithm is effective and effiient to solve the integer programming. The genetic algorithm is one of stochastic search algorithms,

A fuzzy 0-1 integer programming is extended to such fuzzy integer programming as the number of selected variables is decided within some interval. The coding method of a genetic algorithm is improved to solve a fuzzy 0-1 integer programming [28]. In the research to show the effectiveness of the genetic algorithm with improved coding, J. Watada and Y. Mizunuma deal with a simple fuzzy portfolio selection problem with the total 15 bonds. The data treated consists of 15 bonds of Tokyo Stocks 1st Section. The monthly expected return rates for 5 years from January, 1981 are analyzed concerning these bonds. The monthly returns of each bond are calculated based on the first dealing of each month using Nippon Keizai News.

Neural Network Approach

An efficient method for solving a portfolio selection problem and application of the method are proposed for strategic investment into a financial market. A Boltzmann machine is employed to solve the portfolio selection problem efficiently. The Boltzmann machine is an interconnected neural network that is proposed by G. E. Hinton [1]. The Boltzmann machine is a model that improves a Hopfield network [10] using probability rule to update its state of the neuron and the energy function. In the conventional method to solve portfolio selections, the investing rate to each stock is decided to realize the minimum risk under the constraints that the goal rate of an expected return given by a decision maker should be guaranteed.

It is the huge number of stocks, bonds and securities which we should take into the consideration of international investment, we used to make a decision hierarchically in investment using various indices. The index is a parameter to express tendency of stocks in a market of each country. As an application of this method, we propose a strategic approach [49] to investment over different international financial markets. First, a decision maker decides how much should be invested out of the total amount of funds to each of index. After that, a decision maker decides portfolio selection about stocks which compose each index. Furthermore, it is desirable to limit the invested number of stocks. The procedure can be implimented in a multi-stage model in solving limited number of stocks using the Boltzmann machine.

Two-layered Boltzmann Machine It is difficult that a conventional portfolio selection problem, which is based on a mean-variance model, is solved in terms of a mathematical programming method. One of the reasons is because a mathematical programming model becomes a large-scale one since almost all variance-covariances of return rates may not be zero.

An efficient model is proposed to solve the portfolio selection problem, which employs both Hopfield and Boltzmann machines to formulate a Two-Layered Boltzman Machine. It enables us to solve the portfolio selection problem as its highly approximate solution.

J. Watada et al. [47] propose an efficient method solving a portfolio selection problem by transforming its objective function into the energy function since the Hopfield and Boltzmann Machines converge at the minimum point of the energy function. Especially, we formulate a two-layered neural network consisted of both Hopfield and Boltzmann machines in order to effectively and efficiently select a limited number of stocks out of a huge stock market with optimal investment ratio. The Hopfield machine is employed as the upper layer to select the limited number of stocks and the Boltzmann machine is employed as the lower layer to decide the optimal investment ratio over the limited number of stocks selected by the upper layer. The two-layered Boltzmann machine, whose two layeres are inter-connected between the upper and lower machines, can realize an effective method to solve the optimal portfolio selection.

Furthermore, it is desirable to limit the huge number of stocks into several decades for investment. So we show this procedure can be employed in selecting limited number of stocks using a two-layered model. First, we execute the Hopfield layer until its convergence. After this converging, the state of units indicates selected stocks. And using selected units, the subordinate Boltzmann layer shows the investing ratio of each stock. The above algorithms are re-iterated until the number of stocks is obtained, which is previously determined by a decision maker.

It is emphasized that the model proposed here enables us to solve portfolio selection problem effectively and efficiently. Especially, in problems of the real world, the portfolio should be selected out of more than several thousands of stocks. The mathematical programming is complicated computation to solve the mean-variance analysis proposed by H. Markowitz. This model is very effective to obtain the limited number of invested stocks out of the huge stock market.

Chaotic Approach

Recently, the chaotic method is employed to forecast a short-term future using uncertain data. This method makes it possible by restructuring the attractor of given time-series data in the multi-dimensional space through Takens' embeding theory. Never the less, it is hard to obtain the data which come only from a chaotic source. Ordinary, many uncertain time-series data do not come only from the chaotic source, but also from another source. In this paper, we employ the related information in order to remove the influence of the non-chaotic source from the given data. This method makes the forecasting precision higher because the chaotic portion of the given data can be easily abstracted. At the end the effectiveness and usefulness of our method are shown by applying it to the short-term forecasting simulation of economic data.

Recently researches on chaotic phenomena[31,32] are done very widely. Applying the chaotic method to time-series data enables us to forecast short-term future of an event which behaves chaotically. It is to forecast a state in the near future by finding some deterministic structure in a phenomenon that seems to have stochastic noise or no deterministic structure.

This forecasting method is done as 1) to restructure observed time-series data based on Takens' embedding theory[39], and 2) to predict its short-term future trend in the local restructured space using a local vector consisted of recently observed samples. Nevertheless, it is difficult to successfully forecast near future when time-series data are ruled by no low dimensional chaoticity even if the data follows no random process.

In this paper, a forecast by chaos method was performed on the stock prices which are representative economic data. Moreover, by combining related data in the chaotic method, both the proposed one and conventional one are compared in terms of forecast error.

2 Fuzzy Mathematical Programming

The concept of a fuzzy set proposed by L.A.Zadeh [50] in 1965 is employed by H. Tanaka et al [40] to define a fuzzy linear programming. Since then, this area of theoretical researches has been much fertile and productive, and furthermore these results are recently used in applied researches. Fuzzy sets are employed in a fuzzy mathematical programming to define the objective and constraints [2] and to formulate the fuzzy mathematical programming so that a vague aspiration level of a decision maker can be reflected on its solution [52,53].

In this formulation, the fuzzy mathematical programming is defined using real numbers for coefficients of the objective and constraint conditions. Since then under the consideration that the fuzzy aspiration level of the decision maker should not only be considered, but also the coefficients of the objective and the constraint conditions themselves should be vague, the fuzzy mathematical programming is formulated to define coefficients as a fuzzy number [34].

Another model of the fuzzy mathematical programming is formulated to define only the coefficients of the objective and constraints using a fuzzy number without considering an aspiration level which a decision maker has[41].

In this section, basic concepts of a fuzzy mathematical programming, especially of a flexible mathematical programming which are used in formulating the fuzzy portfolio model and its generalized formulation are illustrated.

At first, a fuzzy set proposed by L.A.Zadeh [50] is explained briefly. Next, the maximizing decision employed by R.E.Bellman and L.A.Zadeh [2] is illustrated as a method of decision making in a fuzzy environment. Then, the maximizing decision will be applied to a fuzzy mathematical programming which can be replaced by a conventional mathematical programming [52,53]. In order to simplify its explanation, a formulation of a fuzzy mathematical programming is illsutrated using only a fuzzy linear programming, although a quadratic programming should be employed to solve a port forlio selection problem and a fuzzy portfolio selection.

2.1 Fuzzy Decision and Maximization Decision

R.E.Bellman and L.A.Zadeh define as a decision making in a fuzzy environment a decision set which unifies a fuzzy objective(a fuzzy goal) and a fuzzy constraint given by a decision maker. Let us suppose that fuzzy subsets, which denote a fuzzy objective and a fuzzy constraint, are defined on set of alternatives, X.

Let us denote the fuzzy set for the fuzzy objective by G, the fuzzy set for the constraint by C, and decision set D unifying G and C. Then, decision set D can be defined as intersection set between fuzzy objective G and fuzzy constraint C.

$$D = G \cap C, . \tag{1}$$

Decision set D is a fuzzy set named a fuzzy decision. Its membership function is characterized by the following equation:

$$\begin{aligned}\mu_D(\boldsymbol{x}) = \min(&\mu_G(\boldsymbol{x}), \\ &\mu_C(\boldsymbol{x})) \qquad \forall x \in X\end{aligned} \tag{2}$$

[Definition 2]

Even if the plurality of fuzzy objective and fuzzy constraints are given, the same result holds. In the case where k fuzzy objective $G_1, G_2, \cdots, G_k$ and m fuzzy constraints $C_1, C_2, \cdots C_m$ are given, fuzzy decision D is defined as an intersection:

$$D = \{G_1 \cap G_2 \cap \cdots \cap G_k\} \cap \{C_1 \cap C_2 \cap \cdots \cap C_m\} \tag{3}$$

Then, its membership function is characterized in the following.

$$\mu_D(\boldsymbol{x}) = \min(\mu_{G_1}(\boldsymbol{x}), \mu_{G_2}(\boldsymbol{x}), \cdots, \mu_{G_k}(\boldsymbol{x}), \mu_{C_1}(\boldsymbol{x}), \mu_{C_2}(\boldsymbol{x}), \cdots, \mu_{C_m}(\boldsymbol{x})) \tag{4}$$

The above-mentioned definitions illustrate in nature no deference between the objective and constraint in a fuzzy environment.

Let us explain a maximization decision. The maximization decision means that concerning with member $\boldsymbol{x}$ included in fuzzy decision D, $\boldsymbol{x}$ with maximum membership value should be selected in the decision making. Then, let us denote the maximum value of membership function $\mu_D(\boldsymbol{x})$ of fuzzy decision D by $\mu_D^*(\boldsymbol{x})$. The maximization decision is written in the following equation:

$$\begin{aligned}\mu_D^*(\boldsymbol{x}) &= \max_{x \in X} \mu_D(\boldsymbol{x}) \\ &= \max_{x \in X}\{\min(\mu_G(\boldsymbol{x}), \mu_C(\boldsymbol{x}))\}\end{aligned} \tag{5}$$

In the case where k fuzzy objective and m fuzzy constraints are given, the maximization decision can be denoted as follows:

$$\begin{aligned}\mu_D^*(\boldsymbol{x}) &= \max_{x \in X} \mu_D(\boldsymbol{x}) \\ &= \max_{x \in X}\{\min(\mu_{G_1}(\boldsymbol{x}), \mu_{G_2}(\boldsymbol{x}), \cdots, \mu_{G_k}(\boldsymbol{x}), \\ &\quad hskip0.5cm \mu_{C_1}(\boldsymbol{x}), \mu_{C_2}(\boldsymbol{x}), \cdots, \mu_{C_m}(\boldsymbol{x}))\}\end{aligned} \tag{6}$$

2.2 Fuzzy Objective and Fuzzy Constraints

Let us illustrate a fuzzy mathematical programming using a maximization decision as a fuzzy decision mentioned above. Originally this fuzzy mathematical programming is proposed by H.Tanaka et al [40]. In the case where the membership functions of the fuzzy objective and fuzzy constraints are a linear membership function, the method proposed by H.-J.Zimmermann [52] can give easily its solution to the fuzzy mathematical programming. Therefore, the method proposed by H.-J.Zimmermann will be illustrated in this section. In order to simplify the discussion here, we explain its formulation using a linear programming problem.

In general, a conventional linear programming problem(in the case of a maximizing problem) can be written as follows:

[Problem 2.1]

$$\text{max.} \quad c_1x_1 + c_2x_2 + \cdots + c_nx_n \tag{7}$$

$$\text{s.t.} \quad a_{11}x_1 + a_{12}x_2 + \cdots + a_{1n}x_n \leq b_1 \tag{8}$$

$$a_{21}x_1 + a_{22}x_2 + \cdots + a_{2n}x_n \leq b_2 \tag{9}$$

$$\vdots$$

$$a_{m1}x_1 + a_{m2}x_2 + \cdots + a_{mn}x_n \leq b_m \tag{10}$$

$$x_j \geq 0 \quad j = 1, 2, \cdots, n \tag{11}$$

The fuzzy linear programming problem with fuzzy objective and fuzzy constraints relating to **Problem 2.1** can be defined in the following **Problem 2.2**:

[Problem 2.2]

$$c_1x_1 + c_2x_2 + \cdots + c_nx_n \quad \gtrsim z_0 \tag{12}$$

$$a_{11}x_1 + a_{12}x_2 + \cdots + a_{1n}x_n \quad \lesssim b_1 \tag{13}$$

$$a_{21}x_1 + a_{22}x_2 + \cdots + a_{2n}x_n \quad \lesssim b_2 \tag{14}$$

$$\vdots$$

$$a_{m1}x_1 + a_{m2}x_2 + \cdots + a_{mn}x_n \lesssim b_m \tag{15}$$

$$x_j \geq 0 \quad j = 1, 2, \cdots, n \tag{16}$$

where $\gtrsim$ and $\lesssim$ denote fuzzy inequality "$x \gtrsim a$" means that "x is approximately more than a", and "$x \lesssim a$" means that "x is approximately less than a", respectively.

Fuzzy objective function Eqn(12) of **Problem 2.2** means such fuzzy objective as "approximately more than z_0" in comparison with Eqn(7) of **Problem 2.1**.

In each of constraint equations Eqn(13), Eqn(14), and Eqn(15) of **Problem 2.2** such fuzzy constants as "approximately less than b_1", "approximately less than b_2", and "approximately less than b_m" are treated comparing with Eqn(8), Eqn(9), and Eqn(10) of **Problem 2.1**. Therefore, **Problem 2.2** illustrates a fuzzy decision set denoted by Eqn(1) or Eqn(3).

Let us assume that the fuzzy objective and fuzzy constraints in **Problem 2.2** can be denoted by a linear membership function. Let us denote the necessity and sufficiency levels for the fuzzy objective as z_0^L and z_0^U, respectively and the necessity and sufficiency levels for the fuzzy constraints as b_i^L and b_i^U, respectively, for $i = 1, 2, \cdots, m$.

Fig. 2.1 and Fig. 2.2 illustrate membership functions for the fuzzy objective and fuzzy constraints. As above-mentioned, the membership functions of the fuzzy objective and fuzzy constraints are defined by the following equations:

$$\mu_G(\boldsymbol{x}) = \begin{cases} 1 & ; \sum_{j=1}^{n} c_j x_j \geq z_0^U \\ 1 + \dfrac{\sum_{j=1}^{n} c_j x_j - z_0^U}{z_0^U - z_0^L} & ; z_0^L \leq \sum_{j=1}^{n} c_j x_j \leq z_0^U \\ 0 & ; \sum_{j=1}^{n} c_j x_j \leq z_0^L \end{cases} \tag{17}$$

$$\mu_{C_i}(\boldsymbol{x}) = \begin{cases} 1 & ; \sum_{j=1}^{n} a_{ij} x_j \leq b_i^U \\ 1 - \dfrac{\sum_{j=1}^{n} a_{ij} x_j - b_i^U}{b_i^L - b_i^U} & ; b_i^U \leq \sum_{j=1}^{n} a_{ij} x_j \leq b_i^L \\ 0 & ; \sum_{j=1}^{n} a_{ij} x_j \geq b_i^L \end{cases} \tag{18}$$

Problem 2.2 can be rewritten into **Problem 2.3** using the membership functions for the fuzzy objective and fuzzy constraints. This **Problem 2.3** can be interpreted to express the right hand operation of Eqn(2) or Eqn(4).

[Problem 2.3]

$$c_1 x_1 + c_2 x_2 + \cdots + c_n x_n \quad \geq (z_0^U - z_0^L)\mu_G(\boldsymbol{x}) + z_0^L \tag{19}$$

$$a_{11} x_1 + a_{12} x_2 + \cdots + a_{1n} x_n \quad \leq (b_1^U - b_1^L)\mu_{C_1}(\boldsymbol{x}) + b_1^L \tag{20}$$

$$a_{21}x_1 + a_{22}x_2 + \cdots + a_{2n}x_n \leq (b_2^U - b_2^L)\mu_{C_2}(x) + b_2^L \qquad (21)$$

$$\vdots$$

$$a_{m1}x_1 + a_{m2}x_2 + \cdots + a_{mn}x_n \leq (b_m^U - b_m^L)\mu_{C_m}(x) + b_m^L \qquad (22)$$

$$x_j \geq 0 \quad j = 1, 2, \cdots, n \qquad (23)$$

If the fuzzy decision set, that is, the intersection between the fuzzy objective and fuzzy constraint is taken for one constraint, the feasible solution set can be interpreted to be the same set as a fuzzy decision. Therefore, employing the maximization decision to **Problem 2.3**, **Problem 2.3** can be rewritten into **Formulation 2.1** as mentioned below:

[**Formulation 2.1**]

$$\text{max.} \quad \lambda \qquad (24)$$

$$\text{s.t.} \quad c_1x_1 + c_2x_2 + \cdots + c_nx_n + (z_0^L - z_0^U)\lambda \geq z_0^L \qquad (25)$$

$$a_{11}x_1 + a_{12}x_2 + \cdots + a_{1n}x_n + (b_1^L - b_1^U)\lambda \leq b_1^L \qquad (26)$$

$$a_{21}x_1 + a_{22}x_2 + \cdots + a_{2n}x_n + (b_2^L - b_2^U)\lambda \leq b_2^L \qquad (27)$$

$$\vdots$$

$$a_{m1}x_1 + a_{m2}x_2 + \cdots + a_{mn}x_n + (b_m^L - b_m^U)\lambda \leq b_m^L \qquad (28)$$

$$\lambda, x_j \geq 0 \quad j = 1, 2, \cdots, n \qquad (29)$$

Formulation 2.1 has the same structure as a conventional linear programming. Therefore, this problem can be solved using the conventional algorithm such as a simplex method.

Various types of membership functions which express a vague aspiration level of a decision maker are proposed such as a linear membership function [52,53], a tangent type of a membership function [24], an interval linear membership function [7], an exponential membership function, and an inverse tangent membership function and so on. As a tangent type of a membership function, an exponential membership function, and inverse tangent membership function are a non-linear function, a fuzzy mathematical programming problem defined with a non-linear membership function results in a non-linear programming. Usually the linear membership function is employed in order to avoid non-linearity. Therefore, in this paper a logistic type of a membership function is employed to overcome such deficits which a linear membership function has.

3 Fuzzy Portfolio Selection

The problem treated here is a decision-making under uncertainty in a financial management. Portfolio theory treats a mathematical allocation problem of a given amount of money among several different available investments such as stocks, bonds or securities. This is named a portfolio selection problem. H. Markowitz originally proposed and formulated the mean-variance approach to the portfolio selection. That is, based on the time series of the return rate, the theoretical method decides the best investing rate to each of investments, which minimizes the risk or the variance of the profits to affirm the least rate of the expected return which a decision maker expects.

In a real problem it is difficult to forecast the expected return rate and the variance-covariance of the return rates, and also it is required to calculate the large-scale mathematical programming since almost all covariances may not be zero [23]. Then, instead of portfolio selection, asset allocation and CAPM (capital asset pricing model) are commonly used to decide the allocation of investments [37]. Recently, A. Perold [35] and H. Konno et al. [22] have proposed an efficient computer algorithm for the large-scale of a portfolio selection problem.

In this treatment of a financial management, the satisfaction, which a decision-maker feels, is not considered in solving a portfolio selection, even though two objectives such as the expected return rate and risk are discussed in its decision making. Tabata has pointed out that many methods are proposed that the easily handled objective function is employed to a local and partial problem in a real world without the consideration of maximizing the utility of a decision-maker [38]. In a real financial management the knowledge and experience of an expert are very important in a decision making.

In this paper, a portfolio selection problem is formulated as a mathematical programming with two objectives to minimize risk and maximize the expected return, since the efficient frontier should be considered in the discussion of a portfolio selection [27,29,42]. Moreover, a decision-maker has certain objective values concerning the expected return rate and a certain degree of risk, because he compares the present problem with the past experience and evaluates all portfolios in the selecting and decision-making of portfolios with risk. The objective values of the expected return rate and risk should be vague and uncertain. Therefore, a decision-maker should essentially take such values as a fuzzy number.

In this paper the formulation of a fuzzy portfolio selection is proposed under consideration of an aspiration level of a decision-maker to solve the portfolio selection with two objective.

3.1 Two Objective Portfolio Selection

In the formulation of portfolio selection, M. Markowitz started his discussion with assumption that almost all of decision makers have aversion to risk even if its return may be obtained less. From utility point of view the behaviors of people also have propensity to risk which is denoted by a parabola shape in the plane of the horizon axis of risk and the vertical axis of expected return rate. The parabola has its axis parallel to the axis of risk. Nevertheless, it should be difficult to identify such a utility function because decision markers have different utility functions. Therefore, M. Markowitz has formulated a portfolio selection problem as the following quadratic programming problem under the restriction that the expected return rate is made sure to be more than some amount.

[Formulation 2.1]

$$\left.\begin{array}{l} \min \sum_{i=1}^{n} \sum_{j=1}^{n} \sigma_{ij} x_i x_j \\ \textit{subject to} \\ \sum_{i=1}^{n} \mu_i x_i \geq E \\ \sum_{i=1}^{n} x_i = 1 \\ x_i \geq 0 \quad (i = 1, 2, \cdots, n) \end{array}\right\} \tag{30}$$

where E denotes an acceptable least rate of the expected return, σ_{ij} a covariance between security i and security j , μ_i an expected return rate of security i, and x_i an investing rate to security i.

Figure 1 shows the region of admissible portfolios in the plane of the axes of expected return rate and risk. Each point of the parabola-shaped curve shows the minimum risk for each expected return rate which decision makers aspire.

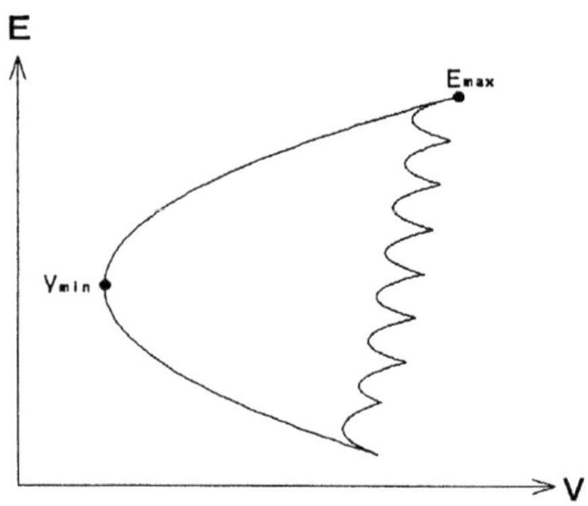

Fig. 1. The region of admissible portfolios in E–V plane

Generally speaking, decision makers should have a convex utility function because they prefer a behavior of risk propensity. Therefore, the optimal solution which the decision makers satisfy can be obtained on the curve $V_{min}E_{max}$

in the region of admissible portfolios which is tangent to the utility function of the decision makers. Nevertheless, as mentioned above, it should be difficult to identify the utility function itself.

Although it is proposed how to measure the partial and local grade of risk propensity which a decision maker has, the attitude of the decision maker toward a risk is easily changed with a new given information. Therefore, even though the attitude of the decision maker toward risk can be identified using a utility function, the effectiveness of the obtained utility function remains only in a short span.

In Formulation 2.1, the optimal solution is searched under the constraint that the expected return rate should be affirmed to be more than the value a decision maker arbitrarily gives. The investing rate to each of securities is decided for the least risk of the solution to the given rate of the expected return. Since the risk is estimated under the condition of fixing the least rate of the expected return, the decision maker cannot be fully satisfied with its solution. Under the consideration that the Pareto region named an efficient frontier exists in the region of admissible portfolios or the curve $V_{min}E_{max}$ as shown in Figure 1, Formulation 2.2 is much proper and reasonable rather than Formulation 2.1.

[Formulation 2.2]

$$\left.\begin{array}{l} \min \sum_{i=1}^{n} \sum_{j=1}^{n} \sigma_{ij} x_i x_j \\ \max \sum_{i=1}^{n} \mu_i x_i \\ \textit{subject to} \\ \sum_{i=1}^{n} x_i = 1 \\ x_j \geq 0 \quad (i = 1, 2, \cdots, n) \end{array}\right\} \tag{31}$$

Formulation 2.2 is a quadratic programming problem with two objective functions of an expected return rate and a certain degree of risk.

Recently an interactive system is proposed to solve a mathematical programming problem with two objectives of Formulation 2.2 [33]. The most beneficial aspect in employing an interactive system is to provide a user with a human-interface, which enables us to solve a trade-off analysis easily. In the conventional interactive method, it is required that all employed values should be decided previously. Therefore, the solution is searched by a cut and try method around an aspiration level that a decision maker should expect.

A decision maker has aspiration levels for both expected return rate and a certain degree of risk. It is difficult to find the solution, which satisfies these aspiration levels. Therefore, a cut and try method should be required to obtain the solution which satisfies these aspiration levels. As such an aspiration level should not be searched locally but globally, the aspiration level is checked according to whether it is satisfied within some range and then the level is expressed as a fuzzy number with such a range. In this paper we employ a fuzzy concept to express aspiration levels of an expected return rate and of risk which a decision maker would expect.

3.2 Non-Linear Membership Function

In order to solve the issue of degeneration mentioned above, we should employ a non-linear membership function such as a tangent one defined by H. Leberling [24], which has asymptotes $\lambda = 1$ and $\lambda = 0$.

In this paper we employ a logistic function for a non-linear membership function as follows :

$$f(\mathbf{x}) = \frac{1}{1 + exp(-\alpha \mathbf{x})} \tag{32}$$

The logistic function has a similar shape as the tangent hyperbolic function employed by H. Leberling, but it is more easily handled than the tangent hyperbola. And also a trapezoidal membership function is an approximation from a logistic function. Therefore, the logistic function is considered much more appropriate to denote a vague goal level, which a decision maker considers.

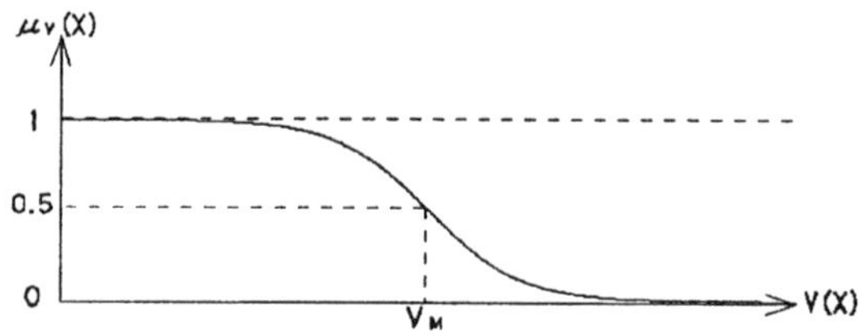

Fig. 2. The logistic membership function of the goal for an expected return rate

The goal rate for an expected return can be described using a logistic membership function in the following :

$$\mu_E(E(\mathbf{x})) = \frac{1}{1 + exp(-\alpha_E(E(\mathbf{x}) - E_M))} \tag{33}$$

where E_M is the mid point where membership value λ is 0.5. Figure 2 shows logistic membership function of the goal rate of an expected return.

The goal for risk can be described using a logistic membership function in the following :

$$\mu_V(V(\mathbf{x})) = \frac{1}{1 + exp(\alpha_V(V(\mathbf{x}) - V_M))} \tag{34}$$

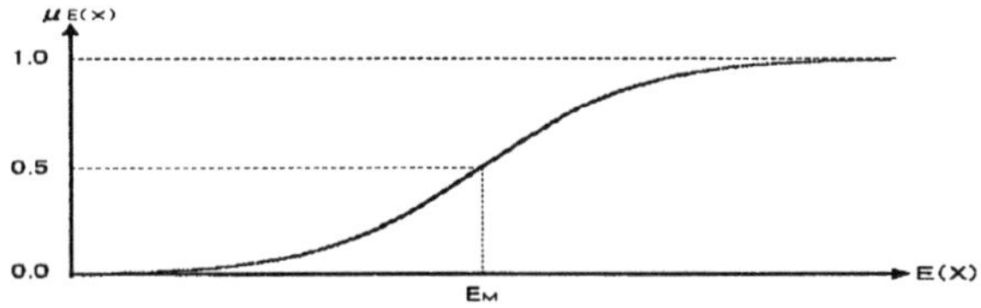

Fig. 3. The logistic membership function of the goal for risk

where V_M is the mid point where membership value λ is 0.5. Figure 3 shows the logistic membership function of the goal for risk.

Notation α_E and α_V determine respectively the shapes of membership functions μ_E and μ_V respectively, where $\alpha_E > 0$ and $\alpha_V > 0$. The larger parameters α_E and α_V get, the less their vagueness becomes.

According to Bellman–Zadeh's maximization principle [2], in terms of the above-mentioned membership functions, the fuzzy portfolio selection can be formulated as follows :

[Formulation 2.3]

$$\left.\begin{array}{l} \max \lambda \\ \textit{subject to} \\ \quad \lambda + exp(\alpha_V(V(\mathbf{x}) - V_M))\lambda \leq 1 \\ \quad \lambda + exp(-\alpha_E(E(\mathbf{x}) - E_M))\lambda \leq 1 \\ \quad \sum_{i=1}^{n} x_i = 1 \\ \quad \lambda \geq 0 \\ \quad x_i \geq 0 \quad (i = 1, 2, \cdots, n) \end{array}\right\} \tag{35}$$

where λ should be larger than 0 since logistic function $f(x)$ has an asymptote $f(x) = 0$.

Substituting $\Lambda = \log \frac{\lambda}{1-\lambda}$, we have

$$\begin{aligned} \Lambda &= \log \frac{\lambda}{1-\lambda} \\ exp(\Lambda) &= \frac{\lambda}{1-\lambda} \\ \lambda &= \frac{1}{1 + exp(-\Lambda)} \end{aligned} \tag{36}$$

Since a logistic function is monotonously increasing, maximizing λ makes Λ maximize, that is, maximizes $\log\{\lambda/(1-\lambda)\}$. Accordingly, Formulation 2.3 is equivalent to Formulation 2.4 as follows:

[**Formulation 2.4**]

$$\left.\begin{array}{l} \max \Lambda \\ subject\ \ to \\ \qquad \alpha_V V(\mathbf{x}) + \Lambda \leq \alpha_V V_M \\ \qquad \alpha_E E(\mathbf{x}) - \Lambda \geq \alpha_E E_M \\ \qquad \sum_{i=1}^{n} X_i = 1 \\ \qquad \Lambda \geq 0 \\ \qquad x_i \geq 0 \quad (i = 1, 2, \cdots, n) \end{array}\right\} \tag{37}$$

[**Theorem 2.1**]

Solution Λ obtained from Formulation 2.4 is equivalent to the solution obtained from Formulation 2.1 or 2.2, which should be the solution on the efficient frontier. It is necessary that parameters α_E and α_V, which determine the figures of membership functions, should be heuristically and experientially decided by experts.

Concerning the setting of values V_M and E_M the method proposed by H. - J. Zimmermann[53] is well-known. In this paper we employ necessity levels V_L and E_L, and sufficiency levels V_U and E_U which are given by decision makers. Since values V_M and E_M denote the mid points at which the membership functions of the expected return rate and risk have 0.5, values V_M and E_M are determined by $\frac{V_L + V_U}{2}$ and $\frac{E_L + E_U}{2}$, respectively. It should be noted that a triangular or trapezoidal membership function shows a necessity level and a sufficiency level at their grades 0 and 1 respectively, on the other hand concerning a non-linear membership function such as a logistic function a necessity level or a sufficiency level may be approximated at the points with grades 0.01 or 0.99, respectively.

When the mid point between the necessity level and the sufficiency level can be interpreted as V_M or E_M from the point of view mentioned above, we have the following theorem concerning parameters α_V and α_E :

[**Theorem 2.2**]

If parameters α_V and α_E concerning a non-linear membership function have the following relation:

$$\begin{array}{l} \frac{\alpha_V}{\alpha_E} = -\frac{E_U - E_M}{V_U - V_M} \\ \left(= -\frac{E_L - E_M}{V_L - V_M} = -\frac{E_U - E_L}{V_U - V_L} = -\frac{E_L - E_U}{V_L - V_U} \right) \end{array} \tag{38}$$

then both the goal for risk and the goal for the expected return rate should have the same measurement of vagueness.

It should be noted that the solutins by logistic membership functions and by linear membership functions are the same when $E_U(X) \ni [E_L, E_U]$ and $V_U(X) \ni [V_L, V_U]$.

Table 1. Expected return of each security

descriptions	bond A	bond B	bond C	bond D	bond E	bond F	bond G
Expected Return	0.0462	0.0097	0.01536	0.0282	0.01929	0.0317	0.0188

Table 2. Variance and covariance among securities

	bond A	bond B	bond C	bond D	bond E	bond F	bond G
bond A	0.0157	-0.0026	0.0005	0.0079	0.0035	0.0013	0.0016
bond B	-0.0026	0.0067	0.0010	-0.0008	0.0014	0.0010	0.0017
bond C	0.0005	0.0010	0.0110	0.0022	0.0011	-0.0007	0.0030
bond D	0.0079	-0.0008	0.0022	0.0119	0.0032	0.0019	0.0017
bond E	0.0035	0.0014	0.0011	0.0032	0.0130	0.0024	-0.0003
bond F	0.0013	0.0010	-0.0007	0.0019	0.0024	0.0093	-0.0002
bond G	0.0016	0.0017	0.0030	0.0017	-0.0003	-0.0002	0.0056

Table 3. Investment ratio of a fuzzy portfolio selection with trapezoidal membership functions

descriptions	bond A	bond B	bond C	bond D	bond E	bond F	bond G
investment ratio	0.2729	0.1521	0.0855	0.0000	0.0021	0.2989	0.1884

Table 4. Membership grade λ, obtained risk and obtained expected return of fuzzy portfolio selection problems with trapezoidal membership functions

λ	obtained risk	obtained expected return
0.8425	0.0029	0.0284

3.3 Numerical Example

Let us exemplify our method using a numerical example of fuzzy portfolio which decides the best portfolio to 7 securities. Table 1 shows the expected

Table 5. Investment ratio of fuzzy portfolio selection problems with logistic membership function

α_V	α_E	bond A	bond B	bond C	bond D	bond E	bond F	bond G
800	600	0.2501	0.1698	0.0902	0.0000	0.0128	0.2815	0.1957
900	550	0.2594	0.1616	0.08775	0.0000	0.0091	0.2883	0.1938
1,000	500	0.2696	0.1542	0.0857	0.0000	0.0041	0.2964	0.1899
1,100	450	0.2812	0.1468	0.0828	0.0000	0.0000	0.3038	0.1855
1,200	400	0.2913	0.1328	0.0799	0.0000	0.0000	0.3120	0.1840

Table 6. Membership grade λ, obtained risk and obtained expected return of fuzzy portfolio selection problems with logistic membership functions

α_V	α_E	λ	obtained risk	obtained expected return
800	600	0.8083	0.0027	0.0274
900	550	0.8253	0.0028	0.0278
1,000	500	0.8376	0.0029	0.0283
1,100	450	0.8451	0.0030	0.0288
1,200	400	0.8476	0.0031	0.0293

return rates of the 7 securities and Table 2 illustrates the variance and covariance among the 7 securities.

Table 3 and 4 illustrate the result that trapezoidal membership functions are employed in the definition of the fuzzy portfolio selection problem, where the necessity and sufficiency levels of the goal for risk are set to 0.007 and 0.002, respectively, and the necessity and sufficiency levels of the goal rate for the expected return are set to 0.02 and 0.03, respectively.

On the other hand, Table 5 and 6 show the obtained result when non-linear membership functions are employed in the definition of the fuzzy portfolio selection problem. The necessity and sufficiency levels of the goal for the risk or the goal rate for the expected return are set to the same values as in the trapezoidal membership function. Therefore,

$$V_M = \frac{0.007 + 0.002}{2} = 0.005$$

$$E_M = \frac{0.002 + 0.003}{2} = 0.025$$

If the obtained membership value of the solution is appropriate and proper, that is, it is included in (0,1), regardless of the shape of a membership function, whether we employ a trapezoidal membership function or a non-linear membership function to the analysis, both solutions are not different so much. Nevertheless, it is possible that the non-linear membership function changes its shape according to the parameter values. Then a decision maker is able to apply his strategy to a fuzzy portfolio selection using these parameters. Therefore, the non-linear membership function is much more convenient than the trapezoidal ones.

4 Conclusion

H. Markowitz originally proposed and formulated the mean-variance approach to the portfolio selection. That is, based on the time series of the return rate, the theoretical method decides the best investing rate to each of investments, which minimizes the risk or the variance of the profits to affirm the least rate of the expected return which a decision maker expects.

In these treatment of a financial management, the satisfaction which a decision maker feels is not considered in solving a portfolio selection, even though two objectives such as the expected return rate and risk are discussed in its decision making. And also in a real financial management the knowledge and experience of an expert are very important in a decision making.

The problem treated here is a decision-making under uncertainty in a financial management. Many problems of decision-making in investment have mainly been studied from optimizing points of view. As the investment is much influenced by the disturbance of a social and economical circumstances, optimization approach is not always the best, because problems used to be ill-structured under uncertain environment. In this chapter, we described the new method in dealing with portfolio selection, that is, the fuzzy approach to the decision making in portfolio selection problems.

The fuzzy portfolio selection enables us to obtain a solution which realizes the best within a vague aspiration level and a fuzzy goal given by membership functions. The vague aspiration, the fuzzy goal and the fuzzy numbers are obtained from the expertise of decision-makers'.

We formulated a portfolio selection problem as a mathematical programming with two objectives to minimize risk and maximize the expected return, since the efficient frontier should be considered in the discussion of a portfolio selection. Moreover, a decision maker has certain objective values concerning the expected return rate and a certain degree of risk, because he compares the present problem with the past experience and evaluates all portfolios in the selecting and decision-making of portfolios with risk. The objective values of the expected return rate and risk should be vague and uncertain. Therefore, a decision-maker should essentially takes such values as a fuzzy number.

We illustrated the formulation of a fuzzy portfolio model under consideration of an aspiration level of a decision-maker to solve the portfolio selection with two objective.

Then we exemplified our method using a numerical example of fuzzy portfolio which decides the best portfolio to 7 securities. We employed non-linear membership functions in the definition of the fuzzy portfolio selection problem. If the obtained membership value of the solution is appropriate and proper, that is, it is included in (0,1), regardless of the shape of a membership function, whether we employ a trapezoidal membership function or a non-linear membership function to the analysis, both solutions are not different so much. Nevertheless, it is possible that the non-linear membership function changes its shape according to the parameter values. Then a decision maker is able to apply his strategy to a fuzzy portfolio selection using these parameters. Therefore, the non-linear membership function is much more convenient than the trapezoidal ones.

References

1. D. H. Ackley, G. E. Hinton & T. J. Sejnowski: "A Learning Algorithm for Boltzmann machines," *Cognitive Sci.* Vol. 9 , 1985
2. R. E. Bellman & L. A. Zadeh: "Decision Making in a Fuzzy Environment," *Management Science*, Vol. 17, No. 4, pp. B141-B164, 1970
3. G. R. Bitran: "Linear Multiple Objective Problems with Interval Coefficients," *Management Science*, Vol.26, No.7, pp.694-706, 1980
4. F. BLack & M. Scholes; "The Pricing of Options and COrporate Liabilities," Journal of Political Economy," 81, pp. 637-654, 1973.
5. D. Dubois & H. Prade: *Fuzzy Sets and Systems: Theory and Applications*, Academic Press, 1980
6. D. Dubois & H. Prade: *Possibility Theory: An Approach to Computerized Processing of Uncertainty*, Plenum Press, 1988
7. E. L. Hannan: "Linear Programming with Multiple Fuzzy Goals," *Fuzzy Sets and Systems*, Vol. 6, pp. 235-248, 1981
8. G.E. Hinton:"Deterministic Boltzmann Learning Performs Steepest Descent in WeightSpace," Neural Computation, pp. 143-150, , 1989
9. J. H. Holland: *Adaptation in Natural and Artificial Systems*, University of Michigan MIT Press, 1975
10. J.J. Hopfield:"Neural netwoks and physical systems with emergent collective computational abilities, " Proc. Natl. Acad. Sci., pp. 2554-2558, , 1982
11. M. Inuiguchi, H. Ichihashi & H. Tanaka: "Fuzzy Programming: A Survey of Recent Developments," *Stochastic versus Fuzzy Approaches to Multiobjective Mathematical Programming under Uncertainty,* eds. R. Slowinski and J. Teghem, Kluwer Academic Publishers, Dordrecht, pp. 45-68, 1990
12. M. Inuiguchi & H. Ichihashi: "Relative Modalities and Their Use in Possibilistic Linear Programming," *Fuzzy Sets and Systems,* Vol.35, No.3, pp.303-323, 1990
13. M. Inuiguchi: "Fuzzy Linear Programming: What, Why and How ?," *Tatra Mountains Mathematical Pulications,* Vol. 13, pp. 123-167, 1997
14. M. Inuiguchi & T. Tanino: "ortfolio selecton under independent possibilistic independent possibilistic information." *Fuzzy Sets and Systems* to appear
15. T. Kaino & K. Hirota; "Derivative of Fuzzy Relations and Its Application to Capital Investment Decision Making Problem," Proc. of IFSA'99, Taipei, pp. 995-998, 1999
16. T. Kaino & K. Hirota; "Differentiation of the Choquet Integral of a Nonnegative Measurable Function," Proc. of FUZZ-IEEE'99, Seoul, Vol. III, pp. 1322-1327, 1999

17. T. Kaino & K. Hirota; "Derivative of Fuzzy Relations and Its Application to FUzzy Sensitivity Analysis," Int. J. of Fuzzy Systems, VOl. 1, No. 2, pp. 129-132, Dec. 1999
18. T. Kaino & K. Hirota; "Differentiation of CHoquet Integral for Nonnegative Measurable Function and its Application to Capital Investment Decision Making," FUZZ-IEEE2000, Texas, 2000
19. T. Kawaura & J. Watada: "Mean-Variance Analysis of Agricultural Management based on a Boltzmann Machine, " Proc. of FuzzIEEE at Seoul, pp.22-25, 1999.
20. W. R. King: "A Stochastic Personnel Assignment Model," *Operations Research*, Vol.13, No.1, pp.67-81, 1964
21. H. Konno & H. Yamazaki: "A MeanAbsolute Deviation Portfolio Optimization Model and Its Application to Tokyo Stock Market," *Management Science*, Vol. 37, No. 5, pp. 519-531, 1991
22. H. Konno & K. Suzuki: "A Fast Algorithm for Solving Large Scale MeanVariance Model by Compact Factorization of Covariance Matrices," *Journal of the Operations Research Society of Japan*, Vol. 35, No. 1, pp. 93-104, 1992
23. H. Konno: "Applications of Mathematical Programming in Financial Optimization The MV Model and Related Topics," *Systems, Control and Information*, Vol. 37, No. 4, pp. 223-229, , 1993 in Japanese
24. H. Leberling: "On Finding Compromise Solutions in Multicriteria Problems Using the Fuzzy MinOperator," *Fuzzy Sets and Systems*, Vol. 6, pp. 105-118, 1981
25. Y. Matsumoto & J. Watada: "Shorttem Prediction by Chaos Method of Embedding Related Data at Same Time," *Journal of Japan Industrial Management Association*, 1998 in Japanese to appear,
26. H. Mizunuma & J. Watada:"Fuzzy portfolio selection - realization of an aspiration level given by a decision maker,"Trans. of the Institute of Systems, Control and Information Engineers 8, pp. 677-684, 1995 (in Japanese)
27. H. Mizunuma & J. Watada: "Solving Portfolio Selection with Fuzzy Goals," *Proceedings of the 6th International Fuzzy Systems Association World Congress*, Sao Paulo, Brazil, July 2228, Vol. 2, pp. 169-172, 1995
28. H. Mizunuma & J. Watada: "Fuzzy Mixed Integer Programming Based on Genetic Algorithm and Its Application to Resource Distribution," *Jouranal of Japan Society for Fuzzy Theory and Systems*, Vol. 7, No. 1, pp. 164-176, 1995 in Japanese
29. H. Mizunuma & J. Watada: "Fuzzy Prtfolio Selection Realization of an Aspiration Level Given by a Decision Maker," *Trans. of the Institute of Systems, Control and Information Engineers*, Vol. 8, No. 12, pp. 677-684, 1995 in Japanese
30. H. Mizunuma, H. Matsuda & J. Watada: "Decision Making in Management Based on Fuzzy MeanVariance Analysis," *Jouranal of Japan Society for Fuzzy Theory and Systems,* Vol. 8, No. 5, pp. 854-860, 1996 in Japanese
31. H. Nagashima, Y. Baba: *Introduction to Chaos*, Baifuu kan, 1992 in Japanese
32. T. Nagashima, Y. Nagai, T. Ogiwara & T. Tsuchiya: "Time series data analysis and Chaos," *Sensing Instrument Control Engineering*, Vol. 29, No. 9, 1990 in Japanese
33. H. Nakayama: "Intaractive MultiObjective Mathematical Programming Methods and Applications," *Communications of the Operations Research Society of Japan*, Vol. 33, No. 8, pp. 375-381, 1991 in Japanese

34. S. A. Orlovsky: "On Formalization of a General Fuzzy Mathematical Programming Problem," *Fuzzy Sets and Systems*, Vol. 3, pp. 311-321, 1980
35. A. Perold: "Large Scale Portfolio Optimization," *Management Science*, Vol. 30, No. 10, pp. 1143-1160, 1984
36. G. Sugihara & R.M. May: "Nonlinear forecasting as a way of distinguishing chaos from measurement error in time series," *Nature*, Vol. 344, pp. 734-741, 1990
37. G. P. Szego : *Portfolio Theory With Application to Bank Asset Management*, Academic Press, Inc., 1980
38. Y. Tabata: "Mathematics of Finance," *Communications of the Operations Research Society of Japan*, Vol. 36, No. 1, pp. 8-12, , 1991 in Japanese
39. F. Takens: "Detecting Strange Attractors in Fluid Turbulence, " ed. by D. A. Rand & L. S. Young: *Lect. Notes in Mathematics*, vol. 898, pp. 366-381, 1981
40. H. Tanaka:"Fuzzy Linear Programming Problems with Fuzzy Number," *Fuzzy Sets and Systems*, Vol. 13, pp. 1-10, 1984
41. H. Tanaka & P. Guo: *Possibilistic Data Analysis for Operations Research*, Studies in Fuzziness and Soft Computing, Vol. 29, Springer Verlag, 1999
42. J. Watada & H. Mizunuma: "Determination of Distribution Centers Location Based on Fuzzy Integer Programming," *Proceedings of the 12th International Conference on Production Research*, pp. 739-740, 1993
43. J. Watada *Fuzzy portfolio selection and its applications to decision making,* Tatra Moutains Math. Publ., Vol. 13, pp. 219-248, 1997
44. J. Watada & H. Mizunuma: "Fuzzy MeanVariance Analysis with Interval Constraints," *7th IFSA World Congress Proc.* Vol. 2, pp. 105-112, 1997
45. J. Watada, H. Mizunuma & H. Matsuda: "Fuzzy Portfolio Selection for Realizing Limited Number of Investment Securities Using Genetic Algorithm, " *Journal of Japan Industrial Management Association*, Vol. 49, pp. 91-99, 1998
46. J. Watada, "Soft-Computing Approaches to Portfolio Slection Problms," *Methods for decision Support in Environment with Uncertainty - Aplications in Economics, Business and Engineering* edited by J. Ramik and V. Novak, Proceedings of The Czech-Japan Seminar, Held in Beskydy, Celandna, Czeck, pp. 35-95, Sept. 5-9, 1999
47. J. Watada & K. Oda, "Formulation of a Two-Layered Bolzmann Machine for Portfolio Selection," InterJournal of Fuzzy Systems, Vol. 2, No. 1, pp. 39–44. 2000
48. T. Watanabe & J. Watada:"The Genetic Portfolio Selection Problem Considering the Investing Pattern of the Preceding Term," Proc. of Japan Industrial Management Association the 1999 in Autumn, pp. 112-113, 1999 (in Japanese)
49. T. Watanabe, K. Oda & J. Watada:"Hierarchical Decision Making of Strategic Investment," *International Journal on Fuzziness, Uncertainly, and Knowledge-Based Reasoning (IJUFKS)*,Vol. 74, pp.429-437, 2000.
50. L. A. Zadeh: "Fuzzy Sets," *Information and Control*, Vol. 8, No. 3, pp. 338-353, 1965
51. L. A. Zadeh: "Fuzzy Sets as a Basis for a Theory of Possibility," *Fuzzy Sets and Systems*, Vol. 1, pp., 1978
52. H. J. Zimmermann: "Description and Optimization of Fuzzy Systems," *International Journal of General Systems*, Vol.2, pp.209-215, 1976
53. H. J. Zimmermann: "Fuzzy Programming and Linear Programming with Several Objective Functions," *Fuzzy Sets and Systems*, Vol. 1, pp. 45-55, 1978
54. H. J. Zimmermann: "Applications of Fuzzy Sets Theory to Mathematical Programming," *Information Sciences*, Vol. 36, pp. 29-58, 1985

Fuzzy Differentials and Deterministic Approaches to Fuzzy Optimization Problems

Seiji Saito[1], Hiroaki Ishii[1], Minghao Chen[2]

[1]Graduate School of Engineering, Osaka University, Suita, 565-0871,Japan
[2]Department of Applied Mathematics, Harbin Institute of Technology, Harbin, People's Republic of China

Abstract We consider some types of fuzzy differentials of fuzzy functions which map from open sets in normed spaces to sets of fuzzy sets. In the field of studying fuzzy differentials, there are many fruitful results, i.e., due to Puri and Ralescu, Goetschel and Voxman, Dubois and Prade,and Furukawa, etc. We introduce some fuzzy differentials which are corresponding to the Dini's derivatives as well as apply a deterministic method to some fuzzy optimization problems.

1 Differentials of Fuzzy Functions

In this chapter we show fruitful results of differentials of fuzzy functions by Dubois and Prade, Geotschel and Voxman, Puri and Ralescu and Furukawa etc. Moreover we deal with the Dini's derivatives of fuzzy functions.

1.1 Fuzzy Functions in $L-R$ Notations

Dubois and Prade [3, 4, 5, 6] define a class of fuzzy numbers with the following kinds of membership functions.

Definition 1.1.1 *Suppose that a function $L:\mathbf{R}\to[0,1]$ satisfies the following conditions $(i)-(iv)$:*

(i) $L(t)=L(-t)$ *for* $t\in\mathbf{R}$;

(ii) $L(0)=1$;

(iii) $L(t)$ *is non-increasing in* $t\geq 0$;

(iv) $0\leq t_0=\sup\{t\in\mathbf{R}:L(t)>0\}<\infty$.

Then the function L is said to be a shape function.

In what follows we consider some types of membership functions as follows:

Definition 1.1.2 *Suppose that functions L and R are two shape functions. Let $\alpha,\beta>0$ and $m\in\mathbf{R}$. Define a function $\mu_M:\mathbf{R}\to[0,1]$ by*

$$\mu_M(t)=\begin{cases} L(\frac{m-t}{\alpha})_+ & (t\leq m)\\ R(\frac{t-m}{\beta})_+ & (t>m).\end{cases}$$

Here $L(t)_+ = \max(L(t), 0)$. *Then* μ_M *is said to be a membership function of the* $L-R$ *fuzzy number* M. *Denote* $M = (m, \alpha, \beta)_{LR}$.

Dubois and Prade deal with the addition, negative element and scalar product on the set of $L-R$ fuzzy numbers.

Theorem 1.1.1 *Suppose that* M *and* N *are* $L-R$ *fuzzy numbers as follows:*

$$M = (m, \alpha, \beta)_{LR}; \quad N = (n, \gamma, \delta)_{LR},$$

where $\alpha, \beta, \gamma, \delta > 0$ *and* $m, n \in \mathbf{R}$. μ_M, μ_N *are membership functions of* M, N, *respectively. Let* $\mu_{M+N}(t) = \max_{x+y=t} \min(\mu_M(x), \mu_N(y))$. *Then we have*

$$\mu_{M+N}(t) = \begin{cases} L(\frac{m+n-t}{\alpha+\gamma})_+ & (t \leq m+n) \\ R(\frac{t-(m+n)}{\beta+\delta})_+ & (t > m+n), \end{cases}$$

or

$$M + N = (m+n, \alpha+\gamma, \beta+\delta)_{LR}.$$

Denote the negative representation of the $L-R$ *fuzzy of* $M = (m, \alpha, \beta)_{LR}$ *by* $-(m, \alpha, \beta)_{LR} = (-m, \beta, \alpha)_{RL}$. *Define the scalar product* cM, *where* $c \in \mathbf{R}$, *as follows:*

$$cM = \begin{cases} (cm, c\alpha, c\beta)_{LR} & (c \geq 0) \\ (cm, -c\beta, -c\alpha)_{RL} & (c < 0). \end{cases}$$

The $L-R$ *fuzzy number* $M = (m, \alpha, \beta)_{LR}$ *is called to be an* L *fuzzy number, where* $L = R$ *and* $\alpha = \beta$ *and we define* $M = (m, \alpha)_L$.

In what follows we treat the fuzzy differential due to Dubois-Prade. They consider $L-R$ fuzzy functions and their derivatives.

Definition 1.1.3 *Suppose that* f *defined on* $\mathbf{R}$ *is an* $L-R$ *valued function, i.e., the value* $f(x)$ *is the* $L-R$ *fuzzy number. It is called to be an* $L-R$ *fuzzy function. Denote* $f(x) = (m(x), \alpha(x), \beta(x))_{LR}$ *and*

$$\begin{aligned} f_\omega^-(x) &= m(x) - L^{-1}(\omega)\alpha(x) \\ f_\omega^+(x) &= m(x) + R^{-1}(\omega)\beta(x), \end{aligned}$$

for $0 \leq \omega \leq 1$.

Suppose that functions $\alpha(x) > 0$ and $\beta(x) > 0$ and $m(x)$ are differentiable in $x \in \mathbf{R}$. Then they define the membership of the derivative $\frac{df}{dx}$ by

$$\mu_{\frac{df}{dx}(x)}(t) = \begin{cases} \sup\{\omega : \frac{df_\omega^\pm}{dx}(x) = t\} & \text{if } \exists \frac{df_\omega^\pm}{dx}(x) = t \\ 0 & \text{if } \nexists \frac{df_\omega^\pm}{dx}(x) = t, \end{cases}$$

where μ is the membership function of the fuzzy number $f(x)$. If

$$\mu_{\frac{df}{dx}(x)}(t) = \begin{cases} L(\frac{p(x)-t}{q(x)})_+ & (t \leq p(x)) \\ R(\frac{t-p(x)}{r(x)})_+ & (t > p(x)), \end{cases}$$

we denote $\frac{df}{dx}(x) = (p(x), q(x), r(x))_{LR}$ provided with $q(x) > 0$ and $r(x) > 0$.

Under some conditions of f they have the following theorem concerning with $\frac{df}{dx}$.

Theorem 1.1.2 *Suppose that two shape functions L and R are monotone and continuous and that $f(x) = (m(x), \alpha(x), \beta(x))_{LR}$, where $\alpha(x) > 0, \beta(x) > 0$ and $m(x)$ are differentiable in $x \in \mathbf{R}$. Then $f_\omega^\pm$ are differentiable in x and the following statements hold:*

$$\begin{aligned} \frac{df_\omega^-}{dx}(x) &= \frac{dm}{dx}(x) - L^{-1}(\omega)\frac{d\alpha}{dx}(x) \\ \frac{df_\omega^+}{dx}(x) &= \frac{dm}{dx}(x) + R^{-1}(\omega)\frac{d\beta}{dx}(x); \end{aligned}$$

Moreover the following cases $(i)-(iv)$ hold for $x \in \mathbf{R}$;
(i) If $\frac{d\alpha}{dx}(x) \geq 0$ and $\frac{d\beta}{dx}(x) \geq 0$, then we have

$$\frac{df}{dx}(x) = \Big(\frac{dm}{dx}(x), \frac{d\alpha}{dx}(x), \frac{d\beta}{dx}(x)\Big)_{LR};$$

(ii) If $\frac{d\alpha}{dx}(x) \leq 0$ and $\frac{d\beta}{dx}(x) \leq 0$, then we have

$$\frac{df}{dx}(x) = \Big(\frac{dm}{dx}(x), -\frac{d\beta}{dx}(x), -\frac{d\alpha}{dx}(x)\Big)_{RL};$$

(iii) If $\frac{d\alpha}{dx}(x) \leq 0$ and $\frac{d\beta}{dx}(x) \geq 0$, then we have

$$\frac{df}{dx}(x) = \Big(\frac{dm}{dx}(x), 0, -\frac{d\alpha}{dx}(x)\Big)_L \cup \Big(\frac{dm}{dx}(x), 0, \frac{d\beta}{dx}(x)\Big)_R,$$

which means the membership function as follows:

$$\mu_{\frac{df}{dx}(x)}(t) = \begin{cases} 0 & (t \leq \frac{dm}{dx}) \\ \max\Big[L\Big(\frac{t-\frac{dm}{dx}}{-\frac{d\alpha}{dx}}\Big)_+, R\Big(\frac{t-\frac{dm}{dx}}{\frac{d\beta}{dx}}\Big)_+\Big] & (t > \frac{dm}{dx}) \end{cases};$$

(iv) If $\frac{d\alpha}{dx}(x) \geq 0$ and $\frac{d\beta}{dx}(x) \leq 0$, then we have

$$\frac{df}{dx}(x) = \Big(\frac{dm}{dx}(x), \frac{d\alpha}{dx}(x), 0\Big)_L \cup \Big(\frac{dm}{dx}(x), -\frac{d\beta}{dx}(x), 0\Big)_R.$$

Remark. When we denote $f(x)$ by $(m(x), \alpha(x), \beta(x))_{LR}$ in the manner of Dubois and Prade, it can be seen that f is differentiable under the conditions that α and β are monotone.

1.2 Parametric Representation of Fuzzy Numbers

Let $I = [0, 1]$. In this section we show main results of Goetschel and Voxman (see [10, 11]). In [10] a fuzzy number is defined as follows:

Definition 1.2.1 *A fuzzy number is identified with a fuzzy set $\mu : \mathbf{R} \to I$ such that there exist $c \leq a \leq b \leq d$ satisfying the following properties (i) - (iii):*

(i) μ is upper semi-continuous;

(ii) $\mu(t) = 0$, outside of an interval $[c, d]$;

(iii) μ is increasing on $[c, a]$, decreasing on $[b, d]$ and $\mu(t) = 1$ for each $t \in [a, b]$.

Denote F_b be a set of all the fuzzy numbers (see fig.1).

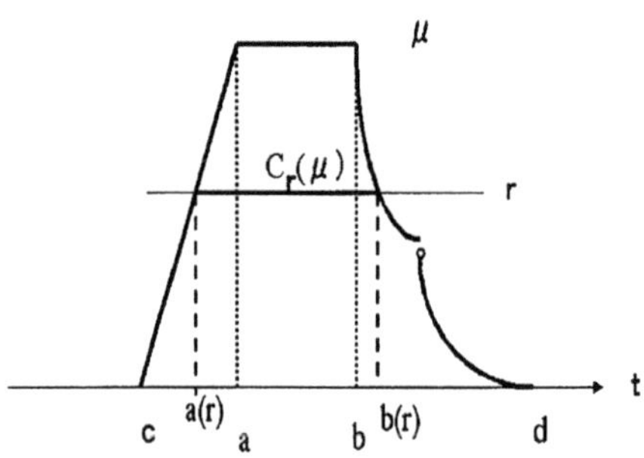

Figure 1: Fuzzy number μ and $C_r(\mu)$

Suppose that $\mu : \mathbf{R} \to I$ is a fuzzy number and for $r \in I$ and define $C_r(\mu)$ by

$$C_r(\mu) = \begin{cases} \{(t, r) : \mu(t) \geq r\} & (r > 0) \\ cl(supp(\mu)) \times \{0\} & (r = 0), \end{cases}$$

where *cl* means the closure. Then it is easily established that μ is a fuzzy number if and only if the following condition (*i*) and (*ii*) hold:

(*i*) $C_r(\mu)$ is a closed and bounded interval of each $r > 0$;

(*ii*) $C_0(\mu) = \{(t, 0) : c \leq x \leq d\}$.

Thus we can identify a fuzzy number μ with the parameter triplet

$$\{(a(r), b(r), r) \in \mathbf{R}^3 : r \in I\},$$

where $a(r)$ and $b(r)$ are the left and right endpoints of $C_r(\mu)$, respectively. This leads to the following characterization of a fuzzy number (see fig.2).

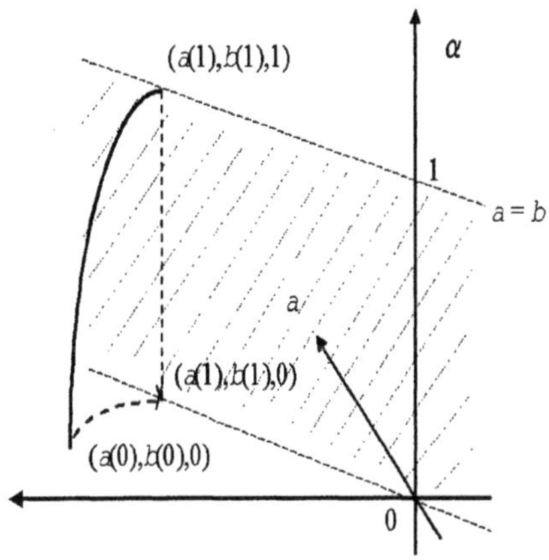

Figure 2: Fuzzy number μ in $\mathbf{R}^3$

Theorem 1.2.1 *Suppose that $a : I \to \mathbf{R}$ and $b : I \to \mathbf{R}$ satisfy the following conditions (i) - (v):*

(*i*) *a is a bounded and increasing function;*

(*ii*) *b is a bounded and decreasing function;*

(*iii*) $a(1) \leq b(1)$;

(*iv*) *For $0 < k \leq 1$ we have $\lim_{r \to k-0} a(r) = a(k)$ and $\lim_{r \to k-0} b(r) = b(k)$;*

(*v*) $\lim_{r \to +0} a(r) = a(0)$ *and* $\lim_{r \to +0} b(r) = b(0)$.

Then μ identified by

$$\mu(t) = \sup\{r : a(r) \leq t \leq b(r)\}$$

is a fuzzy number with the above parameterization. Conversely if μ is a fuzzy number with the above parameterization, then the functions a and b satisfy (i) – (v).

Suppose that μ and ν are fuzzy numbers represented by

$$\{(a(r), b(r), r) \in \mathbf{R}^3 : r \in I\}; \quad \{(c(r), d(r), r) \in \mathbf{R}^3 : r \in I\},$$

respectively. Then it is easily verified that the Dubois-Prade definition (see [3]) of the addition of fuzzy numbers

$$(\mu + \nu)(z) = \max_{x+y=z} \min(\mu(x), \nu(y))$$

is equivalent to the following vector addition of the parametric representation of μ and ν :

$$\mu + \nu = \{(a(r) + c(r), b(r) + d(r), r) \in \mathbf{R}^3 : r \in I\}.$$

In order to represent $-\mu$ Goetschel and Voxman use the following kind of the opposite of μ by

$$\{(-a(r), -b(r), r) \in \mathbf{R}^3 : r \in I\}.$$

They define the scalar product $c\mu$, where $c \in \mathbf{R}$, by

$$\{(ca(r), cb(r), r) \in \mathbf{R}^3 : r \in I\}.$$

Thus the set of fuzzy numbers and the parametric representations of their oppsite form subsets of the vector space

$$\mathcal{V} = \{(a(r), b(r), r) \in \mathbf{R}^3 : r \in I\},$$

where $a, b : I \to \mathbf{R}$ are bounded functions. We define a metric ρ on $\mathcal{V}$ by

$$\rho(\mu, \nu) = \sup\{\max(|a(r) - c(r)|, |b(r) - d(r)|) : r \in I\}.$$

It is also clear that the vector space $\mathcal{V}$ together with the metric ρ form a linear topological space.

In what follows we show the fuzzy differential due to Goetschel and Voxman. A function $f : \mathbf{R} \to F_b$ is said to be a fuzzy function. They define some derivative as follows:

Definition 1.2.2 *Suppose that* $f : \mathbf{R} \to F_b$ *and*

$$f(x) = \{(a(r, x), b(r, x), r) \in \mathbf{R}^3 : r \in I\}.$$

The derivative of f *is defined by*

$$f^{'}(x) = \{\Big(\lim_{h\to 0} \frac{a(r, x+h) - a(r, x)}{h}, \lim_{h\to 0} \frac{b(r, x+h) - b(r, x)}{h}, r\Big) \in \mathbf{R}^3 : r \in I\}$$

provided that these limits exist.

The following theorem due to Goetschel and Voxman is very useful for the representation of $f^{'}$.

Theorem 1.2.2 *Suppose that* $f : \mathbf{R} \to F_b$ *with* $f(x) = \{(a(r,x), b(r,x), r) \in \mathbf{R}^3 : r \in I\}$ *has the derivative* f'. *Let*

$$\eta(x) = \{(\alpha(r,x), \beta(r,x), r) \in \mathbf{R}^3 : r \in I\} \quad (x \in \mathbf{R})$$

be the parametric representation of $f'(x)$. *Then* $\eta(x) \in \mathcal{V}$ *for* $x \in \mathbf{R}$ *and*

$$\alpha(r,x) = \frac{\partial a}{\partial x}(r,x); \quad \beta(r,x) = \frac{\partial b}{\partial x}(r,x)$$

for $r \in I$.

In the next two theorems they establish two simple criteria for the existence of the derivative f'.

Theorem 1.2.3 *Suppose that* $f(x) = \{(a(r,x), b(r,x), r) \in \mathbf{R}^3 : r \in I\}$. *If* $\frac{\partial a}{\partial x}(r,x)$ *and* $\frac{\partial b}{\partial x}(r,x)$ *are continuous , then* $f'(x)$ *exists for each* $x \in \mathbf{R}$.

Theorem 1.2.4 *Suppose that* $f(x) = \{(a(r,x), b(r,x), r) \in \mathbf{R}^3 : r \in I\}$. *If in a neighborhood* $U(x_0)$ *of* $x_0 \in \mathbf{R}$, *the sets* $\{\frac{\partial a}{\partial x}(r,x) : I \times U(x_0) \to \mathbf{R}\}$ *and* $\{\frac{\partial b}{\partial x}(r,x) : I \times U(x_0) \to \mathbf{R}\}$ *exist and are equicontinuous in* x, *then* $f'(x_0)$ *exist for each* $x_0 \in \mathbf{R}$.

Remark. Goetschel and Voxman denote a fuzzy number by a point of $\mathbf{R}^3$ so that the set of fuzzy numbers is a subset of the linear space . In Section 1.5 we make the similar discussion in the case of $\mathbf{R}^2$.

1.3 Linear Space of Fuzzy Numbers

Let both X and Y be reflexive Banach spaces over the field $\mathbf{R}$, U an open set in X. We consider some fuzzy function $f : U \to \mathcal{F}(Y)$, where $\mathcal{F}(Y)$ is a set of all the fuzzy sets $u : Y \to [0,1]$ satisfying the following conditions $(i)-(iii)$ (see [13]):

(i) u is upper semi-continuous on Y;

(ii) u is fuzzy convex, or quasiconcave;

(iii) $L_\alpha(u) = \{y \in Y : u(y) \geq \alpha\}$ is compact for $\alpha > 0$.

Here u is said to be fuzzy convex on $J(\subset Y)$, if for $y_1, y_2 \in J$ and $\lambda \in [0,1]$,

$$u(\lambda y_1 + (1-\lambda)y_2) \geq \min[u(y_1), u(y_2)].$$

For $u, v \in \mathcal{F}(Y)$ and $\lambda \in \mathbf{R}$, they consider the following addition and scalar product:

$$(u+v)(y) = \sup\{\alpha \in [0,1] : y \in L_\alpha(u) + L_\alpha(v)\};$$

$$(\lambda u)(y) = \begin{cases} u(y/\lambda) & \text{for} \lambda \neq 0 \\ 0 & \text{for} \lambda = 0, \ y \neq 0 \\ \sup\limits_{\eta \in Y} u(\eta) & \text{for } \lambda = 0, \ y = 0 \end{cases}$$

where $y \in L_\alpha(u) + L_\alpha(v)$ for $y = y_1 + y_2$, $y_1 \in L_\alpha(u)$ and $y_2 \in L_\alpha(v)$. Furthermore pairs (u, v) and $(u', v') \in \mathcal{F}(Y) \times \mathcal{F}(Y)$ are said to be equivalent if

$$(u, v) \sim (u', v') \Longleftrightarrow (u + v')(y) = (u' + v)(y)$$

for any $y \in Y$. A set of equivalence classes

$$\mathcal{Y} = \{[(u, v)] : u, v, u' \text{ and } v' \in \mathcal{F}(Y) \text{ satisfy } \quad (u, v) \sim (u', v')\}$$

is a linear space with addition and scalar product as follows:

$$[(u, v)] + [(u', v')] = [(u + u', v + v')]$$

$$\lambda[(u, v)] = \begin{cases} [(\lambda u, \lambda v)] & (\lambda \geq 0) \\ [((-\lambda)v, (-\lambda)u)] & (\lambda < 0) \end{cases}$$

for $\lambda \in \mathbf{R}$ and $[(u, v)], [(u', v')] \in \mathcal{Y}$. They denote a norm in $\mathcal{Y}$ by

$$\| [(u, v)] \| = \sup_{\alpha > 0} d_H(L_\alpha(u), L_\alpha(v)).$$

Here d_H is the Hausdorff metric as follows:

$$d_H(L_\alpha(u), L_\alpha(v)) = \max(\sup_{x \in L_\alpha(u)} \inf_{y \in L_\alpha(v)} \| x - y \|, \sup_{y \in L_\alpha(v)} \inf_{x \in L_\alpha(u)} \| x - y \|)$$

and $\| \cdot \|$ is the norm in X. Let an isometric mapping $j : \mathcal{F}(Y) \to \mathcal{Y}$ be $j(u) = [(u, 0)]$. It is said that a fuzzy function f is differentiable at $x_0 \in U$, if

$$(j(f(x))) - (j(f(x_0))) = A_{x_0} h + \omega_{x_0}(h)$$

where $h = x - x_0 \in X$, a mapping $A_{x_0} h : X \to \mathcal{Y}$ is bounded on U and $\omega_{x_0}(h) : X \to \mathcal{Y}$ is a mapping such that

$$\lim_{h \to 0} \frac{\| \omega_{x_0}(h) \|}{\| h \|} = 0 \quad \text{uniformly on } K$$

for each compact set K in the neighborhood of x_0.

Example. Consider a fuzzy function $f : \mathbf{R} \to \mathcal{F}(\mathbf{R})$ such that

$$\begin{aligned} f(x) &= \{(a(r, x), b(r, x), r) : r \in I\} \\ &= (a(\cdot, x), b(\cdot, x)), \end{aligned}$$

where a and b are in $C^1(I \times \mathbf{R})$. Then we have for $h \to 0$

$$\begin{aligned} f(x + h) &= \{(a(r, x + h), b(r, x + h), r) : r \in I\} \\ &= \{(a(r, x) + \frac{\partial a}{\partial x}(r, x)h + o(h), b(r, x) + \frac{\partial b}{\partial x}(r, x)h + o(h), r) : r \in I\}. \end{aligned}$$

Here $\lim_{h \to 0} \frac{o(h)}{h} = 0$ uniformly in $r \in I$. It follows that

$$f'(x) = \{(\frac{\partial a}{\partial x}(r, x), \frac{\partial b}{\partial x}(r, x), r) : r \in I\}.$$

Thus we get $f'(x) = (\frac{\partial a}{\partial x}(\cdot, x), \frac{\partial b}{\partial x}(\cdot, x))$ and $A_x(h) = f'(x)h$.

1.4 Directional Differential of Fuzzy Functions

In this section we treat some kind of the directional differential of the fuzzy function $f: E \to \mathcal{F}_b$ (see [8, 9]),where E is an open subset in $\mathbf{R}^n$. Here $\mathcal{F}_b$ is a set of all the fuzzy sets with bounded supports, each of which are characterized by the membership function μ as follows:

$\mathcal{F}_b = \{\mu : \mathbf{R}^n \to I = [0,1]$ satisfying the following conditions $(i) - (iv)\}$.

(i) μ has a unique point $m \in \mathbf{R}^n$ such that $\mu(m) = 1$;

(ii) $\text{supp}(\mu)$ is a bounded set in $\mathbf{R}^n$;

(iii) μ is fuzzy convex on $\mathbf{R}^n$;

(iv) μ is upper semi-continuous on $\mathbf{R}^n$.

Let $x \in E$ and $h \in \mathbf{R}^n$. For $\alpha \in I = [0,1]$ Furukawa defines $\eta(\alpha)$ and $\xi(\alpha)$ as follows:

$$\begin{aligned}
\eta(\alpha) &= \lim_{\lambda \to +0} \frac{\min f(x+\lambda h)_\alpha - \min f(x)_\alpha}{\lambda} \\
\xi(\alpha) &= \lim_{\lambda \to +0} \frac{\max f(x+\lambda h)_\alpha - \max f(x)_\alpha}{\lambda},
\end{aligned}$$

where $f(x)_\alpha = L_\alpha(\mu_{f(x)})$ as long as it exists. Here $\mu_{f(x)}$ is the membership function of the fuzzy number $f(x)$. Since $f(x+\lambda h)_1$ for any λ is a single set, we have $\eta(1) = \xi(1)$. Let $i(\alpha) = \min(\eta(\alpha), \xi(\alpha))$ and $s(\alpha) = \max(\eta(\alpha), \xi(\alpha))$ for $\alpha \in I$. Suppose that the following assumption holds:
Assumption A. (i) *$i(\alpha)$ is lower semi-continuous on* $(0,1]$ *and* $\lim_{\alpha \to +0} a(\alpha) = a(0)$. *$s(\alpha)$ is upper semi-continuous on* $(0,1]$ *and* $\lim_{\alpha \to +0} b(\alpha) = b(0)$.
(ii) *$i(\alpha)$ is non-decreasing and $s(\alpha)$ is non-increasing on* $(0,1]$.

Then we have a unique fuzzy number μ such that

$$L_\alpha(\mu) = [i(\alpha), s(\alpha)]$$

for $\alpha \in I$. $L_\alpha(\mu)$ is dependent on x and h. Define the directional differential of f as follows:

Definition 1.4.1 *Let $f: E \to \mathcal{F}_b$ and $x \in E, h \in \mathbf{R}^n$. Suppose that there exist $\eta(\alpha), \xi(\alpha)$ for $\alpha \in I$ and that Assumption A holds. Then f is said to be one-sided differentiable at $x \in E$ with respect to an $h \in \mathbf{R}^n$. Define the one-sided directional differential $f'(x;h) \in \mathcal{F}_b$ by*

$$f'(x;h)_\alpha = [i(\alpha), s(\alpha)]$$

for $\alpha \in I$.

In what follows we consider the fuzzy-max order and some convexity of fuzzy functions (see fig.3).

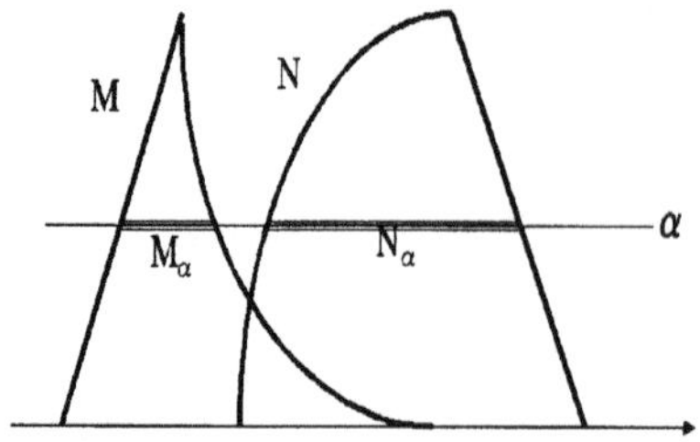

Figure 3: Fuzzy numbers $M \preceq N$

Definition 1.4.2 *Let $M, N \in \mathcal{F}_{\mathbf{b}}$. Define an order relationship by*

$$M \preceq N \Longleftrightarrow (\max M_\alpha \leq \max N_\alpha) \quad \text{and} \quad (\min M_\alpha \leq \min N_\alpha)$$

for $\alpha \in I$. For example $M_\alpha = L_\alpha(\mu_M)$ and μ_M is the membership function of the fuzzy number M. It is said to be the fuzzy-max order.

The order $\preceq$ is a partial order relationship.

Definition 1.4.3 *Let $S \subset \mathbf{R}^n$ be nonempty and convex. A fuzzy function $f : S \to \mathcal{F}_{\mathbf{b}}$ is said to be convex, if*

$$f(\lambda x + (1 - \lambda)y) \preceq \lambda f(x) + (1 - \lambda) f(y).$$

The directional differential is defined as follows:

Theorem 1.4.1 *Let L and R be shape functions (see Section 1.1). Suppose that an $L - R$ fuzzy function $f : S \to \mathcal{F}_{\mathbf{b}}, S \subset \mathbf{R}^n$, is convex and that the parametric representaion of f is as follows:*

$$f(x) = (m(x), a(x), b(x))_{LR}$$

where $m(x) \in \mathbf{R}, a(x) > 0, b(x) > 0$ provided that Assumption A holds. Then we have the following statements (i) and (ii):

(*i*) *$m(\cdot), a(\cdot)$ and $b(\cdot)$ are one-sided directional differentiable on S, i.e., there exists the limit*

$$m(x; h) = \lim_{\lambda \to +0} \frac{m(x + \lambda h) - m(x)}{\lambda}$$

for $x \in S, h \in \mathbf{R}^n$. *So are* $a'(x;h)$ *and* $b'(x;h)$. *Then* $\eta(\alpha)$ *and* $\xi(\alpha)$ *are described by*

$$\begin{aligned}\eta(\alpha) &= m'(x;h) - a'(x;h)t_\alpha^L \\ \xi(\alpha) &= m'(x;h) + b'(x;h)t_\alpha^R\end{aligned}$$

for $x \in S, h \in \mathbf{R}^n$ *and* $\alpha \in I$, *where*

$$\begin{aligned}t_\alpha^L &= \inf\{t \in \mathbf{R} : L\Big(\frac{m(x)-t}{a(x)}\Big)_+ \geq \alpha\} \\ t_\alpha^R &= \sup\{t \in \mathbf{R} : R\Big(\frac{t-m(x)}{b(x)}\Big)_+ \geq \alpha\};\end{aligned}$$

(*ii*) f *is one-sided directional differentiable at* $x \in S$ *with respect to* $h \in \mathbf{R}^n$ *as follows:*

$$\begin{aligned}f'(x) &= (m'(x;h), a'(x;h), b'(x;h))_{LR} && \text{for } a'(x;h) > 0, b'(x;h) > 0; \\ f'(x) &= (m'(x;h), -b'(x;h), -a'(x;h))_{RL} && \text{for } a'(x;h) < 0, b'(x;h) < 0; \\ f'(x) &= (m'(x;h), a'(x;h), 0)_{LR} && \text{for } a'(x;h) > 0, b'(x;h) = 0; \\ f'(x) &= (m'(x;h), 0, -a'(x;h))_{RL} && \text{for } a'(x;h) < 0, b'(x;h) = 0.\end{aligned}$$

Remarks. If a and b have some kind of monotonicity, then the fuzzy function $f(x) = (m(x), a(x), b(x))_{LR}$ is differentiable.

Furukawa analyzes the directional differentials of the $L-R$ fuzzy function $f : \mathbf{R}^n \to \mathcal{F}_\mathbf{b}$. In the case that f is defined on $\mathbf{R}$, the directional differentials mean the Dini's derivatives. In the next section we investigate the Dini's derivatives of fuzzy functions.

1.5 Dini's Derivatives of Fuzzy Functions with Parametric Representation

The following theorem on the completeness of a set of compact and convex sets in $\mathbf{R}^n$ is very interesting (cf. [9]):

Theorem 1.5.1 *Let* $M, N \in \mathcal{F}_\mathbf{b}$ *and*

$$d_\infty(M,N) = \sup_{\alpha \in I} \max(|\min M_\alpha - \min N_\alpha|, |\max M_\alpha - \max N_\alpha|).$$

Then $(\mathcal{F}_\mathbf{b}, d_\infty)$ *is a complete metric space.*

In this section we introduce some representations of fuzzy numbers which have some compactness and convexity as well as we make discussion on the completeness of some linear space, i.e., Banach space, which contains the sets of fuzzy numbers. We treat fuzzy functions with the following representation of

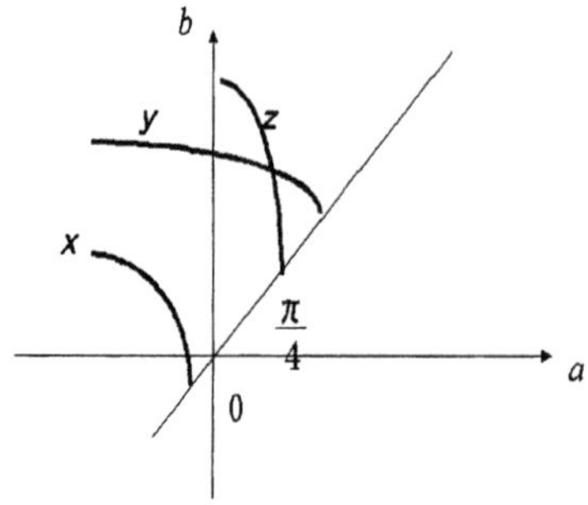

Figure 4: Fuzzy numbers x, y, z

fuzzy numbers (cf. [1]). Consider the following set consisting of pairs of two functions :

$$X = \{x = (a, b) : a \text{ and } b \text{ are bounded functions from } (0, 1] \text{ to } \mathbf{R}\}$$

(see fig.4).

For $x = (a, b)$ and $y = (c, d)$ we denote $x = y$ when $a(\alpha) = c(\alpha)$ and $b(\alpha) = d(\alpha)$ for $\forall\alpha \in (0, 1]$. Let the zero of X be $0 = (a_0, b_0)$ and $a_0(\alpha) = b_0(\alpha) = 0$ for $0 < \alpha \leq 1$. We define the addition and scalar product by

$$x + y = (a + c, b + d) \quad ; \lambda x = (\lambda a, \lambda b)$$

where $\lambda \in \mathbf{R}$. It follows that X is a linear space with the above addition and scalar product.

Let a norm of $x = (a, b)$ be

$$\| x \| = \sup_{0<\alpha\leq 1} \sqrt{|a(\alpha)|^2 + |b(\alpha)|^2}.$$

Then X is a normed space. It follows that X is a Banach space with some consideration.

From *(ii)* and *(iv)* in the definition of $\mathcal{F}_{\mathbf{b}}$ (see Section 1.4), for positive $\alpha \leq 1$ and $\mu \in \mathcal{F}_{\mathbf{b}}$, α-cut set $C_\alpha(\mu) = \{t \in \mathbf{R} : \mu(t) \geq \alpha\}$ is bounded closed, *i.e.*, compact in $\mathbf{R}$. Let $a(\alpha) = \min C_\alpha(\mu)$ and $b(\alpha) = \max C_\alpha(\mu)$. We denote $\mu \in \mathcal{F}_{\mathbf{b}}$ by $\mu = (a, b)$. Then it follows that $\mu \in X$. Thus we have $\mathcal{F}_{\mathbf{b}} \subset X$.

We have the following properties of fuzzy numbers.

Theorem 1.5.2 *(see [9]) Let* $\mu = (a, b) \in \mathcal{F}_{\mathbf{b}}$*, where* $a(\alpha) = \min C_\alpha(\mu)$ *and* $b(\alpha) = \max C_\alpha(\mu)$*.* $a(\alpha)$ *and* $b(\alpha)$ *have the following properties (i) – (iv):*

(*i*) *There exists a unique value of* $a(1) = b(1)$ *;*

(*ii*) *A set* $\{(a(\alpha), b(\alpha)) : \alpha \in I\}$ *is a bounded set in* $\mathbf{R}^2$*, where* $a(0) = \min cl(supp(\mu)), b(0) = \max cl(supp(\mu))$*;*

(*iii*) $a(\alpha)$ *is non-decreasing and* $b(\alpha)$ *is non-increasing;*

(*iv*) $a(\alpha)$ *is lower semi-continuous and* $b(\alpha)$ *is upper semi-continuous.*

Remarks. From the definitions the above addition between fuzzy numbers satisfies the extension principle which are given by Zadeh and many other theoreticians of fuzzy logic.

The polynomials $x^i, i = 2, 3, \cdots$, of $x = (a, b)$ is calculated as follows. $\alpha-$cut sets of membership function μ_x is $L_\alpha(\mu_x) = [a(\alpha), b(\alpha)]$ for $\alpha \in I$. We calculate $x^i, i = 2, 3, \cdots$, in the following cases (a) – (c). By the extension principle, it follows that

$$\begin{aligned} & \mu_{x^i}(\xi) \\ = & \max_{\xi=\Pi_j \xi_j} \min_{1 \le j \le i} (\mu(\xi_j)) \\ = & \max\{\alpha \in I : \xi = \Pi_{j=1}^n \xi_j, \xi_j \in L_\alpha(\mu_x)\}. \end{aligned}$$

When $i = 2$, we find the following relations (see [17]).

(a) If $0 \le a(\alpha) \le b(\alpha)$, then we get

$$L_\alpha(\mu_{x^2}) = [a(\alpha)^2, b(\alpha)^2],$$

thus $x^2 = (a^2, b^2) \in \mathcal{F}_{\mathbf{b}}$.

(b) If $a(\alpha) \le b(\alpha) \le 0$, then we have

$$L_\alpha(\mu_{x^2}) = [b(\alpha)^2, a(\alpha)^2],$$

thus $x^2 = (b^2, a^2) \in \mathcal{F}_{\mathbf{b}}$.

(c) If $a(\alpha) \le 0 \le b(\alpha)$, then it follows that

$$L_\alpha(\mu_{x^2}) = [a(\alpha)b(\alpha), c(\alpha)]$$

where $c(\alpha) = \max(a(\alpha)^2, b(\alpha)^2)$. Here ab is increasing in α and c is decreasing. And $x^2 = (ab, c) \in \mathcal{F}_{\mathbf{b}}$.

In what follows we get the closedness etc of $\mathcal{F}_{\mathbf{b}}$ and we consider the differential of fuzzy functions.

Theorem 1.5.3 $\mathcal{F}_{\mathbf{b}}$ *is closed convex cone in* X*.*

Definition 1.5.1 *Denote a function $f : \mathbf{R} \to X$ by $f(x) = (a(x,\cdot), b(x,\cdot))$. Let $x_0 \in \mathbf{R}$ and $\eta \in X$. f is called to be differentiable at x_0 and $f'(x_0) = \eta \in X$, if for $\forall \varepsilon > 0$, there exists a $\delta > 0$ such that $\forall x : |x - x_0| < \delta$,*

$$\| \frac{f(x) - f(x_0)}{x - x_0} - \eta \| < \varepsilon.$$

Theorem 1.5.4 *Suppose that $f = (a, b)$ is differentiable at x_0. Then f is continuous at x_0. Moreover a and b are differentiable at x_0 and $f'(x_0) = (\frac{\partial a}{\partial x}(x_0,\cdot), \frac{\partial b}{\partial x}(x_0,\cdot))$.*

Theorem 1.5.5 *If both a and b are smooth on $\mathbf{R} \times (0, 1]$, then $f(x) = (a(x,\cdot), b(x,\cdot))$ is differentiable in x.*

Proposition 1.5.1 *Let f is a constant function with the membership function μ, i.e., $f(x) = \mu$, for $x \in \mathbf{R}$. Then f is differentiable on $\mathbf{R}$ and $f'(x) = (0, 0) \in \mathcal{F}_{\mathbf{b}}$ for $x \in \mathbf{R}$.*

Proposition 1.5.2 *Let $f(x) = \mu_1 x + \mu_2$, where $\mu_i \in \mathcal{F}_{\mathbf{b}}($ or $X), i = 1, 2$. Then f is differentiable on $\mathbf{R}$ and $f'(x) = \mu_i \in \mathcal{F}_{\mathbf{b}}($ or $X)$ for $x \in \mathbf{R}$.*

Under fuzzy-max order relationship (see Section 1.4) and some Lipschitz conditions of fuzzy functions we define Dini's derivatives of the functions.

Definition 1.5.2 *(see [8]) Let $f : \mathbf{R} \to \mathcal{F}_{\mathbf{b}}$ and $x_0 \in \mathbf{R}$. f is called to be locally Lipschitzian in x, if there exists a neighborhood $U(x_0)$ of any x_0 and $L(x_0) > 0$ such that*

$$f(x) - L(x_0)|x - x_0| \preceq f(x_0) \preceq f(x) + L(x_0)|x - x_0|$$

for $x \in U(x_0)$.

Suppose that fuzzy function $f(x) = (a(x,\cdot), b(x,\cdot))$ is locally Lipschitzian in x. Then we have

$$\begin{aligned} \sup(f(x) - L(x_0)|x - x_0|)_\alpha &\leq \sup(f(x_0))_\alpha \\ \inf(f(x) - L(x_0)|x - x_0|)_\alpha &\leq \inf(f(x_0))_\alpha \end{aligned}$$

for $\alpha \in I$, i.e.,

$$\begin{aligned} a(x,\alpha) - L(x_0)|x - x_0| \leq a(x_0,\alpha) \leq a(x,\alpha) + L(x_0)|x - x_0|, \\ b(x,\alpha) - L(x_0)|x - x_0| \leq b(x_0,\alpha) \leq b(x,\alpha) + L(x_0)|x - x_0|. \end{aligned}$$

Thus it follows that

$$\frac{f(x) - f(x_0)}{x - x_0} = \Big(\frac{a(x,\alpha) - a(x_0,\alpha)}{x - x_0}, \frac{b(x,\alpha) - b(x_0,\alpha)}{x - x_0}\Big),$$

where $x \neq x_0$ and $\alpha \in I$. Since $a(x,\alpha)$ and $b(x,\alpha)$ are locally Lipschitzian in x, there exist the following Dini's derivatives:

$$\begin{aligned} D^+a(x_0,\alpha) &= \limsup_{x\to x_0+0} \frac{a(x,\alpha)-a(x_0,\alpha)}{x-x_0}; \\ D^-a(x_0,\alpha) &= \limsup_{x\to x_0-0} \frac{a(x,\alpha)-a(x_0,\alpha)}{x-x_0}; \\ D_+a(x_0,\alpha) &= \liminf_{x\to x_0+0} \frac{a(x,\alpha)-a(x_0,\alpha)}{x-x_0}; \\ D_-a(x_0,\alpha) &= \liminf_{x\to x_0-0} \frac{a(x,\alpha)-a(x_0,\alpha)}{x-x_0}. \end{aligned}$$

We have the following of definition of the Dini's derivatives of fuzzy functions:

Theorem 1.5.6 *Suppose that a fuzzy function $f : \mathbf{R} \to \mathcal{F}_b$ is locally Lipschitzian in x. Let $x_0 \in \mathbf{R}$. Denote the Dini's derivatives by*

$$\begin{aligned} D^+f(x_0) &= \limsup_{x\to x_0+0} \frac{f(x)-f(x_0)}{x-x_0}; \\ D^-f(x_0) &= \limsup_{x\to x_0-0} \frac{f(x)-f(x_0)}{x-x_0}; \\ D_+f(x_0) &= \liminf_{x\to x_0+0} \frac{f(x)-f(x_0)}{x-x_0}; \\ D^-f(x_0) &= \liminf_{x\to x_0-0} \frac{f(x)-f(x_0)}{x-x_0}. \end{aligned}$$

Then we have

$$\begin{aligned} D^+f(x_0) &= (D^+a(x_0,\cdot), D^+b(x_0,\cdot)); D^-f(x_0) = (D^-a(x_0,\cdot), D^-b(x_0,\cdot)); \\ D_+f(x_0) &= (D_+a(x_0,\cdot), D_+b(x_0,\cdot)); D_-f(x_0) = (D_-a(x_0,\cdot), D_-b(x_0,\cdot)). \end{aligned}$$

The following example illustrates the Dini's derivatives.
Example. Consider a fuzzy function $f = (a,b) : \mathbf{R} \to \mathcal{F}_b$ such that

$$a(x,\alpha) = \begin{cases} |x|\sin(\frac{1}{x})(\alpha-1) & (x \neq 0) \\ \alpha - 1 & (x = 0). \end{cases}$$

$$b(x,\alpha) = \alpha - 1 \quad (x \in \mathbf{R}).$$

Then it can be seen that f is not differentiable at $x = 0$, but there exist the Dini's differential coefficients $D^{\pm}f(0), D_{\pm}f(0)$.
Remarks. There are two aims of our investigation. One is to discuss some kinds of subdifferentials of fuzzy functions by applying the Dini's derivatives under the following total order relationship:

$$M \leq_m N \Leftrightarrow \int_0^1 \alpha(a(\alpha)+b(\alpha))d\alpha \leq \int_0^1 \alpha(c(\alpha)+d(\alpha))d\alpha,$$

where $M = (a,b)$ and $N = (c,d) \in \mathcal{F}_b$. The other is to establish criteria for optimization problems which consist of nonlinear objective functions and constraints with fuzzy numbers.

By applying the representation of fuzzy numbers in $\mathbf{R}^2$ we analyze nonlinear fuzzy differential equations in the Banach space as well as we get an existence and uniqueness theorem to the fuzzy differential equations in a linear space (cf. [16, 17]).

In [17] we give a definition of integrals of fuzzy functions and define the transition function $e^{\int_{t_0}^{t} p(s)ds}$, where $p : \mathbf{R} \to \mathcal{F}_b$ is a continuous function, which plays an important role in investigating the global attractivity of solutions for initial value problems of fuzzy differential equation

$$\begin{aligned} x' &= p(t)x + q(t) \\ x(t_0) &= x_0 \end{aligned}$$

where $x_0 \in \mathcal{F}_b$ and $p, q : \mathbf{R} \to \mathcal{F}_b$ are continuous functions.

2 Deterministic Method for Fuzzy Optimization Problems

In this chapter we deal with fuzzy optimization problems and some new definitions of optimal solutions for the problems.

2.1 Fuzzy Optimization Problems

In this section we show two examples. One is non-fuzzy convex optimization problem and the other is an optimization problem with fuzzy numbers. Let $\mathcal{F}_b$ be a set of all the fuzzy numbers with bounded supports (see Section 1.4).

Example. Non-fuzzy or fuzzy optimization problem

$$\begin{aligned} &\text{minimize} \quad F(\boldsymbol{x}) \\ &\text{subject to} \quad g_i(\boldsymbol{x}) \leq 0 \quad (i = 1, 2, 3) \end{aligned}$$

where $\boldsymbol{x} = (x_1, x_2)^T \in \mathbf{R}^2$, a fuzzy function $F : \mathbf{R}^2 \to \mathcal{F}_b$ and constraints $g_i : \mathbf{R}^2 \to \mathbf{R}$ as follows (P_u):

$$\begin{aligned} F(\boldsymbol{x}; u) &= ux_1 - x_2; \\ g_1(\boldsymbol{x}) &= -x_1; \\ g_2(\boldsymbol{x}) &= -x_2; \\ g_3(\boldsymbol{x}) &= x_1^2 + x_2^2 - 1. \end{aligned}$$

Here $u = -1$ is a real number or a fuzzy number.

Case 1. If $u \in \mathbf{R}$ and $u = -1$, we get the optimal solution (see fig.5).

$$\boldsymbol{x}^* = (\frac{1}{\sqrt{2}}, \frac{1}{\sqrt{2}})^T.$$

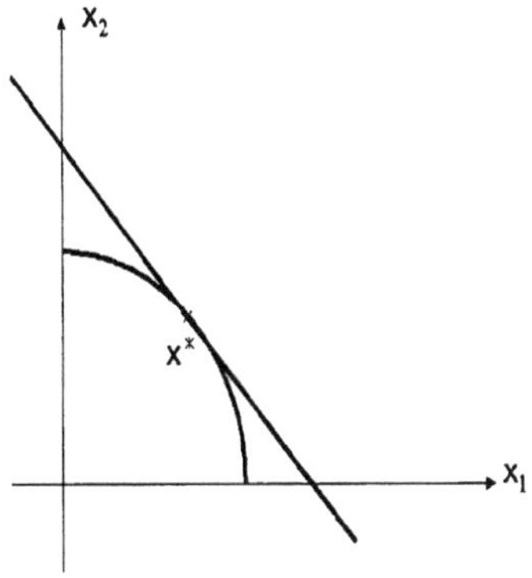

Figure 5: Optimal solution x^*

Case 2. The fuzzy number $u \in \mathcal{F}_{\mathbf{b}}$ and its membership function $\mu_u : \mathbf{R} \to [0,1]$ as follows:

$$\inf L_\alpha(\mu_u) = -1 + p(\alpha), \quad \sup L_\alpha(\mu_u) = -1 + q(\alpha)$$

where $L_\alpha(\mu_u) = \{t \in \mathbf{R} : \mu_u(t) \geq \alpha\}$ and $p(\alpha) \leq q(\alpha)$ for $\forall \alpha$.
Consider the following subproblem (P_y):

$$\begin{aligned} \text{minimize } F(\boldsymbol{x}; y) &= yx_1 - x_2, \quad \boldsymbol{x} = (x_1, x_2)^T \\ \text{subject to } \boldsymbol{x} &\geq 0, \\ g_3(\boldsymbol{x}) &= x_1^2 + x_2^2 - 1 \leq 0, \end{aligned}$$

which is corresponding to the fuzzy optimization problem (P_u), where $y \in \mathbf{R}$ (see fig. 6). We call that a point $\boldsymbol{x}_y^* \in \mathbf{R}$ is an a_0-cut optimal solution of (P_u) for $u \in \mathcal{F}_{\mathbf{b}}$, if there exists an $a_0 > 0$ such that for $a_0 \leq \alpha \leq 1$ and any $y \in L_\alpha(\mu_u)$ there exists an optimal solution to (P_y),

$$x^*(y) = (\frac{-y}{\sqrt{1+y^2}}, \frac{-y}{\sqrt{1+y^2}})^T.$$

In what follows we treat a generalized problem. Consider the following fuzzy optimization problem $(\mathcal{P}_u)$:

$$\begin{aligned} \text{minimize} \quad & F(x; u), \quad x \in \mathbf{R}^n, \\ \text{subject to} \quad & g_i(x) = 0, \ i = 1, \cdots, m, \\ & x \geq 0, \end{aligned}$$

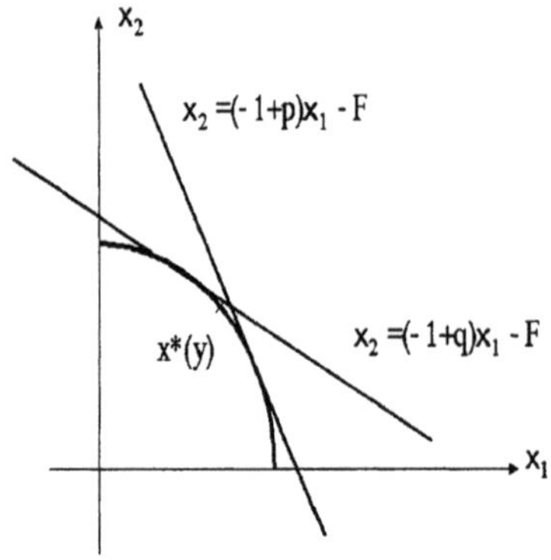

Figure 6: Set of optimal solutions $x^*(y)$ for y

where $u \in \mathcal{F}_{\mathrm{b}}$ and $F, g_i : \mathbf{R}^n \to \mathbf{R}$ are continuously twice differentiable functions.

Definition 2.1.1 *We call that a point $x_y^* \in \mathbf{R}$ is an a_0-cut optimal solution of $(\mathcal{P}_u)$ for $u \in \mathcal{F}_{\mathrm{b}}$, if there exists an $a_0 > 0$ such that for $a_0 \leq \alpha \leq 1$ and any $y \in L_\alpha(\mu_u)$ there exists an optimal solution to the subproblem (P_y):*

$$\begin{array}{ll} \textit{minimize} & F(x;y), \quad x \in \mathbf{R}^n, \\ \textit{subject to} & g_i(x) = 0, \ i = 1, \cdots, m, \\ & x \geq 0. \end{array}$$

We consider the following Lagrangian function for $y \in \mathbf{R}$ in order to give an algorithm for the above problem by some generalized Newton method.

$$\begin{aligned} \mathcal{L}(w;y) &= F(x;y) + c^T g(x) - d^T x, \\ w &= (x^T, c^T, d^T)^T, g = (g_1, \cdots, g_m)^T, \\ c &= (c_1, \cdots, c_m)^T, d = (d_1, \cdots, d_n)^T. \end{aligned}$$

In order that we have a_0-cut optimal solutions of the above problem, we suppose the following conditions which are corresponding to the Karush-Kuhn-Tucker condition.

Assumption A_1. *Let $a_0 > 0$ such that $a_0 \leq \alpha \leq 1$ and $y \in L_\alpha(\mu_u)$. Suppose that there exists the Karush-Kuhn-Tucker point*

$$(w^*)^T = ((x^*)^T, (c^*)^T, (d^*)^T),$$

i.e., K-K-T point, satisfying the following conditions (i)-(iii):

(i) $\nabla_x \mathcal{L}(w^*; y) = 0,$

(ii) $c_i^* g_i(x^*) = 0 \quad (i = 1, \cdots, m);$

(iii) $d_j^* x_j^* = 0 \quad (j = 1, \cdots, n).$

Then we have $r(w^*; y) = 0$, where

$$r(w;y) = \begin{pmatrix} \nabla_x \mathcal{L}(w;y) \\ c_1 g_1(x) \\ \cdots \\ c_m g_m(x) \\ d_1 x_1 \\ \cdots \\ d_n x_n \end{pmatrix}.$$

We denote $w^* = w^*(y)$, since w^* is dependent on $y \in L_\alpha(\mu_u)$. Moreover we suppose that the following conditions in order to show a new algorithm to the new optimal solution by some generalized Newton method.

Assumption A_2. *Let $l = 2n + m$, a K-K-T point $w^*(y) \in D_y$, where*

$$D_y = \{w \in \mathbf{R}^l : \| w - w^*(y) \| \leq \varepsilon\}$$

for $\varepsilon > 0$ and $\| \cdot \|$ is a norm in $\mathbf{R}^l$. Suppose that the following conditions (i)-(v) hold:

(i) *The function $g = (g_1, g_2, \cdots, g_m)^T$ is twice differentiable and its derivative satisfies the following Lipschitz condition:*

$$\| \nabla_x^2 (c_1^T g(x_1)) - \nabla_x^2 (c_2^T g(x_2)) \| \leq K(\| c_1 - c_2 \| + \| x_1 - x_2 \|)$$

for $(x_1, c_1, d_1), (x_2, c_2, d_2) \in D_y$;

(ii) *(complementary slackness, cf. [2]) Let $I_y^* = \{i : x_i^* = 0\}$. When $i \in I_y^*$, then $d_i^* > 0$, where d_i^* is the i-th element of d^* and x_i^* the i-th element of x^* ;*

(iii) *(first-order necessary conditions, cf. [7]) The set*

$$\{\frac{\partial g_i}{\partial x}^T (x^*) : i = 1, \cdots, m\} \cup \{e_i = (0, \cdots, 0, \overset{i}{1}, 0, \cdots, 0)^T : i \in I_y^*\}$$

is linearly independent;

(iv) *(second-order sufficiency conditions, cf. [7])* $\dfrac{\partial^2 \mathcal{L}}{\partial x^2} > 0;$

(v) *Let $0 < \rho < 1$ and $0 < \varepsilon < 1$ satisfy*

$$B_0 \rho + \varepsilon K_0 < \sqrt{2} - 1 \text{ and } 1 - M \varepsilon R_1 > 0$$

and an integer $N_0 \geq 3$ be

$$\left(\frac{B_0\rho + \varepsilon K_0 + 1}{(B_0\rho + \varepsilon K_0)^{-1} - 1}\right)^{N_0-2}$$

$$\leq \frac{\rho - \rho^2}{B_0(\rho^2+1)\varepsilon\left[K + 1 + \sqrt{(K+1)^2 + \frac{8(n+1)K(\rho-\rho^2)}{B_0(\rho^2+1)}}\right]}.$$

Here

$$\begin{aligned} M &= K(1 + 2(n+1)\varepsilon) + 1 \\ R_1 &= \max_{w \in D_y} \| (\nabla_w r(w;y))^{-1} \| \\ R_2 &= \max_{w \in D_y} \| \nabla_w r(w;y) \| \\ K_0 &= \max_{w \in D_y} \| \nabla_x (c^T g(x)) \| \frac{R_1(1+\rho^2)}{1 - M\varepsilon R_1} \\ B_0 &= \frac{R_1(M + \varepsilon R_2)}{1 - M\varepsilon R_1}. \end{aligned}$$

2.2 Algorithm by Generalized Newton Method

By applying the generalized Newton method (see [15]), we get the following algorithm of solving $r(w;y) = 0$ for $y \in L_\alpha(\mu_u)$. Denote a norm for $A = (a_{ij}), 1 \leq i,j \leq l$:

$$\| A \| = \max_j \sum_i |a_{ij}|.$$

Find a sequence $\{(w^{(k)T} = ((x^{(k)})^T, (c^{(k)})^T, (d^{(k)})^T) \in D_y : k = 1, 2, \cdots\}$ such that

$$w^{(k+1)} = w^{(k)} - V^{(k)}(k) r(w^{(k)}; y),$$

where $V^{(k)}(k)$ is closed to the Jacobian matrix $(\nabla_w r(w^*;y))^{-1}$ for the sufficiently large k. We construct two $l \times l-$ matrices $\{U(k) : k = 1, 2, \cdots\}$ and $\{V^{(p)}(k) : k = 1, 2, \cdots; p = 1, 2, \cdots, k\}$. $\{U(k)\}$ is a set of some kind of the initial terms by the generalized Newton method and $\{V^{(p)}(k) : k \geq 1, 1 \leq p \leq n\}$ is the sequence of generalized Jacobian matrices.

Algorithm. *Choose $w^{(1)} \in D_y$.*
For $k = 1, 2, \cdots$, do the following steps.
Step 1. *For $1 \leq k \leq N_0$, find $U(k)$ such that*

$$\| \nabla_w r(w^{(k)}; y) U(k) - I \| \leq \rho,$$

where I is the identity matrix. Put $V^{(0)}(0) = U(k)$ *and go to Step 2.*

For $k \geq N_0 + 1, N_0 + 2, \cdots$, *put*

$$U(k) = V^{(k-1)}(k-1).$$

Go to Step 2.

Step 2. *For* $p = 1, 2, \cdots, k$, *compute* $\{V^{(p)}(k)\}$ *such that*

$$V^{(p)}(k) = V^{(p-1)}(k)[2I - \nabla_w r(w^{(k)}; y)V^{(p-1)}(k)].$$

Step 3. *Compute*

$$w^{(k+1)} = w^{(k)} - V^{(k)}(k)r(w^{(k)}; y).$$

Go to Step 1.

In [12] the authors show an algorithm by generalized Newton method, which is applied by the idea of C.Neumann expansion. In the algorithm one finds a matrix $U(k)$ satisfying the inequality of Step1 for each k. In the above algorithm we find $U(k)$ with $k = 1, \cdots, N_0$. The following theorem plays an important role in our algorithm (cf. [14]). In the same manner of the proof in [14] the proof of the following theorem can be proved.

Theorem 2.2.1 *Under Assumptions* A_1 *and* A_2 *we have the following statements (i) and (ii) for* $a_0 \leq \alpha \leq 1$:

(i) *(superlinear convergence) It follows that* $\{w^{(k)}\}$, *where* $w^{(k)}$ *are K-K-T points dependent on* $y \in L_\alpha(\mu_u), k = 1, 2, \cdots$,

$$\lim_{k \to \infty} \frac{\| w^{(k+1)}(y) - w^*(y) \|}{\| w^{(k)}(y) - w^*(y) \|} = 0;$$

(ii) *Moreover we get*

$$\| \nabla_w r(w^{(N_0+1)}(y); y)V^{(N_0)}(N_0) - I \| \leq \rho$$

and $\| w^{(k+1)}(y) - w^{(k)}(y) \|$ *is decreasing in* $k \geq N_0$.

Remark. In this section we assume that constraints and the objective function of the optimization problem are sufficiently smooth for convenience. If the constraints or objective functions are fuzzy functions and locally Lipschitzian in x, there exist no differentials in the sense of Fréchet. In this case we make use of one-sided differentials, i.e., one in the sense of Gâteaux, and Dini's derivatives of fuzzy functions in order to analyze fuzzy optimization problems and to get establish criteria for the existence and iteration of α_0-cut optimal solutions.

References

[1] Chen,M., Saito,S., Ishii, H. (2000) Representation of Fuzzy Numbers and Fuzzy Optimization Problems. Preprint prepared for " Optimizations: modeling and algorithm" held at the Institute of Statistical Mathematics

[2] Clarke,F.H. (1990) Optimization and Nonsmooth Analysis, Classics in Applied mathematics, SIAM, Philadelphia

[3] Dubois,D., Prade,H. (1978) Operations on Fuzzy Numbers. Internat. J. of Systems **9**, 613–626

[4] Dubois,D., Prade,H. (1982) Towards Fuzzy Differential Calculus Part I : Integration of Fuzzy Mappings. Fuzzy Sets and Systems **8**, 1–17

[5] Dubois,D., Prade,H. (1982) Towards Fuzzy Differential Calculus Part II : Integration of Fuzzy Intervals. Fuzzy Sets and Systems **8**, 105–116

[6] Dubois,D., Prade,H. (1982) Towards Fuzzy Differential Calculus Part III: Differentiation. Fuzzy Sets and Systems **8**,225–233

[7] Fiacco, A. McCormick,G.P. (1990) Nonlinear Programming (Classics in Applied Mathematics). SIAM, Philadelphia

[8] Furukawa, N. (1998) Convexity and Local Lipschitz Continuity of Fuzzy-valued Mapping. Fuzzy Sets and Systems **93**,113–119

[9] Furukawa, N. (1999) Mathematical Methods of Fuzzy Optimization(in Japanese). Morikita Pub., Tokyo, Japan

[10] Goetschel Jr. R., Voxman, W. (1983) Topological Properties of Fuzzy Numbers. Fuzzy Sets and Systems **9**, 87–99

[11] Goetschel Jr. R., Voxman, W. (1986) Elementary Fuzzy Calculus. Fuzzy Sets and Systems **18**, 31–43

[12] Noda, T., Ishii, H. (1998) A General Newton Method for Systems of Nonlinear Equations II. Mathematica Japonica **48**, 447–452

[13] Puri, M.L., Ralescu, D.A. (1983) Differential of Fuzzy Functions. J. Math. Anal. Appl. **91**, 552–558

[14] Saito, S., Ishii, H., On Solving Equations Arising from Optimizations Problems by Some Generalized Newton Method(to be submitted to J. Math. Anal. Appl.).

[15] Saito, S., Ishii, H., Remarks on Some Generalized Newton Method for Solving Nonlinear Equations arising from Fuzzy Optimization Problems. Proc. of IFSA'99.

[16] Saito, S., Ishii, H., Fuzzy Differential Equations in a Linear Space. Proc. of INFORMS-KORMS 2000 (Seoul).

[17] Saito, S., Ishii, H., On Behaviors of Solutions for Fuzzy Differential Equations in a Linear Space (to submitted to European J. Operational Researches).

Order Relations and a Monotone Convergence Theorem in the Class of Fuzzy Sets on $\mathbb{R}^n$

Masami Kurano[1], Masami Yasuda[1], Jun-ichi Nakagami[1], and Yuji Yoshida[2]

[1] Chiba University, Chiba, 263-8522, Japan
[2] Kitakyushu University, Kitakyushu, 802-8577, Japan

Abstract. Concerning with the topics of fuzzy decision processes, a brief survey on ordering of fuzzy numbers on $\mathbb{R}$ is presented and an extension to that of fuzzy sets(numbers) on $\mathbb{R}^n$ are considered. This extension is a pseudo order $\preccurlyeq_K$ defined by a non-empty closed convex cone K and characterized by the projection into its dual cone K^+. Especially a structure of the lattice is presented on the class of pyramid-type fuzzy sets. Moreover, we study the convergence of a sequence of fuzzy sets on $\mathbb{R}^n$ which is monotone w.r.t. the order $\preccurlyeq_K$. Our study is carried out by restricting the class of fuzzy sets into the subclass in which the order $\preccurlyeq_K$ becomes a partial order so that a monotone convergence theorem is proved. This restricted subclass of fuzzy sets is created and characterized in the concept of a determining class. These results are applied to obtain the limit theorem for a sequence of fuzzy sets defined by the dynamic fuzzy system with a monotone fuzzy relation. Several figures are illustrated to comprehend our results.

1 Introduction

Fuzzy set theory has made applications in many fields of management science, operations research and statistics (cf.[7], [13], [18]), in which order relation of fuzzy sets is a fundamental problem in fuzzy optimization or fuzzy decision making. Many methods of ordering fuzzy numbers have been proposed in the literature. Among them a partial order on the set of fuzzy numbers on $\mathbb{R}$, called the fuzzy max order, introduced by Ramík and Řimánek[16] is very interesting in the concerns of pure mathematics because it is a natural extension of the order over real numbers and includes many theoretical and applicable potentials.

First, the fuzzy max order of fuzzy numbers on $\mathbb{R}$ (cf. [6], [16]) is briefly surveyed and extended to a pseudo order on a class of fuzzy sets defined on $\mathbb{R}^n$. The pseudo order for fuzzy sets on $\mathbb{R}^n$ is defined by a non-empty closed convex cone K in $\mathbb{R}^n$ and characterized by the projection into its dual cone K^+. Also, the structure of a lattice is discussed for the class of pyramid-type fuzzy sets (see [11]). For a lattice-structure of the fuzzy max order, see [1], [25]. So, we can imagine the much wider application to the fuzzy optimization problem. Our idea of the motivation originates from a set-relation in $\mathbb{R}^n$ given by Kuroiwa, Tanaka and Ha[12], in which various types of set-relations in $\mathbb{R}^n$ are used in set-valued optimizations.

A convergence theorem for a sequence of fuzzy sets is also a fundamental tool and mathematically interesting for sequential decision analysis in a fussy environment. In fact, the limiting behavior of fuzzy states of dynamic fuzzy system or sequential fuzzy decision process have been studied by developing a suitable convergence theorem of a sequence of fuzzy sets. (c.f. [8], [9], [10], [20], [21], [22], [23]) Also, the theory of metric space of fuzzy sets has been developed by many authors (c.f. [2], [14], [19]), in which several convergence theorems of fuzzy sets are given. On the other hand, in multiple criteria decision making, the rewards from dynamic system are described in terms of fussy sets and the model is often optimized under some order or pseudo order relation among fuzzy sets. In this case, it is more important to study the convergence theorem related to fuzzy order relation.

From this motivation, we study the convergence of a sequence of fuzzy sets on $\mathbb{R}^n$ which is monotone w.r.t. a pseudo order $\preccurlyeq_K$. Our procedure is done by restricting the class of fuzzy sets into the subclass, in which $\preccurlyeq_K$ becomes a partial order and a monotone convergence theorem is proved. This restricted subclass of fuzzy sets is created and characterized in the concept of a determining class. These results are applied to obtain the limit theorem for a sequence of fuzzy sets defined by the dynamic fuzzy system with a monotone fuzzy relation.

The outline for this paper is as follows. Section 2 contains some notations and basic concepts of fuzzy set theory referring to the text books (cf. [3], [15]). The fuzzy max order on $\mathbb{R}$ and its related topics are summarized in Section 3. A pseudo order on the class of fuzzy sets on $\mathbb{R}^n$ is introduced as an extension of the fuzzy max order in Section 4. Its characterization and the structure of a lattice are considered for the pyramid-type fuzzy sets in Section 5. In Section 6, we introduce a concept of determining class and give a convergence theorem for a sequence of convex compact subclass of $\mathbb{R}^n$. In Section 7, these results are applied to obtain a monotone convergence theorem for fuzzy sets on $\mathbb{R}^n$. In Section 8, we consider the limit of a sequence of fuzzy sets defined by the monotone dynamic fuzzy system. Several figures are illustrated to comprehend our results.

2 Notations and Basic Concepts

In this section we describe the notation and basic concepts of fuzzy set theory (cf. [3], [7], [15], [24]).

Let $\mathbb{R}$ be the set of all real numbers and $\mathbb{R}^n$ an n-dimensional Euclidean space. We write fuzzy sets on $\mathbb{R}^n$ by their membership functions $\widetilde{s} : \mathbb{R}^n \to [0,1]$ (see Novák [15] and Zadeh [24]). The α-cut ($\alpha \in [0,1]$) of the fuzzy set $\widetilde{s}$ on $\mathbb{R}^n$ is defined as

$$\widetilde{s}_\alpha := \{x \in \mathbb{R}^n \mid \widetilde{s}(x) \geq \alpha\} \ (\alpha > 0) \quad \text{and} \quad \widetilde{s}_0 := \mathrm{cl}\{x \in \mathbb{R}^n \mid \widetilde{s}(x) > 0\},$$

where cl denotes the closure of the set. A fuzzy set $\widetilde{s}$ is called convex if

$$\widetilde{s}(\lambda x + (1-\lambda)y) \geq \widetilde{s}(x) \wedge \widetilde{s}(y) \quad x, y \in \mathbb{R}^n, \ \lambda \in [0,1],$$

where $a \wedge b = \min\{a, b\}$. Note that $\widetilde{s}$ is convex if and only if the α-cut $\widetilde{s}_\alpha$ is a convex set for all $\alpha \in [0,1]$. Let $\mathcal{F}(\mathbb{R}^n)$ be the set of all convex fuzzy sets whose membership functions $\widetilde{s} : \mathbb{R}^n \to [0,1]$ are upper-semicontinuous and normal ($\sup_{x \in \mathbb{R}^n} \widetilde{s}(x) = 1$) and have a compact support. In the one-dimensional case $n = 1$, $\mathcal{F}(\mathbb{R})$ denotes the set of all fuzzy numbers.

Let $\mathcal{C}(\mathbb{R}^n)$ be the set of all compact convex subsets of $\mathbb{R}^n$, and $\mathcal{C}_r(\mathbb{R}^n)$ be the set of all rectangles in $\mathbb{R}^n$. For $\widetilde{s} \in \mathcal{F}(\mathbb{R}^n)$, we have $\widetilde{s}_\alpha \in \mathcal{C}(\mathbb{R}^n)$ ($\alpha \in [0,1]$). We write a rectangle in $\mathcal{C}_r(\mathbb{R}^n)$ by

$$[x, y] = [x_1, y_1] \times [x_2, y_2] \times \cdots \times [x_n, y_n]$$

for $x = (x_1, x_2, \cdots, x_n)$, $y = (y_1, y_2, \cdots, y_n) \in \mathbb{R}^n$ with $x_i \leq y_i$ ($i = 1, 2, \cdots, n$). For the case of $n = 1$, $\mathcal{C}(\mathbb{R}) = \mathcal{C}_r(\mathbb{R})$ and it denotes the set of all bounded closed intervals. When $\widetilde{s} \in \mathcal{F}(\mathbb{R}^n)$ satisfies $\widetilde{s}_\alpha \in \mathcal{C}_r(\mathbb{R}^n)$ for all $\alpha \in [0,1]$, $\widetilde{s}$ is called a pyramid-type. See Figure 8. We denote by $\mathcal{F}_r(\mathbb{R}^n)$ the set of all pyramid-type fuzzy sets on $\mathbb{R}^n$. Obviously $\mathcal{F}_r(\mathbb{R}) = \mathcal{F}(\mathbb{R})$.

Here we give the extension principle introduced by Zadeh which provides a general method for fuzzification of non-fuzzy mathematical concepts.

The extension principle (cf. Dubois and Prade [3]):

Let f be a map from $\mathbb{R}^{n \times n}$ to $\mathbb{R}^n$ such that $y = f(x_1, \cdots, x_n)$. It allows us to induce a map through f from fuzzy sets $\widetilde{s_i} (i = 1, 2, \ldots, n)$ on $\mathbb{R}^n$ to a fuzzy set $\widetilde{s}$ on $\mathbb{R}^n$ such that

$$\widetilde{s}(y) := \sup_{\substack{x_1, \cdots, x_n \in \mathbb{R}^n \\ y = f(x_1, \cdots, x_n)}} \min\{\widetilde{s_1}(x_1), \cdots, \widetilde{s_n}(x_n)\},$$

where $\widetilde{s}(y) := 0$ *if* $f^{-1}(y) = \phi$.

Applying the extension principle, the addition and the scalar multiplication on $\mathbb{R}^n$ are extended to those on $\mathcal{F}(\mathbb{R}^n)$ as follows:

For $\widetilde{s}, \widetilde{r} \in \mathcal{F}(\mathbb{R}^n)$ and $\lambda \geq 0$,

$$(\widetilde{s} + \widetilde{r})(x) := \sup_{\substack{x_1, x_2 \in \mathbb{R}^n \\ x_1 + x_2 = x}} \{\widetilde{s}(x_1) \wedge \widetilde{r}(x_2)\}, \tag{2.1}$$

$$(\lambda \widetilde{s})(x) := \begin{cases} \widetilde{s}(x/\lambda) & \text{if } \lambda > 0 \\ \mathbf{1}_{\{0\}}(x) & \text{if } \lambda = 0 \end{cases} \quad (x \in \mathbb{R}^n), \tag{2.2}$$

where $\mathbf{1}_{\{\cdot\}}(\cdot)$ is an indicator. By using set operations $A + B := \{x + y \mid x \in A, y \in B\}$ and $\lambda A := \{\lambda x \mid x \in A\}$ for any non-empty sets $A, B \subset \mathbb{R}^n$, the following holds immediately:

$$(\widetilde{s} + \widetilde{r})_\alpha = \widetilde{s}_\alpha + \widetilde{r}_\alpha \quad \text{and} \quad (\lambda \widetilde{s})_\alpha = \lambda \widetilde{s}_\alpha \quad (\alpha \in [0,1]). \tag{2.3}$$

Also, for $\widetilde{s}, \widetilde{r} \in \mathcal{F}(\mathbb{R})$, $\widetilde{\max}\{\widetilde{s}, \widetilde{r}\}$ and $\widetilde{\min}\{\widetilde{s}, \widetilde{r}\} \in \mathcal{F}(\mathbb{R})$ are defined by

$$\widetilde{\max}\{\widetilde{s}, \widetilde{r}\}(y) := \sup_{\substack{x_1, x_2 \in \mathbb{R} \\ y = \max(x_1, x_2)}} \{\widetilde{s}(x_1) \wedge \widetilde{r}(x_2)\} \tag{2.4}$$

and

$$\widetilde{\min}\{\widetilde{s}, \widetilde{r}\}(y) := \sup_{\substack{x_1, x_2 \in \mathbb{R} \\ y = \min(x_1, x_2)}} \{\widetilde{s}(x_1) \wedge \widetilde{r}(x_2)\}. \tag{2.5}$$

The images of $\widetilde{\max}\{\widetilde{s}, \widetilde{r}\}$ and $\widetilde{\min}\{\widetilde{s}, \widetilde{r}\} \in \mathcal{F}(\mathbb{R})$ are illustrated as follows:

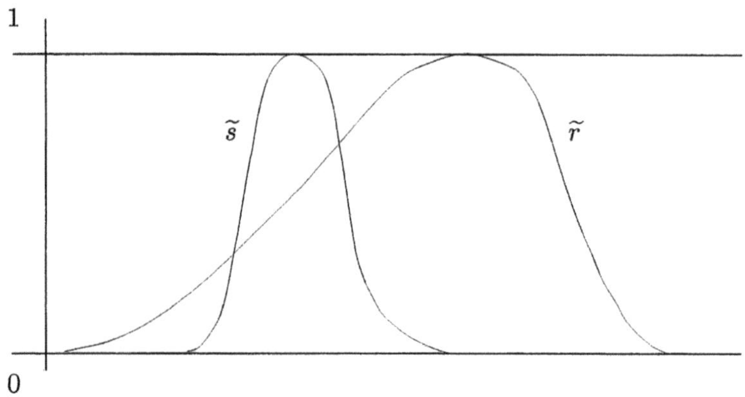

Fig. 1: $\widetilde{s}$ and $\widetilde{r} \in \mathcal{F}(\mathbb{R})$

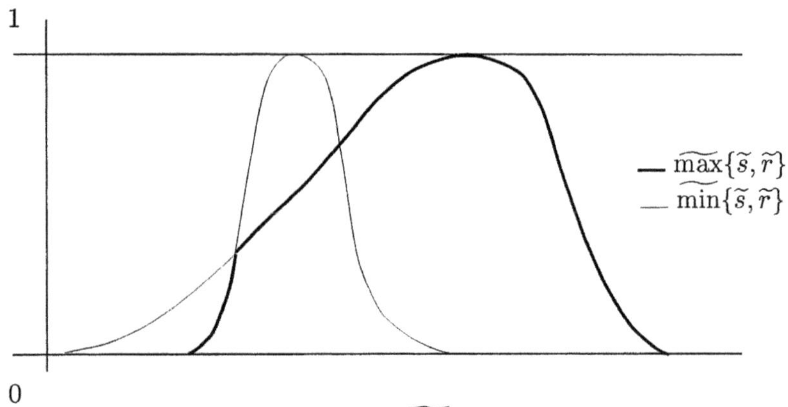

Fig. 2: $\widetilde{\max}\{\widetilde{s}, \widetilde{r}\}$ and $\widetilde{\min}\{\widetilde{s}, \widetilde{r}\} \in \mathcal{F}(\mathbb{R})$

We need a representative theorem (cf. [3], [15]) which is a basic tool for the fuzzy interval analysis.

The representative theorem:

(i) *For any* $\widetilde{s} \in \mathcal{F}(\mathbb{R}^n)$, $\widetilde{s}(x) = \sup_{\alpha \in [0,1]} \{\alpha \wedge \mathbf{1}_{\widetilde{s}_\alpha}(x)\}, \quad x \in \mathbb{R}^n.$

(ii) *Conversely, for a family of subsets* $\{D_\alpha \in \mathcal{C}(\mathbb{R}^n) \mid 0 \le \alpha \le 1\}$ *with* $D_\alpha \subset D_{\alpha'}$ *for* $\alpha' \le \alpha$ *and* $\cap_{\alpha' < \alpha} D_{\alpha'} = D_\alpha$, *if we set* $\widetilde{s}(x) := \sup_{\alpha \in [0,1]} \{\alpha \wedge \mathbf{1}_{D_\alpha}(x)\}$, $x \in \mathbb{R}^n$ *then* $\widetilde{s}$ *belongs to* $\mathcal{F}(\mathbb{R}^n)$ *and satisfies* $\widetilde{s}_\alpha = D_\alpha$, $\alpha \in [0,1]$.

The image of the equation (i) of the representative theorem is illustrated in Figure 3.

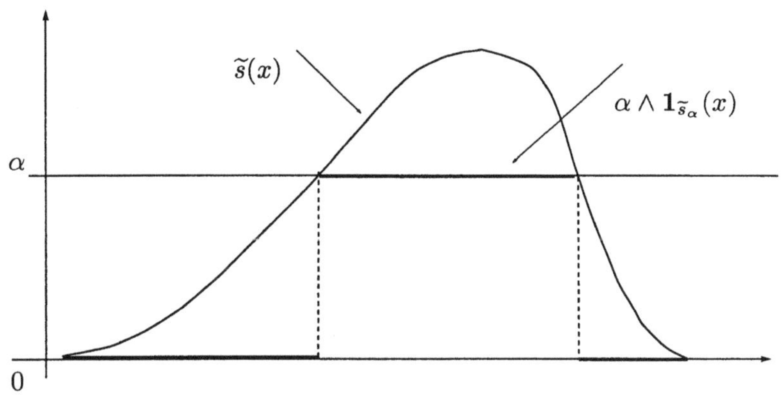

Fig. 3: $\widetilde{s}(x) = \sup_{\alpha \in [0,1]} \{\alpha \wedge \mathbf{1}_{\widetilde{s}_\alpha}(x)\}, \quad x \in \mathbb{R}^n$

3 Fuzzy Max Order on $\mathcal{F}(\mathbb{R})$

In this section, we review a fuzzy max order in $\mathcal{F}(\mathbb{R})$ which is extended to $\mathcal{F}(\mathbb{R}^n)$ in the next section.

The following binary relation $\preccurlyeq$ has been formulated first by Ramík and Řimánek[16]. Let $\widetilde{s}$ and $\widetilde{r}$ be two fuzzy numbers in $\mathcal{F}(\mathbb{R})$. Then $\widetilde{s} \preccurlyeq \widetilde{r}$ if and only if $\sup \widetilde{s}_\alpha \le \sup \widetilde{r}_\alpha$ and $\inf \widetilde{s}_\alpha \le \inf \widetilde{r}_\alpha$ for each $\alpha \in [0,1]$, where $\widetilde{s}_\alpha$ and $\widetilde{r}_\alpha$ are α-cuts of $\widetilde{s}$ and $\widetilde{r}$ respectively and $\widetilde{s}_\alpha := [\inf \widetilde{s}_\alpha, \sup \widetilde{s}_\alpha]$ and $\widetilde{r}_\alpha := [\inf \widetilde{r}_\alpha, \sup \widetilde{r}_\alpha]$. Obviously the binary relation $\preccurlyeq$ satisfies the axioms of a partial order relation on $\mathcal{F}(\mathbb{R})$ and is called the fuzzy max order. Some properties of the relation $\preccurlyeq$ are investigated in Ramík and Řimánek[16].

Proposition 3.1. *Let* $\widetilde{s}, \widetilde{r}$ *be fuzzy numbers in* $\mathcal{F}(\mathbb{R})$.

(i) *The inequality* $\widetilde{s} \preccurlyeq \widetilde{r}$ *if and only if there exist* $m, n, t^* \in \mathbb{R}$ *with* $m \le t^* \le n$, $\widetilde{s}(m) = \widetilde{r}(n) = 1$ *and* $\widetilde{s}(t) \ge \widetilde{r}(t)$ *for any* $t \le t^*$ *and* $\widetilde{s}(t) \le \widetilde{r}(t)$ *for any* $t > t^*$.

(ii) *The following three conditions* (a) *to* (c) *are equivalent:*
(a) $\widetilde{s} \preccurlyeq \widetilde{r}$, (b) $\widetilde{\max}\{\widetilde{s}, \widetilde{r}\} = \widetilde{r}$, (c) $\widetilde{\min}\{\widetilde{s}, \widetilde{r}\} = \widetilde{s}$,
where $\widetilde{\min}$ *and* $\widetilde{\max}$ *are defined in* (2.4) *and* (2.5).

For the fuzzy max order on $\mathcal{F}(\mathbb{R})$, Congxin and Cong [1] proved that the bounded set of fuzzy numbers on $\mathcal{F}(\mathbb{R})$ must have supremum and infimum. The basic proof is as follows. For any sequence of fuzzy numbers $\{\tilde{s}_n\}_{n=1}^{\infty}$, let $\underline{D}_\alpha := \lim_{\alpha' \uparrow \alpha} \sup_{n \geq 1} \inf \tilde{s}_{n\alpha'}$ and $\overline{D}_\alpha := \lim_{\alpha' \uparrow \alpha} \sup_{n \geq 1} \sup \tilde{s}_{n\alpha'}$, where $\tilde{s}_{n\alpha}$ is the α-cut of $\tilde{s}_n$. Then, the family of closed subsets $\{D_\alpha := [\underline{D}_\alpha, \overline{D}_\alpha] \mid \alpha \in [0,1]\}$ satisfies condition (ii) of the representation theorem, so that $\tilde{s}$ defined by

$$\tilde{s}(x) := \sup_{\alpha \in [0,1]} \{\alpha \wedge \mathbf{1}_{D_\alpha}(x)\} \quad (x \in \mathbb{R}) \tag{3.1}$$

belongs to $\mathcal{F}(\mathbb{R})$ and $\tilde{s} = \sup_{n \geq 1} \tilde{s}_n$.

Similarly, the infimum of $\{\tilde{s}_n\}_{n=1}^{\infty}$ is constructed. These results derived the interesting mathematical fact that the continuous fuzzy-valued function on a closed interval has a maximum and minimum. Also, the structure of lattice for fuzzy numbers is discussed in Zhang and Hirota[25].

To be suitable for computations and treatments, a class of fuzzy numbers, called an L-R-fuzzy number, is introduced in many text books.

Let $L, R : [0, \infty) \to [0,1]$ be two non-increasing and not constant functions with $L(0) = R(0) = 1$ and $L(x_0) = R(x_0) = 0$ for some $x_0 > 0$. A fuzzy number $\tilde{s}$ is called an L-R-fuzzy number if there exist real numbers $m, n (m \leq n), \alpha, \beta (\alpha, \beta > 0)$ such that

$$\tilde{s}(x) = \begin{cases} L(\frac{m-x}{\alpha}) & \text{for} \quad x \leq m, \\ 1 & \text{for} \quad m \leq x \leq n, \\ R(\frac{x-n}{\beta}) & \text{for} \quad n \leq x. \end{cases} \tag{3.2}$$

Given functions L, R with the properties in the above definition, the L-R-fuzzy number specified by m, n, α, β is denoted by an ordered tetradic $(m, n, \alpha, \beta)_{L\text{-}R}$, which includes the triangular and trapezoidal fuzzy numbers. Then, the fuzzy max order on the set of L-R-fuzzy numbers is characterized by inequalities of the elements. (cf. [16]).

In particular, the symmetric fuzzy number $\tilde{s} = (m, m, \alpha, \alpha)_{L\text{-}L}$ is called an L-fuzzy number and denoted by $(m, \alpha)_L$. Furukawa[4] extended the L-fuzzy number $(m, \alpha)_L$ with $\alpha > 0$ to the case of $\alpha \in \mathbb{R}$ and proved that for $\alpha\beta \geq 0$ the fuzzy max order $(m, \alpha)_L \preccurlyeq (n, \beta)_L$ if and only if $x_0|\alpha - \beta| \leq n - m$ where x_0 is the zero point of L. Moreover Furukawa [4] introduced the linear operations on the set of extended L-fuzzy numbers by

$$\begin{aligned} (m, \alpha)_L \oplus (n, \beta)_L &= (m + n, \alpha + \beta)_L, \\ \lambda(m, \alpha)_L &= (\lambda m, \lambda\alpha)_L \quad \text{for any scalar} \ \ \lambda \in \mathbb{R}. \end{aligned}$$

The fuzzy max order is proved to be adapted to the above operations. Also Furukawa [5] introduced a parametric order relation on L-fuzzy numbers which is an extension of the fuzzy max order and its total order relation. The fuzzy optimization problems related to the fuzzy max order are dealed with many authors; e.g., Furukawa[5], Kurano et al.[9], Yoshida[22] and others.

4 A Pseudo Order on $\mathcal{F}(\mathbb{R}^n)$

In this section we extend the fuzzy max order on $\mathcal{F}(\mathbb{R})$ to a pseudo order on $\mathcal{F}(\mathbb{R}^n)$ by the argument in [11].

We will review a vector ordering on $\mathbb{R}^n$ by a non-empty convex cone $K \subset \mathbb{R}^n$. Using this K, we can define a pseudo order relation $\preccurlyeq_K$ on $\mathbb{R}$ by $x \preccurlyeq_K y$ if and only if $y - x \in K$. Let $\mathbb{R}^n_+$ be the subset of entrywise non-negative elements in $\mathbb{R}^n$. When $K = \mathbb{R}^n_+$, the order $\preccurlyeq_K$ will be denoted by $\preccurlyeq_n$ and $x \preccurlyeq_n y$ means that $x_i \leq y_i$ for all $i = 1, 2, \cdots, n$, where $x = (x_1, x_2, \cdots, x_n)$ and $y = (y_1, y_2, \cdots, y_n) \in \mathbb{R}^n$.

First we introduce a binary relation on $\mathcal{C}(\mathbb{R}^n)$, by which a pseudo order on $\mathcal{F}(\mathbb{R}^n)$ is given. Henceforth we assume that the convex cone $K \subset \mathbb{R}^n$ is given. We define a binary relation $\preccurlyeq_K$ on $\mathcal{C}(\mathbb{R}^n)$ by abuse of notation. For $A, B \in \mathcal{C}(\mathbb{R}^n)$, $A \preccurlyeq_K B$ means the following (C.a) and (C.b) (cf. [12]):

(C.a) *For any $x \in A$, there exists $y \in B$ such that $x \preccurlyeq_K y$.*
(C.b) *For any $y \in B$, there exists $x \in A$ such that $x \preccurlyeq_K y$.*

Lemma 4.1. *The binary relation $\preccurlyeq_K$ is a pseudo order on $\mathcal{C}(\mathbb{R}^n)$.*

Proof. It is trivial that $A \preccurlyeq_K A$ for $A \in \mathcal{C}(\mathbb{R}^n)$. Let $A, B, C \in \mathcal{C}(\mathbb{R}^n)$ such that $A \preccurlyeq_K B$ and $B \preccurlyeq_K C$. We will check $A \preccurlyeq_K C$ by two cases (C.a) and (C.b). Case(C.a): Since $A \preccurlyeq_K B$ and $B \preccurlyeq_K C$, for any $x \in A$ there exists $y \in B$ such that $x \preccurlyeq_K y$ and there exists $z \in C$ such that $y \preccurlyeq_K z$. Since $\preccurlyeq_K$ is a pseudo order on $\mathbb{R}^n$, we have $x \preccurlyeq_K z$. Therefore it holds that for any $x \in A$ there exists $z \in C$ such that $x \preccurlyeq_K z$. Case(C.b): Since $A \preccurlyeq_K B$ and $B \preccurlyeq_K C$, for any $z \in C$ there exists $y \in B$ such that $y \preccurlyeq_K z$ and there exists $x \in A$ such that $x \preccurlyeq_K y$. Since $\preccurlyeq_K$ is a pseudo order on $\mathbb{R}^n$, we have $x \preccurlyeq_K z$. Therefore it holds that for any $z \in C$ there exists $x \in A$ such that $x \preccurlyeq_K z$. From the above (C.a) and (C.b), we obtain $A \preccurlyeq_K C$. Thus the lemma holds. □

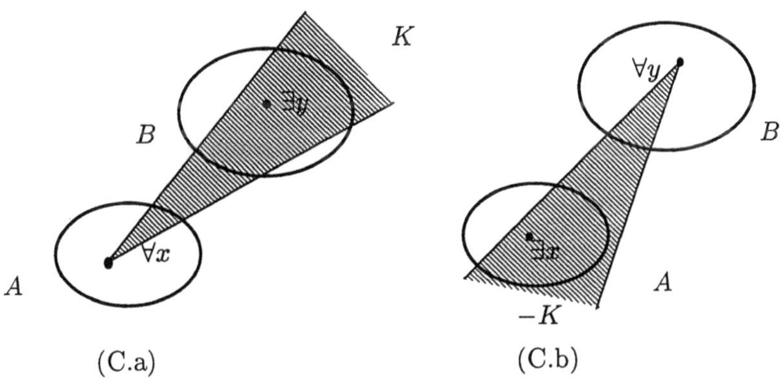

Fig. 4: The binary relation $A \preccurlyeq_K B$ on $\mathcal{C}(\mathbb{R}^2)$

The conditions (C.a) and (C.b) of the binary relation $A \preccurlyeq_K B$ on $\mathcal{C}(\mathbb{R}^2)$ are illustrated in Figure 4.

When $K = \mathbb{R}^n_+$, the binary relation $\preccurlyeq_K$ on $\mathcal{C}(\mathbb{R}^n)$ will be written simply by $\preccurlyeq_n$ and for $[x,y],[x',y'] \in \mathcal{C}_r(\mathbb{R}^n)$, $[x,y] \preccurlyeq_n [x',y']$ means $x \preccurlyeq_n x'$ and $y \preccurlyeq_n y'$.

Next, we introduce a binary relation $\preccurlyeq_K$ on $\mathcal{F}(\mathbb{R}^n)$: Let $\tilde{s},\tilde{r} \in \mathcal{F}(\mathbb{R}^n)$. The relation $\tilde{s} \preccurlyeq_K \tilde{r}$ means the following (F.a) and (F.b):

(F.a) *For any $x \in \mathbb{R}^n$, there exists $y \in \mathbb{R}^n$ such that $x \preccurlyeq_K y$ and $\tilde{s}(x) \le \tilde{r}(y)$.*
(F.b) *For any $y \in \mathbb{R}^n$, there exists $x \in \mathbb{R}^n$ such that $x \preccurlyeq_K y$ and $\tilde{s}(x) \ge \tilde{r}(y)$.*

Note that the notation $\preccurlyeq_K$ denotes the binary relation on $\mathbb{R}^n$, $\mathcal{C}(\mathbb{R}^n)$ and $\mathcal{F}(\mathbb{R}^n)$ with some abuse of notation.

Lemma 4.2. *The binary relation $\preccurlyeq_K$ is a pseudo order on $\mathcal{F}(\mathbb{R}^n)$.*

Proof. It is trivial that $\tilde{s} \preccurlyeq_K \tilde{s}$ for $\tilde{s} \in \mathcal{F}(\mathbb{R}^n)$. Let $\tilde{s},\tilde{r},\tilde{p} \in \mathcal{F}(\mathbb{R}^n)$ such that $\tilde{s} \preccurlyeq_K \tilde{r}$ and $\tilde{r} \preccurlyeq_K \tilde{p}$. We will check $\tilde{s} \preccurlyeq_K \tilde{p}$ by following two cases (F.a) and (F.b). Case(F.a): Since $\tilde{s} \preccurlyeq_K \tilde{r}$ and $\tilde{r} \preccurlyeq_K \tilde{p}$, for any $x \in \mathbb{R}^n$ there exists $y \in \mathbb{R}^n$ such that $x \preccurlyeq_K y$ and $\tilde{s}(x) \le \tilde{r}(y)$, and there exists $z \in \mathbb{R}^n$ such that $y \preccurlyeq_K z$ and $\tilde{r}(y) \le \tilde{p}(z)$. Since $\preccurlyeq_K$ is a pseudo-order on $\mathbb{R}^n$, we have $x \preccurlyeq_K z$ and $\tilde{s}(x) \le \tilde{p}(z)$. Therefore it holds that for any $x \in \mathbb{R}^n$ there exists $z \in \mathbb{R}^n$ such that $x \preccurlyeq_K z$ and $\tilde{s}(x) \le \tilde{p}(z)$. Case(F.b): Since $\tilde{s} \preccurlyeq_K \tilde{r}$ and $\tilde{r} \preccurlyeq_K \tilde{p}$, for any $z \in \mathbb{R}^n$ there exists $y \in \mathbb{R}^n$ such that $y \preccurlyeq_K z$ and $\tilde{r}(y) \le \tilde{p}(z)$, and there exists $x \in \mathbb{R}^n$ such that $x \preccurlyeq_K y$ and $\tilde{s}(x) \le \tilde{r}(y)$. Since $\preccurlyeq_K$ is a pseudo-order on $\mathbb{R}^n$, we have $x \preccurlyeq_K z$. Therefore it holds that for any $z \in \mathbb{R}^n$ there exists $x \in \mathbb{R}^n$ such that $x \preccurlyeq_K z$ and $\tilde{s}(x) \le \tilde{p}(z)$. From the above (F.a) and (F.b), we obtain $\tilde{s} \preccurlyeq_K \tilde{p}$. Thus the lemma holds. □

The following lemma implies the correspondence between the pseudo order on $\mathcal{F}(\mathbb{R}^n)$ for fuzzy sets and the pseudo order on $\mathcal{C}(\mathbb{R}^n)$ for the α-cuts.

Lemma 4.3. *Let $\tilde{s},\tilde{r} \in \mathcal{F}(\mathbb{R}^n)$. $\tilde{s} \preccurlyeq_K \tilde{r}$ on $\mathcal{F}(\mathbb{R}^n)$ if and only if $\tilde{s}_\alpha \preccurlyeq_K \tilde{r}_\alpha$ on $\mathcal{C}(\mathbb{R}^n)$ for all $\alpha \in (0,1]$.*

Proof. Let $\tilde{s},\tilde{r} \in \mathcal{F}(\mathbb{R}^n)$ and $\alpha \in (0,1]$. Suppose $\tilde{s} \preccurlyeq_K \tilde{r}$ on $\mathcal{F}(\mathbb{R}^n)$. Then, two cases (a) and (b) are considered. Case(a): Let $x \in \tilde{s}_\alpha$. Since $\tilde{s} \preccurlyeq_K \tilde{r}$, there exists $y \in \mathbb{R}^n$ such that $x \preccurlyeq_K y$ and $\alpha \le \tilde{s}(x) \le \tilde{r}(y)$. Namely $y \in \tilde{r}_\alpha$. Case(b): Let $y \in \tilde{r}_\alpha$. Since $\tilde{s} \preccurlyeq_K \tilde{r}$, there exists $x \in \mathbb{R}^n$ such that $x \preccurlyeq_K y$ and $\tilde{s}(x) \ge \tilde{r}(y) \ge \alpha$. Namely $x \in \tilde{s}_\alpha$. Therefore we get $\tilde{s}_\alpha \preccurlyeq_K \tilde{r}_\alpha$ on $\mathcal{C}(\mathbb{R}^n)$ for all $\alpha \in (0,1]$ from the above (a) and (b).

On the other hand, suppose $\tilde{s}_\alpha \preccurlyeq_K \tilde{r}_\alpha$ on $\mathcal{C}(\mathbb{R}^n)$ for all $\alpha \in (0,1]$. Then, two cases (a') and (b') are considered. Case(a'): Let $x \in \mathbb{R}^n$. Put $\alpha = \tilde{s}(x)$. If $\alpha = 0$, then $x \preccurlyeq_K x$ and $\tilde{s}(x) = 0 \le \tilde{r}(x)$. While, if $\alpha > 0$, then $x \in \tilde{s}_\alpha$. Since $\tilde{s}_\alpha \preccurlyeq_K \tilde{r}_\alpha$, there exists $y \in \tilde{r}_\alpha$ such that $x \preccurlyeq_K y$. And we have $\tilde{s}(x) = \alpha \le \tilde{r}(y)$. Case(b'): Let $y \in \mathbb{R}^n$. Put $\alpha = \tilde{r}(y)$. If $\alpha = 0$, then $x \preccurlyeq_K x$ and

$\widetilde{s}(x) \geq 0 = \widetilde{r}(y)$. While, if $\alpha > 0$, then $y \in \widetilde{r}_\alpha$. Since $\widetilde{s}_\alpha \preccurlyeq_K \widetilde{r}_\alpha$, there exists $x \in \widetilde{s}_\alpha$ such that $x \preccurlyeq_K y$. And we have $\widetilde{s}(x) \geq \alpha = \widetilde{r}(y)$.

Therefore we get $\widetilde{s} \preccurlyeq_K \widetilde{r}$ on $\mathcal{F}(\mathbb{R}^n)$ from the above Case (a') and (b'). Thus we obtain this lemma. □

The conditions (F.a) and (F.b) of the binary relation $\widetilde{s} \preccurlyeq_K \widetilde{r}$ on $\mathcal{F}(\mathbb{R})$ and $\mathcal{F}(\mathbb{R}^2)$ are illustrated in Figure 5.

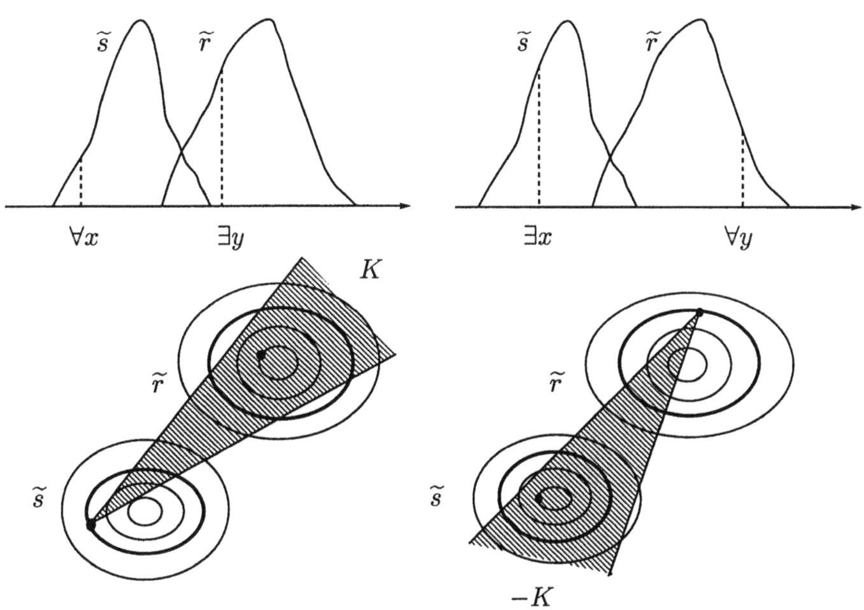

Fig. 5: The binary relation $\widetilde{s} \preccurlyeq_K \widetilde{r}$ on $\mathcal{F}(\mathbb{R})$ and $\mathcal{F}(\mathbb{R}^2)$

For the case of $K = \mathbb{R}_+$, Lemma 4.3 says that the order relation $\preccurlyeq_1$ on $\mathcal{F}(\mathbb{R})$ (that is, $n = 1$) is the fuzzy max order mentioned in Section 3.

Define the dual cone of a cone K by

$$K^+ := \{a \in \mathbb{R}^n \mid a \cdot x \geq 0 \text{ for all } x \in K\},$$

where $x \cdot y$ denotes the inner product on $\mathbb{R}^n$ for $x, y \in \mathbb{R}^n$. For a subset $A \subset \mathbb{R}^n$ and $a \in \mathbb{R}^n$, we define

$$a \cdot A := \{a \cdot x \mid x \in A\} \ (\subset \mathbb{R}^n). \tag{4.1}$$

The definition (4.1) means that $a \cdot A$ is the projection of A on the parallel line with the vector a if $a \cdot a = 1$. It is trivial that $a \cdot A \in \mathcal{C}(\mathbb{R})$ if $A \in \mathcal{C}(\mathbb{R}^n)$ and $a \in \mathbb{R}^n$.

Lemma 4.4. *Let $A, B \in \mathcal{C}(\mathbb{R}^n)$. $A \preccurlyeq_K B$ on $\mathcal{C}(\mathbb{R}^n)$ if and only if $a \cdot A \preccurlyeq_1 a \cdot B$ on $\mathcal{C}(\mathbb{R})$ for all $a \in K^+$.*

Proof. Suppose $A \preccurlyeq_K B$ on $\mathcal{C}(\mathbb{R}^n)$. Consider the two cases (a) and (b). Case(a): For any $x \in A$, there exists $y \in B$ such that $x \preccurlyeq_K y$. Then $y - x \in K$. If $a \in K^+$, then $a \cdot (y - x) \geq 0$ and i.e. $a \cdot x \leq a \cdot y$. Case(b): For any $y \in B$, there exists $x \in A$ such that $x \preccurlyeq_K y$. Then $y - x \in K$. If $a \in K^+$, then $a \cdot (y - x) \geq 0$ and i.e. $a \cdot x \leq a \cdot y$. From the above cases (a) and (b), we have that $a \cdot A \preccurlyeq_1 a \cdot B$.

On the other hand, to prove the inverse statement, we assume that $A \preccurlyeq_K B$ on $\mathcal{C}(\mathbb{R}^n)$ does not hold. Then we have the following two cases (i) and (ii). Case(i): There exists $x \in A$ such that $y - x \notin K$ for all $y \in B$. Then $B \cap (x + K) = \emptyset$. Since B and $x + K$ are closed convex, by the separation theorem there exists $a \in \mathbb{R}^n$ ($a \neq 0$) such that $a \cdot y < a \cdot x + a \cdot z$ for all $y \in B$ and all $z \in K$. Now, we suppose that there exists $z \in K$ such that $a \cdot z < 0$. Then $\lambda z \in K$ for all $\lambda \geq 0$ since K is a cone, and so we have $a \cdot x + a \cdot \lambda z = a \cdot x + \lambda a \cdot z \to -\infty$ as $\lambda \to \infty$. This contradicts $a \cdot y < a \cdot x + a \cdot z$. Therefore we obtain $a \cdot z \geq 0$ for all $z \in K$, which implies $a \in K^+$. Especially taking $z = 0 \in K$, we get $a \cdot y < a \cdot x$ for all $y \in B$. This contradicts $a \cdot A \preccurlyeq_1 a \cdot B$. Case(ii): There exists $y \in B$ such that $y - x \notin K$ for all $x \in A$. Then we derive a contradiction in the similar way to the case (i). Therefore the inverse statement holds from the results of the above (i) and (ii). The proof of this lemma is completed. □

The image of Lemma 4.4 is illustrated in Figure 6.

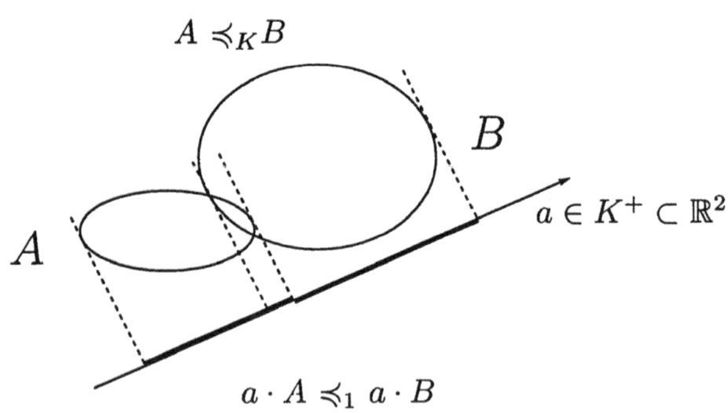

Fig. 6: The image of Lemma 4.4

For $a \in \mathbb{R}^n$ and $\widetilde{s} \in \mathcal{F}(\mathbb{R}^n)$, applying the representation theorem we define a fuzzy number $a \cdot \widetilde{s} \in \mathcal{F}(\mathbb{R})$ by

$$a \cdot \widetilde{s}(x) := \sup_{\alpha \in [0,1]} \{\alpha \wedge \mathbf{1}_{a \cdot \widetilde{s}_\alpha}(x)\}, \quad x \in \mathbb{R}. \tag{4.2}$$

The following theorem gives the correspondence between the pseudo order $\preccurlyeq_K$ on $\mathcal{F}(\mathbb{R}^n)$ and the fuzzy max order $\preccurlyeq_1$ on $\mathcal{F}(\mathbb{R})$.

Theorem 4.1. *For $\widetilde{s}, \widetilde{r} \in \mathcal{F}(\mathbb{R}^n)$, $\widetilde{s} \preccurlyeq_K \widetilde{r}$ if and only if $a \cdot \widetilde{s} \preccurlyeq_1 a \cdot \widetilde{r}$ for all $a \in K^+$.*

Proof. By (4.2) and the representative theorem, we have $(a \cdot \widetilde{s})_\alpha = a \cdot \widetilde{s}_\alpha$ for all $\alpha \in [0,1]$. On the other hand, from Lemmas 4.3 and 4.4, $\widetilde{s} \preccurlyeq_K \widetilde{r}$ if and only if $a \cdot \widetilde{s}_\alpha \preccurlyeq_1 a \cdot \widetilde{r}_\alpha$ for all $a \in K^+$. Thus, noting the definition of the max order $\preccurlyeq_1$ on $\mathcal{F}(\mathbb{R})$, Theorem 4.1 follows. □

The image of Theorem 4.1 is illustrated in Figure 7.

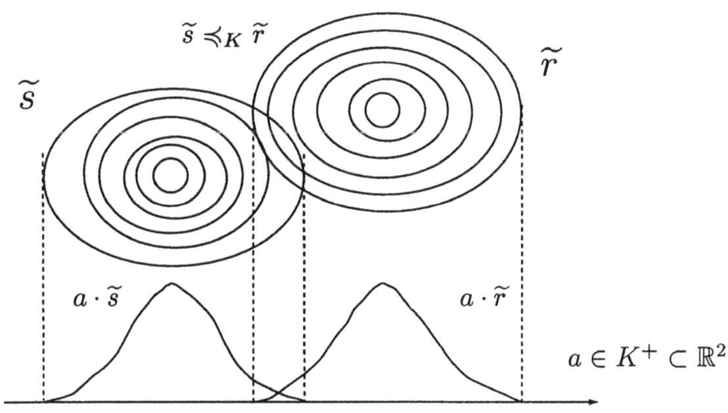

Fig. 7: The image of Theorem 4.1

5 A Pseudo Order on $\mathcal{F}_r(\mathbb{R}^n)$

In this section as a special case of the previous section, we shall investigate the pseudo order $\preccurlyeq_K$ on $\mathcal{F}_r(\mathbb{R}^n)$ for a polyhedral cone K with $K^+ \subset \mathbb{R}^n$. To this end, we need the following lemma.

Lemma 5.1. Let $a, b \in \mathbb{R}^n_+$ and $A \in \mathcal{C}_r(\mathbb{R}^n)$. Then for any scalars $\lambda_1, \lambda_2 \geq 0$, it holds

$$(\lambda_1 a + \lambda_2 b) \cdot A = \lambda_1 (a \cdot A) + \lambda_2 (b \cdot A), \tag{5.1}$$

where the arithmetic in (5.1) is defined in (4.1).

Proof. Let $\lambda_1 a \cdot x + \lambda_2 b \cdot y \in \lambda_1(a \cdot A) + \lambda_2(b \cdot B)$ with $x, y \in A$. It suffices to show that $\lambda_1 a \cdot x + \lambda_2 b \cdot y \in (\lambda_1 a + \lambda_2 b) \cdot A$. Define $z = (z_1, z_2, \cdots, z_n)$ by

$$z_i := \begin{cases} (\lambda_1 a_i x_i + \lambda_2 b_i y_i)/(\lambda_1 a_i + \lambda_2 b_i) & \text{if } (\lambda_1 a_i + \lambda_2 b_i) > 0 \\ x_i & \text{if } (\lambda_1 a_i + \lambda_2 b_i) = 0 \end{cases} \quad (i = 1, \cdots, n).$$

Then, clearly $(\lambda_1 a + \lambda_2 b) \cdot z = \lambda_1 a \cdot x + \lambda_2 b \cdot y$. Since $A \in \mathcal{C}_r(\mathbb{R}^n), z \in A$, so that $\lambda_1 a \cdot x + \lambda_2 b \cdot y \in (\lambda_1 a + \lambda_2 b) \cdot A$. □

Henceforth, we assume that K is a polyhedral convex cone with $K^+ \subset \mathbb{R}^n_+$, i.e., there exist vectors $b^i \in \mathbb{R}^n_+ (i = 1, 2, \cdots, m)$ such that

$$K = \{x \in \mathbb{R}^n \mid b^i \cdot x \geq 0 \text{ for all } \ i = 1, 2, \cdots, m\}.$$

Then, it is well-known (cf. [17]) that K^+ can be written as

$$K^+ = \{x \in \mathbb{R}^n \mid x = \sum_{i=1}^{m} \lambda_i b^i, \ \lambda_i \geq 0, \ i = 1, 2, \cdots, m\}.$$

The above dual cone K^+ is denoted simply by

$$K^+ = \text{cone}\{b^1, b^2, \cdots, b^m\},$$

where cone S denotes the conical hull of set S. The pseudo order $\preccurlyeq_K$ on $\mathcal{C}_r(\mathbb{R}^n)$ is characterized by the pseudo order $\preccurlyeq_1$ on $\mathcal{C}_r(\mathbb{R})$.

Corollary 5.1. Let $K^+ = \text{cone}\{b^1, b^2, \cdots, b^m\}$ with $b^i \in \mathbb{R}^n_+$. Then, for $A, B \in \mathcal{C}_r(\mathbb{R}^n)$, $A \preccurlyeq_K B$ if and only if $b^i \cdot A \preccurlyeq_1 b^i \cdot B$ for all $i = 1, 2, \cdots, m$.

Proof. We assume that $b^i \cdot A \preccurlyeq_1 b^i \cdot B$ for all $i = 1, 2, \cdots, m$. For any $a \in K^+$, there exist $\lambda_i \geq 0$ with $a = \sum_{i=1}^m \lambda_i b^i$. From Lemma 4.1, we have:

$$a \cdot A = \sum_{i=1}^{m} \lambda_i (b^i \cdot A) \preccurlyeq_1 \sum_{i=1}^{m} \lambda_i (b^i \cdot B) = a \cdot B.$$

Thus, by Lemma 4.4, $A \preccurlyeq_K B$ follows. By applying Lemma 4.4 again, the 'only if' part of Corollary holds. □

Lemma 5.2. Let $a, b \in \mathbb{R}^n_+$ and $\tilde{s} \in \mathcal{F}_r(\mathbb{R}^n)$. Then, for any $\lambda_1, \lambda_2 \geq 0$,

$$(\lambda_1 a + \lambda_2 b) \cdot \tilde{s} = \lambda_1 (a \cdot \tilde{s}) + \lambda_2 (b \cdot \tilde{s}), \tag{5.2}$$

where the arithmetic in (5.2) is given in (2.1), (2.2) and (4.2).

Proof. For any $\alpha \in [0, 1]$, it follows from the definition and Lemma 5.1 that

$$\begin{aligned} ((\lambda_1 a + \lambda_2 b) \cdot \tilde{s})_\alpha &= (\lambda_1 a + \lambda_2 b) \cdot \tilde{s}_\alpha = \lambda_1 (a \cdot \tilde{s}_\alpha) + \lambda_2 (b \cdot \tilde{s}_\alpha) \\ &= \lambda_1 (a \cdot \tilde{s})_\alpha + \lambda_2 (b \cdot \tilde{s})_\alpha = (\lambda_1 (a \cdot \tilde{s}) + \lambda_2 (b \cdot \tilde{s}))_\alpha. \end{aligned}$$

The last equality follows from (2.3). The above shows that (5.2) holds. □

The main result in this section is given in the following.

Theorem 5.1. Let $K^+ = \text{cone}\{b^1, b^2, \cdots, b^m\}$ with $b^i \in \mathbb{R}^n$. Then, for $\widetilde{s}, \widetilde{r} \in \mathcal{F}_r(\mathbb{R}^n)$,

$$\widetilde{s} \preccurlyeq_K \widetilde{r} \quad \text{if and only if} \quad b^i \cdot \widetilde{s} \preccurlyeq_1 b^i \cdot \widetilde{r} \text{ for } i = 1, 2, \cdots, m.$$

Proof. It suffices to prove the 'if' part of Theorem 5.1. For any $a \in K^+$, there exist $\lambda_i \geq 0$ with $a = \sum_{i=1}^m \lambda_i b^i$. Applying Lemma 5.2, we have

$$a \cdot \widetilde{s} = \sum_{i=1}^{m} \lambda_i (b^i \cdot \widetilde{s}) \preccurlyeq_1 \sum_{i=1}^{m} \lambda_i (b^i \cdot \widetilde{r}) = a \cdot \widetilde{r},$$

From Theorem 4.1, $\widetilde{s} \preccurlyeq_K \widetilde{r}$ follows. □

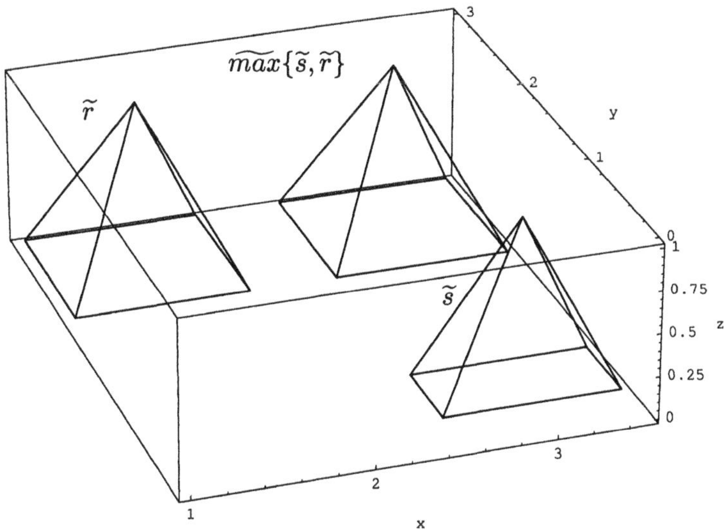

Fig. 8: $\widetilde{\max}\{\widetilde{s}, \widetilde{r}\}$ on $\mathcal{F}_r(\mathbb{R}^2)$

Zhang and Hirota[25] described the structure of the fuzzy number lattice $(\mathcal{F}_r(\mathbb{R}), \preccurlyeq_1)$. When $K = \mathbb{R}^n$, $K^+ = \mathbb{R}^n$ and $K^+ = \text{cone}\{e^1, e^2, \cdots, e^n\}$. So that, by Theorem 5.1, we see that for $\widetilde{s}, \widetilde{r} \in \mathcal{F}_r(\mathbb{R}^n)$, $\widetilde{s} \preccurlyeq_n \widetilde{r}$ means $e^i \cdot \widetilde{s} \preccurlyeq_1 e^i \cdot \widetilde{r}$ for all $i = 1, 2, \cdots, n$. Therefore, by applying the same method as Zhang and Hirota[25], we can describe the structure of the fuzzy set lattice $(\mathcal{F}_r(\mathbb{R}^n), \preccurlyeq_n)$. Figure 8 illustrates $\widetilde{\max}\{\widetilde{s}, \widetilde{r}\}$ for $\widetilde{s}, \widetilde{r} \in \mathcal{F}_r(\mathbb{R}^2)$.

6 Sequences in $\mathcal{C}(\mathbb{R}^n)$

In this section, we introduce the concept of a determining class in which the monotone convergence theorem for the sequences in $\mathcal{C}(\mathbb{R}^n)$ is proved.

A closed cone $K \subset \mathcal{C}(\mathbb{R}^n)$ is said to be acute (c.f. [17]) if there exists an $a \in \mathbb{R}^n$ such that $a \cdot x > 0$ for all $x \in K$ with $x \neq 0$.

We have the following lemma.

Lemma 6.1. *Let K be a closed, acute convex cone and $x_0, y_0 \in \mathbb{R}^n$ with $x_0 \preccurlyeq_K y_0$. Then, $(x_0 + K) \cap (y_0 - K)$ is nonempty and bounded.*

Proof. By $x_0 \preccurlyeq_K y_0$, it follows that $y_0 \in (x_0 + K) \cap (y_0 - K)$. Suppose that $(x_0 + K) \cap (y_0 - K)$ is not bounded. Then, there exists a sequence $\{z_k'\} \subset (x_0 + K) \cap (y_0 - K)$ with $\| z_k' \| \to \infty$ as $k \to \infty$, where $\| \cdot \|$ is a norm in $\mathbb{R}^n$. Since $z_k' \in (x_0 + K)$, for each $k \geq 1$, there exists $z_k \in K$ with $z_k' = x_0 + z_k$. By acuteness of K, there exists $a \in \mathbb{R}^n$ such that

$$a \cdot z_k > 0 \quad \text{for all} \quad k \geq 1. \tag{6.1}$$

Also, from $z_k' \in y_0 - K$, $y_0 - x_0 - z_k \in K$, which implies, together with (6.1), that

$$a \cdot (y_0 - x_0) > a \cdot z_k > 0 \quad \text{for all} \quad k \geq 1. \tag{6.2}$$

It clearly holds that

$$\inf_{\|z\|=1, z \in K} a \cdot z = a \cdot z_0 > 0 \quad \text{for some} \quad z_0 \in \mathbb{R}^n.$$

From (6.2), we have

$$\frac{a \cdot (y_0 - x_0)}{\| z_k \|} > a \cdot \left(\frac{z_k}{\| z_k \|} \right) \geq a \cdot z_0 > 0 \quad \text{for all} \quad k \geq 1.$$

As $\| z_k \| \to \infty$ $(k \to \infty)$, the above inequality leads a contradiction. □

Let ρ_n be the Hausdorff metric on $\mathcal{C}(\mathbb{R}^n)$, that is, for $A, B \in \mathcal{C}(\mathbb{R}^n)$, $\rho_n(A, B) = \max_{a \in A} d(a, B) \vee \max_{b \in B} d(b, A)$, where d is a metric in $\mathbb{R}^n$ and $d(x, Y) = \min_{y \in Y} d(x, y)$ for $x \in \mathbb{R}^n$ and $Y \in \mathcal{C}(\mathbb{R}^n)$. It is well-known that $(\mathcal{C}(\mathbb{R}^n), \rho_n)$ is a complete metric space. A sequence $\{D_\ell\}_{\ell=1}^{\infty} \subset \mathcal{C}(\mathbb{R}^n)$ converges to $D \in \mathcal{C}(\mathbb{R}^n)$ w.r.t. ρ_n if $\rho_n(D_\ell, D) \to 0$ as $\ell \to \infty$.

Definition (Convergence of fuzzy set, [23]).
For $\{\widetilde{s}_\ell\}_{\ell=1}^{\infty} \subset \mathcal{F}(\mathbb{R}^n)$ and $\widetilde{r} \in \mathcal{F}(\mathbb{R}^n)$, $\widetilde{s}_\ell$ converges to $\widetilde{r}$ w.r.t. ρ_n if $\rho_n(\widetilde{s}_{\ell,\alpha}, \widetilde{r}_\alpha) \to 0$ as $\ell \to \infty$ except at most countable $\alpha \in [0, 1]$.

Lemma 6.2. *Let $\{\widetilde{s}_k\}_{k=1}^{\infty} \subset \mathcal{F}(\mathbb{R})$ and $\widetilde{s} \in \mathcal{F}(\mathbb{R})$ such that $\widetilde{s}_k \preccurlyeq_1 \widetilde{s}_{k+1}$ $(k \geq 1)$ and $\lim_{k \to \infty} \widetilde{s}_k = \widetilde{s}$. Then we have $\widetilde{s}_1 \preccurlyeq_1 \widetilde{s}$.*

Proof. Trivial. □

Lemma 6.3. *Let $\{\widetilde{s}_k\}_{k=1}^{\infty} \subset \mathcal{F}(\mathbb{R}^n)$ and $\widetilde{s} \in \mathcal{F}(\mathbb{R}^n)$ such that $\widetilde{s}_k \preccurlyeq_K \widetilde{s}_{k+1}$ $(k \geq 1)$ and $\lim_{k \to \infty} \widetilde{s}_k = \widetilde{s}$. Then we have $\widetilde{s}_1 \preccurlyeq_K \widetilde{s}$.*

Proof. From Theorem 4.1, for all $a \in K^+$ it holds that $a \cdot \widetilde{s}_k \preccurlyeq_1 a \cdot \widetilde{s}_{k+1}$ $(k \geq 1)$. Also, since $(a \cdot \widetilde{s}_k)_\alpha = a \cdot \widetilde{s}_{k,\alpha}$ from (4.2) and $\rho_1(a \cdot \widetilde{s}_{k,\alpha}, a \cdot \widetilde{s}_\alpha) \leq \|a\| \rho_n(\widetilde{s}_{k,\alpha}, \widetilde{s}_\alpha)$ for all $k \geq 1$, we get $\lim_{k\to\infty} a \cdot \widetilde{s}_k = a \cdot \widetilde{s}$ where $\|a\|$ is a norm of a. By Lemma 6.2, it holds that $a \cdot \widetilde{s}_1 \preccurlyeq_1 a \cdot \widetilde{s}$ for all $a \in K^+$. From Theorem 4.1, we have $\widetilde{s}_1 \preccurlyeq_K \widetilde{s}$. □

Let K be a convex cone. The sequence $\{D_\ell\}_{\ell=1}^\infty \subset \mathcal{C}(\mathbb{R}^n)$ is said to be bounded w.r.t. $\preccurlyeq_K$ if there exists $F, D \in \mathcal{C}(\mathbb{R}^n)$ such that $F \preccurlyeq_K D_\ell \preccurlyeq_K D$ for all $\ell \geq 1$ and said to be monotone w.r.t. $\preccurlyeq_K$ if $D_1 \preccurlyeq_K D_2 \preccurlyeq_K \cdots$.

Let $\mathfrak{L} \subset \mathcal{C}(\mathbb{R}^n)$ and $A \subset \mathbb{R}^n$. Then we say that A is a determining class for $\mathfrak{L}$ if it holds that $D = F$ for $D, F \in \mathfrak{L}$ satisfying $a \cdot D = a \cdot F$ for all $a \in A$. For example, the set of unit vectors $\{\mathbf{e}_1, \mathbf{e}_2, \cdots, \mathbf{e}_n\}$ in $\mathbb{R}^n$ is a determining class for $\mathcal{C}_r(\mathbb{R}^n)$, which is the result of Theorem 5.1. Also, by the separation theorem, $\mathbb{R}^n$ is a determining class for $\mathcal{C}(\mathbb{R}^n)$.

Two example are illustrated in Figure 9.

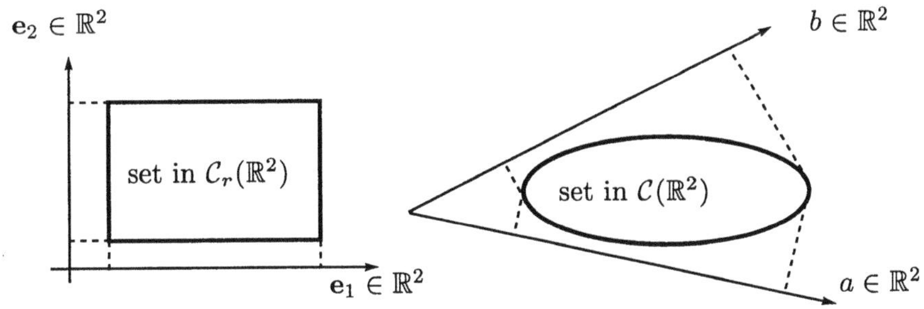

Fig. 9: The example of determining class

Theorem 6.1. *Let K be a closed convex cone of $\mathbb{R}^n$. Suppose that K^+ is a determining class for $\mathfrak{L} \subset \mathcal{C}(\mathbb{R}^n)$. Then, the pseudo order $\preccurlyeq_K$ becomes a partial order in the restricted class $\mathfrak{L}$.*

Proof. It suffices to show that $\preccurlyeq_K$ is antisymmetric in $\mathfrak{L}$. Let $D, F \in \mathfrak{L}$ satisfy that $D \preccurlyeq_K F$ and $F \preccurlyeq_K D$. By Lemma 4.4, $a \cdot D \preccurlyeq_1 a \cdot F$ and $a \cdot F \preccurlyeq_1 a \cdot D$ for all $a \in K^+$. Since $\preccurlyeq_1$ is a partial order, $a \cdot F = a \cdot D$ for all $a \in K^+$, which implies $F = D$ from the determining property of K^+. □

As a simple application of Theorem 6.1, we have the following.

Corollary 6.1. *Let K be a closed convex cone of $\mathbb{R}^n$. Suppose that K^+ is a determining class for $\mathfrak{L}$. Then, any sequence $\{D_l\} \subset \mathfrak{L}$ which is monotone w.r.t. $\preccurlyeq_K$ and satisfies $D_l \subset X$ $(l \geq 1)$ for some compact subset X of $\mathbb{R}^n$ converges w.r.t. ρ_n.*

Proof. Let $\mathcal{C}(X) = \{X \cap D \mid D \in \mathcal{C}(\mathbb{R}^n)\}$. Then, $\mathcal{C}(X)$ is compact w.r.t. ρ_n. So, the sequence $\{D_l\}$ has at most one limiting point. Since $\preccurlyeq_K$ is a partial order from Theorem 6.1, all the limiting points are equal, which completes the proof. □

In order to continue a further discussion, we need the acuteness of the ordering cone K. Then we have the following.

Lemma 6.4. *Let K be a closed, acute convex cone and $D, F, G \in \mathcal{C}(\mathbb{R}^n)$ with $D \preccurlyeq_K F \preccurlyeq_K G$. Let*

$$X := \bigcup_{\substack{x \preccurlyeq_K y \\ x \in D, y \in G}} (x+K) \cap (y-K). \tag{6.3}$$

Then, it holds that $F \subset X$ and X is bounded.

Proof. From $D \preccurlyeq_K F \preccurlyeq_K G$, for any $z \in F$, there exists $x \in D, y \in G$ such that $x \preccurlyeq_K z \preccurlyeq_K y$, which implies $z \in (x+K) \cap (y-K)$.

Now, suppose that X is unbounded. Then, there exists a sequence $\{z_t\} \subset X$ with $\| z_t \| \to \infty$ as $t \to \infty$. By $z_t \in X$, there exists $x_t \in D, y_t \in F$ with $x_t \preccurlyeq_K y_t$ and $z_t \in (x_t + K) \cap (y_t - K)$. Noting that both D and F are compact, there is no loss of generality in assuming that $x_t \to x \in D$ and $y_t \to y \in F$ as $t \to \infty$.

Since $(x_t+K) \cap (y_t-K) \to (x+K) \cap (y-K)$ as $t \to \infty$, $(x+K) \cap (y-K)$ is unbounded. However, from Lemma 6.3, $x \preccurlyeq_K y$, so that $(x+K) \cap (y-K)$ is bounded by Lemma 6.1, which leads to a contradiction. □

Theorem 6.2. *Let K be a closed, acute convex cone of $\mathbb{R}^n$ and $\mathfrak{L} \subset \mathcal{C}(\mathbb{R}^n)$. Suppose that K^+ is a determining class for $\mathfrak{L}$. Then, any sequence $\{D_l\}_{l=1}^{\infty} \subset \mathfrak{L}$ which is bounded and monotone w.r.t. $\preccurlyeq_K$ converges w.r.t. ρ_n.*

Proof. By boundedness of the sequence $\{D_l\}$, there exists $D, G \in \mathcal{C}(\mathbb{R}^n)$ with $D \preccurlyeq_K D_l \preccurlyeq_K G$ for all $l \geq 1$. By Lemma 6.4, there exists a compact subset X of $\mathbb{R}^n$ such that $D_l \subset X$ $(l \geq 1)$. Thus, applying Corollary 6.1, the proof is completed. □

As applications of Theorem 6.2, we have the following Corollaries.

Corollary 6.2. *For any $a \in \mathbb{R}^n$ $(a \neq 0)$, let $K_a := \{\lambda a \mid \lambda \geq 0\}$. Then, any sequence of solid spheres in K_a^+ with monotonicity and boundedness w.r.t. $\preccurlyeq_{K_a}$ converges w.r.t. ρ_n.*

Corollary 6.3. *Any sequence in $\mathcal{C}_r(\mathbb{R}^n)$ with monotonicity and boundedness w.r.t. $\preccurlyeq_n$ converges w.r.t. ρ_n.*

For any $D \in \mathcal{C}(\mathbb{R}^n)$ and $\varepsilon > 0$, the ε-closed neighborhood of D will be denoted by

$$S_\varepsilon(D) := \{x \in \mathbb{R}^n \mid d(x, D) \leq \varepsilon\}, \tag{6.4}$$

which is a compact convex subset of $\mathbb{R}^n$. Note that

$$S_\varepsilon(D) = D + \varepsilon U_0, \tag{6.5}$$

where U_0 is the closed unit ball (cf. [2]).

The following lemma is useful in the sequel.

Lemma 6.5. *The following* (i) *to* (iii) *hold.*

(i) *For any $D, F \in \mathcal{C}(\mathbb{R}^n)$, if $S_{\delta_1}(D) \subset S_{\delta_2}(F)$ for some $\delta_1, \delta_2 \geq 0$, then $S_{\delta_1+\varepsilon}(D) \subset S_{\delta_2+\varepsilon}(F)$ for any $\varepsilon \geq 0$.*
(ii) *For any $D \in \mathcal{C}(\mathbb{R}^n)$ and $\lambda > 0$, $S_\varepsilon(\lambda D) = \lambda S_{\varepsilon/\lambda}(D)$.*
(iii) *For any sequence $\{D_l\} \subset \mathcal{C}(\mathbb{R}^n)$ and $D \in \mathcal{C}(\mathbb{R}^n)$, if $D_l \to D$ as $l \to \infty$, then $S_\delta(D_l) \to S_\delta(D)$ as $l \to \infty$ ($\delta \geq 0$).*

Proof. For any $D, F \in \mathcal{C}(\mathbb{R}^n)$ and $\delta_1, \delta_2 \geq 0$, $S_{\delta_1}(D) \subset S_{\delta_2}(F)$ means from (6.5) that $D + \delta_1 U_0 \subset F + \delta_2 U_0$, so that $D + \delta_1 U_0 + \varepsilon U_0 \subset F + \delta_2 U_0 + \varepsilon U_0$. Since U_0 is convex, $\delta_1 U_0 + \varepsilon U_0 = (\delta_1 + \varepsilon) U_0$ and $\delta_2 U_0 + \varepsilon U_0 = (\delta_2 + \varepsilon) U_0$, which leads to $S_{\delta_1+\varepsilon}(D) \subset S_{\delta_2+\varepsilon}(F)$. Also, $S_\varepsilon(\lambda D) = \lambda D + \varepsilon U_0 = \lambda(D + (\varepsilon/\lambda) U_0)$, so that (ii) follows. For (iii), by the properties of the Hausdorff metric ρ_n (cf. [2]) $\rho_n(S_\delta(D_l), S_\delta(D)) = \rho(D_l, D)$, as required. □

For any closed convex cone $K \subset \mathbb{R}^n$, let $\mathfrak{L}(K^+)$ be the set of all $D \in \mathcal{C}(\mathbb{R}^n)$ satisfying that for any $x_0 \in \mathbb{R}^n$ and $\varepsilon > 0$ with $x_0 \notin S_\varepsilon(D)$ there exists $a \in K^+$ ($a \neq 0$) such that

$$a \cdot y \geq a \cdot x_0 \quad \text{for all} \quad y \in S_\varepsilon(D).$$

The properties of $\mathfrak{L}(K^+)$ are stated in the following lemma.

Lemma 6.6. *The following* (i) *to* (iii) *hold.*

(i) *K^+ is a determining class for $\mathfrak{L}(K^+)$.*
(ii) *$\mathfrak{L}(K^+)$ is closed w.r.t. ρ_n.*
(iii) *For any $D \in \mathfrak{L}(K^+)$, $\lambda D + \mu D \in \mathfrak{L}(K^+)$ ($\lambda, \mu \geq 0$).*

Proof. For (i), suppose that there exist $D, F \in \mathfrak{L}(K^+)$ such that $a \cdot D = a \cdot F$ for all $a \in K^+$ but there exists x_0 with $x_0 \notin D$ and $x_0 \in F$. By $x_0 \notin D$, $x_0 \notin S_\delta(D)$ for some $\delta > 0$. Then, there exists $a \in K^+$ such that $a \cdot x \geq a \cdot x_0$ for all $x \in S_\delta(D)$, so that $a \cdot x > a \cdot x_0$ for all $x \in D$, which implies $a \cdot D \neq a \cdot F$, in a contradiction.

Let $\overline{\mathfrak{L}}(K^+)$ be the closure of $\mathfrak{L}(K^+)$ w.r.t. ρ_n. For any $D \in \overline{\mathfrak{L}}(K^+)$, there exists a sequence $\{D_l\} \subset \mathfrak{L}(K^+)$ such that $\rho_n(D_l, D) \to 0$ as $l \to \infty$.

Now, for each $\varepsilon > 0$, let $x_0 \notin S_\varepsilon(D)$. Obviously there exists $\delta > 0$ with $x_0 \notin S_{\varepsilon+\delta}(D)$. By the definition of the Housdorff metric ρ_n, there exists L (depending on δ) for which $D_l \subset S_\delta(D)$ for all $l \geq L$. Applying Lemma 6.5(i), $S_\varepsilon(D_l) \subset S_{\varepsilon+\delta}(D)$, which implies $x_0 \notin S_\varepsilon(D_l)$ for all $l \geq L$.

Since $D_l \in \mathfrak{L}(K^+)$, by the definition there exists $a^l \in K^+$ such that

$$a^l \cdot x \geq a^l \cdot x_0 \quad \text{for any} \quad x \in S_\varepsilon(D_l). \tag{6.6}$$

Without loss of generality, we can assume that $\| a^l \| = 1$ and $a^l \to a \in K^+$ as $l \to \infty$. As $l \to \infty$ in (6.6), from Lemma 6.5(iii), we get that

$$a \cdot x \geq a \cdot x_0 \quad \text{for any} \quad x \in S_\varepsilon(D). \tag{6.7}$$

The above shows $D \in \mathfrak{L}(K^+)$.

For (iii), observing that $(\lambda + \mu)D = \lambda D + \mu D \quad (\lambda, \mu \geq 0)$, we only need to show $\lambda D \in \mathfrak{L}(K^+)$ for any $\lambda > 0$ and $D \in \mathfrak{L}(K^+)$. For any $x_0 \in \mathbb{R}^n$ and $\varepsilon > 0$ with $x_0 \notin S_\varepsilon(\lambda D)$, from Lemma 6.5(ii) it holds that $\lambda^{-1}x_0 \notin S_{\varepsilon/\lambda}(D)$. That $D \in \mathfrak{L}(K^+)$ implies that there exists $a \in K^+ \quad (a \neq 0)$ such that

$$a \cdot x \geq a \cdot (\lambda^{-1} x_0) \quad \text{for all} \quad x \in S_{\varepsilon/\lambda}(D). \tag{6.8}$$

Obviously, (6.8) leads to $a \cdot x \geq a \cdot x_0$ for any $x \in S_\varepsilon(\lambda D)$, as required. □

Noting that $K^+ = \mathbb{R}^2_+$ when $K = \mathbb{R}^2_+$ in $\mathbb{R}^2$, the sets included in $\mathfrak{L}(\mathbb{R}^2_+)$ are illustrated in Figure 10.

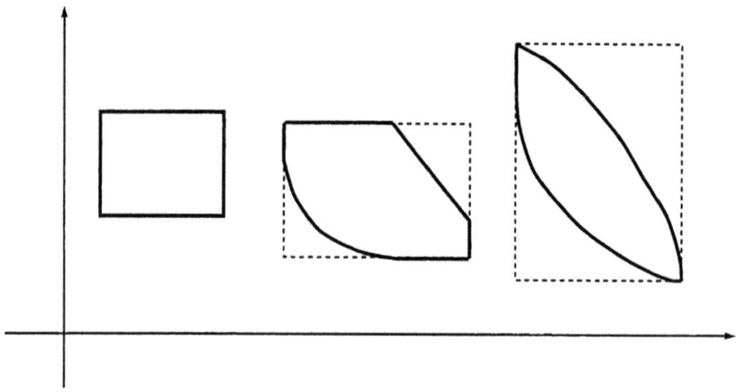

Fig. 10: The example of sets in $\mathfrak{L}(\mathbb{R}^2_+)$

We have the following.

Theorem 6.3. *Let K be a closed, acute convex cone of $\mathbb{R}^n$. Then, any sequence $\{D_l\}_{l=1}^{\infty} \subset \mathfrak{L}(K^+)$ which is bounded and monotone w.r.t. $\preccurlyeq_K$ converges w.r.t. ρ_n.*

Proof. From Lemma 6.3, K^+ is a determining class for $\mathfrak{L}(K^+)$ and $\mathfrak{L}(K^+)$ is closed. Thus, by applying Theorem 6.3, the result follows. □

7 Sequences in $\mathcal{F}(\mathbb{R}^n)$

In this section, the monotone convergence theorem for a sequence in $\mathcal{F}(\mathbb{R}^n)$ is given.

Let $\widetilde{\mathfrak{L}} \subset \mathcal{F}(\mathbb{R}^n)$ and $A \subset \mathbb{R}^n$. Then we call A a determining class for $\widetilde{\mathfrak{L}}$ if it holds that $\widetilde{s} = \widetilde{r}$ for $\widetilde{s}, \widetilde{r} \in \widetilde{\mathfrak{L}}$ satisfying $a \cdot \widetilde{s} = a \cdot \widetilde{r}$ for all $a \in A$.

A natural extension of Theorem 6.1 to fuzzy sets will be given in the following theorem.

Theorem 7.1. *Let K be a closed convex cone of $\mathbb{R}^n$ and $\widetilde{\mathfrak{L}} \subset \mathcal{F}(\mathbb{R}^n)$. Suppose that K^+ is a determining class for $\widetilde{\mathfrak{L}}$. Then, a pseudo order $\preccurlyeq_K$ is a partial order in $\widetilde{\mathfrak{L}}$.*

Proof. Let us show that $\preccurlyeq_K$ is antisymmetric in $\widetilde{\mathfrak{L}}$. For any $\widetilde{s}, \widetilde{r} \in \widetilde{\mathfrak{L}}$ with $\widetilde{s} \preccurlyeq_K \widetilde{r}$ and $\widetilde{r} \preccurlyeq_K \widetilde{s}$, by Theorem 4.4 it holds that $a \cdot \widetilde{s} \preccurlyeq_1 a \cdot \widetilde{r}$ and $a \cdot \widetilde{r} \preccurlyeq_1 a \cdot \widetilde{s}$ for all $a \in K^+$.

Noting $(a \cdot \widetilde{s})_\alpha = a \cdot \widetilde{s}_\alpha$, we have $a \cdot \widetilde{s}_\alpha \preccurlyeq_1 a \cdot \widetilde{r}_\alpha$ and $a \cdot \widetilde{r}_\alpha \preccurlyeq_1 a \cdot \widetilde{s}_\alpha$ for all $a \in K^+$. Since $\preccurlyeq_1$ is a partial order on $\mathcal{C}(\mathbb{R})$, $a \cdot \widetilde{s}_\alpha = a \cdot \widetilde{r}_\alpha$ for all $a \in K^+$, which means $a \cdot \widetilde{s} = a \cdot \widetilde{r}$ for all $a \in K^+$. Thus, that K^+ is a determining class leads to $\widetilde{s} = \widetilde{r}$. $\square$

Let K be a convex cone. The sequence $\{\widetilde{s}_l\} \subset \mathcal{F}(\mathbb{R}^n)$ is said to be bounded w.r.t. $\preccurlyeq_K$ if there exists $\widetilde{u}, \widetilde{v} \in \mathcal{F}(\mathbb{R}^n)$ such that $\widetilde{u} \preccurlyeq_K \widetilde{s}_l \preccurlyeq_K \widetilde{v}$ for all $l \geq 1$ and said to be monotone w.r.t. $\preccurlyeq_K$ if $\widetilde{s}_1 \preccurlyeq_K \widetilde{s}_2 \preccurlyeq_K \cdots$.

In order to obtain the convergence theorem, we need the concept of directionality given in [23]. Denote the surface of the unit ball by $U := \{x \in \mathbb{R}^n \mid \| x \| = 1\}$. Let $V \subset U$. Then, for $D, D' \in \mathcal{C}(\mathbb{R}^n)$ with $D \subset D'$, we call D' V-directional to D (written by $D' \supset_V D$) if there exists a real $\lambda > 0, y \in D$ and $z \in D'$ such that
(i) $d(z, y) = \rho_n(D', D)$ and (ii) $z - y = \lambda v$ for some $v \in V$.

Definition (V-directional). *Let $V \subset \mathbb{R}^n$. For $\widetilde{s} \in \mathcal{F}(\mathbb{R}^n)$, $\widetilde{s}$ is called V-directional if $\widetilde{s}_\alpha \supset_V \widetilde{s}_{\alpha'}$ for $0 \leq \alpha \leq \alpha' \leq 1$.*

Corollary 7.1. *Let K be a closed convex cone of $\mathbb{R}^n$ and $\widetilde{\mathfrak{L}} \subset \mathcal{F}(\mathbb{R}^n)$ be closed. Suppose that K^+ is a determining class for $\widetilde{\mathfrak{L}}$. Let a sequence $\{\widetilde{s}_l\} \subset \mathcal{F}(\mathbb{R}^n)$ be satisfied that*

(a) *$\{\widetilde{s}_l\}$ is bounded and monotone w.r.t. $\preccurlyeq_K$,*
(b) *each $\widetilde{s}_l$ is V-directional for a finite set $V \subset \mathbb{R}^n$ and*
(c) *there exists a compact subset D of $\mathbb{R}^n$ such that $\widetilde{s}_{l0} \subset D$ for all $l \geq 1$, where $\widetilde{s}_{l0}$ is the support or 0-cut of $\widetilde{s}_l$.*

Then the sequence $\{\widetilde{s}_l\}$ converges w.r.t. ρ_n.

Proof. In view of (a) and (c), by the argument similar to the proof of Corollary 6.1, we have that for each $\alpha \in [0,1]$, $\widetilde{s}_{l\alpha} \to \widetilde{s}_\alpha \in \mathcal{C}(\mathbb{R}^n)$ as $l \to \infty$, where $\widetilde{s}_{l\alpha}$ is the α-cut of $\widetilde{s}_l$.

We define $\{\widetilde{s}_\alpha^+\}$ by $\widetilde{s}_\alpha^+ := \bigcap_{\alpha'<\alpha} \widetilde{s}_{\alpha'}$ if $\alpha \in (0,1]$ and $\widetilde{s}_0^+ := \widetilde{s}_0$. Obviously, the family $\{\widetilde{s}_\alpha^+\}$ satisfies the condition (ii) of the representative theorem in Section 2. So, if $\widetilde{s}(x) = \sup_{\alpha\in[0,1]}\{\alpha \wedge \mathbf{1}_{\widetilde{s}_\alpha^+}(x)\}$ for all $x \in \mathbb{R}^n$, it holds $\widetilde{s} \in \mathcal{F}(\mathbb{R}^n)$.

Also, by the same discussion as that in the proof of Lemma 3.2 in [23], we get that $\widetilde{s}_\alpha^+ \supset_V \widetilde{s}_\alpha$ for all $\alpha \in [0,1]$ and $\{\alpha \in [0,1] \mid \widetilde{s}_\alpha^+ \neq \widetilde{s}_\alpha\}$ is at most countable, which implies that $\widetilde{s}_l \to \widetilde{s}$ as $l \to \infty$, as required. □

The following monotone convergence theorem is thought of as an extension of Theorem 6.2 to fuzzy sets.

Theorem 7.2. *Let K be a closed, acute convex cone of $\mathbb{R}^n$ and $\widetilde{\mathfrak{L}} \subset \mathcal{F}(\mathbb{R}^n)$ be closed. Suppose that K^+ is a determining class for $\widetilde{\mathfrak{L}}$. Then, any sequence $\{\widetilde{s}_l\}_{l=1}^\infty \subset \widetilde{\mathfrak{L}}$ which satisfies* (a) *and* (b) *in Corollary 7.1 converges w.r.t. ρ_n.*

Proof. From the definition of boundedness of $\{\widetilde{s}_l\}$, there exists $D, G \in \mathcal{C}(\mathbb{R}^n)$ such that $D \preccurlyeq_K \widetilde{s}_{l0} \preccurlyeq_K G$ for all $l \geq 1$.

By Lemma 6.4, there exists a compact subset X of $\mathbb{R}^n$ with $\widetilde{s}_{l0} \subset X$ for all $l \geq 1$, which implies that the condition (c) in Corollary 7.1 holds. Thus, applying Corollary 7.1, Theorem 7.2 follows. □

Now, for any closed convex cone K, we define $\widetilde{\mathfrak{L}}(K^+)$ by

$$\widetilde{\mathfrak{L}}(K^+) := \{\widetilde{s} \in \mathcal{F}(\mathbb{R}^n) \mid \widetilde{s}_\alpha \in \mathfrak{L}(K^+) \text{ for all } \ \alpha \in [0,1]\}.$$

The previous Lemma 6.6 is extended to that for $\mathcal{F}(\mathbb{R}^n)$ in the following lemma, whose proof is easily done by α-cuts of the corresponding fuzzy sets and leaved to a reader.

Lemma 7.1. *The following* (i) *to* (iii) *hold.*

(i) *K^+ is a determining class for $\widetilde{\mathfrak{L}}(K^+)$.*
(ii) *$\widetilde{\mathfrak{L}}(K^+)$ is closed w.r.t. the convergence defined in Section 6.*
(iii) *For any $\widetilde{s} \in \widetilde{\mathfrak{L}}(K^+)$, $\lambda\widetilde{s} + \mu\widetilde{s} \in \widetilde{\mathfrak{L}}(K^+)$ $(\lambda, \mu \geq 0)$.*

We have the following.

Theorem 7.3. *Let K^+ be a closed, acute convex cone of $\mathbb{R}^n$. Then, any sequence $\{\widetilde{s}_l\}_{l=1}^\infty \subset \widetilde{\mathfrak{L}}(K^+)$ which satisfies* (a) *and* (b) *in Corollary 7.1 converges.*

Proof. From Lemma 7.1, K^+ is a determining class for $\widetilde{\mathfrak{L}}(K^+)$ and $\widetilde{\mathfrak{L}}(K^+)$ is closed. So, applying Theorem 7.2, the results follow. □

8 Applications to Monotone Dynamic Fuzzy Systems

In this section, as an application of the results obtained in the preceding section, we consider a limit theorem for a sequence of fuzzy states defined by the dynamic fuzzy system (cf. [9], [10], [20], [21], [22], [23]) with a monotone fuzzy relation.

Let $\widetilde{q} : \mathbb{R}^n \times \mathbb{R}^n \to [0,1]$ be a continuous fuzzy relation such that $\widetilde{q}(x,\cdot) \in \mathcal{F}(\mathbb{R}^n)$ for each $x \in \mathbb{R}^n$ and $\widetilde{q}(\cdot,\cdot)$ is convex, that is,

$$\widetilde{q}(\lambda x^1 + (1-\lambda)x^2, \lambda y^1 + (1-\lambda)y^2) \geq \widetilde{q}(x^1, y^1) \wedge \widetilde{q}(x^2, y^2) \tag{8.1}$$

for any $x^1, x^2, y^1, y^2 \in \mathbb{R}^n$ and $\lambda \in [0,1]$. From this fuzzy relation $\widetilde{q}$, we define $\widetilde{q} : \mathcal{F}(\mathbb{R}^n) \to \{$the set of fuzzy sets on $\mathbb{R}^n\}$ as follows.

$$\widetilde{q}(\widetilde{u})(y) := \sup_{x \in \mathbb{R}^n} \{\widetilde{u}(x) \wedge \widetilde{q}(x,y)\}, \in \mathbb{R}^n, \tag{8.2}$$

where $a \wedge b = \min\{a,b\}$. Also, for any $\alpha \in [0,1]$, $\widetilde{q}_\alpha : \mathcal{C}(\mathbb{R}^n) \to 2^{\mathbb{R}^n}$ will be defined by

$$\widetilde{q}_\alpha(D) := \begin{cases} \{\, y \mid \widetilde{q}(x,y) \geq \alpha \text{ for some } x \in D\}, & \text{for } \alpha > 0,\ D \in \mathcal{C}(\mathbb{R}^n) \\ \text{cl}\{\, y \mid \widetilde{q}(x,y) > 0 \text{ for some } x \in D\}, & \text{for } \alpha = 0,\ D \in \mathcal{C}(\mathbb{R}^n), \end{cases} \tag{8.3}$$

where cl denotes the closure of a set and $2^{\mathbb{R}^n}$ the set of all closed subsets of $\mathbb{R}^n$. For simplicity, we put $\widetilde{q}(x) := \widetilde{q}(\{x\})$ and $\widetilde{q}_\alpha(x) := \widetilde{q}_\alpha(\{x\})$ for $x \in \mathbb{R}^n$.

The following facts are well-known (cf. [8], [9], [23]).

Lemma 8.1 *The following* (i) *to* (iii) *hold.*

(i) $\widetilde{q}_\alpha(D) \in \mathcal{C}(\mathbb{R}^n)$ *for any* $D \in \mathcal{C}(\mathbb{R}^n)$ *and* $\widetilde{q}_\alpha(\cdot)$ *is continuous in* $\mathcal{C}(\mathbb{R}^n)$ *for each* $\alpha \in (0,1]$.
(ii) $\widetilde{q}(\widetilde{u}) \in \mathcal{F}(\mathbb{R}^n)$ *for any* $\widetilde{u} \in \mathcal{F}(\mathbb{R}^n)$.
(iii) $\widetilde{q}(\widetilde{u})_\alpha = \widetilde{q}_\alpha(\widetilde{u})_\alpha$ *for any* $\widetilde{u} \in \mathcal{F}(\mathbb{R}^n)$ *and* $\alpha \in [0,1]$, *where* $\widetilde{q}(\widetilde{u})_\alpha$ *is the* α*-cut of* $\widetilde{q}(\widetilde{u})$.

The sequence of fuzzy states, $\{\widetilde{s}_t\}_{t=1}^\infty \subset \mathcal{F}(\mathbb{R}^n)$, for the dynamic fuzzy system with fuzzy transition $\widetilde{q}$ is defined as follows.

$$\widetilde{s}_{t+1} = \widetilde{q}(\widetilde{s}_t) \quad (t \geq 1), \tag{8.4}$$

where $\widetilde{s}_1 \in \mathcal{F}(\mathbb{R}^n)$ is the initial fuzzy state.

The problem in this section is to consider a convergence of the sequence $\{\widetilde{s}_t\}_{t=1}^\infty$ defined by (8.4), so that we derive the monotone property of the fuzzy relation $\widetilde{q}$ w.r.t. the pseudo order $\preccurlyeq_K$ defined by the ordering cone K in $\mathbb{R}^n$.

Definition ($\preccurlyeq_K$-monotone). *The fuzzy relation $\widetilde{q}$ is called $\preccurlyeq_K$-monotone if $x^1 \preccurlyeq_K x^2$ $(x^1, x^2 \in \mathbb{R}^n)$ means $\widetilde{q}(x^1, \cdot) \preccurlyeq_K \widetilde{q}(x^2, \cdot)$.*

Remark. Yoshida et al [23] has introduced a monotone property concerning the fuzzy relation $\widetilde{q}$ whose definition is as follows: $\widetilde{q}_\alpha(y) \subset \widetilde{q}_\alpha(x) + \ell(x,y)$ for $x, y \in \mathbb{R}^n$, where $\ell(x,y) := \{\gamma(y-x) \mid \gamma \geq 0\}$. Obviously, if $\widetilde{q}$ is monotone in the sense of [23], then $\widetilde{q}$ is $\preccurlyeq_n$-monotone, but the converse is not necessarily true.

The following lemma is useful for our further discussion.

Lemma 8.2. *Suppose that $\widetilde{q}$ is $\preccurlyeq_K$-monotone. Then, for any $\widetilde{u}, \widetilde{v} \in \mathcal{F}(\mathbb{R}^n)$ with $\widetilde{u} \preccurlyeq_K \widetilde{v}$, it holds that $\widetilde{q}(\widetilde{u}) \preccurlyeq_K \widetilde{q}(\widetilde{v})$.*

Proof. By Lemma 8.1(iii), for any $a \in K^+$, $a \cdot \widetilde{q}(\widetilde{u})_\alpha = a \cdot \widetilde{q}_\alpha(\widetilde{u}_\alpha) \in \mathcal{C}(\mathbb{R}^1)$. So, we write it by the closed interval as follows, $a \cdot \widetilde{q}_\alpha(\widetilde{u}_\alpha) := [\min a \cdot \widetilde{q}_\alpha(\widetilde{u}_\alpha), \max a \cdot \widetilde{q}_\alpha(\widetilde{u}_\alpha)]$ and $a \cdot \widetilde{q}_\alpha(\widetilde{v}_\alpha) := [\min a \cdot \widetilde{q}_\alpha(\widetilde{v}_\alpha), \max a \cdot \widetilde{q}_\alpha(\widetilde{v}_\alpha)]$.

Obviously, for each $\alpha \in [0,1]$, there exists $y^1 \in \widetilde{v}_\alpha$ such that $\min a \cdot \widetilde{q}_\alpha(y^1) = \min a \cdot \widetilde{q}_\alpha(\widetilde{v}_\alpha)$. From Lemma 4.3, $\widetilde{u} \preccurlyeq_K \widetilde{v}$ means $\widetilde{u}_\alpha \preccurlyeq_K \widetilde{v}_\alpha$ for all $\alpha \in [0,1]$, so that there exists $x^1 \in \widetilde{u}_\alpha$ with $x^1 \preccurlyeq_K y^1$. By $\preccurlyeq_K$-monotonicity of $\widetilde{q}$, we have $\widetilde{q}_\alpha(x^1) \preccurlyeq_K \widetilde{q}_\alpha(y^1)$, which from Lemma 6.5 implies $\min a \cdot \widetilde{q}_\alpha(x^1) \leq \min a \cdot \widetilde{q}_\alpha(y^1)$. This leads to $\min a \cdot \widetilde{q}_\alpha(\widetilde{u}_\alpha) \leq \min a \cdot \widetilde{q}_\alpha(\widetilde{v}_\alpha)$.

Now, by taking $x^2 \in \widetilde{u}_\alpha$ with $\max a \cdot \widetilde{q}_\alpha(x^2) = \max a \cdot \widetilde{q}_\alpha(\widetilde{u}_\alpha)$, we can show by the same way as the above that $\max a \cdot \widetilde{q}_\alpha(\widetilde{u}_\alpha) \leq \max a \cdot \widetilde{q}_\alpha(\widetilde{v}_\alpha)$.

Then, we have $a \cdot \widetilde{q}_\alpha(\widetilde{u}_\alpha) \preccurlyeq_1 a \cdot \widetilde{q}_\alpha(\widetilde{v}_\alpha)$ $(\alpha \in [0,1])$. Applying Lemma 4.3, we get $\widetilde{q}(\widetilde{u}) \preccurlyeq_K \widetilde{q}(\widetilde{v})$, as required. □

Assumption A. *The following* (i) *to* (iii) *hold.*

(i) *The ordering cone K is a closed, acute convex one in $\mathbb{R}^n$.*
(ii) *The fuzzy relation $\widetilde{q}$ is $\preccurlyeq_K$-monotone.*
(iii) *There exists a finite subset $V \subset U$ such that, for any $D, D' \in \mathcal{C}(\mathbb{R}^n)$ $(D' \supset D)$, if $D' \supset_V D$ then $\widetilde{q}_{\alpha'}(D') \supset_V \widetilde{q}_\alpha(D)$ for all α, α' $(0 \leq \alpha' \leq \alpha \leq 1)$.*

For any given $\widetilde{u} \in \mathcal{F}(\mathbb{R}^n)$, putting $\widetilde{s}_1 := \widetilde{u}$, we define the sequence $\{\widetilde{s}_t\}_{t=1}^{\infty}$ by (8.4). Then, we have the following.

Theorem 8.1. *In addition to Assumption A, suppose that the following* (iv) *to* (vi) *hold.*

(iv) $\widetilde{u} \in \widetilde{\mathfrak{L}}(K^+)$ *and* $\widetilde{u} \preccurlyeq_K \widetilde{q}(\widetilde{u})$.
(v) $\widetilde{u}_{\alpha'} \supset_V \widetilde{u}_\alpha$ *for all α, α' $(0 \leq \alpha' \leq \alpha \leq 1)$), where V is as in Assumption* A(iii).
(vi) $\{\widetilde{s}_t\} \subset \widetilde{\mathfrak{L}}(K^+)$ *and bounded from above.*

Then, the sequence $\{\tilde{s}_t\}$ *converges and the limit* $\tilde{s} := \lim_{t\to\infty} \tilde{s}_t$ *satisfies the following fuzzy relational equation:*

$$\tilde{s} = \tilde{q}(\tilde{s}). \tag{8.5}$$

Proof. From Lemma 8.2 and Assumption, we observe that the sequence $\{\tilde{s}_t\}$ is bounded and $\preccurlyeq_K$-monotone. Also, we can check that all the assumption in Theorem 7.3 are satisfied. Thus, from Theorem 7.3, we can prove the theorem. □

Theorem 8.2. *In addition to Assumption A, suppose that the following* (iv'), (v) *and* (vi') *hold.*

(iv') $\tilde{u} \in \tilde{\mathfrak{L}}(K^+)$ *with* $\tilde{u}_0 \subset K$ *and* $\tilde{q}(\tilde{u}) \preccurlyeq_K \tilde{u}$.
(v) $\tilde{u}_{\alpha'} \supset_V \tilde{u}_\alpha$ *for all* α, α' $(0 \leq \alpha' \leq \alpha \leq 1)$, *where* V *is as in Assumption* A(iii).
(vi') $\{\tilde{s}_t\} \subset \tilde{\mathfrak{L}}(K^+)$.

Then, the sequence $\{\tilde{s}_t\}$ *converges and the limit* $\tilde{s} := \lim_{t\to\infty} \tilde{s}_t$ *satisfies the fuzzy relational equation* (8.5).

Proof. From Lemma 8.2, $\tilde{s}_{t+1} \preccurlyeq_K \tilde{s}_t$ and $\mathbf{1}_{\{0\}} \preccurlyeq_K \tilde{s}_t \preccurlyeq_K \tilde{s}_1$ for all $t \geq 1$. Applying Theorem 7.3 to the $\preccurlyeq_K$-decreasing case, we can prove the theorem. □

As an example of $\preccurlyeq_K$-monotone fuzzy relation, we put the fuzzy relation $\tilde{q}$ by

$$\tilde{q}(x, y) := \tilde{r}(y) + \beta \mathbf{1}_{\{x\}} \quad (x, y \in \mathbb{R}^n), \tag{8.6}$$

where $\tilde{r} \in \tilde{\mathfrak{L}}(K^+)$ with $\tilde{r}_{\alpha'} \supset_V \tilde{r}_\alpha$ for some finite set $V \subset U$ and α, α' $(0 \leq \alpha' \leq \alpha \leq 1)$ and $0 < \beta < 1$.

Obviously, Assumption A is satisfied for $\tilde{q}$ of (8.6). Also, we observe from Lemma 7.1 that the assumptions (iv) to (vi) in Theorem 8.1 hold for $\tilde{u} = \tilde{r}$. So that by Theorem 8.1, the sequence $\{\tilde{s}_t\}$ defined by (8.4) with $\tilde{s}_1 = \tilde{r}$ converges.

Remark. Note that the fuzzy relation $\tilde{q}$ of (8.6) satisfies the contraction property introduced in [8]. Thus, we see that the limit $\tilde{s} = \lim_{t\to\infty} \tilde{s}_t$ is a unique solution of the fuzzy relational equation (8.5) and given by $\tilde{s} = (1-\beta)^{-1}\tilde{r}$.

Example. We give a one-dimensional numerical example whose fuzzy relation $\tilde{q}$ is given by

$$\tilde{q}(x, y) = (1 - 2|y - (3 - x^{-2})|) \vee 0 \quad (x > 0),$$

where $a \vee b = \max\{a, b\}$ for $a, b \in \mathbb{R}$.

For $\alpha \in [0,1]$, it holds that by (8.3)

$$\widetilde{q}_\alpha(x) = [3 - (1-\alpha)2^{-1} - x^{-2}, 3 + (1-\alpha)2^{-1} - x^{-2}].$$

This is illustrated in Figure 11. So, we observe that $\widetilde{q}$ is $\preccurlyeq_1$-monotone in $(0,\infty) \times (0,\infty)$, also that $\mathbf{1}_{\{1\}} \preccurlyeq_1 \widetilde{q}(\mathbf{1}_{\{1\}})$ and $\widetilde{q}(x,\cdot) \preccurlyeq_1 \mathbf{1}_{\{7/2\}}(x)$.

Applying Theorem 8.1, the sequence $\{\widetilde{s}_t(x)\}$ defined by (8.4) with $\widetilde{s}_1(x) = \mathbf{1}_{\{1\}}(x)$ converges. The convergence is shown in Figure 11 and 12 with the limit $\widetilde{s}(x) = \lim_{t\to\infty} \widetilde{s}_t(x)$, where the α-cut $\widetilde{s}_\alpha$ of the limit $\widetilde{s}(x)$ for $\alpha = 0$ and $\alpha = 1$ are $\min \widetilde{s}_0 = 2.313099034$, $\max \widetilde{s}_0 = 3.414213562$ and $\widetilde{s}_1 = 2.879385242$.

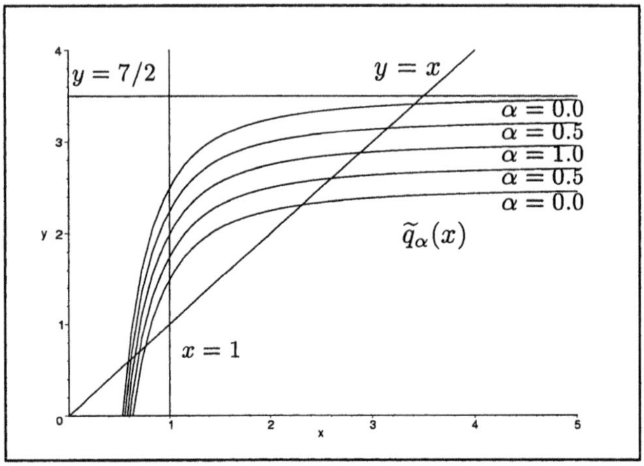

Fig. 11: $\widetilde{q}_\alpha(x)$ and the limit $\widetilde{s}(x)$ of $\{\widetilde{s}_t(x)\}$

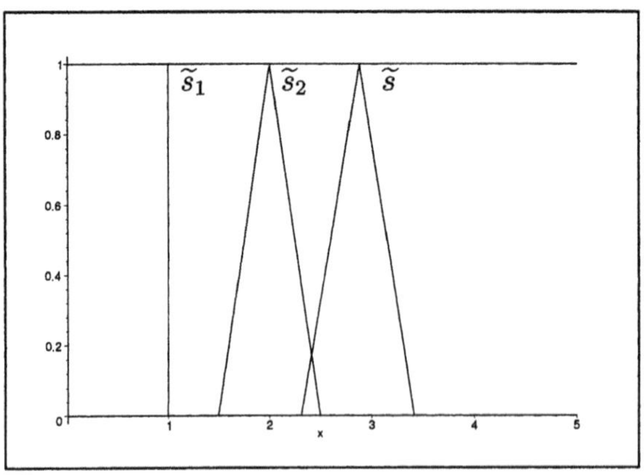

Fig. 12: The sequence $\{\widetilde{s}_t(x)\}$

References

1. Congxin, W., Cong, C. (1997) The supremum and infimum of the set of fuzzy numbers and its application. J. Math. Anal. Appl. **210**, 499–511
2. Diamond, P., Kloeden, P. (1994) Metric Spaces of Fuzzy Sets, Theory and Applications. World Scientific
3. Dubois, D., Prade, H. (1980) Fuzzy Sets and Systems: Theory and Applications. Academic Press
4. Furukawa, N. (1993) An order relation and fundamental operations on fuzzy numbers and their applications to fuzzy linear programming. Bulletin Infor. Cybernetics **25**, 161-179
5. Furukawa, N. (1993) A parametric total order on fuzzy numbers and a fuzzy shortest route problem. Optimization **30**, 367-377
6. Furukawa, N. (1997) Parametric orders on fuzzy numbers and their roles in fuzzy optimization problems. Optimization **40**, 171–192
7. Kaufmann, A., Gupta, M. M. (1988) Fuzzy Mathematical Models in Engineering and Management Science. North-Holland
8. Kurano, M., Yasuda, M., Nakagami, J., Yoshida, Y. (1992) A limit theorem in some dynamic fuzzy systems. Fuzzy Sets and Systems **51**, 83–88
9. Kurano, M., Yasuda, M., Nakagami, J., Yoshida, Y. (1996) Markov-type fuzzy decision processes with a discounted reward on a closed interval. European Journal of Operations Research **92**, 649-662
10. Kurano, M., Yasuda, M., Nakagami, J., Yoshida, Y. (1999) The time average reward for some dynamic fuzzy systems. Computers and Mathematics with Applications **37**, 77-86
11. Kurano, M., Yasuda, M., Nakagami, J., Yoshida, Y. (2000) Ordering of fuzzy sets – A brief survey and new results. Journal of Operations Research Society of Japan **43**, 138-148
12. Kuroiwa, D., Tanaka, T., Ha, T. X. D. (1997) On cone convexity of set-valued maps. Nonlinear Analysis, Theory and Applications **30**, 1487-1496
13. Li, H. X., Yen, V. C. (1995) Fuzzy Sets and Fuzzy Decision-making. CRC Press
14. Nanda, S. (1989) On sequences of fuzzy numbers. Fuzzy Sets and Systems **33**, 123-126
15. Novák, V. (1989) Fuzzy Sets and Their Applications. Adam Hilder, Bristol-Boston
16. Ramík, J., Řimánek, J. (1985) Inequality relation between fuzzy numbers and its use in fuzzy optimization. Fuzzy Sets and Systems **16**, 123-138
17. Stoer, J., Witzgall, C. (1970) Convexity and Optimization in Finite Dimensions I. Springer-Verlag, Berlin and New York
18. Stowinski, R. :editor (1998) Fuzzy Sets in Decision Analysis, Operations Research and Statistics. Kluwer Academic Publishers
19. Syau, Y. R. (1997) Sequences in a fuzzy metric space. Computers and Mathematics with Applications **33**, 73-76
20. Yoshida, Y., Yasuda, M., Nakagami, J., Kurano, M. (1993) A potential of fuzzy relations with a linear structure: The contractive case. Fuzzy sets and Systems **60**, 283-294
21. Yoshida, Y., Yasuda, M., Nakagami, J., Kurano, M. (1994) A potential of fuzzy relations with a linear structure: The unbounded case. Fuzzy sets and Systems **66**, 83-96

22. Yoshida, Y. (1998) A time-average fuzzy reward criterion in fuzzy decision processes. Information Science **110**, 103-112
23. Yoshida, Y., Yasuda, M., Nakagami, J., Kurano, M. (1998) A limit theorem in dynamic fuzzy systems with a monotone property. Fuzzy sets and Systems **94**, 109-119
24. Zadeh, L. A. (1965) Fuzzy sets. Information and Control**8**, 338-353
25. Zhang, K., Hirota, K. (1997) On fuzzy number lattice $(\tilde{R}, \preccurlyeq)$. Fuzzy sets and Systems **92**, 113-122

Advances in the Egalitarist Approach to Decision-Making in a Fuzzy Environment

Didier Dubois and Henri Prade

Institut de Recherche en Informatique de Toulouse (IRIT) – CNRS

Université Paul Sabatier, 118 route de Narbonne

31062 Toulouse Cedex 4, France

***Summary**: This paper proposes a unified approach to decision-making in a fuzzy environment, based on the original idea of Bellman and Zadeh, encompassing fuzzy optimization, fuzzy relational calculus and possibility theory. This approach subsumes the paradigm of constraint-directed reasoning in Artificial Intelligence and allows for flexible or prioritized constraints. More generally the use of Sugeno integral enables to model generalized forms of prioritizing and the inclusion of fuzzy quantifiers in the conjunctive aggregation of local satisfaction levels. It is shown that the egalitarist (maximin) criterion of Bellman and Zadeh must be refined in order to make it Pareto-efficient. Two such refinements called "discrimin" and "leximin" are described. Some results about how to compute such optimal solutions are provided. The proposed framework enables uncertainty to be handled as well. Decision theory is reexamined in the light of possibility theory and Sugeno integral. Older fuzzy pattern matching evaluations turn out to be possibilistic counterparts of expected utility, suitable for a sound modelling of non-repeated decision under uncertainty.*

1 Introduction

The most popular approach to decision-making in the setting of fuzzy sets is the maximin ranking of solutions proposed by Bellman and Zadeh (1970). It consists in maximizing membership to a conjunction of fuzzy sets representing constraints or criteria. This method is natural when fuzzy sets model flexible constraints that cannot compensate with one another. However the obtained ranking of solutions is very coarse. Two refinements to this ordering have been introduced: one focusing on the least satisfied discriminating constraint, and a lexicographical ranking. The latter refines the former and combines utilitarist and egalitarist points of view (Moulin, 1988) on the aggregation of feasibility degrees. Moreover the minimum and maximum operations can be weighted by means of Sugeno integral (Sugeno,

1974, 1977). While the maxmin paradigm makes sense when only flexible constraints represented by fuzzy sets are involved, it no longer always applies when some of the fuzzy sets represent uncertainty. In this situation, a specific decision theory has been developed where criteria make sense for one-shot decisions and reflect the attitude of the decision-maker in front of uncertainty. This paper is a tutorial introduction to these recent developments of Bellman and Zadeh's setting.

2 The calculus of flexible constraints

The notion of constraint is basic in optimization and decision sciences. A constraint prescribes what are the potentially acceptable decisions (the solutions to a problem) and what are the absolutely unacceptable ones: it is an all-or-nothing notion. Moreover, no constraint must be violated, i.e., a constraint is classically considered as imperative, and the violation of a constraint cannot be compensated by the satisfaction of another one. If a solution violates a single constraint, it is regarded as unfeasible. The idea of flexible constraints is to maintain the non-compensatory property of constraints, while introducing:

(i) intermediary levels between feasibility and non-feasibility;

(ii) intermediary levels in the imperativeness of constraints.

This lack of compensation is characteristic of the flexible constraint approach, and contrasts with the multiobjective additive modelling tradition expressing trade-offs and based on weighted arithmetic means (Keeney and Raiffa, 1976).

2.1 Representing flexible and prioritized constraints

Let x be a vector of decision variables ranging on a space U. A solution to a set of constraint is a vector of values x = u. A classical hard constraint C is represented by a classical set of solutions, only using degrees of membership 0 or 1. Introducing intermediary levels of feasibility on a linearly ordered valuation set S (for instance, [0, 1]), C is then called a fuzzy, or soft constraint: $\mu_C(u) = 1$ means that a solution u totally satisfies C while $\mu_C(u) = 0$ means that it totally violates C (u is unfeasible). If $0 < \mu_C(u) < 1$, u satisfies C only partially; $\mu_C(u) > \mu_C(u')$ indicates that C is more satisfied by u than by u'. Hence, like an objective function, a fuzzy constraint rank-orders the feasible decisions. However, contrary to an objective function a fuzzy constraint also models a threshold acting as a veto level (represented by the value 0) beyond which a solution will be rejected. In fact, a fuzzy constraint can be viewed as the association of a constraint (defining the support of C) and a criterion which rank-orders the solutions satisfying this constraint. In this interpretive framework, a membership function is similar to a utility function. A soft constraint C' is looser than another one C if and only if $\mu_C \le \mu_{C'}$, that is, if any solution to C is at least as feasible for C'.

It is often the case that priorities are assigned to constraints. Solutions that satisfy all constraints are selected if any. Otherwise the less prioritary constraints are dropped, and the chosen solution satisfies only higher priority constraints. This decision strategy can be captured in the setting of fuzzy constraints.

A priority level ρ for constraint C can be understood as an estimation of how imperative C is. Then, the *prioritized constraint* (C, ρ), where C is a crisp constraint, can be represented by a special kind of fuzzy constraint C* (Dubois, Fargier and Prade, 1996a):

$$\mu_{C^*}(u) = 1 \text{ if u satisfies C,}$$

$$= 1 - \rho \text{ if u violates C.}$$

Since ρ represents to what extent it is *necessary* to satisfy C, $1 - \rho$ indicates to what extent it is *possible* to violate it. If S is a finite chain, the function $1 - (\cdot)$ is to be replaced by the order-reversing map of S. In other words, any potential solution u that violates C satisfies (C, ρ) to a degree equal to $1 - \rho$. If C is itself a fuzzy constraint with priority ρ, it can be modeled by the fuzzy constraint C* defined by:

$$\mu_{C^*}(u) = \max(1 - \rho, \mu_C(u)).$$

The compatibility of u with (C, ρ) is 0 only if $\rho = 1$ and $\mu_C(u) = 0$, i.e., if constraint C is not satisfied at all but is fully important. Moreover if $\rho = 0$ (C has no importance at all), any solution satisfies C* fully. In the general case, even if C is completely violated, the global level of satisfaction is only upper bounded by $1 - \rho$. In practice, it may be useful in this case to introduce a "safeguard" constraint $\hat{C}$ in case some decision among the ones which violate C should remain unfeasible.

There is a different way of relaxing a constraint (Dubois, Fargier and Prade, 1997), namely by considering that the constraint is sufficiently satisfied if the level of satisfaction for u reaches some threshold θ, i.e., $\mu_C(u) \ge \theta$. Then $\mu_C(u)$ will be changed into an evaluation $\mu_{C'}(u) = 1$. If $\mu_C(u) < \theta$ we may consider that the constraint is satisfied at the level which is actually reached, i.e., $\mu_{C'}(u) = \mu_C(u)$. It is expressed by

$$\mu_{C'}(u) = \theta \rightarrow \mu_C(u)$$

where $a \rightarrow b$ is Gödel implication ($a \rightarrow b = 1$ if $a \le b$, $a \rightarrow b = b$ if $a > b$). Then, we shall speak of a *discounted* constraint. The use of a *relative* level of satisfaction $\mu_C(u)/\theta$ requires a numerical scale and corresponds to Goguen implication. Generally speaking, relaxing a fuzzy constraint C using some importance degree α can be viewed as the modification of μ_C into $\alpha \rightarrow \mu_C$ for some fuzzy implication operation. Prioritized constraints are modelled by Kleene-Dienes implications max(1–a, b). The role of implications in the weighing process was noticed by Yager (1981, 1984). More details on constraint weighting techniques are in (Dubois, Fargier and Prade, 1997). These results show the power of expressiveness of fuzzy constraints.

Example 1: A tutorial course is to be organized. Ideally, it should be composed of not more than 5 sessions (possibly 6 which is less acceptable, or at worst 7). Ideally, there must be 5 lectures (ideally 5, less possibly 4, or 3 in the least acceptable case). Besides, there must be the same number of lectures as exercise sessions (ideally, exactly the same number; a difference of 1 session is "half-acceptable", a difference of 2 being the maximal acceptable difference). This rather self-conflicting problem can be modelled on the preference scale $\{1 > a > b > 0\}$: Let x = nb. of lectures y = nb. of exercise sessions, and i/a be short for $\mu_C(i) = a$.

$$C_1: x + y \in F_1 = \{i/1, i \in [0, 5]\} \cup \{6/a, 7/b\}$$

$$C_2: x \in F_2 = \{5/1, 4/a, 3/b\}$$

$$C_3: |x - y| \in F_2 = \{0/1, 1/a, 2/b\}.$$

2.2 Fuzzy constraint satisfaction

A fuzzy constraint satisfaction problem $\mathcal{P}$ is described by means of m fuzzy constraints $C_1, \ldots, C_m$ and the fuzzy decision set D is then defined by

$$\mu_D(u) = \min_{i=1,m} \mu_{C_i}(u).$$

Note that the use of the combination rule underlies an assumption of *commensurability* between preference levels pertaining to different constraints, i.e., the user who specifies the constraints must describe them by means of a unique preference scale.

The notion of fuzzy set as viewed by Bellman and Zadeh (1970) was meant to represent constraints *as well as* objective functions by fuzzy subsets C of possible decisions. However, this definition of a decision set is not really in accordance with the usual paradigm of multiple-criteria decision-making due to the non-compensatory nature of the minimum operation. Here an optimal solution is one that least violates the most violated constraint. Hence, Bellman and Zadeh's proposal is a constraint-directed view of problem-solving, where constraints are flexible: if there is a solution that completely satisfies all constraints, this solution is optimal. Otherwise $\sup_u \mu_D(u) < 1$, and this indicates that the constraints are partially contradictory. To accept a solution u such that $\mu_D(u) < 1$ means a partial relaxation of some of the constraints C_i (with respect to the constraint corresponding to the core of C_i, i.e., $\{u, \mu_{C_i}(u) = 1\}$). In that sense fuzzy constraints are flexible. The value $\mathrm{Cons}(\mathcal{P}) = \sup_u \mu_D(u)$ is called degree of *consistency* of the problem $\mathcal{P}$. This approach tends to favour solutions that satisfy all constraints to the same extent (even if partially), and to discard solutions that would fully satisfy all constraints but one that would be fully violated. An additive approach would favour the latter kind of solutions. On the contrary, maximizing $\min_{i=1,m} \mu_{C_i}(u)$ tends to select solutions which *equally* satisfy *all* the constraints.

Fuzzy constraint satisfaction is an improvement over standard constraint satisfaction from a modelling point of view. In the presence of very loose constraints, a tool for cleverly picking a solution is needed, as objective functions do. On the contrary when hard constraints in a problem are tight, there is no feasible solution. One way out is to relax the constraints, but automating this process is not so easy and is usually time-consuming. Fuzzy constraints cope with both difficulties since their cores lead to a rather tight problem and their supports to a looser problem.

The notion of optimality involved in the present approach is not new in the literature of decision making. It is known as the maximin strategy and is well-known in game theory as the most cautious strategy for players. It is also well-known in decision-making under uncertainty, where again it is a cautious strategy. Despite these formal analogies, the problem tackled by flexible constraint satisfaction is very different, since index i pertains neither to an opposing player nor to a state of the world. The paradigm most akin to Bellman and Zadeh's is to be found in social choice theory (Moulin, 1988) and $\min_{i=1,m} \mu_{C_i}(u)$ is then an egalitarist social welfare function, $\mu_{C_i}(u)$ being the welfare index of an individual i in situation u.

In the above example 1, it is easy to check that the problem is partially inconsistent : indeed, there is no solution such that $x = y \geq 5$ and $x + y \leq 5$, nor such that $|x - y| \leq 1$, $x \geq 4$ and $x + y \leq 6$. The problem has consistency level b only.

2.3 Sugeno integrals as generalized prioritized conjunctions and disjunctions

Like averaging operations, min and max operations can be "weighted". In the qualitative setting, constraints are more or less relaxable according to their respective levels of importance. This is another way of breaking ties between possible decisions (for instance when $\forall u, \min_i u_i = 0$). Importance acts here as a threshold attached to each fuzzy constraint, either as a priority factor or of discount level as seen in Section 2.1. An example of thresholded min aggregation is thus obtained as the min-based conjunction of prioritized constraints (Yager, 1981; Dubois and Prade, 1986):

$$\mathrm{Wmin}(u) = \min_i \max(1 - \rho_i, u_i).$$

where $\max_i \rho_i = 1$. The corresponding prioritized max operation is then:

$$\mathrm{Wmax}(u) = \max_i \min(\rho_i, u_i).$$

Note that $\max_{i=1,m} u_i \geq \mathrm{Wmin}(u) \geq \min_{i=1,m} u_i$, which indeed expresses a relaxation of constraints and the hybrid nature of the aggregation, between conjunction and disjunction. The same inequalities hold for Wmax. Both aggregations are idempotent. The convention $\max_{i=1,m} \rho_i = 1$ is assumed in order to let the aggregation operation range over the whole of [0, 1]. Denoting by $\mathcal{W}$ the fuzzy set of important constraints (i.e., $\mu_{\mathcal{W}}(C_i) = \rho_i$), Wmin(u) (resp. Wmax(u)) expresses a strong type of inclusion (resp. a degree of intersection) of $\mathcal{W}$ in(resp. with) the fuzzy set $\mathcal{S}_u$ of constraints satisfied by choice u, $\mathcal{S}_u$ (where $\mu_{\mathcal{S}_u}(C_i) = u_i$).

Weighted min and max are particular cases of Sugeno integrals. Namely let g be a set-function on {1,..., m} where g(T) is the weight of the group of constraints T. If T is a subset of T' it is assumed that $g(T) \leq g(T')$ so that $g(T \cup T') \geq \max(g(T), g(T'))$ and $g(\{1,\ldots,m\}) = 1$. Indeed, the importance of a set of constraints is at least as great as the importance of any of its subsets. The Sugeno integral (Sugeno, 1974, 1977) leads to the following aggregation:

$$S_g(u) = \max_{i=1,m} \min(u_{\sigma(i)}, g(\{\sigma(i),\ldots, \sigma(m)\})$$

$$= \min_{i=1,m} \max(u_{\sigma(i)}, g(\{\sigma(i+1),\ldots, \sigma(m)\})$$

using an increasing reordering of vector u according to a permutation σ. $S_g(u)$ is actually the median of the 2m − 1 terms $\{u_1,\ldots, u_m, g(\{\sigma(2),\ldots,\sigma(m)\}),\ldots, g(\{\sigma(m)\})\}$(Dubois and Prade, 1980). Sugeno integrals are applied in subjective evaluation (Ishii and Sugeno, 1985). Marichal (2000) has shown that $S_\sigma(u)$ can also be written in a form involving all priority levels of all subsets of constraints:

$$S_g(u) = \max_{i=1,m} \min(\min_{i \in T} u_i, g(T))$$

$$= \min_{i=1,m} \max(\max_{i \in T} u_i, g(\bar{T})),$$

where $\bar{T}$ denotes the complement of T. Thus, more flexibility is offered for the representation of constraint importance since one can set the importance of a group of constraints almost independently as any of its subset. One can express that a set of constraints is much more important than each of them (complementary constraints), or not more important than the most important of them (redundant constraints).

The weighted min and max are special cases of Sugeno integrals where g is a necessity measure and a possibility measure, respectively (see for instance Grabisch et al., 1992). Namely, letting $\rho_i = g(\{i\})$

$$S_\Pi(u) = \max_i \min(\rho_i, u_i) \text{ for Wmax}$$

$$S_N(u) = \min_i \max(1 - \rho_i, u_i) \text{ for Wmin.}$$

If g(T) only depends upon the cardinality of T, so that $g(\{\sigma(i),\ldots, \sigma(m)\}) = \phi_i$ (and $\phi_{m+1} = 0$) one gets the ordered weighted min and max (see, e.g., Dubois et al., 1988), of the form:

$$\text{OWmin}(u) = \min_{i=1,\ldots,m} \max(\phi_{i+1}, u_{\sigma(i)}),$$

$$\text{OWmax}(u) = \max_{i=1,\ldots,m} \min(\phi_i, u_{\sigma(i)}),$$

whose values coincide. It corresponds to the requirement that a decision with rating vector u satisfies 'at least k', or more generally 'most' constraints (rather than 'all' the constraints or more generally all the important constraints). For instance, the requirement that "at least k" constraints should be satisfied will be modelled by k weights equal to 1, i.e., $\phi_i = 1$ if $1 \le i \le k$, $\phi_i = 0$ for $i \ge k + 1$ (ϕ_i is going to be used as the weight associated with the i-th most satisfied constraint). More generally the set of weights can be derived from a fuzzy quantifier of the form "most": a fuzzy subset Q of integers s.t. $\mu_Q(0) = 0$, $\mu_Q(i) \le \mu_Q(i + 1)$, $\mu_Q(m) = 1$; then define $\phi_i = 1 - \mu_Q(i - 1)$, for $i = 1,\ldots, m + 1$.

For a detailed study of Sugeno integral and its characterization as an aggregation operation, see Marichal (2000), Dubois et al. (1998a). For the mathematics of continuous Sugeno integral, see Wang and Klir (1992).

2.4 Fuzzy constraint propagation

The search for solutions can exploit branch and bound methods that are guided by preference levels. This combinatorial problem can benefit from local propagation schemes extensively developed in the constraint satisfaction literature (Tsang, 1993). Fargier (see Fargier et al., 1995; Dubois et al., 1996a) has proved that the calculus of fuzzy restrictions proposed by Zadeh (1975) provides a sound basis for the local propagation of preference in fuzzy constraint satisfaction problems (CSP). Projecting a fuzzy constraint on the domain of a variable is based on the maxmin composition. When the fuzzy domain of each decision variable in a fuzzy CSP cannot be further restricted, via such projection, the problem is said to be arc-consistent, thus extending the classical arc-consistency notion. Combination being associative, commutative and idempotent, we can compute an equivalent problem which is arc-consistent using a local propagation scheme. More generally all constraint propagation algorithms that have been developed for crisp constraints can be easily adapted to the local propagation of preference in the noncompensatory idempotent approach to fuzzy constraint satisfaction. More details appear in Fargier et al. (1995), Dubois et al. (1996a).

Example 1 (continued): Let us project C_1 and C_3 on the domain of x:

$$\mu_{C'}(x) = \max_{y = 1,\dots 7} \min(\mu_{F_1}(x+y), \mu_{F_3}(|x-y|))$$

$$= \max_{y = 1,\dots 7} \min(\mu_{F_1}(x+y), \mu_{F'_3}(x-y))$$

where $F'_3 = \{-2/b, -1/a, 0/1, 1/a, 2/b\}$

$$= \max_{u,\, v:\, x = (u+v)/2} \min(\mu_{F_1}(u), \mu_{F'_3}(v))$$

Hence we can use fuzzy arithmetics and compute (using integer division):

$$F' = (F_1 \oplus F'_3)/2 = \{i/1, i \in [0, 2]\} \cup \{3/a, 4/b\}$$

Hence $x \in F' \cap F_2 = \{4/b, 3/b\}$. We can then directly check that the problem is partially inconsistent.

Existing tools for constraint satisfaction such as constraint logic programming can be directly used to handle fuzzy constraints through the notion of level-cutting. Namely the level of consistency of a FCSP can be obtained as follows by invoking a classical CSP program (call it CONSAT) that can tell if a set of constraints is consistent or not, and provide a solution, if any. Let $\mathrm{supp}(C) = \{u : \mu_C(u) > 0\}$ be the weakest crisp constraint induced from C, and $C_\alpha = \{u : \mu_C(u) \geq \alpha\}$ be the α-cut of C

Procedure:

Input: a FCSP $\{C_1, \dots, C_k\}$

Test CONSAT(supp(C_1),..., supp(C_k))

If inconsistent: stop.

$\alpha = 1$; $\beta = 0$

Do until impossible or $|\alpha - \beta|$ small enough

Choose $\gamma : \beta < \gamma < \alpha$ (e.g., $\gamma = (\alpha + \beta)/2$)

Test CONSAT($\{(C_1)_\gamma,\ldots,(C_k)_\gamma\}$)

if inconsistent: $\alpha := \gamma$

if consistent: $\beta := \gamma$

End Do

Output: The optimal consistency level (it is γ if the scale is finite and greater but very close to it on [0, 1]) and a solution satisfying all constraints at least at this level.

The output of this procedure can also be viewed as the standard CSP $\{(C_1)_\gamma,\ldots,(C_k)_\gamma\}$ itself, where constraints have been parcimoniously relaxed so as to allow for a solution. In the above example 1, only $\{(C_1)_b,(C_2)_b, (C_3)_b\}$ is consistent.

2.5 Difficulties with min-optimal solutions

Using minimum as an aggregation operation, the global level of satisfaction of a set of fuzzy constraints is the level of satisfaction of the least satisfied one(s). As a result, many possible decisions may receive the same global evaluation, although it would be possible to distinguish between them by considering the individual levels of satisfaction of each constraint.

Example 1 (continued): There are 6 maximin decisions (x,y) easily obtained from the arc-consistency step above, proving that x = 3 or 4:

	C_1	C_2	C_3
$s_1 = (3, 1)$	1	b	b
$s_2 = (3, 2)$	1	b	a
$s_3 = (3, 3)$	a	b	1
$s_4 = (3, 4)$	b	b	a
$s_5 = (4, 2)$	a	a	b
$s_6 = (4, 3)$	b	a	a

It is clear that it is not very reasonable not to discriminate between these solutions, since, for instance, s_2 satisfies the first two constraints to the same degree as s_1 but it is better for C_3.

3 Refinements of min-based rankings

A natural way of ranking the solutions is the well-known Pareto ordering, which, in the fuzzy context, *corresponds to a fuzzy inclusion.*

$$u \geq_P v \Leftrightarrow \forall i, \mu_{C_i}(v) \leq \mu_{C_i}(u),$$

It simply expresses the obvious (and generally accepted) requirement that a solution is at least as good as another one if the former satisfies each constraint at least as much as the latter. Let $u_i = \mu_{C_i}(u)$ for the sake of brevity. Clearly, the Pareto-ordering is a partial ordering: many decisions can be incomparable. It is worth noticing that the min-ordering defined by $u \succcurlyeq_{min} v$ if and only if $\min_i u_i \geq \min_i v_i$, satisfies a weak Pareto principle (if $u_i \geq v_i$ for i = 1, m, then $u \succcurlyeq_{min} v$). However, although there always exist a min-optimal solution which is Pareto-optimal, and conversely, there may exist Pareto-optimal solutions which are not min-optimal, and min-optimal solutions which are not Pareto-optimal. For instance, in the above example1 solutions s_1 and s_4 are clearly not Pareto-optimal. In order to keep only Pareto-optimal solutions to a fuzzy constraint satisfaction problem, the ranking of solutions must be refined.

3.1 Discrimin

The discrimination power of the min-ordering is low, while the Pareto-ordering often leads to incomparabilities. We consider a refinement of both these orderings by comparing the decisions on the basis of constraints that make a difference for the solutions. We have called it "discrimin ordering". Let $\mathcal{D}(u,v) = \{C_i \in \mathcal{C} / u_i \neq v_i\}$ be the set of constraints which are satisfied by u and v to a different extent. (Fargier et al., 1993) define:

$$u >_D v \Leftrightarrow \min\{u_i : C_i \in \mathcal{D}(u,v)\} > \min\{v_i : C_i \in \mathcal{D}(u,v)\}.$$

The "discrimin" refinement is based on the idea that the constraints on which two decisions receive the same evaluation, have no importance when comparing the decisions. It consists in practice in focusing on the lowest satisfaction degrees among the constraints satisfied *at different degrees* by the competing decisions. Thus, decisions are compared on the basis of the least satisfied *discriminating* constraints.

The relation $>_D$ is irreflexive and transitive: it is a strict partial ordering. It can be verified that it is a refinement of both $>_{min}$ and of the Pareto ordering. This ordering of solutions was actually first proposed by Behringer (1977) with a totally different definition (see the discussion by Dubois and Fortemps (1999)). Note that in the previous example, s_1 and s_4 are discrimin-dominated by s_2. Other solutions are discrimin-maximal.

The discrimax relation is defined similarly just changing min into max in the definition of $u >_D v$.

3.2 Leximin

There is another refinement of the egalitarist maximin ordering: the leximin ordering (e.g., Moulin, 1988). The idea is to represent vectors of satisfaction levels by ranked multi-sets of satisfaction degrees. Let u be a vector of satisfaction degrees, and let σ be a permutation such that $u_{\sigma(1)} \leq u_{\sigma(2)} \leq \ldots \leq u_{\sigma(m)}$ obtained by reordering the components of u. Define the leximin ordering $>_L$ as :

$$u >_L v \text{ iff } \exists\, k \leq m \text{ such that } \forall\, i < k,\ u_{\sigma(i)} = v_{\sigma(i)} \text{ and } u_{\sigma(k)} > v_{\sigma(k)}.$$

Two decisions are indifferent if the corresponding reordered vectors are the same.

The leximin-ordering is a refinement of the discrimin ordering, hence of both the Pareto-ordering and the min-ordering (Dubois, Fargier and Prade, 1996b):

$$u >_D v \Rightarrow u >_L v.$$

Leximin-optimal decisions are always discrimin-maximal decisions, and thus indeed min-optimal and Pareto-maximal: $>_L$ is the most selective among these preference relations. Converse implications are not verified. The leximin ordering can discriminate as much as any symmetric aggregation function. For instance in the above example solutions s_2 and s_3 are leximin optimal and cannot be distinguished by a symmetric aggregation. The leximin-ordering tends to favor solutions that violate as *few* fuzzy constraints as possible (where 'few' refers to a fuzzy cardinality evaluation; see (Dubois, Fargier and Prade, 1996b)).

Leximin optimality has been first introduced in numerical analysis for the purpose of approximating functions in the sense of the Chebyshev norms (Rice, 1962), (Descloux, 1963). The leximin solution can be interpreted as the limit of optimal solutions to other multiattribute objective functions. Namely the following result has been proved (Dubois Fargier, Fortemps and Prade. 1997):

Proposition: *Let $\{f^n_p : p > 0;\ n = 1, 2, \ldots\}$ be a family of n-place monotonic continuous and commutative aggregation functions with real parameter p , from $(0, 1)^n$ to $(0, 1)$ such that :*

i) $f^n_p = g_{(i,n)}(f^i_p, f^{n-i}_p)$ *for some function* $g_{(i,n)}$, $\forall n \in \mathbb{N}, n > 0, \forall i, 1 \leq i \leq n.$

ii) $lim_{p \to +\infty} f^n_p = min$.

Let x^p *be the supposedly unique solution to the maximization of* $f^n_p(x)$ *over a convex subset V of* $[0, 1]^n$. *Let* x^∞ *be the optimal leximin solution over V (provably unique when V is convex). Then,* $lim_{p \to +\infty} x^p = x^\infty$.

This result generalizes a theorem in numerical analysis pertaining to the convergence of L_p-norms towards the Chebyshev norm. It is also proved that the leximin ordering can be represented by some ordered weighted averaging operations (OWA, see Yager , 1988; Yager and Kacprzyk, 1997) when the scale of preference levels is finite (Dubois, Fargier and Prade 1997). OWA operations are linear convex averages where the values to be aggregated are reordered like for the leximin, and weights are allocated after the reordering of values. In the infinite case, the representation result of leximin ordering by OWA's holds only in the limit on convex subsets of $[0, 1]^n$, where again the OWA optimal solution converges towards the leximin solution (Dubois Fargier, Fortemps and Prade. 1997).

These results show that the leximin ordering is very natural in the scope of fuzzy (maxmin, egalitarist) optimization. Note that one can define leximax orderings in a similar way, by ranking the values to be aggregated in decreasing order instead of the increasing one.

3.3 Computing improved solutions to FCSP's

An important issue is how to compute discrimin and leximin optimal solutions. The starting point of a generic algorithm that finds all such solutions is the fact that a maximin optimal solution is generally not Pareto-optimal when the optimal level of satisfaction Cons($\mathcal{P}$) of a fuzzy CSP $\mathcal{P}$ is not 1. By definition, the crisp CSP defined by $\mu_{C_j}(u) \geq \alpha$, $\forall j$ is unfeasible for $\alpha >$ Cons($\mathcal{P}$). Hence we are led to find maximal subsets of constraints for which the level of satisfaction can be strictly higher than Cons($\mathcal{P}$). The complements of these sets, called *critical* in the following, contain constraints that are simultaneously forced to be satisfied at level at most α.

Formally, a subset $\mathcal{C}$ of fuzzy constraints is said to be *saturated* if $\exists u$, $\mu_{C_j}(u) =$ Cons($\mathcal{P}$), $\forall$ $C_j \in \mathcal{C}$ and $\mu_{C_j}(u) >$ Cons($\mathcal{P}$) otherwise. A subset $\mathcal{C}$ of fuzzy constraint is said to be *critical* if $\mathcal{C}$ is a minimal saturated set (in the sense of inclusion). Constraints in a critical set are said to be critical. Then a general technique that yields all the discrimin optimal solutions is given by Dubois and Fortemps (1999) :

Procedure: Disc($\mathcal{P}$) (where $\mathcal{P}$ is a FCSP)

- find the level of consistency of $\mathcal{P}$:

$\alpha = \text{Cons}(\mathcal{P})$

- find all critical subsets of constraints : $\{ \mathcal{C}_1,\ldots, \mathcal{C}_k\}$

- for each $\mathcal{C} \in \{\mathcal{C}_1,\ldots, \mathcal{C}_k\}$ define the problem $\mathcal{P}'$ with constraints $C'_1,\ldots, C'_k$:

  if $C_j \in \mathcal{C}$, $C'_j = \{u, \mu_{C_j}(u) = \alpha\}$

  if $C_j \notin \mathcal{C}$: $C'_j = C_j \cap \{u, \mu_{C_j}(u) > \alpha\}$

  - solve $\mathcal{P}'$ so generated using Disc($\mathcal{P}'$)

- the procedure stops when all generated problems are classical CSP's.

This method achieves several parallel defuzzifications of the FCSP. At each step critical constraints are defuzzified, that is, changed into crisp constraints[1]. Each solution to a terminal classical CSP is discrimin-optimal. For leximin optimal solutions the procedure is similar, but the notion of minimality for sets of saturated constraints should be expressed in terms of cardinality, and the solutions found by the procedure must be leximin-ranked in a last step. This procedure is highly combinatorial but it highlights the nature of discrimin-maximal solutions.

Many FCSP's can be viewed as *classical CSP's with fuzzy domains,* that is, a FCSP where the all fuzzy constraints are of the form $x_i \in F_i$ for some fuzzy subset F_i of the domain D_i of a decision variable. For these problems, subsets of critical constraints become subsets of critical variables. All problems where fuzzy constraints are of the form $f_j(x_1, x_2, x_3, \ldots) \in F_j$ for some functions f_j are such, since this fuzzy constraint can be put under the form $t = f_j(x_1, x_2, x_3, \ldots)$ (crisp constraint) and $t \in F_j$ (fuzzy domain for the new variable t).

A FCSP is said to be *simple* if:

– it can be put under the form of a classical CSP with fuzzy domains;
– the critical set of variables is unique at each step of the procedure;
– the values of critical variables are completely determined at each step (that is the

[1] In the literature of fuzzy control, the term "defuzzification" stands for the selection of a representative value from a fuzzy set. It is a misnomer since the word "defuzzification" suggest the deletion of the fuzziness from a fuzzy set, hence the "crispification" of a fuzzy set, which is done here. Strictly speaking, defuzzifying a fuzzy set should yield a standard set, not a single value. Defuzzification, in the usual meaning, should rather be called "selection" or "decision". This anomaly is due to the fact that many people mix up the notion of fuzziness (gradual membership) and set-valuedness (lack of specificity).

solution to $\mu_{F_i}(x_i) = \text{Cons}(\mathcal{P})$ is unique).

For simple FCSP's the discrimin optimal solution is unique. Noticeable classes of simple FCSP are explored in detail by Dubois and Fortemps, (1999) (see also Fortemps (1997)'s dissertation) and briefly pointed out here:

– Convex mathematical programming problems with fuzzy domains. Noticeably, fuzzy linear programming problems in the sense of Zimmermann (1978) have unique discrimin-optimal solutions;

– Fuzzy scheduling problems with no resource limitations where earliest starting dates of tasks, durations of tasks, and due-dates are flexible and decision variables include both starting times and durations (Dubois, Fargier and Prade, 1995). They are particular instances of a more general class of numerical FCSP's called *isotonic*, where the set of variables is partitioned into two sets of left and right variables respectively, and each constraint is of the form $f_j(x_L) \le g_j(x_R)$ where x_R is a vector of right variables and x_L of left variables. Functions f_j and g_j are isotonic, and variables have fuzzy domains with increasing membership functions for left variables and decreasing membership functions for right variables. For PERT-CPM problems, left variables are starting times and durations of activities. Right variables are ending times thereof.

Example 2: a scheduling problem:

Suppose that three tasks T1, T2, T3 must be performed where T1 must precede both T2 and T3. The problem is to determine optimal starting times and durations of the tasks. Each task is best performed if it is allocated at least 4 hours. In any case not less than 2.

Denote (a, b, c) a triangular fuzzy number with core b and support (a, c). The feasible domain for durations is thus $(2, 4, +\infty)$. Task T1 can start at time $t = 0$. Task T2 should be finished best before $t = 4$ hours, and T3 before $t = 6$ hours. All tasks should be finished before 8 hours in any case. The feasible due dates are $(-\infty, 4, 8)$ and $(-\infty, 6, 8)$. Let s1, s2, s3 be the starting times of tasks and d1, d2, d3 their durations, to be decided upon. The consistency of the problem is the maximal value of the least among

$\mu_{(2,4,+\infty)}(d1)$, $\mu_{(2,4,+\infty)}(d2)$, $\mu_{(2,4,+\infty)}(d3)$, $\mu_{(-\infty,4,8)}(s2 + d2)$,

$\mu_{(-\infty,6,8)}(s3 + d3)$, such that $s1 \ge 0$, $\min(s2, s3) \ge s1 + d1$.

The reader can check that $\text{Cons}(\mathcal{P}) = 0.5$. However defuzzifying the duration values for membership .5 leads to d1= d2 = d3 = 3, and suggests s1 = 0 , s2 = 3, s3 = 3. However this solution can be improved.

Note that the sequence T1, T2 cannot be moved without decreasing the feasiblity below 0.5 (which enforces an actual due-date of 6). Hence s1, s2, d1, d2 are critical variables whose values are fixed and T1, T2 define a critical path in the usual sense. Now T3 can be much better performed by optimizing the FCSP with variables s3 and d3, defined by $s3 \ge 3$, $s3 + d3$ being limited by the fuzzy set $(-\infty, 6, 8)$, and d3 by $(2, 4, +\infty)$. A simple calculation shows that the optimal maxmin solution is unique and is s3 = 3, and d3 = 3.5 with membership grade .75. This way, the discrimin-optimal solution to the overall problem has been constructed.

4 Applications of discrimin / leximin

The applications of the leximin/leximax and discrimin/discrimax orderings can be found in multicriteria fuzzy optimization and also in artificial intelligence for the purpose of handling inconsistency in propositional knowledge bases. Potential applications of discrimin and leximin orderings also include querying problems in databases, for the purpose of improving the ranking between retrieved items matching a fuzzy multiattribute request.

4.1 Refinements of possibility theory

It is tempting to exploit discrimin and leximin orderings within possibility theory itself, for achieving a finer-grained representation of qualitative uncertainty (see Dubois, Fargier and Prade, 1998). It enables possibility and necessity orderings of events to be refined on the basis of the only knowledge of the underlying possibility distribution, and without necessarily resorting to the use of numbers.
Recall (Zadeh, 1978, Dubois and Prade, 1988, De Cooman, 1997) that a possibility measure on a (here finite) set U is defined by means of a normalized possibility distribution π describing what are the more or less possible values of a parameter. The possibility of an event A is $\Pi(A) = \max_{u \in A} \pi(u)$ and the necessity of event A is $N(A) = 1 - \max_{u \notin A} \pi(u) = 1 - \Pi(\bar{A})$ where $\bar{A}$ is the complement of A, and π denotes the possibility distribution associated to Π.

Two events A and B cannot be discriminated using the dual pair (N, Π) as soon as $\Pi(A) = \Pi(B)$ and $N(A) = N(B)$, which occurs quite often, namely, as soon as

$$\max_{u \in A} \pi(u) = \max_{u \in B} \pi(u) < 1 \text{ or}$$
$$\max_{u \notin A} \pi(u) = \max_{u \notin B} \pi(u) < 1.$$

The equality $\Pi(A) = \Pi(B)$ may be due to a high value of $\Pi(B \cap A)$. However in the spirit of the discrimin relation, this weight should not affect the comparison between A and B, since it is common to both. The same reasoning applies to $\Pi(\bar{B} \cap \bar{A})$ with respect to the equality $N(A) = N(B)$. Only $\bar{B} \cap A$ and $B \cap \bar{A}$ should matter in telling A from B. Let us introduce the relation $>_{\Pi L}$ on 2^U, different from although closely related to the original necessity and possibility orderings modelled by N and its dual Π:

$A >_{\Pi L} B$ iff $\Pi(\bar{B} \cap A) > \Pi(B \cap \bar{A})$.
$A \geq_{\Pi L} B$ iff not $(B >_{\Pi L} A)$.

The relation $>_{\Pi L}$ is a refinement of both possibility and necessity orderings in the sense of a discrimax ordering since the term $\Pi(B \cap A)$ common to A and B is deleted from the comparison. More precisely, let $\vec{a}$ be the vector $(a_1, \ldots, a_n)$ such that, denoting $U = \{u_1, u_2, \ldots, u_n\}$ in the finite case: $a_i = \pi(u_i)$ if $u_i \in A$; $a_i = 0$ otherwise; $\vec{b}$ is defined from B and π similarly. Then :

$A >_{\Pi L} B \Leftrightarrow \vec{a} >_{\text{Discrimax}} \vec{b}$.

These relations are purely ordinal, yet being as much discriminant as comparative probability orderings (Fishburn, 1986) with which they share many properties.

$A \subseteq B \Rightarrow A \leq_{\Pi L} B$ (monotony);
$A \cap (B \cup C) = \emptyset \Rightarrow (B \geq_{\Pi L} C \Leftrightarrow A \cup B \geq_{\Pi L} A \cup C)$ (additivity);
$A \geq_{\Pi L} B \Leftrightarrow \bar{B} \geq_{\Pi L} \bar{A}$ (self duality).

If A is a proper subset of B then $B >_{\Pi L} A$ always hold for positive possibility distributions. The possibilistic relation $\geq_{\Pi L}$ is called *possibilistic likelihood* and $A \geq_{\Pi L} B$ reads "A is at least as likely as B", so as to emphasize the self-duality. However, because of the lack of transitivity of the indifference relation, we cannot generally represent such relations by means of probability measures, nor can we assume properties that are usually derived from comparative probabilities. However, the leximax extension of a possibility measure is a genuine comparative probability relation on finite sets and can be represented by a special class of numerical probabilities (Dubois, Fargier, Prade, 1998).

4.2 Inconsistency handling in possibilistic logic

Consider layered, possibly inconsistent, knowledge bases in propositional logic, of the form $\mathbf{K} = L_1 \cup \ldots \cup L_n$, such that formulas ϕ_{ik} in L_i have the same level of priority or certainty and are more reliable than ϕ_{jl} if L_j where $j > i$. Formulas of L_1 are the most credible beliefs and those in L_n are the least important ones.

Due to inconsistency, the problem of selecting a maximal consistent subbase arises. There exist two criteria for defining such preferred subbases of **K**: set-inclusion (Brewka, 1989) or cardinality (Dubois et al.,1992; Benferhat et al., 1996).

A consistent subbase $M = M_1 \cup \ldots \cup M_n$ is an *inclusion-preferred subbase* of K iff there does not exist a consistent subbase $N = N_1 \cup \ldots \cup N_n$ of K such that: $\exists i \leq n$,

where $M_i \subset N_i$ and for $j < i$, $N_j = M_j$. For any $i = 1, \ldots, n$, M_i is a subset of L_i.
A consistent subbase $M = M_1 \cup \ldots \cup M_n$ is called a *lex-preferred subbase* of **K** iff there does not exist a consistent subbase $N = N_1 \cup \ldots \cup N_n$ such that: $\exists i \leq n$, where $|N_i| > |M_i|$ and for $j < i$, $|N_j| = |M_j|$ where $|M|$ is the cardinality of M.
Define a complete preordering on **K** via a weight assignment that accounts for the priority of the layers, namely $\mu(\phi_{ij}) > \mu(\phi_{kl})$ iff $i < k$. Viewed from a semantic perspective these weights are degrees of necessity induced by a possibility distribution on interpretations. Here, for mathematical convenience, we view these weights as a distribution μ on the set **K** of formulas, with a syntactic point of view. Then it is easy to check that the selection of interesting consistent subbases can rely on the discrimax and leximax orderings:

Proposition: *$M = M_1 \cup \ldots \cup M_n$ is an inclusion-preferred subbase (resp. lex-preferred) of K iff M is a maximal element of $\{N \mid N$ consistent, $N \subset$ **K**$\}$ for the discrimax (resp. the leximax) likelihood relation induced by μ on subsets of **K**.*

5 Handling preference and uncertainty conjointly

In the general case, decisions are made in an uncertain environment. In the Savage (1954) framework, the consequence of a decision depends on the state of the world in which it takes place. But an agent does not always know the state of the world when making a decision. For instance, in a restaurant, one must choose our dishes without being totally sure that the food is good. The usual approach to decision-making under uncertainty is based on representing uncertainty on states by a unique probability distribution and the decision-maker by a utility function on consequences. Then decisions are selected on the basis of expected utility.

However such an approach makes more sense in the scope of repeated decisions whose results compensate, since in the case of risk-neutral decision-makers, an average gain is computed. When uncertainty is just due to a lack of information and only the result of the present decision matters (as in the restaurant), the idea of average is less attractive. For this reason we have developed a purely possibilistic approach to decision under uncertainty that addresses this kind of situation.

5.1 Preference vs. uncertainty: why bother?

We shall assume that both the preference profile of decision makers and their uncertainty can be modelled by possibility distributions. It may be strange to do so since possibility measures are often understood as a tool for representing uncertainty. However in the founding paper by Zadeh (1978) it is not so clear that the purpose is to model uncertainty. In natural language, the term "possibility" refers as often to the idea of feasibility ("it is possible TO do something") as well as to uncertainty ("it is possible THAT something happens"). The feasibility interpretation of possibility has been used in the previous sections of this paper. In that view, a degree of necessity qualifies the priority of a constraint while, in the other view, it reflects the certainty of a statement. Hence the calculus of possibility bears two distinct interpretive settings that cannot be told apart just looking at the mathematics.

This situation is a bit dangerous because there is a great temptation to confuse uncertainty and preference in a fuzzy approach, as sometimes found in the literature. Not making the distinction may lead to the wrong approach to modelling fuzzy decision problems as shown now, on an example from scheduling theory, published elsewhere.

Example 3 (Dubois et al. 1995)

Suppose Tom wants to attend a meeting in the morning at 8 a.m. He wants to know when to get up, so as to arrive on time. He has to take the bus to reach the venue of the meeting, and the bus ride takes about 1 hour. Besides he does not want to leave his house too early, say before 7, and in any case not earlier than 6:30 h. Clearly the time when he leaves his house is his choice. He can express preferences on this decision variable by means of a linear fuzzy interval R with a nondecreasing membership function, lower modal value 7 and support [6.5, 12]. As for the travel time, Tom has no control on it. It depends on the waiting time (not more than 15 mn) and the traffic situation, which never causes more than a 15 mn delay. His experience suggests that the usual overall travel time (including the wait at the bus stop) is 1 hour. But if Tom is lucky (no wait, no traffic jam) it can take only 45 mn. and, if unlucky, 1 hour and 15mn. This information builds up a triangular fuzzy number T that models the uncertainty about the travel time; it does not reflect preference. Tom has preference on his arrival time: he would like to arrive at 8 or before, but certainly not after 8:15 a.m.This makes up the fuzzy arrival time D. How can Tom choose his actual starting time? Treating all these pieces of information in a symmetric way (without separating uncertainty and preference the problem becomes one of finding both s and t which maximize the membership of the starting time, the driving time, and the arrival hour, i.e., $\max_{s,t} \min(\mu_R(s), \mu_T(t), \mu_D(s+t))$). This problem is trivially solved by letting s = 7 and t = 1 with membership 1. But it is not a sound solution to the problem because in many cases the travel will take more than one hour and Tom will be in trouble.

5.2 Possibilistic criteria for one-shot decisions

The usual framework for decision under uncertainty is as follows: Let U be a set of states and X a set of possible consequences. A decision d is a function from U to X stating for each state the consequence of the decision. The decision-maker has some knowledge of the actual state and some preference on the consequences of his decision. It makes sense if information about the state is sparse, to represent the incomplete knowledge on the state by a possibility distribution π on U with values in a plausibility valuation set L and the decision-maker's preference on X by means of another possibility distribution μ with values on a preference valuation set S. Here μ is viewed as a utility function.

The level of preference of a decision d whose consequence in state u is x = d(u) for $u \in U$, can be evaluated by combining the plausibilities $\pi(u)$ and the utilities $\mu(x)$ in a suitable way. Two quatitative criteria that evaluate the worth of decision d have been put forward in the literature. They presuppose that a commensurability assumption between plausibility and preference is made. Namely, there exists a totally ordered set V with top 1 and bottom 0, and order preserving mappings η_L and η_S from L and S to V, respectively, such that for any

$\alpha \in L, \beta \in S$, we can define $\alpha \geq \beta \Leftrightarrow \eta_L(\alpha) \geq \eta_S(\beta)$.

Moreover, $\eta_L(0) = \eta_S(0) = 0$ and $\eta_L(1) = \eta_S(1) = 1$.

In the following we shall assume that L and S are subsets of V. Then the two preference functionals are respectively:

- a pessimistic criterion : $\mathcal{U}_*(d) = \min_{u \in U} \max(\eta(\pi(u)), \mu(d(u)))$

(the mapping η is the order reversing automorphism in V.)

- an optimistic criterion $\mathcal{U}^*(d) = \max_{u \in U} \min(\pi(u), \mu(d(u)))$

If S = L = [0, 1], once can choose $\eta(a) = 1 - a$. These criteria are clearly based on the necessity and the possibility of fuzzy events, they are respectively weighted min and max, and are special cases of Sugeno integrals. The optimistic criterion has been first proposed by Yager (1979) and the pessimistic criterion by Whalen (1984), and also used in Inuiguchi et al. (1989).

Maximizing $\mathcal{U}_*(d)$ means finding a decision d all the highly plausible consequences of which are also highly preferred. The definition of "highly plausible" is decision-dependent and reflects the compromise between high plausibility and low utility expressed by the order-reversing map between the plausibility valuation set L and the utility valuation set S. The pessimistic evaluation $\mathcal{U}_*(d)$ is small as soon as there exists a possible consequence of d which is both highly plausible and bad with respect to preferences. This is clearly an uncertainty-averse and thus a pessimistic attitude. It generalizes the max-min Wald criterion in the absence of probabilistic knowledge since if π is the characteristic function of a subset A of states, $\mathcal{U}_*(d)$ is the utility of the worst consequence of states in A, however unlikely they are. But the possibilistic criterion is less pessimistic. It focuses on the idea of usuality and relies on the worst *plausible* consequences induced by the decision. Some unlikely states are neglected by a variable thresholding and the threshold is determined by comparing the possibility distributions valued on L and S via the mapping η. If $\mathcal{U}_*(d) = a$, and $A(d) = \{u, \pi(u) \geq \eta(a)\}$ is the set of plausible states in the context of decision d, then $\mathcal{U}_*(d) = \min_{u \in A(d)} \mu(d(u))$.

On the contrary, $\mathcal{U}^*(d)$ corresponds to an optimistic attitude since it is high as soon as there exists a possible consequence of d which is both highly plausible and highly prized. It generalizes the maximax optimistic criterion.

For binary acts the expression of the possibilistic preference functionals is rather simple: let xAy denote a decision that gives consequence x if A occurs and y otherwise, and assume x is preferred to y ($\mu(x) > \mu(y)$). Observe that $N(A) = \eta(\Pi(\bar{A}))$ so that:

$$\mathcal{U}_*(xAy) = \max(\mu(y), \min(N(A), \mu(x))) = \min(\mu(x), \max(N(A), \mu(y))).$$

Note that this is the median of $\{\mu(x), N(A), \mu(y)\}$, thus contrasting with expected utility, which is a mean. This form of the pessimistic possibilistic preference functional is easy to understand: if the agent is sure enough that A occurs ($N(A) > \mu(x)$) then the rating of the act xAy is $\mu(x)$. If the agent has too little knowledge ($\max(N(A), N(\bar{A})) < \mu(y)$), then cautiousness prevails and the rating is $\mu(y)$, the worst case. Of course the same happens if the agent is at least somewhat certain that $\bar{A}$ occurs. If the agent's certainty that A occurs is positive but not extreme, the rating reflects the certainty level and is equal to N(A). Similarly, the optimistic possibilistic preference functional of the binary act takes the simplified form :

$$\mathcal{U}^*(xAy) = \max(\min(\Pi(A), \mu(x)), \mu(y)),$$

and can be interpreted similarly as the median of $\{\mu(x), \Pi(A), \mu(y)\}$, but here the utility is $\mu(x)$ as soon as he agent believes that obtaining x is possible enough ($\Pi(A) > \mu(x)$).

A more general preference functional is Sugeno integral of the utility function μ with respect to a monotonic set function g describing the state of knowledge of the decision-maker. The corresponding preference functional for binary acts is again of the form

$$\mathcal{U}^*(xAy) = \max(\min(g(A), \mu(x)), \mu(y)).$$

It clearly indicates that the attitude of the decision-maker in front of uncertainty is modelled by the choice of the uncertainty function. For instance an uncertainty neutral decision-maker can be modelled, in the face of total ignorance by a constant set-function over all non-empty proper subsets of U, such that g(A) is the mid-point of V.

The commensurability assumption between uncertainty and preference exploited in the model, is natural as long as it makes sense to compare uncertain binary acts xAy and sure consequences, as made clear in the above cases.

Possibilistic counterparts of the expected utility theory nicely fit the setting of flexible constraint propagation. as suggested by the Tom's appointment example, where a pessimistic attitude is more natural:

Example 3 (continued)

Assuming that the specifications for the starting time R, the travel time T, and arrival time D are intervals, what Tom wants to find is a starting time s that does not force him to get up too early (hence $s \in R$) such that whatever the travel time (hence for any $t \in T$) he arrives on time at the meeting ($s + t \in D$). Mathematically this means:

$$\exists\, s, \text{ s.t. } s \in R \text{ and } \forall t, \text{ if } t \in T \text{ then } s + t \in D.$$

When R, T, D are fuzzy sets it comes down to finding s that maximizes $\min(\mu_R(s), \inf_t \max(1 - \mu_T(t), \mu_D(s + t)))$.

The maximization and minimization are the fuzzy counterpart of the universal ($\forall$) and existential ($\exists$) quantifiers; and $\max(1 - a, b)$ is a multiple-valued implication. Clearly, the term $\inf_t \max(1 - \mu_T(t), \mu_D(s + t))$ represents a pessimistic possibilistic preference functional and is equal to the degree of necessity of the fuzzy event $s + t \in D$ given the uncertain information $t \in T$. The calculation is detailed in (Dubois et al. 1995). The reader can check that the optimal satisfaction level is .75, and that the optimal time for Tom to start safely enough is $6.875 = \mu_R{}^{-1}(.75)$ (= 6: 52' 30" a.m.). This result presupposes that the travel time does not exceed 1.1875 (= 1h 11' 20"); note that this is very likely. Moreover taking these conditions for granted, Tom will arrive at his meeting not later than $\mu_D{}^{-1}(.75) = 8.0625$ (= 8: 03' 45" a.m.). Note that this solution sounds quite reasonable in practice. The previous solution assumed a very optimistic attitude.

5.3 Axiomatic justifications

The pessimistic criterion has been axiomatically justified by Dubois and Prade (1995) in the style of von Neumann and Morgenstern (1944) utility theory. The idea is that if the uncertainty on the state is represented by a possibility distribution π, each decision induces on the set of consequences X a possibility distribution π_d such that $\pi_d(x) = \Pi(d^{-1}(x))$ is the plausibility of getting x under decision d. So ranking decisions comes down to ranking possibility distributions on X.

Assume the decision-maker supplies an ordering between possibility distributions on X, thus expressing his attitude in front of risk, that is, in front of various possibilities of happy and unhappy consequences in X. The question is to propose axioms on the ordering between possibility distributions on X that make it representable by the ranking of decisions according to the above pessimistic or optimistic criteria. Let $(\lambda/\pi, \mu/\pi')$ denote the "qualitative lottery" yielding π with plausibility λ and π' with plausibility μ. Of course, $\max(\lambda, \mu) = 1$. The following are the pessimistic axioms (Dubois, Godo et al., 1999):

1: The set of possibility distributions is equipped with a complete preordering structure, where $\succcurlyeq$, $\sim$, $\succ$ are the weak preference, indifference and strict preference, respectively.

2: *Independence*: $\pi 1 \sim \pi 2 \Rightarrow (\lambda/\pi 1, \mu/\pi) \sim (\lambda/\pi 2, \mu/\pi)$

3: *Continuity:* if $\pi \succ \pi'$ then $\exists\, \lambda \in L, \pi' \sim (1/\pi, \lambda/X)$

4: *Reduction of lotteries*: $(\lambda/x, \mu/(\alpha/x, \beta/y)) \sim (\gamma/x, \delta/y)$

where $\gamma = \max(\lambda, \min(\mu,\alpha))$ and $\delta = \min(\beta,\mu)$

5: *Risk aversion*: $\pi \geq \pi' \Rightarrow \pi' \succcurlyeq \pi$.

The risk aversion axiom states that the less informative is π, the more risky is the situation: The worst epistemic state is total ignorance. Continuity says that if the rating of π is greater than the one of π', then the latter is equivalent to having some uncertainty level on π. It can be proved that if the knowledge is represented by a subset A of possible states, then $\exists\, x \in A, x \sim A$. This property, violated by expected utility, suggests that contrary to it, the pessimistic possibilistic preference functional is not based on the idea of average and repeated decisions, but makes sense for one-shot decisions. A dual set of axioms can be devised for the optimistic criterion (see Dubois, Godo et al. 1999). The latter can be used as a secondary criterion, for breaking ties between decisions which are equivalent w.r.t. the pessimistic criterion.

An alternative axiomatic justification has been developed in the style of Savage (Dubois, Prade and Sabbadin, 1998a, b). The problem is one of representing the preference relation of an agent over the set $D = X^U$ of potential decisions by means of a preference functional whose form is dictated by the properties of this preference relation $\succcurlyeq$. An example of such a set of axioms for the pessimistic possibilistic preference functional is as follows (here, dAd' denotes a decision that coincides with d if A occurs and d' if not):

S1. $(D, \succcurlyeq)$ is a complete preorder

S2. There exist two decisions d and d' where d is strictly preferred to d'$(d \succ d')$.

S3. If **x** and **y** denote *constant acts* that yield consequence x and y for any state and for any decision d and any event A: **x** $\succcurlyeq$ **y** implies **x**Ad $\succcurlyeq$ **y**Ad.

S4. If d $\succ$ d' and d $\succ$ d" where d' is a constant act, then d $\succ$ d'$\vee$ d"

S5. If d' $\succ$ d and d" $\succ$ d then d'$\wedge$ d"$\succ$ d.

If the preference relation over D satisfies the above axioms then there exists a possibility distribution on U, a utility function on X and an common scale V for plausibility and preference such that the ordering of acts can be represented by the pessimistic preference functional $\mathcal{U}_*$, namely:

$$d \succ d' \text{ if and only if } \mathcal{U}_*(d) > \mathcal{U}_*(d').$$

The optimistic criterion can be justified likewise, moving the constant act condition from axiom S4 to S5. In fact axioms S1, S2, S3 are enough to show that the uncertainty on states is captured by a monotonic (Sugeno) set-function. We have also proved that S1, S2, S3, S4, and S5, both restricted to constant acts d', are enough to show that the preference relation $\succ$ is representable by a Sugeno integral (Dubois, Prade and Sabbadin, 1998a). S5 ensures the min-decomposition of the uncertainty measure (which is then a necessity function).

The pessimistic nature of S5 can be guessed from its equivalent form: d'Ad $\succ$ d implies d $\succcurlyeq$ dAd'. If decision d is improved by d' when A occurs it means that A is sure enough to occur and d is good enough too on A, so that there is no way of improving decision d by changing it in case A does not occur (the agent neglects this possibility).

5.4 Applications

There are numerous applications of the possibilistic preference functionals. In fact these expressions have been widely used in the past for the purpose of fuzzy pattern matching, starting with Cayrol et al (1982). The utility function μ then represents the description of a fuzzy prototype and the possibility distribution π represents some ill-known object. The possibilistic preference functionals then represent the certainty and the possibility that the object fits the description of the prototype. These indices have been used for a long time for triggering fuzzy rules in expert systems and for handling fuzzy queries to incomplete databases (see Dubois and Prade, 1988). In scheduling, the pessimistic possibilistic preference functional has been exploited to define robust schedules for sets of tasks under limited resources, when there are preferences about starting times and due-dates and uncertainty about task durations (Dubois, Fargier and Prade, 1995). More recently the similarity between possibilistic and probabilistic decision theory has been exploited in the study of multiple-stage decision processes for the purpose of planning under possibilistic uncertainty. More precisely two extreme cases have been studied: the case when at each stage no new observation of the state is available, and the result of actions is not fully known in advance; then an optimal sequence of state-independent decisions is searched for that maximizes the pessimistic possibilistic preference functional (Da Costa Pereira et al. 1997). The other case is the search for an optimal policy made of a tree of conditional decisions when the state is observable at each stage (Sabbadin, Fargier and Lang, 1998). The case of partial observability is under study. It seems that possibilistic Markov decision processes are less computationally expensive than their probabilistic counterparts when the plausibility scale is finite (Sabbadin, 2000).

6 Conclusion and open problems

These results, summarizing some five years of research, suggests that the maximin approach to decision is potentially very effective from an algorithmic and fruitful from an application-oriented point of view. Bellman and Zadeh's proposal leads to a simple approach to valued constraint satisfaction problems provided that Pareto-optimal maximin solutions are computed. It is one possible treatment of some multiple-criteria decision-making problems where compensation is not permitted between the goals. Fuzzy constraints are a natural notion to be added to decision support systems. It is more qualitative than utility-based approaches and more expressive than pure relational methods to multiple criteria decision-making as done in constraint logic programming. Moreover all standard CSP software can be readily used to solve FCSP's via level-cutting. The framework is also rich enough to accommodate uncertainty on top of graded preference. There are several open problems in this direction:

i) Improving fuzzy dynamic programming (e.g. Esogbue and Kacprzyk, 1998 for a survey) using discrimin and leximin concepts. It is clear that the Bellman principle stating that all subsolutions of an optimal multistage solution is optimal does not hold for min-optimal solutions. But it is recovered by discrimin maximality and leximin optimality (Fortemps, 1997). How to efficently compute such solutions?

ii) Possibilistic logic inference evaluates a proof path by the weight of the weakest link (Dubois, Lang, Prade, 1994). One could refine the evaluation of conclusions by means of the discrimin and leximin notions and build a more powerful weighted logic.

iii) The possibilistic preference functionals suffer from a lack of discriminating power just as the min-based ordering, as already pointed out by Dubois and Prade (1997). The discrimin and leximin relations apply to vectors, hence apply to preference profiles on the set of consequences. On the other hand the refinements of possibility theory presented in section 4.2 yield a refined ordering of events. Improving the discriminating power of the possibilistic preference functionals may be addressed by extending the possibilistic likelihood relations to fuzzy events. A first proposal along this line is in Fargier and Sabbadin (2000). Of interest are also the variants of possibilistic preference functionals criteria using triangular norms and co-norms, for which axiomatic justifications would be meaningful.

References

Behringer F. 1977 On optimal decisions under complete ignorance: A new criterion stronger than both Pareto and maxmin. *Europ. J. of Operations Research,* 1:295-306.

Bellman R. Zadeh L.A. 1970. Decision making in a fuzzy environment. *Management Science,* 17: B141-B164.

Benferhat S., Dubois D., Prade H. 1996. Reasoning in inconsistent stratified knowledge bases. *Proc. of the 26 Inter. Symp. on Multiple-Valued Logic (ISMVL'96)*, Santiago de Compostela, Spain, 29-31 May, 184-189

Brewka G. 1989 Preferred subtheories: an extended logical framework for default reasoning. *Proc. of the 11th Inter. Joint Conf. on Artificial Intelligence (IJCAI'89)*, Detroit, Aug. 20-25, 1043-1048.

Cayrol M., Farreny H. and Prade H. (1982). Fuzzy pattern matching, *Kybernetes*, **11**, 103-116.

Da Costa Pereira C., Garcia F., Lang J., Martin-Clouaire R. 1997 Planning with nondeterministic actions: a possibilistic approach. *Int. J. Intell. Syst.*, 12, 935-962.

De Cooman G 1997 Possibility theory — I: Measure- and integral-theoretics groundwork; II: Conditional possibility; III: Possibilistic independence. *Int. J. of General Systems*, 25(4):291-371 .

Descloux J. 1963 Approximations in l^p and Chebyshev approximations, *J. Indust. Appl. Math.* ,11: 1017-1026.

Dubois D., Fargier H., Fortemps P., Prade H. 1997a. Leximin optimality and fuzzy set-theoretic operations. *Proc. of the 7th World Congress of the Inter. Fuzzy Systems Assoc. (IFSA'97)*, Prague, July, 55-60.

Dubois D., Fargier H., Prade H. 1995 Fuzzy constraints in job-shop scheduling. *J. of Intelligent Manufacturing* , 64, 215-234.

Dubois D., Fargier H., Prade H. 1996a. Possibility theory in constraint satisfaction problems: Handling priority, preference and uncertainty. *Applied Intelligence*, 6: 287-309.

Dubois D., Fargier H., Prade H. 1996b Refinements of the maximin approach to decision-making in fuzzy environment. *Fuzzy Sets and Systems*, 81:103-122.

Dubois D., Fargier H., Prade H. 1997 Beyond min aggregation in multicriteria decision: (Ordered) weighted min, discrimin and leximin. In:Yager R.R., Kacprzyk J. Eds., *The Ordered Weighted Averaging Operators* , Kluwer , Boston, 181-192.

Dubois D., Fargier H., Prade H. 1998 Possibilistic likelihood relations, *Proc.7th Int. Conf. on Information Processing and Management of Uncertainty (IPMU98)*, Paris, 1196-1203.

Dubois D., Fortemps P. 1999. Computing improved optimal solutions to fuzzy constraint satisfaction problems. *Eur. J. Operational Research.*, 118 (1), 95-126.

Dubois D., Godo L., Prade H., Zapico A. 1999 On the possibilistic decision model: from decision under uncertainty to case-based decision. *Int. J. of Uncertainty, Fuzziness, and Knowledge-based Systems*, 7, 631-670.

Dubois D., Lang J., Prade H. 1992 Inconsistency in possibilistic knowledge bases: To live with it or not live with it. In *Fuzzy Logic for the Management of Uncertainty*, L.A. Zadeh, J. Kacprzyk, eds., New York: Wiley, 335-351.

Dubois D., Lang J., Prade H. 1994 Automated reasoning using possibilistic logic: semantics, belief revision and variable certainty weights, *IEEE Trans. on Data and Knowledge Engineering*, 6(1), 64-71

Dubois D., Prade H. 1980 *Fuzzy Sets and Systems — Theory and Applications*. New York: Academic Press.

Dubois D., Prade H. 1986 Weighted minimum and maximum operations in fuzzy set theory. *Information Sciences*, 39:205-210.

Dubois D., Prade H. 1988 *Possibility Theory*. Plenum Press, New York.

Dubois D., Prade H. 1995 Possibility theory as a basis for qualitative decision theory. *Proc. of the 14th Inter. Joint Conf. on Artificial Intelligence (IJCAI'95)*, Montréal, Canada, Aug. 20-25, 1924-1930.

Dubois D., Prade H. 1997 Towards possibilistic decision theory. In *Fuzzy logic in Artificial Intelligence (Proc. IJCAI'95 Workshop, Montreal)*, T.P. Martin, A. L. Ralescu, Eds, LNAI 1188, Springer Verlag, Berlin, 240-251.

Dubois D. Prade H. Sabbadin R. 1998a Qualitative decision theory with Sugeno integrals, *Proc. 14th Conf. on Uncertainty in AI*, Madison, Wisconsin, 121-128

Dubois D. Prade H. Sabbadin R. 1998b Decision-theoretic foundations of qualitative possibility theory. Invited research review. *16th Eur. Conf. on Operational Research*, Brussels, July 1998. To appear in *Eur. J. Operational Research*, 2001.

Dubois D., Prade H., Testemale, C. 1988 Weighted fuzzy pattern matching. *Fuzzy Sets and Systems*, 28:313-331.

Esogbue A.O. Kacprzyk J. 1998 Fuzzy dynamic programming. In *Fuzzy Sets in Decision Analysis, Operation Research and Statistics* (R. Slowinski, Ed.), The Handbooks of Fuzzy Sets Series, Kluwer, Boston, 281-310.

Fargier H., Dubois D., Prade H. 1995 Problèmes de satisfaction de contraintes flexibles: Une approche égalitariste. *Revue d'Intelligence Artificielle*, 9(3):311-354.

Fargier H., Lang J., Schiex T. 1993. Selecting preferred solutions in fuzzy constraint satisfaction problems. *Proc. of the 1st Europ. Congress on Fuzzy and Intelligent Technologies (EUFIT'93)*, Aachen, Germany, Sept. 7-10, 1128-1134.

Fargier H., Sabbadin R. (2000) Can qualitative utility criteria obey the sure thing principle? *Proc. 8th Int. Conf. on Information Processing and Management of Uncertainty (IPMU00)*, Madrid, 821-826.

Fishburn P. 1986 The axioms of subjective probabilities. *Statistical Science* 1, 335-358.

Fortemps P. 1997 *Fuzzy Sets for Modelling and Handling Imprecision and Flexibility.* Ph. D. Thesis, Faculté Polytechnique de Mons, Belgium.

Grabisch M., Murofushi T., Sugeno M. 1992. Fuzzy measure of fuzzy events defined by fuzzy integrals. *Fuzzy Sets and Systems*, 50: 293-313.

Inuiguchi M., Ichihashi, H. and Tanaka H. 1989. Possibilistic linear programming with measurable multiattribute value functions. ORSA J. on Computing, 1(3), 146-158.

Ishii K., Sugeno M. 1985 A model of human evaluation process using fuzzy measure. Int. J. Man-Machine Stud. 22: 19-38

Keeney R. Raiffa H. (1976) *Decisions with Multiple Objectives.* J. Wiley, New-York.

Marichal J.-L. 2000 On Sugeno integral as an aggregation function, *Fuzzy Sets and Systems*, 114, 347-367

Moulin H. 1988 *Axioms of Cooperative Decision-Making.* Cambridge, UK: Cambridge University Press.

Rice, J. 1962 Tschebyscheff approximation in a compact metric space. *Bull. American Math. Soc.*, 68:405-410.

Sabbadin R. 2000 Empirical comparison of probabilistic and possibilistic Markov decision processes algorithms. *Proc. 14th European Conference on Artificial Intelligence* (ECAI2000), Berlin, (W. Horn, Ed.), IOS Press, Amsterdam, 586-590.

Sabbadin R., Fargier H., Lang J. 1998 Towards qualitative approaches to multistage decision-making, *Int. J. Approx. Reas.*, 19 : 441-471.

Savage L.J. 1954. *The Foundations of Statistics.* 2nd edition, 1972, Dover, New York.

Sugeno M. 1974. *Theory of fuzzy integrals and its applications.* Doctoral Thesis, Tokyo Inst. of Technology.

Sugeno. M. 1977 Fuzzy measures and fuzzy integrals — A survey. In M. M. Gupta, G.N. Saridis, and B.R. Gaines, editors, *Fuzzy Automata and Decision Processes*, pages 89-102. North-Holland, Amsterdam.

Tsang E. 1993. *Foundations of Constraint Satisfaction.* Academic Press, New York

von Neumann J. Morgenstern O. 1944. *Theory of Games and Economic Behavior.* Princeton Univ. Press, NJ.

Wang Z-Y, Klir G 1992. *Fuzzy Measure Theory*, Plenum Press, New York.

Whalen T. 1984. Decision making under uncertainty with various assumptions about available information. *IEEE Trans. on Systems, Man and Cybernetics*, 14: 888-900.

Yager R.R. 1979. Possibilistic decision making. *IEEE Trans. on Systems, Man and Cybernetics*, 9, 388-392.

Yager R.R. 1981. A new methodology for ordinal multiobjective decisions based on fuzzy set. *Decision Sciences*, 12, 589-600.

Yager R.R. 1984 General multiple objective decision making and linguistically quantified statements. *Int. J. of Man-Machine Studies*, 21:389-400.

Yager R.R. 1988 On ordered weighted averaging aggregation operators in multi-criteria decision making. *IEEE Trans. on Systems, Man and Cybernetics*, 18:183-190.

Yager R.R., Kacprzyk J. Eds. 1997 *The Ordered Weighted Averaging Operators* , Kluwer , Boston.

Zadeh L.A. 1975. Calculus of fuzzy restrictions. In: *Fuzzy Sets and their Applications to Cognitive and Decision Processes* (L.A. Zadeh, K.S. Fu, K. Tanaka, M. Shimura, eds.), Academic Press, New York, 1-39.

Zadeh L.A. 1978. Fuzzy sets as a basis for a theory of possibility. *Fuzzy Sets and Systems*, 1: 3-28.

Zimmermann H.J. 1978. Fuzzy Programming and linear programming with several objective functions. *Fuzzy Sets and Systems* 1: 45-55.

www.ingramcontent.com/pod-product-compliance
Ingram Content Group UK Ltd.
Pitfield, Milton Keynes, MK11 3LW, UK
UKHW020138290926
15471UKWH00003B/576
9783662003527